THE CAMBRIDGE COMPANION TO
FICTION IN THE ROMANTIC PERIOD

While poetry has been the genre most closely associated with the Romantic period, the novel of the late eighteenth and early nineteenth centuries has attracted many more readers and students in recent years. Its canon has been widened: alongside Jane Austen, Walter Scott, Mary Shelley, and Thomas Love Peacock, a remarkable range of popular works from the period have been rediscovered and reread intensively. An overview of British fiction written between roughly the mid-1760s and the early 1830s, this Companion is an ideal guide to key authors and genres, the novel's historical and cultural contexts, and its later critical reception. The contributors to this volume showcase the new scholarship of this period, charting the ways its social, political, and intellectual redefinitions created new fictional subjects, forms, and audiences.

A complete list of books in the series is at the back of this book

THE CAMBRIDGE
COMPANION TO

FICTION IN THE
ROMANTIC PERIOD

EDITED BY

RICHARD MAXWELL
Yale University

KATIE TRUMPENER
Yale University

CAMBRIDGE
UNIVERSITY PRESS

CAMBRIDGE UNIVERSITY PRESS
Cambridge, New York, Melbourne, Madrid, Cape Town, Singapore, São Paulo

Cambridge University Press
The Edinburgh Building, Cambridge CB2 8RU, UK

Published in the United States of America by Cambridge University Press, New York

www.cambridge.org
Information on this title: www.cambridge.org/9780521681087

First published 2008

Printed in the United Kingdom at the University Press, Cambridge

A catalogue record for this publication is available from the British Library

Library of Congress Cataloging in Publication data
The Cambridge companion to fiction in the romantic period / edited by
Richard Maxwell and Katie Trumpener.
Includes bibliographical references (p. 265) and index.
ISBN-13: 978-0-521-86252-3 (hardback: alk. paper)
ISBN-10: 0-521-86252-3 (hardback: alk. paper)
ISBN-13: 978-0-521-68108-7 (pbk: alk. paper)
ISBN-10: 0-521-68108-1 (pbk: alk. paper)
1. English fiction – 18th century – History and criticism. 2. English fiction – 19th century –
History and criticism. 3. Romanticism – Great Britain. 4. Great Britain – Intellectual
life – 18th century. 5. Great Britain – Intellectual life – 19th century. 6. Books and reading –
Great Britain – History – 18th century. 7. Books and reading – Great Britain – History –
19th century. 8. Gothic revival (Literature) – Great Britain. 9. English literature – Irish
authors – History and criticism. 10. English literature – Scottish authors – History and
criticism. I. Maxwell, Richard, 1948– II. Trumpener, Katie, 1961– III. Title: Fiction
in the romantic period.
PR858.R73C36 2007
823'.709–dc22   2007014639

ISBN 978-0-521-86252-3 hardback
ISBN 978-0-521-68108-7 paperback

CONTENTS

ILLUSTRATIONS

NOTES ON CONTRIBUTORS

MARTHA BOHRER is Assistant Professor of English Literature at North Central College in Naperville, Illinois. She has published previously on Gilbert White and Maria Edgeworth and the representation of rural places. She is currently writing a book on the influence of natural history, Romantic nature poetry, and anecdotal rural fiction on the development of the novel in the Romantic Period.

MARSHALL BROWN is Professor of Comparative Literature at the University of Washington and editor of *Modern Language Quarterly: A Journal of Literary History*. He is the author of *The Shape of German Romanticism* (1979), *Preromanticism* (1991), *Turning Points: Essays in the History of Cultural Expressions* (1997), and *The Gothic Text* (2004). His next book, *"The Tooth That Nibbles at the Soul": Essays on Poetry and Music*, is under contract with the University of Washington Press.

JILL CAMPBELL teaches in the English department at Yale University and is the author of *Natural Masques: Gender and Identity in Fielding's Plays and Novels* (1995). She is currently completing a book on satire and self-representation in the writings of Lady Mary Wortley Montagu, Lord Hervey, and Alexander Pope. Her next book involves the interplay between literary texts and aspects of daily life, including newspaper advertising, reading to children, and hymn-singing.

IAN DUNCAN is Professor of English at the University of California, Berkeley. He is the author of *Modern Romance and Transformations of the Novel* (1992) and *Scott's Shadow: The Novel in Romantic Edinburgh* (2007). He has edited Scott's *Rob Roy* and *Ivanhoe* for Oxford World's Classics and James Hogg's *Winter Evening Tales* (2002), and is a co-editor of *Scotland and the Borders of Romanticism* (2004).

INA FERRIS is a Professor of English at the University of Ottawa. Her publications include *The Romantic National Tale and the Question of Ireland* (2002) and *The Achievement of Literary Authority: Gender, History, and the Waverley Novels* (1991). She recently edited Charlotte Smith's *The Old Manor House* (2006), and is at work on a project on antiquarian genres in the Romantic period.

PAUL KEEN teaches English at Carleton University. He is the author of *The Crisis of Literature in the 1790s: Print Culture and the Public Sphere* (1999) and the editor of *The Popular Radical Press in Britain, 1817–1821* (2003) and *Revolutions in Romantic Literature: An Anthology of Print Culture, 1780–1832* (2004).

GARY KELLY holds the Canada Research Chair in Language and Literature in Society at the University of Alberta. Kelly is the author of many books on Romantic fiction and poetry, including *English Fiction of the Romantic Period, 1789–1830* (1999), *The English Jacobin Novel, 1780–1805* (1976), *Women, Writing, and Revolution, 1790–1827* (1993), and *Revolutionary Feminism: The Mind and Career of Mary Wollstonecraft* (1992). He is the general editor of the six-volume collection *Bluestocking Feminism: Writings of the Bluestocking Circle, 1738–1785* (1999). He is currently preparing an edition of Gothic fiction by women.

DEIDRE SHAUNA LYNCH is Professor of English at the University of Toronto. She is the author of *The Economy of Character: Novels, Market Culture and the Business of Inner Meaning* (1998) and, more recently, the co-editor (with Jack Stillinger) of the Romantic period volume of *The Norton Anthology of English Literature*.

RICHARD MAXWELL is the author of *The Mysteries of Paris and London* (1992) and editor of Dickens's *A Tale of Two Cities* (2000) and of *The Victorian Illustrated Book* (2002). His essay on discovered manuscripts and the history of the novel appears in *Il romanzo* (2003). He has been working on a manuscript about the history of historical fiction. He teaches in the Comparative Literature Department at Yale University.

ANN WIERDA ROWLAND is an Assistant Professor at the University of Kansas and has published articles on William Wordsworth, Walter Scott, and the Romantic ballad revival. She is completing a book on Romantic ideas of childhood and their importance to the emergence of Britain's national and vernacular literary culture.

WILLIAM ST CLAIR is a former Senior Research Fellow of Trinity College, Cambridge. His books include *Lord Elgin and the Marbles* (1967), *The Godwins and the Shelleys* (1989), *The Reading Nation in the Romantic Period* (2004), and, most recently, *The Grand Slave Emporium* (2006).

KATIE TRUMPENER is Professor of Comparative Literature and English at Yale University. Her first book, *Bardic Nationalism: The Romantic Novel and the British Empire* (1997), won the MLA First Book Prize and the British Academy's

Rosemary Crashay prize. Her book on postwar German cinema and the Cold War will be published by Princeton. She is working on a book about the early history of children's literature.

JAMES WATT is Lecturer in English at the University of York. He is the author of *Contesting the Gothic: Fiction, Genre, and Cultural Conflict, 1764–1832* (1999), and has edited the Oxford World's Classics edition of Clara Reeve's *The Old English Baron* (2003). His current project is a literary and cultural history of British orientalisms *c.* 1750–*c.* 1830.

CHRONOLOGY: LITERATURE, CULTURE AND HISTORY IN THE ROMANTIC PERIOD

1759   Laurence Sterne's *Tristram Shandy* published in York (London publication follows, 1760)

1760   Accession of George III to the throne of Great Britain

1762   Catherine the Great seizes power in Russia
Richard Hurd, *Letters on Chivalry and Romance*
James Macpherson, *Fingal: An Ancient Epic Poem*
Horace Walpole tours the gardens at Stourhead

1763   End of the Seven Years' War

1764   Death of William Hogarth
"Musing among the ruins of the Capitol," Edward Gibbon determines to write *The Decline and Fall of the Roman Empire* (published 1776–88)

1765   [Oliver Goldsmith?], *The History of Little Goody Two-Shoes*
Thomas Percy, *Reliques of Ancient English Poetry*
Horace Walpole, *Castle of Otranto*

1766   Jean-Jacques Rousseau in Derbyshire, where he begins writing his *Confessions* (published 1776–88)
Oliver Goldsmith, *The Vicar of Wakefield*

1767   Adam Ferguson, *Essay on the History of Civil Society*

1768   Captain Cook sails for the Pacific (returning 1771)

1769   Famine in Bengal: *c.* 10 million people die

1770   Benjamin West, *The Death of General Wolfe*

1771   Henry MacKenzie, *The Man of Feeling*
Tobias Smollet, *Humphry Clinker*

1773   Boston Tea Party

1774   Perpetual copyright declared illegal
Goethe, *Sorrows of Young Werther*

1776   (American) Declaration of Independence
Adam Smith, *The Wealth of Nations*

1777   Thomas Chatterton, *Poems, Supposed to Have Been Written at Bristol, By Thomas Rowley*

1780   Gordon Riots in London

1781   Friedrich von Schiller, *Die Raüber*

1782   Helenus Scott, *The Adventures of a Rupee*
Pierre Laclos, *Les Liaisons Dangereuses*

1783   George Crabbe, *The Village*
Sophia Lee, first part of *The Recess* (completed 1785)

1785   James Boswell, *Journal of the Tour to the Hebrides*
Clara Reeve, *The Progress of Romance*

1786   Death of Frederick the Great of Prussia
William Beckford, *Vathek*

1788   John Soane's Bank of England (destroyed 1833)

1787   Charlotte Brooke, *Reliques of Irish Poetry*
Wolfgang Amadeus Mozart and Lorenzo da Ponte, *Don Giovanni*

1789   The fall of the Bastille
Gilbert White, *Natural History of Selborne*

1790   Edmund Burke, *Reflections on the Revolution in France*
For the first time, J. W. M. Turner exhibits a painting at the Royal Academy

1791   William Blake, *Marriage of Heaven and Hell*
James Boswell, begins publishing *The Life of Samuel Johnson* (completed 1799)
Thomas Paine, *The Rights of Man* (completed 1792)

1792   Mary Wollstonecraft, *Vindication of the Rights of Women*
Thomas Paine, *The Rights of Man*

1793   Louis XVI executed in France
        William Godwin, *Enquiry Concerning Political Justice*
        Charlotte Smith, *The Old Manor House*
        Tom Paine's Jests

1794   William Godwin, *Adventures of Caleb Williams*
        Thomas Holcroft, *Hugh Trevor*
        Ann Radcliffe, *The Mysteries of Udolpho*

1795   Warren Hastings acquitted by House of Lords in East India
        Company scandals
        Hannah More begins publishing her *Cheap Repository Tracts*

1796   Vaccination for smallpox introduced by Edward Jenner
        Elizabeth Hamilton, *The Letters of a Hindoo Rajah*
        Robert Bage, *Hermsprong*

1797   Thomas Bewick, *History of British Birds*, Vol. I (Vol. II,
        1804)
        Abbé Barruel, *Memoirs, Illustrating the History of Jacobinism*

1798   Charles Brocken Brown, *Wieland*
        William Wordsworth and Samuel Taylor Coleridge publish
        Lyrical Ballads
        Thomas Malthus, *Essay on the Principles of Population*
        United Irishmen's Uprising

1799   Alexander von Humboldt begins five years of exploration in
        South America (*Voyage aux régions équinoxiales de Humboldt
        et Bonpland*, published 1805–34)

1800   Act of Union with Ireland
        Maria Edgeworth, *Castle Rackrent*

1801   Thomas Jefferson elected President of the United States by the
        House of Representatives
        After years of leading a slave rebellion, Toussaint L'Overture
        controls all of Haiti. (In 1802, he is overthrown by Napoleon,
        who restores slavery.)

1802   Madame Tussaud's exhibition of wax figures opens in London
        (her Baker Street Museum 1835)
        Walter Scott, *Minstrelsy of the Scottish Border* (Vols. I and II; 3rd
        volume published 1803)
        Frances Jeffrey founds the *Edinburgh Review*

William Cobbet begins to write the *Weekly Political Register*
François René Chateaubriand, *Génie du christianisme*

1803   Louisiana Purchase negotiated by Thomas Jefferson
Humphry Repton, *Observations on the Theory and Practice of Landscape Gardening*

1804   Napoleon crowns himself Emperor of France
Beethoven, the "Eroica" Symphony

1805   Sarah Catherine Martin, *The Comic Adventures of Old Mother Hubbard and her Dog*
Ludwig van Beethoven, *Fidelio*
The Battle of Trafalgar (and the death of Nelson)

1806   Abolition of the Holy Roman Empire
Lady Morgan, *The Wild Irish Girl*

1807   Abolition of the slave trade in the British Empire
Charles and Mary Lamb, *Tales from Shakespeare*

1808   Statutory copyright period extended from fourteen years to twenty eight years (further extensions in 1814 and 1842)
Goethe, *Faust I*

1809   *Quarterly Review* founded

1810   George Crabbe, *The Borough*
Jane Porter, *The Scottish Chiefs*
Jane and Ann Taylor, *Hymns for Infant Minds*

1811   The future George IV becomes Regent, replacing his deranged father
Jane Austen, *Sense and Sensibility*

1812   Napoleon's invasion of Russia and devastating retreat from it
War of 1812 (between Britain and the United States)
Thomas Rowlandson, *The Tour of Dr. Syntax* (sequels 1820, 1821)

1813   Jane Austen, *Pride and Prejudice*

1814   Napoleon exiled to Elba
Duke of Sutherland begins clearances of tenants on his estates, replacing them with sheep
Jane Austen, *Mansfield Park*

Walter Scott, *Waverley*
Mrs. Sherwood, *Little Henry and His Bearer*

1815   Napoleon escapes from Elba and is defeated at Waterloo; Louis XVIII returns to France
Jacob and Wilhelm Grimm, *Kinder und Hausmärchen*
John Nash begins to remodel the Royal Pavilion at Brighton for George IV (finished 1823)

1816   Jane Austen, *Emma*
Walter Scott, *Old Mortality*

1817   Walter Scott, *Rob Roy*
James Mill, *The History of British India*
Blackwood's Edinburgh Magazine launched

1818   Jane Austen, *Northanger Abbey*, *Persuasion* (published posthumously)
Susan Ferrier, *Marriage*
Thomas Love Peacock, *Nightmare Abbey*
Walter Scott, *The Heart of Midlothian*
Mary Shelley, *Frankenstein*
Ludwig van Beethoven, *Hammerklavier* Sonata

1819   The Peterloo Massacre
Lord Byron, *Don Juan* (cantos I and II)
Mary Russell Mitford, *Our Village*
Washington Irving, *The Sketch Book*
Theodore Géricault, *The Raft of the Medusa*

1820   Accession of George IV to the throne of Great Britain
John Keats, *Lamia, Isabella, Even of St. Agnes, Hyperion, and Other Poems*
Charles Robert Maturin, *Melmoth the Wanderer*
Percy Shelley, *Prometheus Unbound*

1821   Pierce Egan, *Life in London*
John Galt, *Annals of the Parish*
Jean Champollion deciphers the Rosetta Stone

1822   George IV visits Scotland (and Scott, who orchestrates the trip)
Lord Byron, *The Vision of Judgement*
John Galt, *The Provost*

Introduction

This *Companion* offers an introduction to British fiction written between roughly the mid-1760s and the early 1830s. Across Europe, these seventy years encompass a large number of artistic works conceived in Romantic styles: symphonies by Ludwig van Beethoven, picturesque landscape gardens, paintings by Eugène Delacroix, the visionary domestic architecture of Sir John Soane, and the Gothic novel. Yet many novels and tales of these decades are not identifiably Romantic in style or sensibility. On the whole, the era may be characterized less by a unifying artistic sensibility than it is by a spirit of experimentation, and an overall political situation, a civic unrest traceable throughout Europe and North America.

The period was turbulent. The Russians, under Catherine the Great, fought the Ottoman empire (1768–74), while waging a less direct battle against their allies, the Bourbons of France, and fomenting political unrest on a European scale. One country affected was Greece, where Catherine's agents helped start a revolution against Turkish rule; the conflict lasted decades, becoming celebrated for its horrors and heroism. Catherine's domestic troubles included the peasants' revolt led by Pugachev (a Cossack soldier and pretender to the Russian throne, executed in 1775). Meanwhile, as historian Franco Venturi observes, rebellions and insurrections of many different kinds broke out all over Europe, especially "in unexpected and peripheral places."[1] Among the countries affected were Corsica, Montenegro, Bohemia, Geneva, Denmark, and Sweden, each in turn seeming to provide another view of a confusing new world in revolt against old forms of social order. The culminating event of these decades of crisis was, of course, the French Revolution (beginning in 1789), with the long, bloody aftermath of the Napoleonic Wars, but the French upheaval was not an isolated event; almost everywhere in Europe, from the mid-eighteenth century onwards, a major realignment seemed to be under way.

Older portrayals of the Romantic period often suggested its relative insulation from instability. Many recent historians and critics disagree. Venturi's multi-volume *The Eighteenth Century of Reforms* [*Settecento riformatore*] sees "the problem of the organization of liberty itself" defining "the Britannic world" (i.e., England, Scotland, Ireland, and the various American colonies).[2] Marilyn Butler's *Romantics, Rebels, and Reactionaries* (1981) makes a related argument; between 1760 and 1830, Butler suggests, both Britain and its American colonies were caught up in the period's questioning spirit. Britain had vigorous radical movements, embodied initially in the figure of John Wilkes (the self-described "friend of liberty" who defied George III's minister Lord Bute) and exacerbated by the social transformations wrought during the Industrial Revolution, whose "making of the English working classes" also spawned a formidable Jacobin movement, based not only in London but in various provincial centers: the failed United Irishmen's Uprising of 1792, most spectacularly, was to have precipitated a French Jacobin invasion of Ireland.

If, during the earlier eighteenth century, Britain had managed to neutralize the influence of the exiled Stuart pretenders (the nearest local equivalents to charismatic rebels like Pugachev), its sway over certain outlying or colonized regions – Scotland, Ireland, India – remained an open question. The Seven Years War wrested North America from the French but soon afterwards, in the American Revolution (1776), much of the Continent was lost to Britain. Two decades later, British politics were reframed by the ambitions of a general and emperor just on the other side of the English Channel. Napoleon's advancement of revolutionary principles through military force or imperial decree changed the Continent's legal and social structure – and might perhaps have changed that of England too, had the great French leader managed to invade (by means of balloons, as some surmised he would), or merely to prevail at home. No less than Continental Europeans, then, the inhabitants of the British Isles felt themselves a part of a great international cataclysm, stretching, in the long view, from Catherine's plots of the 1760s and 1770s through the Napoleonic era and into the politically shaky period that followed victory at Waterloo, culminating, on the British side of the Channel, in the Reform Bill of 1832 (the first step on the way to a full franchise).

Like politics, fiction in Britain was part of a lively and much larger European and transatlantic scene. This larger context has been mapped out recently by Alain Montandon's absorbing *Le Roman au XVIIIe siècle en Europe*, a synthetic overview still lacking an English-language equivalent.[3] This *Companion* cannot undertake such large-scale comparative work, except on a very occasional basis and on an abridged scale. But it would be a mistake to lose sight of the rest of European fiction during this era, especially since contemporaries generally kept it in mind.

Thanks to recent bibliographical researches, some of their attentiveness can be quantified. Between 1770 and 1799, as a recent, authoritative, bibliography observes, "More than a tenth of all novel titles first published in Britain ... were translations from Continental novels."[4] There were excellent reasons for the substantial presence of literary imports. Just across the Channel, French prose fiction had been a prominent, sophisticated, and highly theorized genre as early as the reign of Louis XIV, and throughout the eighteenth century, fashions and trends in the novel were typically established in France, despite both the domestic and international importance of British novelists like Daniel Defoe, Henry Fielding, Samuel Richardson, Laurence Sterne and Tobias Smollett. In Germany, moreover, a late eighteenth-century efflorescence of fiction produced a second rival to English and English-language fiction; indeed, a number of the period's most ambitious experimental novelists, such as Jean Paul, were animated by Sterne's example. Meanwhile, a range of brilliant German writers linked fictive prose narrative with prestigious forms of philosophical discourse, creating subgenres like the fantastic tale (E. T. A. Hoffmann), the novella (Goethe, Heinrich von Kleist, Novalis), and the reflexive *Bildungsroman* – most spectacularly exemplified by Goethe's *Wilhelm Meister's Apprenticeship* (1795–6, whose belated, somewhat bowdlerized English translation by Thomas Carlyle appeared in 1824). Further afield, significant works of fiction were produced, during the late eighteenth and early nineteenth centuries, in the former American colonies, in Nova Scotia and Upper Canada, in India, and in Van Diemen's Land; this very new body of literature at once extended the reach of the British tradition and competed with it (James Fenimore Cooper, for example, becoming an influential international rival to Walter Scott, almost, in certain cases, a replacement for him). Finally, the discovery and widespread adaptation of the popular Eastern tale, initiated by Antoine Galland's *Thousand and One Nights* (1704–8), continued to shape prose fiction almost everywhere in the Western world, its Romantic-period reception particularly inflected by ruminations about the nature and future of French and British colonial expansion.

Despite its (geographically) insular situation, the British sense of the novel was cosmopolitan. Yet if the permeability of the literary scene reflected the virtue of intellectual curiosity, it also signalled a particular weakness. British fiction of the late eighteenth and early nineteenth centuries notably failed to produce one of those omnicompetent figures – like Johann Wolfgang von Goethe, Jean-Jacques Rousseau, or René Chateaubriand on the Continent – who seemed to tower over as well as to embody the age. As intellectuals who initially made their mark in other fields (poetry, drama, political philosophy, and perhaps above all autobiographical life-drama), these legendary characters seemed to try out novel-writing as a diversion from higher or more pressing matters, thus adding enormous lustre to the enterprise of prose fiction. After Samuel Johnson (d. 1784), Britain lacked such figures; Lord Byron came closest in some ways, but he chose to compose his great Regency novel (*Don Juan*) in verse. This lack is symptomatic. Despite its popularity, prose fiction during most of the Romantic period had less glamor, and less status, in the British context, than in many other national traditions. The novel would attain greater prestige only during the second and third decades of the nineteenth century, when the balance of literary trade would shift from British imports to British exports, and when anglophone fiction, correspondingly, began to attract wider international attention. The presiding genius of the upturn was Scott, whose artistic (and financial) achievements are repeatedly chronicled in this volume. Yet his triumphs come towards the end of the Romantic period. For most of this era, British novels and tales were ugly ducklings; their swanlike qualities would be mostly recognized in retrospect, and indeed the process of discovery is still in progress, with new candidates for revaluation offered on a surprisingly regular basis.

The *Companion*'s first two chapters present complementary extensions of this Introduction. Chapter 1, "The historiography of fiction in the Romantic period," details how the field of British fiction managed over several successive generations to acquire a decodable history, a substantial (and extendable) canon, a usable bibliography, and, eventually, some genuine prestige and presence of its own, beyond the omnipresent Scott. Chapter 2, "Publishing, authorship, and reading," emphasizes the questions of copyright and intellectual property that underlay the new ways the British began producing, circulating, and reading prose fiction during the Romantic period.

Subsequent chapters address the range of ways in which the period's social, political, and intellectual redefinitions created new fictional subjects, forms, and audiences. Various chapters describe the emergence of distinctive Irish and Scottish fictional traditions; the novel's links with colonialism and orientalism; the rise of fiction addressed to working-class readers, and to children; new forms of women's (and self-consciously feminist) fiction; and the impact of new scientific practices and of vogues for the sentimental and the Gothic on the shape of fictional worlds and forms. In some chapters, familiar figures like Jane Austen, Maria Edgeworth, Thomas Love Peacock, William Godwin, Mary Shelley, and James Hogg take on new contours in the company of their numerous and prolific contemporaries. Other chapters immerse the reader in the period's full range of fiction-writing. The recent upsurge of scholarship on Romantic-era fiction, working to reassess its depth, breadth, triumphs, and peculiarities as a period corpus, implicitly counters both older histories of the novel, which used to treat the Romantic period as one of virtual eclipse for the novel as a form, and older accounts of the Romantic period, which slighted fiction altogether in favor of poetry.

Several chapters here address one of the Romantic period's biggest (yet most-often ignored) conundrums: the complex relationship of poetic and prose narrative. The Romantic period is the last (even in Britain) in which poetry is more popular than prose; Scott's own shift from one medium to another both embodied and precipitated a great transformation. Yet poets such as George Crabbe need to be read along with the prose novelists of local, regional, or village life, Byron read with (and against) the sentimentalists. As chapter 6 on poetry in fiction insists, moreover, mixed forms and generic mixing were a central feature of the Romantic period; poetry inserted into a novel often served to encapsulate its fictional quintessence.

The image used on the front cover of this book, Francis Danby's *Landscape Near Clifton* (1821–2) depicts a mountainous scene in terms reminiscent of the period's famous landscape poetry. Yet this prospect functions, simultaneously, as a bookscape, a place where reading aloud, and the collective appreciation of literature help bind a marital, familial, or intellectual community. Chapter 5 in this volume describes the way the emerging naturalist study of locale, habitat, and ecosystem became a new organizing principle in the construction of fictional worlds. Danby's painting evokes literary reading as a communal, organic activity. Yet some of the volume's essays, in contrast, understand the novel as a means of articulating new, exclusive forms of social identity – and sometimes also as arenas for political strife.

The Romantic novel is a genre in transition during an era of transition. And the coincidence of formal and historical changes, formal and political experiments, now seems part of the fascination of this epoch in the novel's history. The *Companion* evokes familiar and unfamiliar frames of reference in its efforts to elucidate an extraordinary period in literature. By the end of the eighteenth century, the novel might have come and gone; it was nowhere more contingent, it often appeared, than on British ground. Instead, during the Romantic period, prose fiction opened up many new possibilities, firmly establishing itself as the pervasive and privileged medium for anglophone literature.

NOTES

1 Franco Venturi, *The End of the Old Regime in Europe, 1768–1776: The First Crisis*, trans. R. Burr Litchfield (Princeton: Princeton University Press, 1989), p. ix.

Our historical account draws largely from this book (itself only part of *Settecento riformatore*).

2 Venturi, *The End*, p. 377.

3 See Alain Montandon, *Le Roman au XVIIIe siècle en Europe* (Paris: Presses Universitaires de France, 1999).

4 Garside, Peter, James Raven, and Rainer Schöwerling, *The English Novel 1770–1829: A Bibliographical Survey of Prose Fiction Published in the British Isles*, 2 vols. (Oxford: Oxford University Press, 2000), vol. I, p. 56.

I

RICHARD MAXWELL

The historiography of fiction in the Romantic period

There is widespread agreement that the Romantic period exists as a meaningful span of time – even if it is defined less by Romanticism *per se* than by a strong revolutionary trend. By contrast, the fiction written in the Romantic period has only occasionally been treated as an integral subject. It is true that Walter Scott never disappeared from view (even when most people stopped reading him), that Jane Austen had strong admirers from the beginning – including Scott – and that the creature of Mary Shelley's *Frankenstein* became a general byword and remains one, even or especially for people who don't know the book *Frankenstein* itself. A few other writers, such as Maria Edgeworth and Thomas Love Peacock, managed to keep readers and reputations. However, that doesn't make quite enough books to constitute a larger entity called "fiction of the Romantic period." For an era rich both in brilliant experimentation and achieved masterpieces, this one has tended to drop off the map, despite various attempts during the last two centuries to demarcate it.

Such recovery efforts and their often equivocal success will be the focus of this chapter, which looks at four moments – windows of opportunity – when for one reason or another the idea of a body of fiction produced during the Romantic period and conceivable as an overall topic of inquiry and opportunity for reading came into focus. One such moment is early (1785); one, around 1830, provides a sort of instant retrospect; one occurs just after World War I, marking a decisive turn in modern literary studies; one is the present – which is to say, the last few decades, culminating in the publication of Peter Garside, James Raven, and Rainer Schöwerling's *The English Novel: 1770–1829*. Taken as a sequence, these episodes – of collective memory kicking in, even if only temporarily – can be used to introduce the problematic historiography of fiction in the Romantic period.

The Progress of Romance

One of the early English-language books to single out prose fiction as a significant kind of literature was Clara Reeve's *The Progress of Romance, through times, countries, and manners; with remarks on the good and bad effects of it, on them respectively; in a course of evening conversations* (1785). Reeve's main competition was French; Pierre-Daniel Huet's letter to the Abbé Segrais, "De l'origine des romans," "Upon the Original of Romances" (1670) was not only a study as broad and ambitious as her own, but one that had been widely available in the English language for half a century or more before *Progress*. Moreover, the French had kept their lead in sophistication, as Reeves might have observed if she had encountered the *Bibliothèque universelle des romans* (224 volumes, 1775–89), unfolding just across the Channel in a seemingly endless series of tomes during the same decade as *Progress* and by far the most comprehensive effort of the eighteenth century to imagine what a history of novel and romance might look like. Reeves, however, was unjustly scornful of Huet and probably did not know about the *Bibliothèque* (Vol. I, pp. 91ff). She is friendlier towards a recent run of English studies of literary history, such as James Beattie's *Dissertation on Fable and Romance* and Thomas Warton's *History of English Poetry*, although, as she points out, neither Beattie nor Warton focus on prose works. As for the *Critical* and *Monthly Reviews*, operating since the reign of George II, she has read them (and quotes them at length) but doubts their historical sense; she is especially irritated by one reviewer's insistence that he has "no relish for the Romances of the last Century" since he is "sufficiently satisfied with those of the present" (Vol. I, p. 82).

That leaves the field open for her own efforts. Reeve was a well-known novelist, and *The Progress of Romance* is nearly a novel in itself; adapting its format from Madame de Genlis's *Theatre of Education*, it recounts a series of chats among Hortensius, Sophronia, and Euphrasia, each of whom has a characteristic voice and moral or intellectual position on the announced topic of prose romance.[1] Euphrasia is Reeves's de facto heroine; the twelve discussions occur at her home, where she takes the lead in providing a history of romance, as well as in defending its integrity. A romance, she says, is a "wild, extravagant, fabulous Story" (Vol. I, p. 6). It is to be closely associated with epic and it has an admirable hero; it constitutes, indeed, a "Heroic fable" (Vol. I, p. 13). The romance and the novel, she suggests, are separate genres, the first tending towards idealization, the other more realistic (Vol. I, p. 111); moreover, there are many kinds of romances, such as the ancient Greek and Roman ones, the medieval chivalric romances, and the fifteenth- or sixteenth-century kind (mostly by French writers like Madeleine de Scudéry).

Having highlighted the fruitful distinction between wild romance and the more settled, everyday novel, Euphrasia and her friends complicate this opposition. Romances are what precede novels, in a less modern, probably more warlike, state of society; once a polite and Augustan civilization is established, romance becomes novel, a process of metamorphosis and also of sublimation. The old world of romance lurks inside the new world of the novel, but is in every sense contained by it. Then again, the three friends seem at times to prefer a different account, whereby novel and romance coexist as alternate, autonomous possibilities in their own, contemporaneous world; moreover, some works combine the tendencies of both. In either accounting, the wild and everyday tend to blend, with unpredictable aesthetic or ethical results; Reeve's narrative thus spotlights the ways that both prose and prosiness can coexist with that apparently archaic kind of narrative where anything can happen, where wildness prevails without difficulty. Over the long run, prose is the medium where the Romantic and novelistic consort together most effectively.

Reeve's line of argument falters towards the end, but she offers an extensive list. She knows ancient novelists like Heliodorus, understands their importance for the foundational Renaissance innovators (above all, Miguel de Cervantes), tries to bring Middle Eastern story types into her discussion, and follows developments in novel and romance up through her own moment, while making frequent recommendations for the benefit of those ardent, even obsessive readers whom she imagines as her core audience. *The Progress of Romance* thus doubles as a model for conversationalists and a handbook for browsers in the bookstore (who, in Reeve's presentation, are assured terrific bargains if they seek oldish romances). There is a good deal of anxiety about which books are morally improving and which are not. On the whole, *Progress* is notable not for its occasional fears but its sustained intellectual adventurousness; the study of romance and novel appears a great undertaking – hardly a waste of time on trivial "trash" (p. 6), as Hortensius initially implies. Given that so much eighteenth- (and nineteenth-) century criticism continues to harp on the trashiness of prose fiction, *The Progress of Romance* is a bold and independent book.

As a work of 1785, *The Progress of Romance* cannot yet have a full concept of fiction in the Romantic era, but it provides the necessary basis for such an idea. *Progress*'s links between old romances and new ones create a formidable, praiseworthy body of writing, a tradition in which a romancer like Reeve herself might thrive. *Progress* was to remain the primary synthetic work of its time – the best anglophone equivalent to the *Bibliothèque universelle*. This is not, however, to say that Reeve's work had immediate success. In 1790, five years after its publication, she said that she still had

300 or 400 unsold copies out of the 1,000 printed; she blamed the London booksellers, who had little faith in literary productions from the provinces. (Reeve lived in Ipswich, where she supported herself by her pen.) Moreover, fourteen years later (in 1804), she refused to support a publishing scheme for a new edition.[2] Reeve died in 1807; it would be another eight years until the publication of Walter Scott's *Waverley*. The success of that book was the real and lasting confirmation of her original decision to focus on prose as distinguished from verse romance. But *Waverley*'s triumph created problems of its own for the overall visibility of fiction from the Romantic era.

From Scott's Magnum Opus to Bentley's Standard Novels

An admirer of Reeve, Scott was first famous as the author of exciting narrative poems; driven out of the field, he claimed, by Lord Byron's even greater success as a poet, he then made a further career as the dominant novelist of his day. It was Scott who made prose the default medium of fictional narrative in the nineteenth century, thus confirming the guiding intuition of *The Progress of Romance*.[3] "During the Romantic period, the 'Author of Waverley' sold more novels than all the other novelists of the time put together," William St Clair points out.[4] Eventually, Scott's position as an unmatchable moneymaker among novelists became a curse as well as a blessing. He was a partner in the publishing firm of Scott & Ballantyne; partnership law (unlike limited liability, a later standard) put all business and personal assets at risk.[5] In 1826, a bad year for the economy, Scott & Ballantyne went bankrupt, leaving Scott himself personally or (in his opinion) morally liable for (at least) £126,000. He spent the rest of his life working to repay it. (The debt was liquidated in 1833, shortly after his death.)

Scott's most ambitious and effective effort to write himself out of bankruptcy was the Magnum Opus edition of the Waverley novels. Working with Robert Cadell (a fellow bankrupt from the 1826 disaster), Scott projected a collected Waverley that would include new introductions and notes, a corrected text, and newly commissioned illustrations. From mid-1829, one volume a month appeared, most volumes containing half a novel; within four years, the set had been completed. These are handy little books – a wonderful way to read Scott and, by the standards of the late Romantic period, a cheap one.

The Magnum Opus helped shape the future of fiction publishing during the rest of the nineteenth century.[6] (It is even more interesting studied in conjunction with the edition of the novels that followed it, the Abbotsford, conceived and supervised by Cadell.) One of the important early effects of the Magnum was to serve as a model for Bentley's Standard Novels. Such projects were not new; in 1810, Anna Barbauld had supervised and written introductions to an extensive set of reprints (Barbauld's British Novelists, fifty volumes); Scott had followed suit a decade later as the introducer of Ballantyne's Novelist's Library (issued 1821–4, ten volumes). However, both the Barbauld and Ballantyne collections are largely retrospective; Barbauld starts from Richardson's *Clarissa* and works up, slowly, to Maria Edgeworth's *Belinda*, while Scott's editorial project concentrates entirely on novels of previous generations. Bentley's Standard Editions took an altogether different form.

Inspired by the sensational success of the Magnum Opus, Bentley worked hard to associate his series with Scott. The first known advertisement presents it as "Standard Novels – A Companion to the Waverley Novels." Moreover, Bentley bought the rights to Ballantyne's Novelist's Library, intending to reprint Scott's introductions along with the novels he had chosen. When Scott's executors blocked this move, Bentley shifted his strategy, deciding that the Standard Novels would concentrate on more or less contemporary books – first, those published a minimum of seven years ago and then even more recent works. Echoing the Magnum Opus, Bentley's series asked writers to provide new introductions and notes, and to establish definitive texts. This approach was partly an effort to secure copyright for James Fenimore Cooper's American novels, but it then became a general strategy for the series as a whole. As a consequence, the Standard Novels acquired the same *summa*-like aura of scholarly definitiveness and artistic authority that Cadell and Scott had generated for the Magnum Opus; also as in Magnum, this aura came at a relatively low cost (6 shillings per volume, each volume generally containing a whole novel).[7]

The first, and by far the most important, series of Bentley's Standard Novels ran from 1831 to 1855 and contained 126 volumes. The first half or so of this run (up to around 1838) constitutes a biased, lively, and influential survey of fiction in the Romantic era. There were three William Godwin novels, six Austens, four Peacocks, twenty-one James Fenimore Coopers (a strong American link: Cooper, one suspects, standing in for Scott). Edward Bulwer-Lytton had three novels, Edgeworth only one: her *Helen* (first published 1834) a latish addition of 1838. Captain Marryat was represented by eleven volumes – mirroring his contemporary popularity – while two now-forgotten figures of the 1830s, Theodore Hook and G. P. R. James (a further Scott stand-in) were represented by six and five volumes respectively. Madame de Staël was represented by *Corinne* (first published 1807), René Chateaubriand by *The Adventures of the Last of the Abencerages* (first published 1826), Alessandro Manzoni by *The Betrothed* (first published 1825–7; Bentley's only acknowledgment of France and Italy). A section of Friedrich von Schiller's *The Ghost Seer* (first published 1786–8) filled out a volume dominated by *Frankenstein* (first published 1818), and another section was paired with Charles Brocken Brown's *Edgar Huntly* (first published 1799), thus dramatizing links between anglophone and German horror. A previous generation of Gothicists, William Beckford, Horace Walpole, and M. G. Lewis, were bundled into a compact volume of supremely elegant terrors. Three James Morier novels and Thomas Hope's *Anastasius* (first published 1819) waved the banner of Byronic orientalism. Susan Ferrier made it into the series with *Marriage* (first published 1818); two other important Scots, John Galt and Michael Scott, would also have been included if Bentley had been able to buy the necessary rights from William Blackwood in Edinburgh, but he only offered £175 for a slew of their fiction and Blackwood turned him down.

Bentley's Standard Novels did a great deal to make affordable fiction available, offering a new kind of alternative to the circulating libraries on which many middle-class readers relied (and would continue to rely, during most of Victoria's reign). At the same time, the effect of the Standards was often to suppress rather than encourage the reading of fiction from the Romantic period. In a usefully discouraging rebuttal to the enthusiasm of Bentley's previous chroniclers, St Clair notes that whereas the price of the Waverley novels kept dropping during the decades after 1830, Bentley seems to have been much more reluctant to broaden his audience still further by narrowing profit margins on individual volumes. The result was that, if Scott's fiction had dominated the market during his lifetime, it dominated it even more after his death. Bentley sat on the rights he had bought (and which he kept, in many cases, for a generation); meanwhile, the Waverley novels circulated through the anglophone world in every imaginable form (as though the tormented ghost of their author were still doing everything it could to pay off debts).[8] It is a slight overstatement to say that prose fiction in the Romantic period became the novels of Walter Scott. But there were noticeable tendencies in that direction.

The Popular Novel in England 1770–1800

In 1920, Jane Austen's fortunes were rising and Walter Scott's were on the wane. R. W. Chapman's 1923 critical edition of Austen was, Kathryn Sutherland suggests, the "first such treatment of a popular English novelist." The classically trained Chapman had thought about what such an edition would require during his World War I stint as a gunner in the Balkans; the care he lavished on Austen, Sutherland argues, was in part a reaction to his experience of the War. Seemingly the chronicler of quiet villages, insulated from the turbulence of the Napoleonic era, Austen provided "a refuge from our own historically sated present."[9] One correlative of this reading is that, if the Waverley novels fared less well in the postwar period, it might have been because they were so clearly saturated with history; more palpably, more measurably, Great Britain was saturated with them. Not everyone rejected the ubiquitous Scott; Virginia Woolf's *To the Lighthouse* offers a thoughtful appreciation of *The Antiquary*, mediated through the mind of the aging Mr. Ramsay, a leftover Victorian Sage, standing in for Woolf's own father, Leslie Stephen. All the same, the Author of Waverley was a problem; by the early twentieth century, he had become the writer whom everyone read as a child, and then he became the writer whom everyone was supposed to read as a child, except that most didn't want to any more. There would be no comprehensive critical edition of Scott until the end of the twentieth century, when devolution made him into an important, if equivocal, icon of Scottish nationalism. Meanwhile, the Waverley novels went into the attic.

Austen and Scott were monuments (compact or crumbling). The rest of fiction in the Romantic period seemed less monumental. Its apparent lack of weight was emphasized by one of its best early historians, J. M. S. Tompkins, whose magisterial study of *The Popular Novel in England 1770–1800* (1932) declares:

> Between the work of the four great novelists of the mid-eighteenth century and that of Jane Austen and Scott there are no names which posterity has consented to call great, but there is a large body of fiction which fed the appetite of the reading public, reflected and shaped their imaginations, and sometimes broke out into experiment and creative adventure. In this tract a generation of readers took their pleasure, and it is the conditions of this pleasure that I have tried to make out.[10]

Tompkins did not exactly apologize for focusing on little-known and generally unremembered novels, but did feel it necessary to explain why they were still worth studying. Her method was to read deeply and broadly in a literature that seemed ephemeral to many contemporaries, as well as to most later critics. The sheer density of her researches helped her evoke a whole world of "popular taste" with unusual vividness and precision. It was clear to her, however, that she could only accomplish this task by skirting around Austen, Scott, and perhaps a few others. "These spirits would have been too strong ... if I had suffered them to intrude."

One of the essential ways in which Tompkins managed to bracket out stronger spirits was by ending her study in 1800. For most purposes, this is not an especially logical place to stop; the French Revolution is over, but its immediate consequences, as manifested by the Napoleonic Wars, are just in the process of unfolding, and the novel – a form deeply open to politics and history – is mixed up in this process irretrievably. For Tompkins, nonetheless, it is a serious consideration that she cannot afford to let Austen, much less Scott, appear on the scene of her idyllic, miniaturized world of minor writers. Minor novelists consort well enough with one another; placed next to the greats, they become practically invisible. Clara Reeve was not nearly so severe, or so anxious, in her list-making; Richard Bentley was cheerfully eclectic, assembling a good range of recent works by a combination of luck, taste, and judgment about what the public would be willing to buy. More sheltered than either of these predecessors from the practical world of publishing and authorship, Tompkins had a fuller, denser sense of the past than they did, but she also experienced great difficulty integrating small works with larger ones, in fact, she was unwilling on principle to do so.

In taking this stance, she was not alone. A decade later, the first edition of *The Cambridge Bibliography of English Literature* identified seven "first-rank" novelists working during the Romantic era: Frances Burney, Beckford, Austen, Scott, Edgeworth, Peacock, and Marryat. By contrast, its authors of "minor fiction" (there are hundreds of them) included not only the writers that Tompkins wanted to shelter from Austen and Scott, but a range of better defined figures, including Galt, Charles Maturin, Sydney Owenson (Lady Morgan), and Mary Shelley ("minor," perhaps, because she seemed to have written only one major book). Godwin appeared as an "essayist and pamphleteer," hardly a novelist at all (although his fictional works were scattered among the eighteenth-century listings). James Hogg, author of that perennially alarming masterpiece, *Confessions of a Justified Sinner*, was categorized mainly as a poet.

Tompkins demonstrates that every book from the past might tell us something important; moreover, in her hands, this kind of historical significance no longer seems dry or abstruse. As a result, *Popular Fiction* is still the best overall book about the novels of its period: densely, circumstantially knowledgable, and seldom condescending to the writers under study. Yet it cannot countenance the prospect of a synthetic, integrated overview of its subject. Tompkins does not brood about the divide between major and minor, which is presented as an inevitable condition of things. In some ways, retrospectively, she seems caught in a distinctive period dilemma, strongest during the interwar period (though also noticeable after World War II, when Trollope graduated to the idyllic Austenian slot). As a general principle, if some writers are to be monumentalized, above all for reasons of national security, then others must be kept out of view. Under these circumstances, there can be no meaningful act of comprehensive survey. During the early twentieth century, the idea of fiction in the Romantic period thus had to suffer a drastic, though temporary, bifurcation.

2000: *The English Novel 1770–1829*

Since the mid-twentieth century, three developments (at least) have reshaped the scholarly sense of what constitutes fiction in the Romantic era. First, almost all the "minor" authors just mentioned have acquired – or reacquired – substantial identities. It is true that Marryat has sunk further out of sight than before; perhaps this is because so much of his work belongs to that still-elusive decade, the 1830s – or perhaps it's not at present clear how to read maritime and military fiction. The others have been treated more apprecia-tively. Godwin has been revalued as a master of Gothic and historical materials. There were *Frankenstein* admirers from an early point, Scott pro-minent among them, but Shelley too has been revealed as much more than a one-novel writer. Available in a pathbreaking new edition, Hogg's work can now be seen as offering a sharp, sustained challenge to the vision of history and society offered by the Waverley novels. Lady Morgan (in association with Edgeworth) has benefitted from a resurgence of interest in nationalism as well as in fiction by women. Sophia Lee's *The Recess* (1783–5; warmly treated by Tompkins) has long been considered a book of historical signifi-cance, since it was popular and often imitated; back in print, in a strong scholarly edition, it now seems a major imaginative accomplishment. Neither Maturin nor Radcliffe needed rediscovery, but a heightened interest in Gothic fiction during the waning decades of the twentieth century has helped intensify curiosity about their work and its original context. Galt, finally, is still a bit of a dark horse, but his regional works have gained new respect, as well as new editions; the recent republication of a book as ambitious but little-known as *Bogle Corbet* (1831; beginning in Jamaica and ending in Canada, after exploring the impact of the Industrial and French revolutions in Scotland) might give a larger sense of his considerable range.

As the variety of writers in the limelight has widened, so has the sense of fictional genres in the period. It has never been hard to identify late eighteenth-century fiction with the Gothic and early nineteenth-century fiction with the historical novel; however, both these modalities now seem more diverse, and more divided against themselves, than they used to. Meanwhile, a succession of other generic types has been recovered for general discussion. Scott's version of historical fiction proves to be in dialogue with the Irish "national tales" of Edgeworth, Lady Morgan and others, as well as with a variety of considerably more transient projects, such as the "scandal" novels of 1807–8.[11] The Jacobin novels of the Revolutionary period turn out to be more than matched by a sustained anti-Jacobin backlash; a later strain of conservative fiction is defined by Hannah More's evangelical *Coelebs in Search of a Wife* (1808), which spawns both direct imitations (or refutations) and further experiments in moral austerity, such as Mary Brunton's *Self-Control* (1811) and *Discipline* (1814). This development of a broad interest in genre cuts two ways. It grounds very well-known books in largely forgotten fashions and fads of another day – for example, Austen's *Mansfield Park* (1814) in the work of writers like Brunton. Simultaneously, it brings once celebrated, now somewhat obscure, books into the spotlight; they acquire (or reacquire) a kind of celebrity, if only by association. The cumulative effect is to blur, without eliminating, the sort of distinction that the *Cambridge Bibliography* wanted to make when it set up its "major" and 'minor' lists. (And indeed, the third edition of the book has given up this distinction altogether.)

The late twentieth-century book that epitomizes these trends most effectively is Gary Kelly's *English Fiction of the Romantic Period 1789–1830* (1989). Kelly's Romantic period begins perhaps a little late; it ends late too, allowing him to include a strong discussion of "silver-fork" novels (on high society) and Newgate Novels (on crime), two types of fiction often lost in the no-man's-land between Romantic and Victorian studies. In addition he provides a highly original treatment of what he calls "the Romantic quasi-novel," including such under-read works as Legh Richmond's *Annals of the Poor* (1809–14), Thomas Frognall Dibdin's *Bibliomania; or, Book Madness: A Bibliographical Romance* (1809), Thomas Moore's *Memoirs of Captain Rock* (1824), as well as Moore's verse narratives, and the "Noctes Ambrosianae" composed by the circle of writers associated with *Blackwood's Magazine* (1822–35). Conversely, all this boundary-stretching does not prevent Kelly from singling out Austen and Scott as writers especially deserving of comprehensive and intensive treatment; where, for Tompkins, the simultaneous treatment of monumental with forgotten authors seemed impossible, it has now become an integral feature of historically sensitive (and historically ambitious) reading.

A third development encourages a yet more drastic rethinking of fiction in the Romantic period. *The English Novel: 1770–1829*, edited by Peter Garside, James Raven, and Rainer Schöwerling, "records the first editions of all known novels in English published in the British Isles" during the specified fifty-nine years. Garside and his colleagues are necessarily wary about just what counts as a novel, and make certain important exclusions from this category. Nonetheless, after their excisions, a good deal is left to record. Volume I (1770–99) lists 1,421 novels; Volume II (1800–29) lists 2,256. (In both cases, the figures include translations.) Many of these books have seldom or never been noticed since their original publication and reviews (and their path through the circulating libraries of the British Isles). In other words, the field of works that constitutes British fiction in the

Romantic period is now known to consist of some 3,600-odd books. What would it mean to explore them in their totality?

The editors base much of their analysis on statistics. With frequent assistance from charts and graphs, they demonstrate how many novels were published year by year, pinpointing such periods of "optimum production" as 1808–10 (279 titles) and 1823–5 (277 titles); the rate at which novels moved from two-volume to three-volume and from duodecimo (tiny) to quarto (huge) formats; how many authors chose anonymity; how many lied about their gender identities (to borrow Garside's transsexual example, a "Bengal Officer" may be a lady, or "A Lady" a Bengal officer); how much money novelists made from their work (Ann Radcliffe and Walter Scott substantial amounts; most other writers, rather little); and at what rate English translations of foreign novels filtered into the anglophone world. It is usefully disorienting to discover that the ten "most productive authors of novels, 1800–1829" are – in order of productivity – Sir Walter Scott, Barbara Hofland, Mary Meeke, August Lafontaine, Frances Lathom, Stéphanie Genlis, Catherine George Ward, John Galt, Sarah Greene, and Louisa Stanhope. Scott's position at the head of the list comes as no surprise, but relatively few readers will recognize each and all of the other nine. Meeke, Stanhope, and Lathom published with the popular Minerva Press, which produced various kinds of light reading, including an extensive line in the Gothic. Genlis and Lafontaine are both French imports, she a versatile celebrity author (former mistress of Orléans Egalité, tutor of the future Louis-Philippe), he another Minerva specialist. Much of Barbara Hofland's best work is for children. There are, of course, other ways yet to measure what people were reading: numbers of editions, print-runs, and numbers of times a given copy was perused. Not all of this is reconstructible, but each such determination provides an illuminating glance into the world – the market – of late eighteenth- and early nineteenth-century fiction. Working with these figures, one starts to get a fresh sense of the system; something of the density of Tompkins's *Popular Novel* is restored, though in a more methodical and perhaps more authoritative way. In certain ways, indeed, Scott and Austen seem much closer to their times than ever before, since their novels play off readerly expectations established by a wide range of recovered contemporary work.[12]

This new bibliography of English-language fiction in the Romantic era is unlikely to be bettered; that makes it more important than ever to remember what's still missing. As the editors observe, in the late eighteenth and early nineteenth centuries, "novel" was a flexible term. However, for practical purposes as well as theoretical ones, it does have limits. The editors exclude on principle "religious tracts, chapbooks, literature written only for children and juveniles, and very short separately issued tales. Collections of tales are included; separate verse tales are not" (p. 4). They also tend to avoid the scandal-mongering *roman à clef* (as recently laid bare in Iain McCalman's *Radical Underworld*) and tale collections with an ethnographic bent, like the Irish or Scottish compilations of William Croker and Alan Cunningham; perhaps both these subgenres are too much like non-fiction. Short stories published in magazines exclusively are also not counted, which means that certain important fictional types, like the *Blackwood's* tale, are much less visible than they were to contemporary readers.

These exclusions noted, the range of late eighteenth-century and early nineteenth-century novels available for study is now larger than ever before – both literally (since Garside et al. have uncovered a considerable number of previously unrecorded titles) and in the terms of practical, everyday discussion among those who study the period intensively. There is simply more that seems potentially meaningful. This full view could perhaps seem overwhelming, but in context it is curiously intimate. The point is driven home by a remarkable survival from the period. Over the last decade, especially, a number of professional Romanticists have been fascinated with "Die Fürstliche Bibliothek" (the Princely Library) at Castle Corvey in Germany. The Princely Library contains almost 2,500 English novels published between 1790 and 1834; that's about three times as many as are available in early editions at any other location and much more than half of all those that are known to exist, or to have existed. This section of the library was assembled by Victor Amadeus, the Langrave of Hesse-Rotenburg and his second wife Elise, with the help of Dr. Möller, a Göttingen bookseller. Elise died in 1830 and Victor in 1834. Their heirs neither carried on in their spirit, nor dispersed or sold the books that had been accumulated.

The editors base their descriptions and analysis on the books at Castle Corvey, supplementing Corvey as needed from other sources. However, Corvey is interesting for more than its bibliographical value. The combination of physicality and (near) comprehensiveness is haunting. Some current-day collectors and scholars have the luxury of reading Scott and his contemporaries in the old two- or three-volume editions (which are not only a pleasure to handle, but provide important clues to structure and tone lost in modern reprints), or in the equally informative Magnum Opus. That the Corvey collection is as close as it is to a complete run – that one can encounter this large a proportion of the English-language novels published during the Romantic period, and encounter them, moreover, in one princely but nonetheless circumscribed library – gives additional pause for thought. Victorian fiction would not fit into the library of Castle Corvey. Conversely, few inquirers, even the most ambitious, are going to make their way through all of what's in the castle, but the range and variety are still comprehensible without an impossible degree of strain – and the books can be assembled in a human-scaled succession of spacious rooms. The Romantic era is effectively the latest historical period (for the anglophone world, at least) in which the extent of novel production, the totality of the product, can assume a relatively compact – Corveyesque – form.

The Spirit of the Beehive

Victor Erice's film *The Spirit of the Beehive*, a landmark in the history of the Spanish New Wave, appeared in 1973, towards the end of Franco's regime. *Spirit* recounts a tale from the early years of that long-lasting government. It is 1942; the place is a remote Spanish village, where a philosopher and his family are living in a kind of voluntary retreat from the public sphere. The philosopher tends bees and meditates upon their social habits (which he finds disturbing). His wife dreams of a lost love. Left largely to their own devices, his two young daughters have a lot of time on their hands. They see an old print of James Whale's *Frankenstein* (1931), the famous film version in which Boris Karloff with a high forehead and a bolt through his neck receives, inadvertently, a criminal brain rather than the good brain that the well-intentioned scientist meant to implant in him. This is not Mary Shelley's plot, of course. Her tale of a universally rejected outcast had been constructed as an argument for a society where even the most revolting outcast could gain social acceptance. By contrast, Whale's cautionary narrative recalls the theatrical "Frankensteins" that toured during most of the nineteenth century, preaching a moral about the vanity of human presumption and the danger that science will challenge divine will, thus blaspheming against it.

Struck less by the overall point of the film than by its local and often felicitous oddities – like a curious scene where the creature plays with a small child, then accidentally drowns her – the two girls make up a fantasy about the creature, imagining him as a spirit who haunts the woods and will come if called; it is not clear whether his coming would have desirable consequences, but it might. This is first the idea of the older daughter, Isobel; then the younger one, Ana, takes it over and it becomes her ruling obsession, while Isobel looks on stunned and tries to be part of a game that's gotten beyond her. The rest of the film is mostly about waiting in a spirit of messianic expectation. Eventually the Messiah comes, or at least the creature does. Fleeing through the wood, Ana sees him face to face, and as he bends down towards her, she closes her eyes, she waits for his healing or deathly touch ...

Ana and Isobel learn *Frankenstein* at a distance. They do not read the book, they see the film, itself more influenced by theatrical adaptations than by Mary Shelley's original. Moreover, they don't have enough knowledge about art or fiction or narrative, or for that matter philosophy, to grasp what's supposed to be going on. Their refashioning of Whale's movie involves certain wild misunderstandings which then prove to have their own intrinsic power, leading the girls ever further from the movie that was their original inspiration. How could any of their forbidden games ever circle back to that now-distant original? The strange thing is that by the time *Spirit* concludes, it has proven to be the most faithful among the many adaptations of Shelley's novel, not in its narrative, certainly, but in the approach to politics and society enacted by the children, especially Ana. Like Mary Shelley, Ana is a philosopher's child. Ludicrously, there is a scene where she tries to shave with her father's razor, but even this farce has its weight; she proves her father's daughter. As Ana learns, first from her beekeeper parent, then from the imaginary creature who seems to mimic his awkward gait and to whom she transfers her affections, there are powerful models for how to live in a world where one is an outcast, an internal exile either by genealogy or choice. The film, like the novel, asks us to see things from the outcast's perspective, and to make the pertinent deductions from that philosophical experiment.

Fiction in the Romantic era has proven a rich field of inquiry; Reeve, Bentley, Tompkins, and the editors of the Oxford bibliography have recovered a multitude of books for reading, discussion, and study. *The Spirit of the Beehive* allows its viewer to imagine, if only in passing, a drastically different version of the post-Richardson, pre-Victorian novel. This heritage has been compacted; in fact, it seems to have shrunk to a single book, a book, moreover, that isn't even available directly, but that can – indeed, must be – communicated through layers of mediation (as is the monster's story in *Frankenstein*, a tale within a tale within a tale that gains in point with every mile it travels and every listener it reaches). Erice's scenario intimates that if a novel is sufficiently powerful, it works, and even works best, from a distance. Just a hint of it, transmitted indirectly, brings it to the right receiver: call her Ana. Fiction in the Romantic era can be conceived under the sign of romance and novel, as Reeve argued; or presented as a vast publishing project, a potentially endless series, as in Scott's Magnum Opus or Bentley's Standard Editions; or as a self-enclosed world, protected from greatness and thereby achieving a peculiar greatness of its own, as Tompkins supposed; or (perhaps most satisfyingly) it can be Castle Corvey. But, then again, it might also be thought of as a remote but powerful source, amplified in influence through its very inaccessibility. This would be the Romantic reading of fiction in the Romantic period.

NOTES

1 A generation later, Thomas Peacock would use a similar format in a series of more fully realized conversation novels: *Nightmare Abbey, Headlong Hall, Crotchet Castle, Gryll Grange.*

2 This information on the publishing history of *Progress* derives from Gary Kelly's entry on Reeve in *The Dictionary of National Biography.*

3 Karl Kroeber's *Romantic Narrative Art* (Madison: University of Wisconsin Press, 1960) still offers the best account of how and why this happened.

4 William St Clair, *The Reading Nation in the Romantic Period* (Cambridge: Cambridge University Press, 2004), p. 224.

5 For a clear and concise account of Scott's bankruptcy, see David Hewitt's article on Scott in *The Dictionary of National Biography.*

6 For more on this, see Jane Millgate's *Scott's Last Edition* (Edinburgh: Edinburgh University Press, 1987).

7 See Michael Sadleir's analysis and bibliography in *XIX Century Fiction: A Bibliographical Record*, 2 vols. (London: Constable & Co. and Berkeley: University of California Press, 1951), Vol. II, pp. 91ff., and Royal Gettmann's account of the Standard Novels in his *A Victorian Publisher: A Study of the Bentley Papers* (Cambridge: Cambridge University Press, 1960), p. 46.

8 See St Clair, *Reading Nation*, p. 363.

9 Kathryn Sutherland, "On Looking into Chapman's *Emma*," *Times Literary Supplement* (January 13, 2006), pp. 12–13.

10 J. M. S. Tompkins, *The Popular Novel in England 1770–1800* (Lincoln: University of Nebraska Press, 1961), p. v.

11 See Ina Ferris, *The Achievement of Literary Authority: Gender, History, and the Waverley Novels* (Cornell: Cornell University Press, 1991); Katie Trumpener, *Bardic Nationalism: The Romantic Novel and the British Empire* (Princeton: Princeton University Press, 1997); Peter Garside, "Popular Fiction and National Tale: Hidden Origins of Scott's *Waverley*," *Nineteenth-Century Fiction* (1991), pp. 30–53; Peter Garside, "The English Novel in the Romantic Period," in Garside, James Raven, and Rainer Schöwerling, *The English Novel 1770–1829: A Bibliographical Survey of Prose Fiction Published in the British Isles*, 2 vols. (Oxford: Oxford University Press, 2000), Vol. II, p. 42.

12 Some of Franco Moretti's highly theorized work on the history of the novel was avowedly inspired by the researches of Garside et al., *The English Novel*, Vol. I, p. 4, suggesting how close the link can be between bibliography and the most ambitious kinds of large-scale historical criticism.

2

WILLIAM ST CLAIR

Publishing, authorship, and reading

The economic conditions within which works of prose fiction were printed for sale in Great Britain during the Romantic period were set by a legal decision of 1774. In that year, following a struggle that had lasted for decades, the House of Lords, acting as the supreme court for civil cases in Great Britain, confirmed that the practice of perpetual intellectual property, which had been a central feature of the English book industry since around 1500, was unlawful – indeed that it had been unlawful for over sixty years. Since the passing of the Act of Parliament of 1710, commonly known as the Act of Queen Anne, the court determined, the only intellectual property regime permissible under the law of Great Britain was the precise set of statutory provisions laid down in that Act. Queen Anne's Act had formally recognized that an exclusive right to make printed copies of a text for sale – "copyright," although the word was not used – is an authorial right that comes into being with the act of composition.

The statute gave an author the legal right to assign his or her copyright to a publisher for a period of fourteen years, with provision for a possible further fourteen years if the author were still alive at the end of the first fourteen. Provision had been made for a transitional period after the Act first came fully into force, but after 1774, the maximum length of time during which an intellectual property holder could exercise a monopoly right to sell printed copies was twenty-eight years "and no longer" in all circumstances.[1] Queen Anne's Act applied, with a handful of exceptions (mainly official religious texts whose status was laid down in other legislation), to all texts printed in Great Britain since the arrival of printing.

For a few years after 1774, it was not certain that the court's decision could be made to stick in practice. The main London book publishers acting in concert had seen off attempts by outsiders and insiders to exercise their statutory rights on many occasions since 1710, and in 1774 they again mobilized their political and financial power. Many within the industry expected that the decision of 1774 would either soon be formally reversed or that means would be found to frustrate or circumvent it. For example, the main firms, who operated many other restrictive business practices besides perpetual intellectual property, instituted a system of "honorary" copyrights among themselves, and continued to buy and sell expired copyrights as if nothing had happened. For a time they had some success in resisting the decision. However, by around 1780, it was clear that, on this occasion, they would not succeed. Publishers from Scotland, where the courts had correctly applied the 1710 Act since it came into force, flooded the English market with reprints of texts that lay outside the terms of the Act, selling them at about half or two-thirds the English prices and making large inroads into the market. Newly founded English firms, entering the book market for the first time, started to reprint out-of-copyright texts in competition with the former intellectual property holders, with the Scottish publishers, and with other reprinting firms.

By 1780 the publishing industry in Great Britain had become divided into two sectors with entirely different economic characteristics. One sector published works that had entered the public domain under the terms of Queen Anne's Act in conditions of economic competition. The other sector published newly written copyrighted works within the terms of the same Act at monopoly prices. By around 1800 the mainstream English industry had itself adapted to the new conditions, with the largest firms, such as Longman, operating in both sectors. By that time too, the Scottish book industry became part of a British book industry with London and Edinburgh as competing centers operating within the same nationwide intellectual property regime. In 1801, Ireland, which had hitherto been a separate jurisdiction from Great Britain, and where the absence of intellectual property restrictions had enabled a large offshore reprinting industry to develop, became part of an enlarged United Kingdom subject to the same intellectual property regime as Great Britain. The offshore reprint business whose books, when sent to England, had provided some, albeit illegal, alternative to high English prices, was brought to an end.

The two sectors of this new British publishing industry were subject to sharply divergent economic pressures. In the copyrighted sector, it was in the commercial interest of publishers to sell small numbers of the books at high prices, and then, if demand continued, to reprint at lower prices for a slightly wider market. As with other monopolistic industries, especially those selling capital not consumption goods, the pressures were to stay high on the demand curve and to tranche down slowly during the limited period of monopoly ownership.[2] In the competitive, public domain sector, the pressures on publishers were to gain an advantage over other publishers who were offering the same or similar texts. A publisher could gain such an advantage by making his books more attractive as objects of sale. But the main area of competition was price. A publisher could reduce the price at which his books could be profitably sold by reducing his manufacturing costs, by, for example, printing in a smaller format, using cheaper paper, or employing new technology.

The technological limits within which book publishers were constrained were the same across the industry. In essentials, the technology of text-copying by print had remained largely unchanged since the fifteenth century. Movable metal type, each piece made individually by hand by a skilled craftsman, was set by hand by skilled printers who copied by eye. After the setting of the print came the inking, the drying, and the pressing of the sheets, and then the folding, the stitching, and the binding. The paper was made by hand, sheet by sheet. The battlefields of Europe were picked over before the blood was dry for every scrap of cloth that could be sold in the rag fairs and on to the international markets. The cast-off smocks of Hungarian shep-herds, the shirts of Italian sailors, and the bonnets of Irish ladies all made their way to the booming paper mills which were springing up along many British rivers. Boiled, bleached, and smoothed, the paper from which most British books of the Romantic period were made remains white and spotless after 200 years, shaming all subsequent books. Paper was expensive and heavily taxed, and the watermarks reveal their date of manufacture to within a few months. Most books published in the Romantic period were manu-factured entirely by hand, with the use of hand-held tools, by skilled men who had served a long apprenticeship in their trade. The types, the paper, the ink, the press, the binding were all manufactured without the aid of machin-ery or of mechanical power.

The printers, who were legally liable for the lawfulness of the texts to be printed, sometimes asked for changes. They were also the final authority on spelling and punctuation, and often made changes without the author's consent. William Godwin, noted for the punctiliousness of his punctuation, was still complaining that his wishes were not respected fifty years after he wrote his first book. When a book was to consist of more than one volume, the printing was frequently contracted out simultaneously to more than one firm. For example, the three volumes of Lady Caroline Lamb's *roman à clef*, *Glenarvon* (1816), published anonymously, were each printed by different printers. Splitting the printing saved time and provided some protection against proofs being stolen and sold to pirate publishers abroad. When the printing of some of Austen's novels was divided, the different printers used different type fonts, a matter of little importance for books intended primar-ily for commercial renting, in which each volume went out to a different borrower.

When time was short, the writing, the printing, and the proof-correcting often proceeded simultaneously. One reason why some of Walter Scott's Waverley novels were weak in artistic unity and contained many minor inconsistencies is that they were sent to be printed in sections as they were written. With movable type it was possible to make corrections and changes during all the stages of the manufacturing. Since the publishers and book-sellers continued to sell whatever they had until the reprinted sheets arrived, there are often textual variations among books which appear to be from the same edition, as well as corrections, and new errors in subsequent editions.

Apart from standard works such as school text-books, it was usual for the publishers to order editions with typical print runs of 500, 750, 1,000, or occasionally 1,500, or 2,000, and to order a reprint, much the same range as in earlier centuries when the market, economy, and population were only a fraction of the size they had since become. If a work was to be reprinted for a second or a subsequent edition, the author was encouraged to correct, revise, and add to the previous text, usually by marking up a copy of the previous printed version. A second or subsequent edition might then be noted on its title page as "revised" or "corrected," but often there was no overt indication that textual changes had been made. Textual differences between editions were intrinsic to the technology of manufacture by movable type. Since every edition was a new investment, with opportunities for corrections, additions, revisions, and new paratexts, movable type encouraged instability between editions.

Authors often wished to revise their texts and publishers encouraged amendments and additions as a means of maintaining or renewing interest. In 1811 Scott's publishers were advertising that *The Lady of the Lake* was in its ninth edition, *The Lay of the Last Minstrel* in its twelfth, and *Marmion* in its seventh. Murray too liked to give the public the impression that any edition of Byron sold out as soon as it was put on sale. On examination, however, some of the later editions turn out to have been made, wholly or in part, from unsold sheets of earlier printings, dinner leftovers re-heated for next day's lunch, made more appetizing by a few fresh garnishes, a new preface, or new notes, but sometimes with nothing but the title-page changed to a new date. Sometimes, the publishers pretended to editions which had never actually existed. In the case of Hannah More's novel *Coelebs in Search of a Wife*, for example, we find editions numbered 3rd, 5th, 7th, and 9th but none with even numbers. These ancient selling practices, found throughout the era of movable type, were known as "lifting a book."

By the 1810s, a new form of text-copying began to be applied to the manufacture of reprints. Stereotype plates were made after the text of a book had been set up in movable type and the proofs corrected. By taking a plaster mould of the type into which molten metal was then poured, it was possible to make a durable metal plate, in effect a duplicate of each sheet of movable type. After a number of copies had been printed from the first edition made by movable type, and the types put back in the cases for use on the next order, as many copies as were required could be run off from the plates. The plates could then be put in store, to be brought out and used for making reprints. Stereotyping was only adopted in the mainstream book industry in London after the process had been pioneered and introduced by outsider firms. In 1807, it was said that the cost of commissioning a set of stereotype plates was the equivalent of printing an extra 750 copies of the first edition by traditional movable type methods. At that time, it was suggested, only about twenty or thirty titles could justify the investment. The first titles to be selected for the technology in the 1810s were those for which a continuing large demand was expected at that time, reference works and dictionaries, and the best-selling anthologies and abridgments, of out-of-copyright texts, including school text-books, and the archival record tends to confirm that many of the titles selected for stereotyping turned out to have a long life with many reimpressions made from the plates over many years.

By 1839 it was said that 100,000 impressions could be taken from one set of plates, and with care a million, and the invention of paper moulds and electrotypes soon afterwards raised the potential output figures even higher. As had been the case with the shift from manuscript to movable print, the new copying technology had effects on reading patterns which went far beyond the reductions in the unit cost of manufacturing extra copies of particular texts. With movable type, the industry was normally obliged to utilize the expensive hand-made type as frequently as possible, seldom keeping type standing for more than a few days or weeks, before it had to be put back in the cases for use in printing other orders. Long initial print runs were rare and often resulted in heavy remaindering. With stereotyping, by contrast, although the initial costs of setting up a text remained the same, and the costs of making the plates was extra, once the plates were made, the movable type was not needed again. Since the melt-down value of the plates as scrap was low, they could be kept in store until it was certain that they would never be needed again. For the first time in history, a publisher could plausibly promise never to let a title go out of print.

The new technology altered the balance of economic incentives between publishing new titles and reprinting existing titles. For any level of printing/reprinting output, therefore, stereotyping enabled the printer to operate with less of the most expensive component of his fixed capital, namely the hand-made types. Furthermore, since reimpressions could be manufactured quickly without the need for new editing, typesetting, and proof-reading, the working capital required in making reprints was lower than in the days of movable type, as were the risks to unsold stocks from fire and water. Text-copying by movable type had tended to stabilize texts within editions, but promote instability between editions. Stereotyping ensured that texts were also stable from edition to edition. Authors were still permitted, and sometimes encouraged, to add a new preface, which could be added to the previous version, and publishers frequently changed the title-pages and sometimes the illustrations. But as far as the main text was concerned, once it had been inscribed on a durable plate, the difficulties and expense of correcting or amending it were prohibitive, and it was, literally, set in metal. Gone were the days when authors could rewrite from edition to edition. As far as readers were concerned, printed texts came increasingly in one version only, fixed once and for ever, not at the moment when the author or editor laid aside his or her pen, but when the production manager in the printing shop passed the proofs as fit for stereotyping. Although corrections and additions to the plates could be made, some plates carried their errors for the remainder of their material lives, which could be half a century or more. The arrival of stereotyping was to have as profound an effect on the whole system of texts, books, prices, access, and reading as any change since the arrival of print.

The effects of 1774 on price, access, and readership, are observable and quantifiable across the whole range of print producton of the Romantic period, not only prose fiction, verse, plays, essays, and other imaginative literature, but the vast body of non-fictional works. The patterns that emerge are fully in line with what elementary economic theory of monopoly and competition would predict. In the out-of-copyright sector, minimum prices dropped, sales soared, and access and readership widened dramatically. For example, in the case of Defoe's *Robinson Crusoe*, first published in 1719, the archival records of publishers and printers show that, although it had been regarded as a best-seller from the day it was published, within about five years of 1780, it had sold more copies than in the previous sixty.

In the out-of-copyright sector, as economic theory would again have predicted, prices were largely determined by manufacturing costs, the longer texts costing more to manufacture. But even when some of the cost factors, such as paper and taxes, rose, as they did during the war and later, minimum prices continued to fall. Table 1 shows some typical prices.

Meanwhile, in the copyrighted sector, we see a quite different pattern of price, access, and, therefore, of potential readership. As the minimum price of out-of-copyright fiction halved, halved again, and went on falling, the price of copyrighted fiction doubled, and then tripled, as can be seen from Table 2. Since the general value of money relative to other goods and services

Table 1 *Typical retail prices of out-of-copyright novels, before rebinding, in shillings*

1800–1810	Daniel Defoe's *Robinson Crusoe*	5 to 3.5, falling
1810	Samuel Johnson's *Rasselas*	1
1810	Horace Walpole's *Castle of Otranto*	1
1823	Walpole's *Castle of Otranto* (Limberd's edition)	0.5
1820	Tobias Smollett's *Roderick Random*	3.5

Table 2 *Retail prices of new three-volume novels, boards, before rebinding, in shillings*

1790 to 1800	about 9	
1800 to 1810	about 12	
1801 (Austen's) *Sense and Sensibility*	15	
1813 (Austen's) *Pride and Prejudice*	18	
1814 (Scott's) *Waverley*	21	
1816 (Austen's) *Emma*	16	
1816 (Scott's) *The Antiquary*	24	
1818 (Mary Shelley's) *Frankenstein*	[short]	16.5
1818 (Thomas Love Peacock's) *Melincourt*	18	
1818 (Scott's) *Rob Roy*	24	
1819 (Thomas Hope's) *Anastasius*	31.5	
1821 (Scott's) *Kenilworth*	31.5	
All subsequent Waverley novels in three volumes	31.5	
1840 51 out of 58 new novels	31.5	

was falling during much of the nineteenth century, the stabilization of prices at thirty-one shillings and sixpence (31.5 shillings) represented a continuing rise in real price terms.

During most of the Romantic period, it was normal for all books to be rebound in leather before they were read, a factor that widened the differential further, the out-of-copyright sector books being, on the whole, smaller in size and in number of volumes than the three-volume format in which most new novels were published from the 1820s. In general, in terms of length of reading matter or of hours of potential reading, the out-of-copyright authors were available in mainstream bookshops at about a tenth of the prices of newly published works. Outside the mainstream bookshops, prices were even lower.

To understand the book prices of the period, and the potential customers that they imply, we need to construct a standard which reflects not only the relative and absolute levels of prices of goods and services, but the social and economic structures and expectations of the time. For this purpose we can use the rates of pension that were established in 1816 for officers of the armed forces after the long wars came to an end. A figure of 100 shillings a week would be the typical income of a senior retired commander in the Royal Navy with some independent income, that is, a reasonable but not extra-vagant income for a member of the upper or upper-middle classes. Against the standard of 100 shillings a week, we can regard the prices of books expressed in shillings as percentages. Thus, by the 1820s, a new three-volume novel cost about a third of the weekly income of a gentleman. Hazlitt's life was transformed when he married a widow with "an independence of nearly £300 a year," near to my suggested standard, and was able to make his first trip abroad. We can estimate the impact of these prices on the book-buying patterns of younger sons, clergymen, officers, doctors, merchants, widowed ladies on annuities, journalists, university students, and the large cons-tituency of potential readers whose income lay between 100 and, say, 50 shillings.

Letitia Landon, for example, one of the most famous and financially successful authors of the later Romantic period, lived on £120 a year, less than 50 shillings a week. For this group, buying a new novel would be a high, in many cases prohibitive, slice of the weekly budget. Lower down the socio-economic scale, the printers, the highest-paid skilled workers in the country, were paid about 36 shillings a week from 1810. Carpenters were paid about 25 shillings. Lawyer's clerks in London were paid about 10 shillings and sixpence (10.5 shillings). For the vast majority of the reading nation, the only books they could hope to buy, if any at all, were reprints of out-of-copyright texts.

For the first time in English publishing history, the 1774 decision per-mitted formal canonization, that is, the publication of books by different authors in uniform editions under titles such as "The English Classics" and "The British Novelists." Of the many hundreds of works of prose fiction that had been published, however, only a small minority were selected to be reprinted even when all restrictions had been lifted. The canon of prose fiction that emerged included at its core *Robinson Crusoe*, *Gulliver's Travels*, *The Pilgrim's Progress*, the works of Richardson, Fielding, Smollett, Sterne, Johnson's *Rasselas*, and Goldsmith's *Vicar of Wakefield*. These, and some other eighteenth-century works, were published in uniform series by many competing firms, some operating from outside London, notably Harrison, Hogg, Nicholson, Cooke, Sharpe, and Whittingham. The mainstream firms established their own series, "Walker's Classics," priced above the minimum, which they later followed with another series, published by Dove, and then another published by Scott and Webster. By the 1820s many of the titles had been stereotyped, enabling prices to be further reduced. Although the names of the authors were generally noted in these lists, novels were mainly listed and advertised by title. A few translations, notably *Don Quixote* and *Gil Blas*, were so closely integrated into the editions of English classics as to be regarded as part of the national canon.

In the public domain sector, texts could be freely anthologized, abridged, and adapted. *Gulliver's Travels* was usually purged. *Robinson Crusoe* was drastically adapted for a widening constituency of children of all ages, and provoked imitations, spin-offs, and parodies. Many books were sold in installments, as a form of consumer credit, usually at sixpence (0.5 shillings) a week. By the 1820s, *Robinson Crusoe* could be bought in full for as little as a penny (0.08s.) a part. Publishing in parts also affected the nature of the reading experience. Just as new novels were frequently read as serials, rented by a family, a volume at a time, from commercial circulating libraries, so the much wider reading constituencies who could now afford to buy out-of-copyright fiction, including children, read the older novels in installments. As Hazlitt remembered from his childhood, "Tom Jones ... came down in numbers once a fortnight in Cooke"s pocket edition ... The world I found ... was to me a dance through life, a perpetual gala day."[3]

The volumes, normally small and portable, could be read outside, important to those who had to snatch their reading opportunities, but could also be carried in a pocket or a handbag, an important consideration for some constituencies, such as women of the higher income classes, whose reading normally occurred in the semi-public space of the drawing room. As John Clare remembered of his childhood, "I read the old novels and poems again and again ... At this time there were published charming little volumes of verse and prose, as Walker's Classics, one of which was generally in my pocket."[4] Even in the cheapest editions, the out-of-copyright novels normally contained at least one illustration, usually the work of some notable modern artist, that was engraved in copper or woodcut. Since newly published fiction was almost always unillustrated, this feature also affected the reading experience. As Leigh Hunt wrote of his schooldays, confirming the appeal of the illustrations: "I doted on their size; I doted on their type, on their ornaments, on their wrappers containing lists of other poets, and on the engravings."[5] The rapid expansion of the reading of printed literature that was released by 1774 was matched by an expansion in the viewing of fine reproductions of works of art.

In 1808, at a time when the economic and cultural consequences of 1774 had not yet worked their way through, the publishers' campaign to reverse the decision had its first success. The statutory copyright period was extended from fourteen years to twenty-eight years in all circumstances. In 1814 the period was extended to cover the life of the author. Then in 1842, when many of the famous works of the Romantic period were still in copyright, a new Copyright Act extended the copyright period to either the author's lifetime plus seven years or to forty-two years from publication, whichever was the longer. A regime that had restricted copyright to about one generation, was replaced by one of about three generations. Given the lag after 1774, while the industry wondered whether the decision could be made to stick, the short legal copyright set out in the Act of 1710 was, therefore, only observed in England for about twenty-five years.

In practice only a limited range of texts slipped through what I have called "the brief copyright window." We can regard them as forming a canon, which I have called the "old canon" on which 1774 conferred the gifts of low and falling prices, widening access, and larger readerships. When it was first made available during the brief copyright window, the old canon, although mainly the printed texts of a remoter past, also contained a proportion of works written only a few decades earlier. If the 1710 Act had continued in force, the old canon would have been continuously replenished, refreshed, and updated by works falling out of copyright. However, when, after 1808, the brief copyright window came to an end, the number of titles coming out of copyright dropped sharply. As the publishers drove up the price of newly written books, the old canon, held fast within the ever tightening economic constraints, stood unchanged, gaining in authority, falling in price, gradually extending its penetration ever deeper and wider into the expanding reading nation, but becoming more obsolete with every year.

Alongside the eighteenth-century novels, amongst the largest group of prose texts to be reprinted as old canon classics were collections of essays such as *The Spectator* and *The Tatler* with an explicit moral message. A large body of conduct literature, much of it reprinted seventeenth- and early eighteenth-century texts, gave advice on how to lead a pious life, offered comfort in tribulation, illness, and bereavement, and guided readers on how to prepare for death. Many old canon conduct books composed later in the eighteenth century offered advice on reading, as did the many conduct books first composed and published in the Romantic period. The explosion of reading that began in the late eighteenth century included an explosion of warnings against the risks of uncontrolled, unsupervised, unselected, and desultory reading. Novels and romances that took their readers into attractive alternative worlds, and potentially undermined their assent to the religious, political, social, and gender structures and customs of society, were regarded by many as particularly harmful. To combat these perceived threats, many novels were little more than conduct literature disguised as fiction.

Of all the many changes brought about by 1774, the one with the most long-lasting consequences was to steep British readers, including children, of the post-Enlightenment urban and industrialized nineteenth century in the pre-Enlightenment rural religious culture as it had been imagined and celebrated by writers of the previous century. Almost everyone in the Romantic period about whose reading we know anything, from lord to cottager, appears to have been familiar with old canon authors. It was the first truly national literature, available not only to men and women of the traditional reading classes but to a rapidly growing constituency who could choose to find sixpence (0.5 s.) from their income to buy a book. Reprinted on local provincial presses, anthologized, abridged, incorporated into schoolbooks, and carried to the villages by chapmen and "numbers" salesmen, the old canon reached far more deeply into the reading nation than any texts written during the period. The old canon texts made their way into the village schoolroom, to the smoke room of the ale house, to the inglenook of the shepherd, to the wallets of ploughmen in the fields, the weaver at his handloom, and artisan at his bench, the bored lady, and the unhappy schoolboy. During the Romantic period the reading nation was probably, to a large extent, commensurate with the reach and availability of these texts.

In traditional literary history, which is often conventionally arranged as a chronological parade of canonical authors, and which usually presents works of literature as autonomous objects of aesthetic appreciation, the literature written by one generation is presented as succeeding its immediate predecessor. A history of reading, by contrast, shows instead a reading nation in which different layers of readers interacted with texts of differing degrees of modernity and obsolescence within their economic circumstances and cultural horizons. Any attempt to understand the writings of the Romantic period, whether we consider texts, authors, readers, or possible impact on the construction of mentalities, will be incomplete without an appreciation of how deeply the so-called Romantic age was steeped in the texts of the old canon, although the fact is recorded in plentiful detail not just in the publishing statistics but in the biographical and historical record. To take *Robinson Crusoe* as an example, according to Hazlitt, "Next to the Holy Scriptures, it may safely be asserted that this delightful romance has ever since it was written excited the first and most powerful influence upon the juvenile mind of England."[6] *Robinson Crusoe*, believed by many to be a genuine autobiography, and commended as a tale of Christian virtue, hard work, and perseverance, eventually rewarded with a large fortune made from the profits of overseas trade, was probably amongst the most influential pieces of prose fiction that was read during the Romantic period in the sense of helping to shape the mentalities of readers. By contrast, although Hazlitt was a professional lecturer on English literature and published extensively on the writings of his contemporaries, including the "English novelists," he seems to have been entirely unaware of the works of Austen.

The effects of the changing intellectual property regime on prices, on access, and therefore on readerships can be traced from author to author. Some of Frances Burney's novels, notably *Evelina*, went out of copyright during the brief copyright window and became cheap and plentiful. Of the six novels by Austen, *Sense and Sensibility*, *Pride and Prejudice*, and *Mansfield Park* were in copyright for twenty-eight years, until 1839, 1841, and 1842, but *Emma*, *Northanger Abbey*, and *Persuasion*, which qualified for the 1842 extension, remained privately owned, and only available at premium prices, until 1857 and 1860. Scott's verse romances, mostly published before 1810, went out of copyright, in their unrevised versions, at various dates in the mid-1830s. By 1839, *The Lay of the Last Minstrel*, *Marmion*, and *The Lady of the Lake* could be purchased for less than one shilling each, and minimum prices continued to fall rapidly. With Scott's prose romances, on the other hand, the intellectual property wheel of fortune favored the producer's interest. The 1842 Act came into effect on 1 July, just six days short of twenty-eight years from the date when the first copies of *Waverley* had been put on sale in 1814. As the then three owners looked at their records, they were delighted to discover that the last-minute delays which had caused annoyance in 1814 gave them a windfall bonanza in 1842. When the Stationers' Company registry opened its doors for business in London on July 1, 1842, the owners were the first in the door, and they registered not only *Waverley* and all the Waverley novels but virtually all Scott's prose writings and a corpus of revised "author's versions" of the poems. The copyright for the Waverley novels was prolonged at least until 1856, or in the case of Scott's revised editions, until 1871 and in some cases until 1876. Similarly patterns of texts, prices, and access, depending upon the date of first publication, the date of death of the author, and the effects on each printed text of the changes of 1808, 1812, and 1842, can be seen across all the new writings of the Romantic period. In every case I have looked at I find the same direct correlation between intellectual property, price, and access, and the same rapid sensitivity of the price mechanism. Anyone wishing to understand the readership of an individual work would be well advised to consider its intellectual property status, a factor that was often decisive in determining the extent to which it was reprinted or not and at what price. In the case of *Frankenstein*, for example, in order to protect their general pricing structures, the owners refused to allow another publisher to reprint it although it was then out of print, a dog-in-a-manger attitude that appears to have been common.

In addition to the private intellectual property regime, that is, a state-conferred and state-guaranteed monopoly selling right, the British state operated a wide range of direct textual controls on what could be legally printed and distributed. During the Romantic period these controls were unusually fierce and comprehensive. The laws relating to "seditious" and "obscene" libel limited discussion of political and sexual matters. Those relating to "blasphemous" libel protected from criticism the privileged status of the official English religion, both as a collection of ideas and as an ecclesiastical institution. Private intellectual property and state textual controls were closely allied – the publisher of any work that risked being prosecuted either by the state or by private groups bringing private prosecutions could not be sure that his private intellectual property rights would be upheld by the courts. During the Romantic period, a time of international crisis when many previously accepted ideas were losing adherents, the main British publishers, as well as authors and their advisers, practiced self-censorship that went beyond the formal prohibitions of the law. *Frankenstein*, for example, was turned down by several publishers for fear that it would cause offense to Christians.

One of the many differences between the two sectors of the publishing industry was in their attitude towards abridgments. Since about 1600 the English book industry had, with some exceptions, not permitted abridgments of texts that they regarded as being in their private ownership on the grounds that they would undermine the market in the main unabridged texts. The effect until 1774 was to divide the English reading nation sharply into two and to confine the fictional reading of those at the lowest tranches of the book market and reading public to chapbook versions of old romance, many of them abridgments of longer literary texts made before the 1600 clampdown. By around 1800, however, abridgments of the old canon were available at comparably low prices, and the old chapbook canon that had lasted for more than 200 years disappeared, like the dinosaurs, in a sudden mass extinction. In the copyrighted sector, by contrast, the prohibition on abridgments continued to be an essential feature. For example, while they were in private ownership, there were no abridgments or chapbook versions of the Waverley novels, texts that cry out for shortening, nor of any of the many other novels that failed to pass through the brief copyright window.

The differences brought about by the restrictions on abridgment emerge vividly when we look at the patterns of access for so-called 'Gothic' fiction. From the 1780s to the 1810s, such works were often initially published anonymously in three or more volumes by the Minerva Press and other publishers closely associated with the commercial circulating libraries. By around 1800 "Gothic" fiction was also available in so called "blue books," chapbooks consisting normally of thirty-six to seventy-two pages with at least one illustration, sold at prices of one shilling or sixpence (0.5s.) by firms such as Arliss. In 1803, for example, the schoolboy Percy Bysshe Shelley was reading them by the dozen. English "blue books," with their echo of the popular "bibliothèque bleu" in France that the authorities of church and state eventually suppressed because of their perceived threat to mainstream political and religious ideologies, have been even more heartily despised than the Minerva Press texts of which they are derivatives. The rapid tailing off of the publication of blue book Gothic by the 1810s has been attributed to a change in taste, but can be more precisely explained as a drying up of access to longer mainstream texts. By the 1830s, the popular sector, that by that time could, by applying new technology adapted from the newspaper industry, profitably sell whole novels at prices as low as twopence (0.16s.) was obliged to go to France, Germany, and the United States to find abridgable and adaptable prose fiction, foreign texts not yet having any copyright protection in the United Kingdom.

Popular audiences did however have some access to recently written fiction through another medium, the theatre. Although intellectual property in printed texts was rigidly enforced, and piracy of mainstream texts was rare, there was, as yet, no legal intellectual property in performance. Until the Dramatic Copyright Act of 1833, a theatre wishing to put on a commercial production of a printed play did not need to obtain the permission of the holder of the copyright. Furthermore, during the Romantic period, many works of literature, including many novels, were adapted for the stage almost as soon as they appeared. Unlike printed literature, theatrical performances, that were usually scripted by professional adapters, were subject to direct pre-censorship, and many works were altered so drastically in order to conform with the censorship as to be scarcely recognizable. *Frankenstein* was altered so that the main message was lost, but every single night of performance of one of the adaptations brought a version of the story of the man-made monster to more men and women than the book did in ten or twenty years.

As far as newly written novels are concerned, there are records of about 3,000 titles of new works of prose fiction being published during the period.[7] However, number of titles is a poor indicator of production and of readership. For that we need reliable records of print runs, sales, the markets at which they were aimed, and information about the extent to which a copy of a book might have had multiple readers. Most of the novels produced during the period, for example, were designed not only to be sold to personal buyers and readers but to commercial libraries who would then rent them out to those who paid membership and borrowing fees. From the names used at the time, "circulating libraries," "proprietary libraries," "subscription libraries," "public libraries," "book societies," "reading societies," "book clubs," "literary societies," and others, it is not possible to separate the commercial renting libraries from the libraries formed by groups of citizens under their own ownership and control. There were almost no free libraries. "Public libraries" were only public in the sense that they were open to all customers able and willing to pay. I use the convention of using the term "circulating libraries" to describe the commercial renting sector.

As the London publishers admitted to a Parliamentary inquiry in 1818, their predecessors had tried to prevent the growth of a renting sector. At some time in the mid-eighteenth century, however, they suddenly reversed their policy. By the 1820s there were about 1,500 circulating libraries in Britain. Almost every town had at least one, and resorts favored by the leisured classes, such as Bath, Cheltenham, and Brighton, had several. The question why book renting took off when it did and not at some other time before or after has not yet been fully answered. Part of the explanation may be that the industry solved the problem of how to prevent the growth of an effective second-hand market. At a time when a single volume of one new novel would have cost more than a week's income for most of the population, and when there was a market even for single, damaged, and incomplete books of other kinds, it is hard to believe that second-hand copies of new novels would have had no value. What we may be seeing are the results of restraints on resale, a restrictive trade practice, whereby the producers make it a condition of giving trade discounts that the goods must be sold back in part exchange or that they should not be resold until after a certain period of time has passed. In other words it was part of the conditions within which they were produced that they should be effectively removed from potential readers after their initial circulation. Documentary evidence for this business practice is plentiful for the Victorian age.

Although books other than novels may have been as much as half the total holdings in some circulating libraries, the business of most was not to provide a comprehensive book lending facility for the local community, but to rent out the latest novels and romances when they first appeared, and to replace them frequently with more recent titles. The main circulating library owners were also book publishers, and from the beginning the close interdependence between the producing and the renting sectors and their customers affected the texts. During the 1790s, the Minerva Press published about one third of all the novels published in London. The renting sector decisively influenced the conditions in which new English novels were written, the textual limits, the material format, the price and therefore the extent of access, and the social composition of readerships. Although circulating libraries widened the amount of reading among the upper income groups, they did little to deepen it down the socio-economic scale. In England, commercial circulating libraries were the main medium of reading for nearly a century, but membership never widened beyond the aristocratic, professional, and business classes. Although the libraries maintained a nationwide network, they never reached more than about 1 percent of the population.

Authors of the Romantic period normally wrote their drafts on paper with a quill pen while seated at a desk. A few dictated to an amanuensis. Whatever the initial transfer from mind to paper, the composing of a text was seldom a solitary activity, but involved family, friends, publishers, and advisers. The novels of Austen and Susan Ferrier were initially composed to entertain their families without any expectation that they would be published in print, or so the authors claimed. But authors of long works who aspired to a larger readership needed to find a publisher to arrange the financing, the manufacture, the distribution, and the sales. The main publishing centers were London and Edinburgh, but although postage was expensive, authors no longer needed personal meetings.

Most manuscripts were turned down. *Pride and Prejudice* was rejected by return of post. Nor did having a contract necessarily ensure that a work was published. Austen bought back the manuscript and intellectual property rights to *Northanger Abbey* six years after they had been sold to a publisher who in the meantime had let the matter lie. By taking out options in this way, publishers could, if not quite corner a market, put a squeeze on competitors, but on the whole, the record suggests, most works accepted for publication were published not long after. The rhetoric of Romanticism, mainly devised and developed in Victorian times, stressed the uniqueness and autonomy of the "creative" author, and some writers who did not depend financially on their pens, notably Byron, fiercely defended their independence. In practice, however, most authors were obliged to operate within a commercial system, with textual controls and pressures to self-censor, in which they, their advisers, and their publishers attempted to judge what the market wanted and how best to supply it.

A common type of contract, as it had been for centuries, was for the author to sell the copyright to a publisher outright for a lump sum. Under this type of contract, the publisher met all the costs of manufacture and publication, and the author had no further financial claim. Another traditional type of contract involved the publisher buying the copyright for an edition of a certain agreed size, say 500 or 1,000 copies, with another fee to be negotiated if a second edition were agreed upon. From the author's point of view, such a contract could be preferable to an outright sale of copyright, although in practice only a few authors benefited. A third common type of contract was for a sharing of the net profits between publisher and author, either by half or in some other proportion, after all the costs of publishing had been met. Under this arrangement the publisher accepted the costs and risks of production, but paid no advance. Profit-sharing contracts were attractive to publishers, but for authors they raised suspicions. Since, in striking the declared profit to be divided, all costs of every kind, capital and current, were netted against the receipts from the sales of the declared first edition, publishers had an incentive to understate the income and to overstate the costs. It was especially difficult for authors to judge whether the stated figures for the costs of printing and paper were reasonable, and they were often taken in. The accounts that the publisher John Murray prepared for Austen in calculating her share in the profits of *Emma* are as fictional as the novel.[8]

Finally, for authors who could not find a publisher willing to risk any of his own money, there was publishing "on commission" in which it was the author who was the investor who accepted all the costs and the risks, and the publisher who took a royalty on sales. "On commission" publishing was therefore the reverse of normal modern publishing practice, in which the publisher accepts the costs and the risks and the author receives a royalty, a type of contract which was virtually unknown in the Romantic period. Thomas Campbell told the story of how God came to London to offer to sell the copyright of the Bible. Colburn, the first publisher he approached, whose main line was in circulating library novels about high society, disliked the stables and carpenters, wanted the characters to be made aristocratic, and asked for the story of King Herod and Salome to be expanded. Longman, to whom God went next, said he did not think sales would be high. He told Him "that he would be very happy to print it at his Lordship's expense on commission."[9]

Unlike verse publication, where "on commission" publishing was probably the main type of contract in the Romantic period, enabling hundreds of otherwise unknown poets to see their compositions in book form, the publishing of novels seems to have been almost always a commercial enterprise, with both authors and publishers making some money, however small, on every book. Only a few novels are known to have been published at the author's expense, although in many cases publication was made conditional upon the author drumming up subscriptions in advance. In the 1760s, when circulating libraries first became common, the going rate for the outright sale of a manuscript of a novel with its copyright was very low. George Lowndes, for example, who was both a publisher and a circulating library proprietor, paid the authors of novels between £5 and £10 a title, depending on length.

By the turn of the eighteenth century the going rate was a little higher: an archive of copyright contracts of George Robinson shows an average payment to authors of about £25 in a wide range. Some authors, notably Mary Meeke and Frances Lathom, wrote large numbers of novels, probably receiving only a modest payment for each one. The £250 paid to Burney for *Cecilia* in 1795 was highly exceptional. By the middle of the Romantic period, however, the prices paid to authors were rising in line with the rising retail prices to readers. By 1824 even as relatively little known an author as "the author of Marriage" (Susan Ferrier) was able to obtain £1,000 for the copyright of *The Inheritance*, to be published anonymously.

But if writers of novels were receiving larger financial rewards, they were still more like piece workers than independent "authors," and most novels of the period were still published, as had been a custom in the eighteenth century, without the author being named. A few saw their names on the title-pages of their later works, but anonymity seems to have normal, particularly for first books. Although a high proportion of the novelists of the Romantic period were women, therefore, this was not obvious or known to readers at the time. Successful anonymous novelists seldom kept their secret for long, but it was one thing for family and friends to know, another for potential customers in the provinces ordering from bookshop and library catalogues. (Austen's) *Sense and Sensibility* (1811) was attributed on the title page to "a Lady," *Pride and Prejudice* (1813) was by "the author of Sense and Sensibility," *Mansfield Park* (1814) by the "the author of Pride and Prejudice," as was *Emma* (1816). During the Romantic period you could not go to a circulating library and ask for works by Miss Austen. Why there should have been a tendency towards greater anonymity at the time when the rhetoric of Romanticism strove to celebrate artists and writers as unique and independent creative geniuses needs an explanation. The main driving force was probably the ongoing attempt by the publishers and the circulating libraries to impose greater similarity, regularity, and predictability on the nature and habit of novel-reading, in other words to turn novels into uniform and mutually substitutable commodities, and the renting and reading of them into a regular habit.

From the surviving archival record it emerges that the normal print run for a routine new novel was about 500 copies, or sometimes 750, or 1,000, with only a small minority ever being reprinted. And although each copy might have been rented to a number of readers in succession – a multiplier that can be estimated for some titles – on such a small production base the number of readers per copy can seldom have been great. Given the numbers of circulating libraries, these production figures confirm that only a minority took even a large sample of what was produced. After 1814, one name dominated the

Table 3 *New novels and romances: estimated sales excluding collected editions, exports, imports, and piracies, in thousands of copies*

(Scott's) *Guy Mannering* (1815) to 1836	50
(Scott's) *Waverley* (1814) to 1836	40
(Scott's) *Rob Roy* (1818) to 1836	40
About twenty other Waverley novels	10 to 30 each
(Burney's) *Camilla* (1796)	4
Individual novels by Burney, John Galt, William Godwin, Maria Edgeworth, Ferrier, Amelia Opie, Jane Porter, Ann Radcliffe, and probably others	low thousands
(Burney's) *The Wanderer* (1814)	3.5
Most copies wasted	
(Austen's) *Pride and Prejudice* (1813) until mid-1830s	2 to 3
(Austen's) *Emma* (1815), sales before mid-1830s	2
Of which sold at unremaindered prices	1.5
(Mary Shelley's) *Frankenstein* (1818), sales to 1831	1
(James Hogg's) *Confessions of a Justified Sinner* (1824)	1
Most new novels published by Colburn, Longman, and others during the Romantic period	0.5 or 0.75

age, "the author of Waverley," not publicly acknowledged to be Sir Walter Scott, the famous poet, until 1827. The extent of his dominance is shown by the figures in Table 3.

Every circulating library worthy of the name took each new Waverley novel as soon as it came out, often several copies. Some London circulating libraries, it was said in 1826, were "obliged to have from fifty to seventy copies of each novel when it comes out." The demand for borrowing so outran supply that we hear of circulating libraries sometimes splitting volumes in half, to make six volumes per title instead of three. Shops which had never previously handled books went into commercial book lending exclusively to hire out Waverley novels. Not every reader who handled a volume, we can be sure, read it through or went on to the next volume, but few men and women who read any new books at all did not read Waverley novels at least in part, and many read every title as it came out. It was a publishers' joke that a man had been discovered at a London party who had not read the Scotch novels. The larger the sales, the record shows, the more a book was also rented. The bigger the sales, therefore, the bigger the multiplier needed to convert to readership. The predominance of Scott over all the other modern literary authors turns out to be many times greater than we might have estimated from the production and sales figures, huge though these are.

In 1828 the then owners sharply reduced the price of Waverley novels, bringing about a further huge increase in sales. It was partly their success which persuaded the publisher Richard Bentley to begin his innovative series of Bentley's Standard Novels. Bentley realized that, if he could buy cheaply the tail-ends of copyrights of out-of-print novels, he could start a uniform series which would take a second tranche from libraries and individuals who had not bought first time round. Bentley's Standard Novels, which began in the 1830s, included works by many excellent recent authors whose works had then become unavailable: Austen, Beckford, Burney, Edgeworth, Ferrier, Galt, Godwin, Peacock, and others. With the exception of the Waverley novels, Bentley made himself the owner of almost all the best fiction of the Romantic period and later of the 1830s. With a new title coming out every few weeks, he provided several years' worth of continuous serial reading, a delayed, carefully selected, series of most of the best fictional writing of recent times. Since Bentley innovatively arranged the series by name of the author, the names of Jane Austen, Susan Ferrier, John Galt, and others appeared for the first time on the title-pages. Bentley did for Romantic period novels what the editors of the initial old canon series had done at the end of the previous century, namely to establish an authoritative, carefully chosen, series of original works, and make it available more cheaply. And novels such as Hogg's *Justified Sinner* and Godwin's *Mandeville*, which failed to be selected, disappeared from public attention until the twentieth century.

Bentley insisted that the author should correct errors and supply new material either in the text or as a paratextual preface or notes. Even if the changes were minimal, the revisions allowed him to claim a new copyright which, if not valid in law, would normally be respected within the industry. If authors were reluctant to revise their texts, Bentley would provide a professional reviser to do the work. If, as in the case of Austen, the author was dead, Bentley asked a member of the author's family to write a memoir. Although, at an initial price of six shillings, Bentley's Standard Novels were less than a fifth of the price of new novels, they were not cheap by absolute terms. In the 1830s, a single Bentley's Standard Novel cost about half the weekly wage of a clerk or skilled manual worker. Bentley's novels were more expensive than Waverley novels whose sales were far higher. They were twice as expensive as reprints of out-of-copyright novels of similar length. Within his chosen market, Bentley positioned himself as far upmarket as he could go.

The books were tightly printed in one volume, and sold already bound in cloth, thus saving customers the usual further cost of rebinding; they each included an engraved frontispiece. The texts of some titles had to be abridged in order to fit the one volume format. Almost all were stereotyped. Although, over time, the plates became worn and the books became harder to read, the plates could occasionally be repaired to prolong their useful life. If the old pre-1842 regime had continued, Bentley could have extended his list almost indefinitely, adding, say, Dickens, Trollope, Thackeray, and the other mid-Victorian novelists to his list as their works went out of copyright. But after the ending of brief copyright in 1842, he was boxed in. With the new longer copyright regime, publishers were no longer willing to let him have copyrights cheap – they wanted to exploit them themselves. The supply of tail-end copyrights fell to a trickle and the latter titles of Bentley's Standard Novels were less distinguished than their predecessors.

At the same time, some authors such as Mary Shelley were still alive at the time of the Copyright Act of 1842. Bentley and his heirs thus found themselves windfall owners of a range of excellent, but increasingly obsolete, intellectual properties and also of the increasingly obsolescent plant from which copies could be manufactured. Bentley and his successors brought the price down from six to three shillings and sixpence (3.5 s.) to two shillings and sixpence (2.5 s.), but then stopped. Why they did not tranche down further, as the publishers of the Waverley novels did with success, is not known, but the effects of this single publishing decision on the later reading of the novels of the Romantic period were enormous. In the case of the Waverley novels, the further lowering of price took the texts to a reading nation of several millions. In the case of the other novels of the period, readerships remained confined to the upper tranches.

With all the main novels of the Romantic period there is, therefore, both a clear starting point, the date of first publication, and an easily recognizable publishing break point in the 1830s, within which to make comparisons. On one side are each and all of the Waverley novels whose immediate sale was often in the range 6,000 to 10,000 for every title. On the other side are all the other novels of the period, whose immediate sale in the Romantic period was usually in the range 500 to a maximum of about 1,500. With novels as with poems, by sales as well as by reputation, the dominant author of the Romantic period, and indeed of the Victorian period, was Walter Scott. During the Romantic period, the "Author of Waverley" sold more novels than all the other novelists of the time put together. Even by about 1850, as Table 4 shows, no novel by any other recent novelist, including Austen, had achieved cumulative sales of 8,000, a number which several Waverley novels reached in the first week.

Because many thousands of books of verse are known to have been printed during the Romantic period, it is sometimes assumed that verse was the preferred reading of the age, and that at the end of the Romantic period, there was a shift in public taste in which the reading of "poetry" gave way to

Table 4 *Novels of the Romantic period: estimated total book production during the period and later, in thousands of copies*

(Austen) 6 novels to 1830s	10 to 12
(Scott) 25 Waverley novels to 1829	500
Austen's 6 novels to about 1860	40
Scott's 25 Waverley novels to 1860s?	2,000 to 3,000

the reading of prose fiction. However, the fact of a book's having been noted in a bibliography as having been printed is no guarantee that it was produced in more than a tiny edition, let alone that it was widely sold, circulated, or read. When quantified, the apparent shift from verse to prose does not appear nearly so sharp as traditional parade models of literary history imply. Seen in a longer time horizon, verse and prose publication were proceeding in opposite directions. The authors of verse still came from the aristocracy or gentry, were proud to be named, and wanted to reproduce copies for friends at their own expense, either in manuscript or with the help of print. With novel publishing, by contrast, previously anonymous, genderless, low-skilled, low-paid, piece-workers were successfully claiming a more explicit acknowledgment of their role in the production process, and a greater financial share in the rewards from the market. The poetry of the Romantic period was supply-pushed by authors and patrons. Novels were demand-led by book purchasers, by commercial borrowers, and by readers. Verse was moving socially and materially downwards, the books in which it was published reducing in size from quarto to octavo and then to duodecimo. The novel was moving upwards from duodecimo to octavo. Verse publishing saw the expiry of the traditions of the guild and the early modern periods. The publishing of novels was a fully commercial enterprise.

* * *

In the United States, the structures that governed the publishing, pricing, and therefore the readership, of prose fiction were different from those in Britain as they were for all printed texts. In 1790, the federal government erected an intellectual property regime modeled, in part, on Queen Anne's Act. However, in what was the single most important structural determinant of American reading for nearly a century, the new law gave copyright protection only to the works of local American authors.

All the printed writings in English that had originated in Great Britain, old and new, were now available to be reprinted in the United States without the need to obtain permission from or pay fees to authors or copyright holders. Virtually every mainstream book published in Britain during the Romantic period was reprinted at once in the United States, often by more than one publisher simultaneously. Despite the attempts to develop a distinctively local American literature, reading in the United States during the period still coincided, to a large extent, with reading in Britain. Indeed the asymmetrical protectionist intellectual property regime helped to continue the dominance of texts written in Britain.

And, in sharp contrast with the situation in Britain, there was no price differential between the old and the new. The American reprints of newly written fiction were tightly printed by hand from movable type, manufactured in small format on poor quality paper, and sold at less than half the British prices. Some texts were adapted to fit the smaller format. Waverley novels, for example, which had been padded out to fit the British three-volume convention, were depadded into two volumes to meet the local conditions. Whereas the British publishers of newly written copyrighted works started at the top of the perceived demand curve and slowly tranched down, the American reprint publishers positioned themselves initially far lower down the curve, aiming to sell more copies at prices that were determined by manufacturing costs. The result was that Americans of the Romantic period had cheaper access to the literature being written in Great Britain than most of their contemporaries across the ocean. They also had access to illustrations copied or cloned from British books.

As in Britain, the novelist who had, by far, the largest sales was Scott. When in 1832, shortly after his death, the British publishers appealed to the United States Senate to agree to international copyright, they drew a picture of the cruel treatment which the Americans had inflicted on the most famous author of the age in his hour of need by refusing to make any payment. In 1820, it was said, boats had been sent out from American ports to look out for the ship carrying the first copy of *Rob Roy*. For the four volumes of *The Fortunes of Nigel*, nine printing shops were put simultaneously to work and the reprints were ready for sale in three days. In histories of American literature arranged as a parade of authors, Scott usually features only as a footnoted influence on James Fenimore Cooper. In histories of American reading, or in any attempt to assess how far American mentalities were influenced by reading, he must be regarded as one of the most influential. According to Mark Twain, the pervasive reading of the works of Sir Walter Scott in the states of the American South and the neo-chivalric ideologies that they celebrated "had so large a hand in making Southern character, as it existed before the [American Civil] war, that he is in great measure responsible for the war."[10]

NOTES

1 Much of this chapter is summarized from my longer study, *The Reading Nation in the Romantic Period* (Cambridge: Cambridge University Press, 2004) with some corrections and updatings.

2 Explained with worked examples in William St Clair, *The Political Economy of Reading* (London 2005), available free online under Creative Commons.

3 In "On Reading Old Books" in *The Plain Speaker*.

4 Mark Storey, ed., *The Letters of John Clare* (Oxford: Clarendon Press, 1985), p. 35.

5 *The Autobiography of Leigh Hunt* (1860 edition), p. 76.

6 From his memoir of "The Life of Daniel De Foe" prefixed to *The Works of Daniel De Foe* (London, 1840) Vol. I, p. cviii.

7 See Peter Garside, James Raven, and Rainer Schöwerling, general eds., *The English Novel, 1770–1829: A Bibliographical Survey of Prose Fiction Published in the British Isles* (Oxford: Oxford University Press, 2000).

8 For the actual figures, see St Clair, *The Reading Nation*.

9 Quoted by Royal A. Gettman, *A Victorian Publisher, A Study of the Bentley Papers* (Cambridge: Cambridge University Press, 1960), p. 9, and in *The Reading Nation*, p. 164.

10 *Life on the Mississippi* in *Mississippi Writings* (New York: The Library of America, 1982), pp. 500–1.

3

DEIDRE SHAUNA LYNCH

Gothic fiction

Gothic fictions of the Romantic period are constructed as curious compounds of the unknown and the too well-known. On the one hand, these narratives traded in obscurity and mystery. This trade (and attendant turn away from the novel of modern life) had gotten underway, vexingly enough, at precisely the historical moment when it looked as if an educated populace, weaned from superstition, schooled in the empiricist protocols of the Scientific Revolution, would at last be ready and able to see the world in its true colors. Gothic fictions reacquainted that populace with the perverse pleasures of *un*certainty. Thus, for instance, the preference in many of these books for envisioning landscapes in those atmospheric conditions that Ann Radcliffe, virtuoso of picturesque description, evokes: her heroine admires the vista at times when "the progress of twilight, gradually spreading its tints . . ., steal[s] from the eye every minuter feature of the scene," or when "long billows of vapour" are seen "excluding the country below, and now opening, and partially revealing its features." The prospect conjured up in such passages discloses only enough for us to know that mystery is almost literally in the air. The Enlightenment assumption that truth is the product of an unmediated encounter between the eye and its object got sidelined when the novel acquired *atmosphere* (a word that Romantic-period Britons were already learning to use to identify a text's mood-creating tone, and which we continue to apply to texts that give us the chills).[1]

On the other hand, even as they took possession of the settings where their characters could be left in the dark (caverns, dungeons, secret passages), and even as they perfected the machinery of plot twists, digressions, and deferrals that placed their audience in that state too, Gothic fictions somehow produced a nation of *knowing* readers. Gothic readers could look up from their books and issue arch predictions about what they all too clearly saw coming. This knowingness bespoke the repeatability of this fiction's formulae. Especially after Radcliffe's triumph with her third novel, *The Romance of the Forest* (1791), book after book arranged (in the words of a reviewer) to annex "enchanted forests and castles" for "the province of fiction" and make "use of them for the purpose of creating surprise."[2] This meant that, in ways that made their mysteriousness predictable, the revenants haunting these sites kept coming back, at an egregiously accelerated rate. (At the peak moment for the mode, 1795, these fictions accounted for 38 percent of the novels published.)[3] Astonishment had become a commodity manufactured on an assembly line, or so disenchanted critics seem to complain during the period, anticipating twentieth-century critiques of mass culture. The repetition compulsion of a reading public who also appeared willing to keep coming back – expecting new surprises in the same, familiar format – likewise aroused acerbic criticism.

When Walter Scott recounts his search for a subtitle for his *Waverley*, he is caustic about such shopworn options as "a Tale of Other Days" and "a Romance from the German." What novel-reader in 1814 could possibly be so "obtuse," Scott asks, as not to anticipate, once cued by the first option, "a castle ..., of which the eastern wing had long been uninhabited, and the keys ... lost"? Whose brain would not, encountering the second, instantly image forth "a secret and mysterious association of Rosycrucians and illuminati, with all their properties of black cowls, caverns, daggers, ... and dark-lanterns"?[4] This is, of course, satire. Scott establishes his own originality as he decries the conventionality of his rival novelists, who for decades had deployed subtitles of this ilk with gusto. But these acknowledgments of the over-familiarity of Gothic materials – or, perhaps more precisely, of the potboilers' characteristic intertwining of surprises and samenesses – may also, strange to say, be found inside Gothic fictions themselves. Even the novel usually said to inaugurate the Gothic tradition, Horace Walpole's *The Castle of Otranto* (first published in 1764, acquiring the subtitle "A Gothic Story" in its second edition a year later), asks whether the thrills that it delivers to the reader can be sustained in the face of those sensations' oversupply – a question writ large across the mode's subsequent history. (In 1757 the downside to knowing too much had already troubled Edmund Burke as he discussed the vicissitudes of aesthetic sensation. "It is our ignorance of things that ... chiefly excites our passions," Burke writes in his *Philosophical Enquiry into ... the Sublime and the Beautiful*: "Knowledge and acquaintance make the most striking causes affect but little.")[5] Thus, in a line whose understatement and formality make it almost campy, the narrator informs us that Manfred, *Otranto*'s villain, is now "almost hardened to preternatural appearances"; at this point, in apparent fulfillment of a prophecy foretelling the fall of his house, Manfred has already seen his son dashed to pieces by a gargantuan helmet that tumbles from the sky, but faced with another "new prodigy" (an equally outsized sword), he "surmounted the shock."[6]

Radcliffe's *Mysteries of Udolpho* (1794) also ponders its enchantments' staying-power. Following her escape from Udolpho, where unexplained coincidences and mysterious voices predicting peril have led her almost to doubt her sanity, the heroine discovers her experience repeating itself. Her new place of refuge may likewise harbor supernatural forces. "'I perceive,' said Emily smiling, 'that all old mansions are haunted.'"[7] The smile prompts us to smile. It as if Emily herself were amused by her creator's hyperbolic plotting – and as if Radcliffe were anticipating her book's future lampooning.

This chapter will scrutinize this knowingness, scrutinize how knowledge itself is a topic for the Gothic, so as to help demonstrate why Romantic-period Europe found in this mode of fiction-writing one of its chief vehicles for political, philosophical, and aesthetic inquiry, despite the mode's reputation among critics and canonical Romantic authors for silliness and social irresponsibility. It will assess Gothic fictions across three adjacent microperiods. During the two-and-a-half-decade-long gestation period for the mode that follows the publication of *Otranto*, Walpole's model for producing "artificial terror" is assimilated into the culture of the novel only haltingly.[8] During the 1790s, Radcliffe's eminently imitable successes endow the Gothic with an almost scary degree of popularity, even while the import of lurid German terror novels elevates the fear factor in literature to unprecedented heights. The opening three decades of the nineteenth century, finally, are often identified as the moment when market saturation and the public's newfound preference for Scott's historical novels extinguish the mode, but, given the diversification of the book market and the emergence of new sorts of literary annuals, magazines, and chapbooks, Gothic authors might be said, instead, to be practising their trade in mystery in more formats than ever.[9] Throughout the Romantic period, the Gothic remains a vehicle for engaging questions posed by philosophers like Burke and David Hume: questions about the relationship of knowledge to belief (timely in an era of revolution when the political instrumentality of that particular mode of belief called ideology was explicitly theorized for the first time), questions about the relationship of knowing to feeling, or imagination to delusion, and questions about the powers of the mind. For the Gothic is especially interested in the minds of readers, and the psychological powers of auto-hallucination on which the reading act depends.

***

The recycling of second-hand material that *Waverley* jokily identifies as the fate awaiting the Gothic was actually inscribed in the tradition's genetic code. This was thanks to Walpole, who had intervened into the history of fiction by resurrecting a past that novelists were supposed to have put behind them. Walpole's second, 1765 preface declared *Otranto* an experimental hybrid, both of modern fiction, fettered by its adherence to probability and "common life," and of "ancient romance," which, however unnatural, did grant the imagination liberty.[10] Trickily equivocal, Walpole in *Otranto* does two things at once. He asserts the novelty of his enterprise – like Henry Fielding in the 1740s, he styles himself the founder of a new province of writing – yet, contrariwise, he allies that enterprise with the antiquity-hunting that figures such as Richard Hurd and Thomas Warton were undertaking, from the 1750s through the 1780s, under the banner of the romance revival. In rehabilitating Edmund Spenser's *Faerie Queene* (long faulted for its unclassical irregularity and scant resemblance to the epic), the witchery and fairy lore of Shakespeare, and the obscure medieval narratives that had nourished Spenser and Shakespeare with accounts of magic and marvel, the mid-eighteenth-century antiquarians and poets pieced together an oppositional literary aesthetic: one that flouted orthodox visions of cultural progress, and one that they promoted as a sublime if uncouth alternative to the languid literature of modernity. They advocated regression, from a world of "good sense" – where imagination had to accommodate humdrum truth if she were to be "admitted to good company" – and back to "a world of fine fabling."[11] Many eighteenth-century British novelists had declared their books means of reintroducing readers to nature, after reams of improbable fictions had diverted them from it. *Otranto* turned the clock back again. This impudent response to the early novel's habit of equating realism, literary modernity, and literary morality linked Walpole's book to the romance revivalists' campaign.

"Confused remembrance" is a psychological condition often investigated in Gothic fiction – the hazy sense of half-knowledge, or déjà vu, that orphans (the mode's favourite protagonists) experience when they explore a desolate castle, or contemplate an old portrait, and find it both strange and tantalizingly familiar. These books are plotted so that this exploration and contemplation prefigure denouements in which providence reveals family secrets and re-establishes disrupted genealogies. It turns out that it is their own family histories – balefully estranged – that the protagonists have encountered in these episodes. The portraits, whose lineaments look so much like their own, depict their true parents. They themselves are the legitimate heirs to the properties that sheltered them when, at the desperate moments in their histories, they were homeless or hiding from their persecutors. At the end of Clara Reeve's *The Old English Baron* (1777–8) the gates of Lovel Castle thus open magically, apparently "of their own accord," to receive the hero, who was raised as a peasant but has been revealed as the Castle's rightful master.[12]

In the later eighteenth century, romance is regarded in something of the manner of these edifices – as a legacy, neglected or lost but at last recovered, that is the ancestral birthright of the reading nation. (The nationalist motives of its promoters made the revival of romance a precocious form of heritage industry.) To some extent Gothic fictions are set up to enable the British public to probate that literary inheritance. Hence their writers' choice of medieval or Renaissance settings, an arrangement that enables their ordinarily incredulous readers to participate imaginatively in their ancestors' belief in romance's marvels.

Hence, too, the density of the books' intertextual allusions to earlier British literature, or to the so-called graveyard poetry of the mid-eighteenth century that made archaic romance its inspiration. It is as if these books about ghost-seeing also sought to keep open lines of communication with the literary dead. This allusiveness is manifested most flamboyantly, in the 1790s and after, within the quotation-heavy, verse-studded works of Radcliffe and her imitators. Every chapter within novels like *Udolpho* or Matthew Lewis's *The Monk* (1796) or Eleanor Sleath's *The Nocturnal Minstrel* (1810) opens with a mood-enhancing epigraph, usually from Shakespeare, Milton, Robert Blair, or William Collins. The narratives also carefully preserve the verses their protagonists compose at moments of inspiration. Such practices elevated the tone of the Gothic novel. They also made it resemble, formally, another byproduct of the romance revival, the literary anthology organized on historicist principles.

Bizarrely, however, the novels adorned by these quotations from the history of English poesy unfold, as often as not, *outside* Britain, in Catholic Europe – priest-ridden Italy or Spain – or Germany's Black Forest (*The Mysterious Hunter*, Figure 1). Indeed, through the Romantic period, fidelity to the romance origins of the national culture leads, as if cultural memory were structured like a Moebius strip, to its opposite, to a confrontation with otherness and outlandishness. This is the paradox inscribed in the very term "Gothic." In the period's historical debates, "Gothic" could denote, confusingly, both the native and the foreign, both the folkloric roots of British culture *and* the Oriental fantasies that Europeans had encountered during their Crusades against the Saracens. This doubleness energizes Gothic fiction. In its presentation of bygone horrors, it provokes a sensation of "confused remembrance" precisely by intermingling the *here and now* with the *then and there*, the familiar – quotations from verse that the modern reader has already read; sensible protagonists who apprehend their experiences as that modern reader would in their place – with the strange – the preternatural events, the bygone superstitions and the foreign institutions of oppression that make these protagonists suffer.

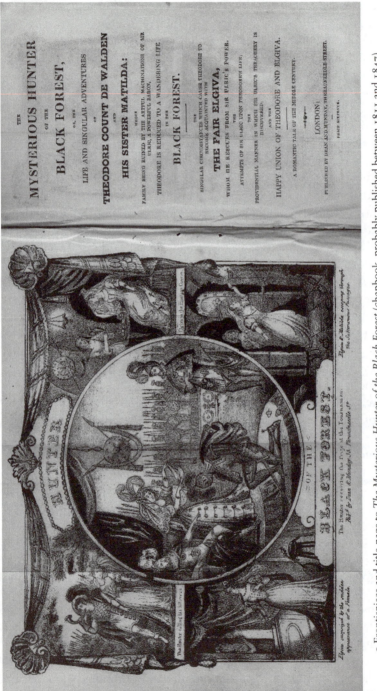

1 Frontispiece and title-page to *The Mysterious Hunter of the Black Forest* (chapbook, probably published between 1811 and 1847).

The Gothic's sleight of hand, in short, is both to locate lost origins and relocate them, banishing them beyond home's borders. For this reason, modern commentators often assert that its exhumations of the skeletons in history's closet and resurrections of archaic, unsocialized passions must have *reassured* a complacent British public. "It could never happen here": this is supposed to have been the message delivered by narratives chronicling tyrannical Italian and Spanish inquisitors, bloodthirsty German robbers, and the various fratricides, patricides, and matricides with whom their stories were regularly entangled.

The mode's message may indeed be a conservative reaffirmation of the status quo. Yet, in the wake of the French Revolution, the moment when historical reality starts supplying even more shock effects than this fiction can, some contemporaries advance an antithetical account of the mode: Gothic fictions are regarded as if they themselves incarnate the insurrectionary energies that menace the *ancien régime*'s structures of political subordination. By the 1790s even the sheer size of the readership drawn to Gothic fiction sometimes scared conservatives, supplying them with evidence that, in British literary culture as in the political arena of Jacobin France, the mob had taken the lead. The sudden influx into this expanded book market of terror novels translated from the German was similarly frightening for some, seeming to betoken Britain's vulnerability to invasion by alien political principles. Yet another assessment of the politics of the Gothic has been developed by modern feminist critics as they consider the unsettling manner in which supernatural occurrences are finally explained away by Radcliffe and her imitators. The plot that Radcliffe pioneers in *A Sicilian Romance* (1790) and that Eliza Parsons's *The Castle of Wolfenbach* (1793), Francis Lathom's *The Midnight Bell* (1798), and countless others recycle is structured so that, in these books' closing pages, heroines at last discover the truth behind the mysterious noises and sights that have earlier all but convinced them that the dead do walk. They learn that in fearing these apparitions they have been imposed upon: the ghosts are in actuality living women – sometimes these heroines' mothers – who have *feigned* their deaths so as to escape being murdered by their husbands, and who have then kept their existence secret by exploiting the superstitions of the surrounding populace. This revelation restores a world ruled by natural rather than supernatural causes. But aspects of that world might well seem as frightening as the delusions such denouements expel. In *A Sicilian Romance* the marchioness Mazzini, long supposed dead, is discovered by her daughter as an emaciated prisoner in the underground cell beneath the castle where once she was the mistress. When she recounts her story, the narrator tells us that "it entirely dissipated the mystery which had so long enveloped the . . . castle." But the story begins with a lament: "'Oh! why,' said the marchioness, 'is it my task to discover to my daughter the vices of her father?'"[13] Perhaps the appeal of such plotting for Britain's female readership was not that it transported them to an exotic past, but rather that it afforded them insight into their lives in the here and now. This variety of Gothic gave voice to a truth whose expression was increasingly censored in modern-day Britain, the truth about the continued existence of patriarchal coercion.

However, the Gothic mode's turn to the world elsewhere that Catholic Europe represented for British readers should not be seen simply as a device for masking the unseemliness of such insights. Romance's etymological and representational connection to the Church of Rome is deliberately exploited by Gothic writers as they investigate the mechanisms of power – the deceptive devices of priestcraft, to use the term favored by English Protestants – used in Europe's Catholic kingdoms to enforce a uniformity of belief among their subjects and to base their political unity on that adherence to doctrine. Such investigations obviously carried political resonances for an era of democratic revolutions. (Monarchical government had, after all, abruptly entered the category of things – like ghosts or devils or miracles or God – that an individual might or might not believe in. Hence Edmund Burke in 1790 castigating the Jacobins for overvaluing rationality, taking enlightened demystification too far, and thus recklessly abandoning the appeals to the "moral imagination" to which governments owe their legitimacy. They had stripped away the "pleasing illusions" in which power must veil itself, Burke declared, and so had left "laws ... to be supported only by their own terrors.")[14]

But through their interest in the romancing practiced by the Church of Rome – and their reiteration of the Protestant critiques that faulted the papists' ceremonies and spectacles for how they played on devotees' passions – Gothic writers find a way of exploring aesthetic questions as well. From exploring zealots' relationship to their religious creed or superstitious peasants' relationship to ghost belief, it is a short step, in the most compelling Gothic writing, to exploring the enlightened reader's complicated relationship to the illusions of fiction. For the act of reading something *as* fiction is predicated on a reader's capacity to deploy belief in a subtle, supple way, to fall "almost simultaneously into enchantment and disenchantment."[15]

Back in 1764, Walpole's preface to the first edition of *Otranto* inaugurated this line of investigation. This unsigned preface, in contrast to the one that Walpole added a year later, presented his text not as his fiction, but as a certain William Marshall's translation of a sixteenth-century Italian book "found in the library of an ancient catholic family in the north of England." It speculates that the author of this romance was a crafty priest, who – anticipating that the power of the printing press would soon dispel "the empire of superstition" – had determined, nonetheless, to "confirm the populace in their ancient errors" via his account of the horrors that divine wrath unleashes on Manfred's accursed house.[16] Later Gothic writers keep returning to that crafty priest and his bamboozling of the credulous. When, for instance, the reader of Lewis's *Monk* follows Father Ambrosio into his private chamber after he delivers a sermon that has made all Madrid tremble with their consciousness of sin, we learn enough to realize that the priest secretly exults in his skill at manipulating his listeners' feelings. Yet by the end of Lewis's novel – after Ambrosio has broken through his religious prejudices, acted on his lusts, and turned serial killer – such debunking of belief has an ambiguous status. A major source of that ambiguity is the fact that Matilda, the figure inside the book who is most fluent in the idiom of the Enlightenment, and who has seduced Ambrosio both with talk about the slavery of superstition and with sex appeal, is revealed to have been a devil all along. (Lewis's decision to cast Satan as the most successful plotter of all indicates just how far he was willing to go to escalate the shock effects of the Gothic mode. Not for him a conclusion like Radcliffe's that soothes readers' frayed nerves by restoring ordinary reality; in the frenzied closing pages of *The Monk*, as in those of *Zofloya, or, the Moor* (1806) by Lewis's emulator Charlotte Dacre, the Devil gets the last word.)

The 1795 translation of Friedrich Schiller's *The Ghost-Seer* inaugurated the vogue in Britain for German tales of terror; like Lewis's protagonist, Schiller's hero, a German prince sojourning in Italy, also careens back and forth like a puppet on a string between credulity and skepticism, in a narrative that breaks off just shy of the moment that will make his conversion to Catholicism a *fait accompli*. To read *The Ghost-Seer* is to be delivered over and over again into uncertainty. One is never quite sure of how to distinguish what is real from what is instead illusion wrought by the Prince's tormentors. Every act of demystification that checks the Prince's fascination with the occult – and propensity to become the dupe of priestcraft – looks, on a second view, to be drawing the would-be ghostseer further into a web of lies. The Prince gets walked through various proofs demonstrating that the first ghost he sees was a special effect created by a fraudster who is a dab hand with phosphorus and a magic lantern. These proofs, however, leave tantalizingly unexplained the status of the second apparition that appears hard on the heels of the first.

With its hall of mirrors plot, *The Ghost-Seer* exemplifies with particular egregiousness how Gothic fiction both condemns irrational superstition and exploits it, both fears the plots that it associates with crafty priests and *uses* them.[17] The hero of the sixpenny chapbook *The Monks of St. Andrews* (*c.* 1808–27) is, despite being a man of the Middle Ages, fully cognizant of these eighteenth-century lessons about the government of belief. At the story's end, when this Abbot of St. Andrews is revealed as the former Lord Alphonzo, the rightful possessor of the Castle of Haldenstein who was left for dead years before by a rapacious enemy, we learn that the plot that the book unravels is of Alphonzo's own devising: it has been designed to play on the usurper Ferdinand's superstitions. "[L]etters of lambent flame" appear on the castle walls and terrorize Ferdinand into repentance. He believes this handwriting on the wall to be of celestial penmanship. But when the provenance of those letters of flame is exposed – "a chemical preparation" – so, too, is the secret behind the enthralling power exerted by the letters on the pages we ourselves have perused (*The Monks of St. Andrews*, Figure 2).[18] Our situation as readers redoubles the character's. Hack-work that it is, *The Monks of St. Andrews* manages in thirty-six efficient pages to reprise the peculiar structure of address developed by works like *Udolpho* and *The Ghost-Seer*, its more respectable predecessors. It too aligns the out-plotted victims of superstition *in* the Gothic book with the readers who, confined on the rack of suspense, may feel themselves to be the duped victims *of* the Gothic book.

The many episodes when characters in Gothic fictions decide to entertain themselves with fictions likewise testify to the mode's defining interest in how it feels to read. Hence Radcliffe's Emily testing, at an anxious moment, whether circumstances will prevail "over the taste and powers of the mind" or whether instead she might manage one more time "to lose the sense of her own cares, in the visionary scenes of the poet"; hence Emily's servant Ludovico picking up an old Provençal tale ("strongly tinctured with the superstition of the time") to while away the hours as he keeps watch in the haunted castle.[19] And there is also the scene of reading that is included in the first story within a story in Charles Maturin's 1820 *Melmoth the Wanderer*, a book whose frame narrative recounts how a nineteenth-century Irishman discovers his family connection to an outcast, also named Melmoth, who long ago sold his soul to the Devil. The manuscript that young Melmoth discovers among the family papers, recounting the story of the encounter between his ancestor and an unlucky Englishman named Stanton 150 years earlier, includes this episode: "Stanton ... as usual seized the first book near him, and began to read. It was a volume in manuscript, – they were then much more common than now. The first lines struck him as indicating insanity in the writer ... It is singular that Stanton read on, without suspicion of his own danger, quite absorbed in *the album of a mad-house*, without ever reflecting on the place where he was." What ensues, of course, is Stanton's belated discovery that the lock has been turned on the door of the room in which he has been reading, and that he is now the fellow inmate of

2 *The Monks of St. Andrews, or, Castle of Haldenstein: A Romance. By the Author of the "Treacherous Minstrel"* (chapbook, probably published between 1808 and 1827).

the maniac writer. Stanton has tumbled inside the world of his dangerously absorbing book.[20]

Gothic scenes of reading bring to the fore the intimacy between this fiction and the discussions in which Romantic-period philosophers developed their new concept of the aesthetic, their new concern with registering the kind of knowledge embodied by art and the kind of cognition, somatic as well as mental, involved in art's appreciation. Philosophers and Gothic novelists alike take an interest in the psychology of reception, in the way sympathy can make our experience of another's tribulation feel as vivid as our own, in the way this feeling kicks in regardless of whether that other is real or fictional, in the strange power fiction has to transport its beholder from this world, and in the conditions under which (as with Radcliffe's Emily) that power fails.

Burke's *Enquiry into . . . the Sublime and the Beautiful* is often mentioned in this connection. Aiming to *know* something about the sensation of terrible uncertainty, the *Enquiry* enumerates how, variously, vacuity, darkness, solitude, and silence produce it. Burke's volume becomes, accordingly, the recipe-book from which Gothic writings will be concocted for the next seven decades. Another aesthetic inquiry, "On the Pleasure Derived from Objects of Terror," by brother and sister John and Anna Laetitia Aikin, extends the premises of the *Enquiry* so as to elaborate a full-dress vindication of the taste for wildly fanciful reading. "A strange and unexpected event awakens the mind, and keeps it on the stretch," the Aikins write in 1773, celebrating *Otranto* (alongside other romances) in quasi-medical terms, as an occasion for a kind of bracing psychological calisthenics.[21]

The Aikins' essay is upbeat, an early Romantic account of imaginative transcendence: "where the agency of invisible beings is introduced" into a narrative, they comment (in a passage indebted to Burke), "our imagination darts forth, and explores with rapture the new world which is laid open to its view."[22] But a more ignoble account of the self can be glimpsed at the edges of Romantic-period aesthetic discussion, as at the edges of the Gothic; the technophobic science fiction that is Gothic fiction's descendant will bring it to center-stage. This is the consumer of fiction conceived of as a kind of "sensory-response machine."[23] Gothic fiction can remind us of what is spookily mechanical, volitionless, about readers' responsiveness. Like pornographic fiction, which also made its British debut in the mid-eighteenth century, the mode is designed, thanks to the bait and switch tactics it implements through its narration of suspense, to provoke physiological sensation – to quicken the readerly pulse, for a start, and more generally to make bodies, without minds' say-so, do untoward things. Often, accordingly, the investigations of the reading process that the Gothic authors undertake end up furthering the mode's broader interest in morbid psychology, in "the way the human mind can . . . go astray" – as Schiller puts it, in language allying *The Ghost-Seer*'s story of the Prince's mental disintegration with the period's new psychological case histories.[24] In *The Monk* Ambrosio is easy prey because the demon Matilda is so adept at psychological manipulation, able to dominate her victim through his appetite for sensory gratification. Lewis might be seen as reinserting into the tale of terror the carnal elements in aesthetic discourse that Radcliffe omitted in her dematerializing, spiritualizing adaptation of Burke. (Burke had in fact observed that moralists too frequently attributed "the cause of feelings which merely arise from the mechanical structure of our bodies ... to certain conclusions of the reasoning faculty.")[25] Sensory bombardment is Lewis's modus operandi in *The Monk*, but when Radcliffe's heroines contemplate sublime nature (often, as noted earlier, under conditions in which nature is, in fact, hard to see) they become, as she likes to say, all pensiveness, all mind.

To some extent Lewis's materialist and fatalist account of mental vulnerability prevails. The political panics of the 1790s were conducive to his pessimism. The influence of books on the mind – a phenomenon generally lauded in the heyday of Enlightenment confidence about how education would underwrite social amelioration – had come to seem troubling at a moment when those same books looked to be sponsoring outright revolution. Indeed, the malice toward his audience that Maturin smuggles into *Melmoth* when, as we have seen, he makes a madhouse the staging ground for reading suggests how, as time went on, Gothic writers of books appeared to many (themselves included) to be taking on the lineaments of Gothic villains. The link between the two parties was their shared penchant for messing dangerously with others' vulnerable minds; both were connoisseurs of agony. Critical discourse on the Gothic retains into the nineteenth century the quasi-medical cast that we can see in the Aikins' aesthetics, but makes the text's operations on the reader's body seem less like therapy than like the actions of mad scientists. Samuel Taylor Coleridge's epithet for Schiller – "Convulser of the Heart" – is in this mode, as is the *Critical Review*'s declaration in 1805 that "the writers of the German school have introduced a new class [of fictions], which may be called the *electric*." "Every chapter contains a shock, and the reader not only stares, but starts, at the close of every paragraph."[26]

And if such references to narratives' electro-shock treatments of their consumers bring to mind the experimentation practiced in *Frankenstein* (1818), we do well to remember, in addition, that to tell his life-story Mary Shelley's experimenter actually begins with an account of how he, a vulnerable reader, fell prey to a sinister book. His dangerous ambition is traceable, Victor Frankenstein asserts, to the fatal moment when a work of medieval alchemy made an untimely appearance on the eighteenth-century stage and chance directed it into his hands. (The premise that modern philosophers like Rousseau had caused the French Revolution by means of their authoring haunts *Frankenstein*, and informs the text's ambiguous politics, but in positioning Victor as that anachronistic thing, a living "disciple of Albertus

Magnus and Paracelsus" in an "enlightened and scientific age," Shelley connects this problem of influence to the Gothic's signature theme of a primitive past that will not stay past.)[27] Shelley apparently enjoys conceiving of books as assailing unsuspecting readers (as choosing them rather than being chosen). Introducing her 1831 revision of the novel, she replays Victor's story and traces her own composition to a moment when "[s]ome volumes of ghost stories fell into [her] hands." Victor's monster is likewise a reader, one who by hazard happens on the books to which he ascribes his mis-education. Another book that chooses its reader is found in the American Charles Brockden Brown's *Wieland* (1798), a text deeply influential for Shelley: this story of a fanatic who believes he enjoys direct communication with God, and of his victimization by an emissary of a malevolent secret society, gets underway when Wieland senior chances "to light upon a book written by one of the teachers of the Albigenses," a "volume [that] had lain for years in a corner of his garret, half buried in dust and rubbish."[28]

But the Gothic mode in general has a penchant for making words seem eerily mobile, detachable from their contexts of origin, and for recording the interpretive difficulties arising from that decontextualization. (Think of frantic Ferdinand striving to assign an author to the handwriting on the wall.) The dead keep speaking in the Gothic – in medieval books of alchemy, in moldering manuscripts found in ruined castles – but the effects of distance and the physical depredations of time on these texts leave the protagonists who read the dead desperately uncertain, paranoid even, about what is being said and about why they in particular are fated to receive these messages. One might think in this connection of the mysterious voices that the protagonists hear and which they almost never succeed in tracing back to particular bodies – voices that could belong to spectres, or (as in *Wieland*) to conniving ventriloquists, but might also be the characters' hallucinations. All these instances of disorder in the relations between signifiers and signifieds, and between causes and effects, serve to create situations of extreme interpretive agitation – situations whose agonies are perfected in those German and German-influenced tales of terror in which secret societies of revolutionary conspirators appear, through their superhuman "sway over the minds of men," to *cause* everything – to cause all of history even – but who, "behind the impenetrable veil of mystic concealment," never can clearly be seen to be *doing* anything.[29]

Characterization is not the Gothic authors' strong suit. Psychology experiments probing the powers of the mind are, but there never seems, within their fictions, to be enough selfhood *per se* to go around. The plot motifs outlined above appear almost programmatically designed to undermine orthodox notions of the individual as the origin and cause of action, along with orthodox notions of causality. Characters, imperfectly individuated, never as self-contained as they would like to be, tend uncannily to resemble one another. The most recent visitor to a haunted castle will find her will stymied and her fate repeating the previous occupant's. And every one is hemmed in by the past. This curtailing of individual agency and autonomy may suggest that, for all their extravagance and fantasy, we could do worse than look to Gothic fictions if we wish to identify how Romantic culture provides the first drafts for modern narratives of social determinism. Historical novels of the early nineteenth century are often said to have extinguished the taste for Gothic mystery and restored the public to its senses; but Walter Scott's fascination with the friction between the laws of social change and the ideals of individual responsibility, his interest in the limits of agency of an Edward Waverley, enmeshed as that hero is within the business of common life, suggest how well he attended to the Gothic vision of history as a welter of uncontainable and malevolent forces.

On the other hand, we might return to the Aikins' commentary on the pleasures of terror to recall the challenge the Gothic mode posed to the orthodox ways of understanding what was fictional – as opposed to historical – about fiction. By endorsing Walpole's blend of the old and new romance, the Aikins, after all, deviate abruptly from a tradition of vindications of the novel that for half a century had depended on re-assimilating fiction to history, on highlighting how the novel's verisimilitude made it a vehicle for a knowledge that could educate readers for real life. In the late eighteenth century the Gothic – resurrecting superseded worlds in which marvels as yet retained their believers – raised the prospect that a fiction's authority might derive from alternate sources, not from its mimetic accuracy, plausibility, or didactic force, but from its performative efficacy – its capacity to affect readers. Notably, both Radcliffe and Maturin are drawn to Cervantes and his trademark creation, the quixotic and deluded reader who consumes narrative as literal truth: in *The Italian* (1797) Radcliffe even replays the episode that Cervantes centered on Don Quixote's destruction of the puppet theatre.[30] Those allusions to the first European novel can be understood as the means by which these novelists thematized their own position within the cultural history of reading. They also read as the writers' acknowledgment that narrative concerning those things (ghosts, portents, necromancy, diablerie) in which we moderns cease to believe once we close our books might function as a forum in which readers learn that "poetic faith" – that "willing suspension of disbelief" or "unaccountable operation of the mind between disbelief and conviction" – on which the recognition of fiction *as* fiction depends.[31]

Historically, that recognition was a long time coming. As recent scholarship on the early novel has emphasized, only in the mid-eighteenth century do novels begin to renounce claims to historical veracity (in the first edition of *Otranto*, presented as an antiquarian find, Walpole had yet to do that relinquishing).[32] Only then does the problem of differentiating kinds of untruth – differentiating lying from fiction-writing – start to look as though it were solved. Here, perhaps, lies the primary achievement of the Gothic fictions discussed in this chapter. Gothic fictions often call themselves romances, and use the generic epithet militantly, to declare themselves anachronisms (throwbacks) in both literary history and the history of belief. But as *modern* romances, whose stories of superstition and delusion illuminate how fiction is grounded in consensual illusion, they also help complete the rise of the novel.

NOTES

1 Radcliffe, *The Mysteries of Udolpho*, ed. Bonamy Dobrée (Oxford: Oxford University Press, 1998), pp. 598; 43. See the *OED*, 2nd edn., s.v. "atmosphere"; and Jayne Lewis, "'No Colour of Language': Radcliffe's Aesthetic Unbound," *Eighteenth-Century Studies* 39 (2006), pp. 377–90.

2 William Enfield, anonymous review of *The Romance of the Forest*, *Monthly Review*, 1791, cited in Peter Garside, James Raven, and Rainer Schöwerling, *The English Novel, 1770–1829: A Bibliographical Survey of Prose Fiction Published in the British Isles*, Vol. I, ed. James Raven and Antonia Förster (Oxford: Oxford University Press, 2000), p. 543.

3 Robert Miles, "The 1790s: The Effulgence of the Gothic," in *The Cambridge Companion to Gothic Fiction*, ed. Jerrold E. Hogle (Cambridge: Cambridge University Press, 2002), p. 42.

4 *Waverley*, ed. Claire Lamont (Oxford: Oxford University Press, 1986), pp. 3–4.

5 *Philosophical Enquiry into ... the Sublime and Beautiful*, ed. James T. Boulton (Notre Dame, Indiana: University of Notre Dame Press, 1958), p. 61.

6 *The Castle of Otranto*, ed. W. S. Lewis (Oxford: Oxford University Press, 1966), p. 66.

7 *Udolpho*, p. 491.

8 One sign that Walpole's "Gothic Story" was initially regarded more as an *outré* spoof than as an example on which future fictions might capitalize is that few of his successors coveted his subtitle. Granted, Clara Reeve would in 1777 subtitle her conscious imitation of *Otranto* "A Gothic Story," but "romance" was the label under which most of the novelists studied here announced themselves. As a classification for fiction "Gothic novel" was to gain currency only in the twentieth century.

9 See Franz J. Potter, *The History of Gothic Publishing, 1800–1835* (Basingstoke: Palgrave Macmillan, 2005), p. 51.

10 *Otranto*, p. 9.

11 Richard Hurd, *Letters on Chivalry and Romance*, ed. Edith J. Morley (London: Henry Froude, 1911), p. 154.

12 *The Old English Baron*, ed. James Trainer (Oxford: Oxford University Press, 2003), p. 115.

13 *A Sicilian Romance*, ed. Alison Milbank (Oxford: Oxford University Press, 1993), p. 175.

14 *Reflections on the Revolution in France*, ed. Conor Cruise O' Brien (Harmondsworth: Penguin, 1982), p. 171.

15 Simon During, *Modern Enchantments: The Cultural Power of Secular Magic* (Cambridge: Harvard University Press, 2002), p. 65.

16 *Otranto*, p. 5.

17 Similar accounts of the double-dealing the mode practices are developed in Anne McWhir, "The Gothic Transgression of Disbelief: Walpole, Radcliffe and Lewis," in *Gothic Fictions: Prohibition/Transgression*, ed. Kenneth W. Graham (New York: AMS Press, 1989), p. 37; E. J. Clery, *The Rise of Supernatural Fiction, 1762–1800*, Cambridge Studies in Romanticism (Cambridge University Press, 1995), pp. 148–55.

18 Anon., *The Monks of St. Andrews* (London: J. Bailey, n. d.), p. 28.

19 *Udolpho*, pp. 383; 552.

20 Charles Robert Maturin, *Melmoth the Wanderer*, ed. Alethea Hayter (Harmondsworth: Penguin, 1977), pp. 89–90.

21 "On the Pleasure Derived from Objects of Terror," *The Norton Anthology of English Literature*, 8th edn., Vol. D, *The Romantic Period*, ed. Jack Stillinger and Deidre Shauna Lynch (New York: W. W. Norton, 2006), p. 584.

22 *Ibid.*, p. 584.

23 Robert Miles, *Gothic Writing: A Genealogy, 1750–1820* (London: Routledge, 1993), p. 162.

24 Friedrich von Schiller, *The Ghost-Seer*, trans. Andrew Brown (London: Hesperus, 2003), p. 5. This passage, which opens Schiller's revised version of the novella, does not appear in the earliest English translations.

25 *Enquiry*, p. 45.

26 *Collected Letters of Samuel Taylor Coleridge*, ed. Earl Leslie Griggs (Oxford: Clarendon, 1956), Vol. I, p. 122; anon. review, cited in Devendra P. Varma, Introduction to Laurence Flammenberg [pseud.], *The Necromancer* (London: Folio, 1968), p. viii.

27 *Frankenstein*, ed. Maurice Hindle (Harmondsworth: Penguin, 1992), p. 45.

28 *Frankenstein*, p. 7; *Wieland*, ed. Jay Fliegelman (New York: Penguin, 1991), p. 8.

29 Karl Friedrich August Grosse, *Horrid Mysteries*, trans. Peter Will (London: Folio Press, 1968), p. 3 (first English translation 1796).

30 Miguel de Cervantes Saavedra, *Don Quixote de la Mancha*, trans. John Rutherford (New York: Penguin, 2001), p. 666 (Vol. II, ch. 26); Radcliffe, *The Italian*, ed. Frederick Garber (Oxford: Oxford University Press, 1981), p. 274.

31 Samuel Taylor Coleridge, *Biographia Literaria*, ed. James Engell and W. Jackson Bate (Princeton: Princeton University Press, 1983; first published 1817), Vol. II, p. 6; David Hume, *The Natural History of Religion*, ed. H. E. Root (Stanford: Stanford University Press, 1957; first published 1757), p. 60.

32 See Catherine Gallagher, *Nobody's Story: The Vanishing Acts of Women Writers in the Marketplace* (Berkeley: University of California Press, 1994); Margaret Russett, *Fictions and Fakes: Forging Romantic Authenticity* (Cambridge: Cambridge University Press, 2006).

4

RICHARD MAXWELL

The historical novel

The historical novel begins as a French genre. Its formative instance, *The Princess of Cleves* (1678), was the work of Madame de Lafayette, a sophisticated insider at the court of Louis XIV. *Cleves* is focused on a disastrous moment in French history, when Henry II died from injuries suffered at an anachronistically feudal tournament, thus accelerating the country's path towards the Wars of Religion (1562–98), fought over freedom of religion and the division of power among various cliques. This national crisis is counterpointed with the heroine's dazzling debut at court and the irresolvable love dilemmas that develop out of it. The fictive princess is held up as both exemplary and inimitable: an impossible figure of virtue in a corrupt world collectively headed for disaster.

Until the early nineteenth century, *Cleves* remained the most famous and widely read example of historical fiction. A generation later, the abbé Prévost developed a second persuasive version of this long-lived but elusive genre. A much less respectable character than Lafayette, Prévost fled to Holland and England in an effort to avoid various theological and financial quandaries. Partly as a result of his exile, he became fascinated with English, Scottish, and Irish history, which provide the main historical mooring for his three great novels of the 1730s: *Memoirs and Adventures of a Man of Quality* (1728–31), *The English Philosopher, or the History of Monsieur Cleveland* (1731–9), and *The Dean of Killerine* (1735–40).

Lafayette is the ultimate insider, Prévost a quintessential outsider. Lafayette writes with classic concision, from and about an exclusive center of power; her plots observe – or subtly challenge – the established literary rules of probability, or *vraisemblance*. (It was fiction that was supposed to be probable whereas in history anything could happen; historical fiction was situated on the cusp between these two aesthetics.) Prévost's approach is more open and improvised than hers. Taking heart from the mid-seventeenth-century fashion for the huge romances of Madeleine de Scudéry – a fashion against which Lafayette herself had reacted – he spins his tales sentimentally, and at length, about a global range of people and places. Moreover, he is capable of asking his readers to believe just about anything; *Cleveland*, most spectacularly, is the supposed autobiography of an illegitimate son of Oliver Cromwell, who spends his juvenile years hiding in a huge cave with his mother, then (on his emergence) embraces the cause of Charles II, thus initiating a lifetime of political intrigue, erotic confusion, and maritime adventure. The technique of making up fictions that seem like history because of their startling extravagance (rather than despite it) becomes a self-conscious feature of Prévost's work, outdoing Lafayette's subtler violations of *vraisemblance* through sheer narrative bravado.

The huge stylistic and thematic gaps between *Cleves* and *Cleveland* should not obscure their similarities. Both books spin tales within a frame of famous historical names and dates; each presents itself as a biography or (in *Cleveland's* first-person rendering) an autobiography; and each tends to highlight the glamor of the Stuarts, a mobile, elusive, and ultimately tragic dynasty of kings and queens. It is Prévost who writes most explicitly about the formal demands of such an undertaking:

> a particular history [une histoire particulière] has several characteristics peculiar to it ... the goal of a particular history being nothing but to make known the action, quality, inclinations and manners of a person of one or the other sex, all the public events that belong to general history must not be introduced except when they are found to be mixed with those that one is trying to recount.[1]

To the extent that a historical narrative is particularized, readers see the surrounding political and social landscape in a bit of a blur: such a landscape is depicted clearly and at length only when it elucidates the life of a chosen protagonist. The historical novel tends to imitate this approach, emphasizing a biographical form of narrative but (often abruptly) widening its focus when it turns to the description of major historical events.

The works of both Lafayette and Prévost were soon transplanted. *Cleves* was translated early into English, and was adapted as a play for the London stage. Prévost's novels were more centrally *about* British history than Lafayette's work, and even more deeply rooted within it; his efforts to explain British culture and literature to the French (in his periodical *Le pour et contre*), his role as translator of Richardson's *Clarissa*, and his formative Stuart-obsession, make him a pioneering adherent of comparative literary and political studies. Inspired by British culture, and written (partly) on British soil, *Cleveland* and its ilk are in some ways British literature, though their language of origin happens to be French; the novels were embraced enthusiastically by a later generation of anglophone writers.

Even aside from the special case of Prévost, it is often hard to tell where French historical fiction ends and English historical fiction begins. Very early instances of the latter, such as *The Amours of Edward IV: A Historical Novel* (1700) are either translations or close imitations: Who knows which? Throughout the first half of the eighteenth century, the prestige of historical fiction fluctuates on both sides of the Channel, almost all the leading indicators coming from France rather than England, even when it is English, or occasionally Scottish, history that is evoked. Among the best-known English instances, Daniel Defoe's books, like *Memoirs of a Cavalier* (1719) or *Memoirs of the Plague Year* (1722), are perhaps the freshest – and have certainly worn well, in their vivid, unsentimental evocations of famous historical events as experienced by quirky, characterful narrators. Even Defoe, however, has a significant French predecessor: Courtilz de Sandras, author of circumstantial, racy faux-memoirs like the *Memoirs of M. d'Artagnan* (1700).

The anonymously published *Longsword Earl of Salisbury: An Historical Romance* (1762), probably by Thomas Leland, has occasionally been identified as the first real English historical novel.[2] *Longsword* treats the efforts of a medieval English knight to return to his native domains after a long military campaign in France and to subdue a usurper who wants to seize his lands and marry his wife. The book has identifiable historical sources; however, the sense of chronology is much less specific than in Lafayette, Prévost, or Courtilz. Moreover, the basic situation, that of *The Odyssey*, has been attached to the thirteenth century only vaguely. At times, the book's murkiness becomes a curious strength. Sailing around in the English Channel, tossed from adventure to adventure, both hero and reader lose all sense of where they are; this nightmarish aura of placelessness seems to accentuate the value of home, this narrative's goal.

Two years after *Longsword*, Horace Walpole published *The Castle of Otranto* (1764). Insofar as any one book can establish a genre, *Otranto* establishes Gothic fiction. A little less conspicuously, the book rethinks the historical novel. Taking, perhaps, certain hints from Prévost, especially from his fondness for the improbable extravagances of romance, *Otranto* opens up literary, historical, and philosophical possibilities that would remain vital through the eighteenth and much of the nineteenth century.

The preface published with the first edition of *Otranto* – a major document in the theory of fiction – establishes Walpole's revisionary ambitions. Here he plays the part of a learned, slightly pedantic antiquary, but his pedantry proves to have basic implications for the way that novels evoke historical time. In the opening sentence, its writer claims to have discovered *Otranto* rather than composed it. "It was printed at Naples, in the black letter, in the year 1529. How much sooner it was written does not appear."

Manuscript-discovery narratives are frequent in eighteenth-century fiction and almost always conventional. This one is unusually rich; it has a kind of verbal density more often associated with lyric poetry. Thus, having evoked the image of an old and difficult-to-decipher tome, the writer proceeds to spotlight the process by which this dusty, mysterious volume came into existence: its passage from manuscript to print. The book itself has a history, and this history must be laid out in successive stages, conceived as a process. Moreover, by inquiring into the gap between the book's writing and its publication, we learn to confront other, even more significant gaps:

> Miracles, visions, necromancy, dreams, and other preternatural events, are exploded now even from romances. That was not the case when our author wrote; much less when the story itself is supposed to have happened. Belief in every kind of prodigy was so established in those dark ages, that an author would not be faithful to the manners of the times, who should omit all mention of them. He is not bound to believe them himself, but he must represent his actors as believing them.[3]

In this important passage, there are wonderful, yet treacherous, mid-sentence slippages between the old sort of romance and the new (the latter confined by the rules of probability, the former open to fantastic variations); alternately, Walpole shifts among belief as it existed in the (uncertain) time of the author, the time in which the romance is set, and the time in which he, the discoverer of the manuscript, presents it to his contemporaries. The point is to subordinate the predominantly French obsession with probability to a more time-bound sense of *manners*. Since manners differ from age to age, our criteria for belief and probability must shift too. In other words, readers of *Otranto* are pressed to cultivate a historical sense, so that they can accept in an old book events that they would reject, had the book been composed during a later era. Walpole speculates that the original author – himself separated from the age that he was writing about – was a historical novelist in just this sense. He included weird events in his narrative to emphasize the past's foreignness, its distance from the present. In turn, this fictional author's efforts suggest a good deal of Walpole's own literary project. *Otranto* is famous for bizarre, obscurely allegorical moments, as when, in the opening pages, a giant helmet, a hundred times the size of a normal one and covered with black feathers, falls upon and crushes the Prince of Otranto's fifteen-year-old son. Such incidents (inspired in large part by Walpole's reading of such esoteric fare as the sixteenth-century *Three Princes of Serendip*, with its giant marauding Hand) interest the student of Gothic literature because they represent an intrusion of the irrational or impossible into an everyday world. For the student of historical fiction, these same supernatural moments signify a radical experiment in understanding and evoking historical time: the past as a place where they do things differently – and, more important yet, think differently about the world and the things that happen there. Like Lafayette and Prévost, Walpole is playing with the aesthetics of *vraisemblance*; in a more roundabout and eccentric way than theirs, he describes improbable occurrences as a way of creating a sense of history, which is now presented as an alien, mysterious, and nearly indecipherable world of the past.

From an early twenty-first-century point of view, *Otranto* is boring and fascinating at the same time. Relatively few readers would now value it for its story (about a guilty usurper avenged by supernatural means); the underlying project, to evoke an archaic way of thinking, was original in its moment and remains remarkable today. Perhaps the book is best appreciated as a small part in a much larger pattern of literary, artistic, and social work, including the author's learned *Historical Doubts* (where he demonstrates his skills in historical detection), his enormous, cosmopolitan correspondence, and above all his house – Strawberry Hill, a real-life Gothic castle, and the prototypical example of what would later be called the "Romantic Interior."

When Clara Reeve published *The Old English Baron* (1777/8), she tried to turn Walpole into a realist and a moralist. *Baron* is often identified as a Gothic novel, where the term "Gothic" suggests fear, mystery, and intrigue. There is some truth in this characterization; *Baron* includes a castle with a convincingly ghostly secret chamber (later imitated by Scott, among others). However, Reeve's preface to her second edition, like Walpole's to his first, highlights another, equally important kind of Gothicism to which the author is committed. Reeve begins by acknowledging that her work is *Otranto's* "literary offspring ... written upon the same plan, with a design to unite the most attractive and interesting circumstances of the ancient romance and modern novel." Such a composition is "Gothic" because it affords "a picture of Gothic times and manners." *Baron* is set in a specific late medieval past, typified by such chivalric institutions as trial-by-combat – featured at the pivotal moment of Reeve's Otrantesque plot, about a lost heir who is restored to his inheritance – as well as by a more sparing, understated version of Walpole's supernatural thrills. Reeve puts greater emphasis than Walpole on sociological and legal institutions of the past, less on ghostly visitations and apparitions or the questions about belief and probability that such plot-features raise; at the same time, her "Gothic" England is more idealized than *Otranto's*. For Reeve, it seems, much of the point of traveling back into an imagined, faraway era is that it makes a convincing setting for a benign hero like the eponymous Baron. Apparently, virtue is more comfortable, more at home, in a distant period.[4] When chronologically remote (yet anchored by homey details), it is relatively easy to believe in. Morally, at least, the past was better than the present.

Reeve's solution to the challenge of imitating Walpole is both sensible and a little disappointing. Transforming *Otranto* from a singular *tour de force* into a prototype for the antiquarian historical novel remained an unfulfilled goal. Indeed, practically speaking, many of Reeve's contemporaries avoided the Walpole alternative altogether, instead returning to Prévost as their main model. The two writers who did this most programmatically – Sophia Lee and William Godwin – also wrote the most successful English historical novels of the late eighteenth century.

Lee's *The Recess* (1783–5) forms itself closely on Prévost's *Cleveland*. If the earlier book narrates the fugitive struggles for survival and recognition of one of Cromwell's bastard sons, and then (in a tale-within-the-tale) the even more fevered struggles of that bastard's half-brother, Lee more than matches this accomplishment by narrating the lives of the two secret daughters of Mary, Queen of Scots. Struck especially by the opening chapters of *Cleveland*, where the hero and his mother take refuge from Cromwell's agents in an enormous Somerset cave, Lee has her two heroines grow up in the subterranean "recess" of the title; only gradually and by accident learning who they are. First Queen Elizabeth, then in the next reign King James, pursue them relentlessly, fearing that one or the other of them might make a claim on the throne. Separated during a raid on the recess, each of the sisters ends badly – but not before their life-stories (the one narrative ensconced within the other) have provided a remarkable succession of thrilling adventures.

Prévost invented the modern sentimental romance; Lee rivals and even surpasses his emotional intensity by adopting a device with which Reeve and various others had already experimented. *The Old English Baron* is supposedly transcribed from a partly destroyed or unreadable original, whose editor supplies ellipses or bridging explanations where her source fails her. *The Recess* does the same kind of thing, but by couching each sister's manuscript in the first person, it identifies gaps and blanks with fainting spells, periods of dizziness (a device shrewdly adapted from sentimental fiction by writers like Laurence Sterne and Henry Mackenzie). These moments of vertigo are experienced by the sisters (who sometimes, at moments of extremity, literally faint); they also seem to belong to the narrative, as though a story itself could have moments of treacherous forgetfulness. By this means, Lee emphasizes that history is shot through with treacherous blanks: suppressions of knowledge (and crimes against justice) that sustain the power of the state.

William Godwin briefly (and unsuccessfully) courted Sophia Lee's sister and sometime co-author Harriet; his literary link with the Lees is that, no less than Sophia, he modeled his historical novels and his accompanying theory of the genre on the work of Prévost. One of the most valuable documents in Godwin's thinking about historical fiction did not reach print until long after the author's death. This is the essay "Of History and Romance" (1797), originally intended for a second volume of his essay-collection, *The Enquirer*. Godwin proposes that the "genuine purpose of history" is "to understand the machine of society, and to direct it to its best purposes." He asks whether "individual" or "general" history can best fulfill this function. The distinction between "individual" and "general" echoes Prévost's distinction between "particular" and "general" in *Marguerite d'Anjou* (which, along with *Cleveland*, Godwin had studied while moving from writing philosophy to writing history, three years previously). Prévost spells out the rules of particular history. Godwin goes further, making a passionate, often transgressive case for the superiority of individual history, especially from the novelist's point of view. In Godwin's not altogether conventional interpretation, general history should be identified with learned, indeed antiquarian, investigations of subjects like "eloquence," "taxation," or "the succession of archons and the adjustment of olympiads." (An archon is an ancient ruler, an Olympiad is one of the four-year periods between Olympic games by which the Greeks computed time; together these words evoke the techniques of eighteenth-century chronology.) By contrast, individual or particular history takes, above all, a biographical form. What makes biography so effective is that it allows us to estimate realistically the social capacities of humankind. If we can see close up what people are truly capable of, then we can decide how the machine of society itself should be directed. Godwin's case for particular over general enquiries then shades into a case for fictional over non-fictional representations of historical events and phenomena. Getting to the heart of history and learning how to use it is less a matter of establishing facts than it is of presenting truths about human nature in a vivid, circumstantial manner. "The noblest and most excellent species of history, may be decided to be a composition in which, with a scanty substratum of facts and dates, the writer interweaves a number of happy, ingenious and instructive inventions, blending them into one continuous and indiscernible mass." This, notes Godwin, is what Prévost meant by "historical romance." And it is (implicitly) the mode in which he himself intends to strike out.[5]

Godwin's first novel was the brilliant *Adventures of Caleb Williams* (1794), his greatest success with contemporary readers, as with later generations. However, it is his second novel, *St. Leon* (1797), and the much later *Mandeville* (1817) that best embody the practice proposed by "Of History and Romance." A glance at *St. Leon* will suggest something of Godwin's accomplishment in his second vocation of novelist. Like Walpole and Reeve, he writes a doubly "Gothic" tale; it is both terrifying and obsessed with late-medieval chivalry. Much in the manner of Prévost's flawed, fascinating protagonists, St. Leon tells his own story, providing an engrossing (and implicitly unreliable) account of his life thus far. He is born into a distinguished French family. At the age of fifteen, he is "present as a spectator at the celebrated meeting between Francis the First and Henry the Eighth, king of England, in a field between Ardres and Guines." This event, he admits, helped form him; indeed, he never quite gets over its expensive but deceptive glamor.[6] Godwin both celebrates the charisma of a chivalric culture intent on the proper conduct of love and war, and demonstrates the potential for violent self-destruction just beneath that elegant kind of surface. Here, at least briefly, he seems closer to Lafayette than to Prévost.

Initially, St. Leon fails out of a lack of self-discipline; he is a compulsive gambler who takes his family down with him. So much for the honor and virtue of the warrior class. Meanwhile, the various countries through which he flees (France, Switzerland, Spain; later on, Hungary and the Ottoman Empire) exhibit the opposite failing; each of them is marred by its own socially specific variety of despotic over-control. This plot-scheme would not necessarily need a supernatural element to make it work; Godwin provides one, and by this means strengthens the book immeasurably. In effect, he finds a way to adopt the elixir-of-life plot, so popular, in so many variants, during the later eighteenth century, to the purposes of historical fiction.[7] Having exhausted almost all his resources, having brought wife and children as well as himself to a point of desperation, St. Leon meets a sinister, ageless, wandering outcast who passes on to him the fatal secret of how to achieve immortality and manufacture endless wealth.

The book's characteristic *frisson* develops from the novelist's shrewd handling of the elixir plot. The mysterious stranger's entrance is postponed until the hero has lived (and ruined) much of his life. Thus Godwin does just the opposite of what Goethe manages in *Faust I*; he goes out of his way, over the course of many chapters, to establish a non-supernatural literary decorum. When St. Leon's tempter finally arrives, he challenges this decorum; when St. Leon himself uses the elixir, turning himself young again, he disrupts the frame of the book even more drastically. It is a built-in limit of autobiography that it continues as long as its narrator, and no longer. However, St. Leon's lifespan has become potentially infinite. Particular history thus expands to encompass general history; biography is no longer limited by human mortality but claims the same interminable extensiveness as its rival, the history of the polity at large. Since Godwin sends the new St. Leon to Hungary and Turkey, he expands his book's spatial range almost as suddenly, almost as shockingly, as its timeline, and at virtually the same moment. The geographical and historical novel are shown to go hand in hand. The subsequent, concluding chapters, in which our hero tries to establish himself as the intimate friend of his son, without revealing his true identity, link this rearrangement of time–space coordinates to a disturbing warpage of family life.

Insofar as it treats the past, every historical novel reverses time or creates the illusion of doing so. In *St. Leon*, such an enterprise seems to mirror, distortedly, the hero's own longings and actions. The author tries to live backwards, into the sixteenth century, as a way of comprehending the "social machine"; the protagonist tries to live forwards, past his own generation and even into eternity, pursuing by this means a parallel project of investigation and (eventual) self-education. (His daughter, Mary Shelley, would take up this theme once more in *The Last Man*, 1826.) On the one side, we are led to consider the powers of fiction as imagined by a particular kind of philosopher, one who has recently converted from systematic, abstract investigation to casual, circumstantial, and fictive narrative. On the other, we are asked to imagine what it would be like to live out history rather than to recall it, or to reconstruct it through an intricate literary game.

The novels of both Godwin and Lee engage the mass political ferment across Europe during the last decades of the eighteenth century. Godwin manifests his interest more fully than Lee does; not only was the French Revolution the central event of his intellectual life, most of his fiction allegorizes his effort to affirm its positive side without accepting the politics of Terror. More pious and more conservative, Lee shows little enthusiasm for Jacobinism. *The Recess* does feature an effective evocation of a slave rebellion in the West Indies, but its main line of narrative puts it on the side of dispossessed aristocrats; within a decade of its publication, it could well have been read as an elegy for French *émigrés*, bereft of country, fortune, and power, permanently in flight.

A slightly later generation of novelists pushed Prévostian historical romance towards an even more charged relation to contemporary history. The reasons for this shift are historical as well as aesthetic. From the 1790s onwards, as war spread across Europe, the population of Great Britain divided into those who stayed at home and those who fought abroad. The best-known representation of this split is perhaps Jane Austen's *Persuasion* (1818) with its suffering, waiting heroine and its sunburnt sailors returning from their bloody, immensely profitable maritime exploits. But the gap is everywhere, producing remarkable interactions between real-life events and fictional evocations of them.

There is, for instance, the case of the Porter family. The Porters were descended from distinguished Irish forebears, including Endymion Porter,

Charles I's Groom of the Bedchamber. The eldest son of the Napoleonic generation was Robert Ker Porter, who grew up in Edinburgh. There he met Flora MacDonald (the legendary heroine of Scottish Jacobites, for her role in assisting the escape of Prince Charles Edward, after the insurrection of 1745). MacDonald encouraged him to pursue an artistic career. In his early twenties, he became an accomplished military painter; his breakthrough work was "The Storming of Seringapatam," a huge panoramic painting (designed to surround viewers, producing a powerful you-are-there illusion). The siege of Seringapatam was a key event in the British project to remove the French from India and simultaneously subdue local rulers. Robert worked fast to satisfy public interest in this victory: Seringapatam fell during 1799, while his painting was exhibited in London just a year later. He thus became a great pioneer in the field of military panorama painting, a genre which was to have a substantial future over the course of the nineteenth century. The form of the panorama proved especially useful for conveying the strategic, logistical and geographic complexities of large battles from the apparent position of an eyewitness; a surviving engraving shows just how vividly and lucidly Robert evoked the 1799 assault. In the words of Thomas Dibdin, "You looked a second time, and the figures moved, and were commingled in hot and bloody fight. You saw the flash of the cannon, the glitter of the bayonet, the gleam of the falchion. You longed to be leaping from crag to crag with Sir David Baird who is hallooing his men on to victory! Then, again, you seemed to be listening to the groans of the wounded and the dying – and more than one female was carried out swooning."[8]

Jane Porter was not among these susceptible spirits. On the contrary, she was delighted with her brother's virtuoso performance. "I could not conceive that he could cover that immense space with the subject he intended, under a year's time at least, but – and it is indeed marvellous! – he did it in SIX WEEKS." As this emphasis on speed underscores, a war panorama was not just an aesthetic object but a journalistic report. Promptness counted, as did vividness, command of detail, and (a special strength of this format) great clarity in presenting the spatial position of a huge variety of actors. Jane's novels carry on in a similar spirit. Russia had recently invaded and eviscerated Poland (1794); the ambitious war scenes in chapters 7–9 of *Thaddeus of Warsaw* (1803) show a military eye for the topographic placement of soldiers, as well as considerable flair for describing the way that a battle develops and for the way that troops move about over a particularized terrain. *The Scottish Chiefs* (1810), which treats the legendary heroes Wallace and Bruce, repeats and extends this success. Prose fiction is hardly the ideal medium for such kinetic representations, but Jane convincingly marries strategic movement to the forces of history.

Jane, and in her immediate wake her sister Anna (*The Hungarian Brothers*, 1807; *Don Sebastian*, 1809), were fascinated by the idea of national resistance movements (Scots against England, Poles against Russia, and so forth). This is, of course, a widespread interest of the time; Byron's support for Greek independence affords the most famous radical version, but there was also a Tory taste for cheering on rebels against governments of occupation. It helped if the governments in question had been installed by Napoleon; the novels of the Porter sisters stage tacit confrontations with the great French commander and emperor, who, for his part, did Jane the honor of banning *The Scottish Chiefs*. This gesture suggests that a book like *Chiefs* could seem firmly grounded in the present moment, even though set in a chivalric past. In the 1831 preface to *Thaddeus*, Jane went so far as to claim that she had invented the practice of "biographical romance." (Apparently, she hadn't read Prévost, Lee, and Godwin.) She would have been better off claiming to have helped turn historical fiction in a certain sort of strategic, landscape-oriented, and panoramic direction – thus intimidating the greatest general of her day.

Prevented by war, as well as by physical infirmities, from even leaving the country (until after Waterloo), Walter Scott traveled most effectively in his mind. Inspired by diagrams of Indian sieges, he adapted, when young, "the childish expedient of arranging shells, and seeds, and pebbles, so as to represent encountering armies."[9] What Jane Porter learned from her brother Robert's panorama of Seringapatam, Scott learned from the huge range of literary and historical works available to an Edinburgh reader circa 1800. Scott is by far the most scholarly of major anglophone novelists. His talent for popularizing erudition – prominent already in his vast range of pre-novelistic publications – gave him a decisive advantage over every other antiquary of his generation.

Scott is often seen as a innovator. But he was also a great synthesizer; he knew what everyone before him had done and found a way to put it all together, without losing a purposeful overall direction distinctively his. Closest to home, Scott drew on the Scottish Enlightenment school of historiography that had grown up in the wake of the crisis of 1745; according to this tradition, societies develop through distinctive phases, an idea that Scott appropriates in both obvious and subtle ways. But this is not the only useful frame of reference for understanding his work. Familiar with the French tradition of historical fiction, he worked out his own version of particular history as adapted to the purposes of the novel. No less than Lafayette, Prévost, and their later-eighteenth-century successors, he invented fictive heroes or heroines who seemed to stray in and out of history, as defined by famous people, events, and dates; thus Waverley, an imaginary hero seduced by the powers of imagination, yields to the charisma of Charles Edward, only to retreat from the rigors of revolution, just in time to avoid political disgrace (not to mention capital punishment). Further, even more than Reeve, Scott appreciated *Otranto* as a landmark experiment in the practice of antiquarian historical fiction; throughout his life as a novelist, Walpole's book remained his most important point of departure. He too designed an intricate novelistic machine through which he could make readers feel that they had been projected back among the manners and social institutions of a previous era; like Walpole, as well, he linked this accomplishment to the erection of a fantastical "Romantic Interior" (his house, Abbotsford), designed to display objects, to hold a vast range of books, and to embody not only its creator's literary eminence but the ideas of the Gothic and the chivalric to which his fiction was so often addressed. Finally, in the spirit of the Porters, Scott presented large-scale events intensively. Readers of the Waverley novels are immersed in history. The past seems to surround such readers (panoramically); there are complex but clear dispositions of a multitude of figures, arranged to tell a vivid story with the quality of a crisis, of an emergency that must be confronted urgently and on all sides. Also like the Porters (and even more like his great Irish contemporary Maria Edgeworth), Scott found a way to encompass and evoke the energies of national identity, energies that had been called up by the French Revolution, by the subsequent Napoleonic invasions of countries all over Europe, and by the growing sense of a global, transnational polity, sustained through empire, maritime trade, and linguistic or historical learning. On these grounds, the historical novel and the national tale, a closely adjacent genre, would shape and reshape each other over the first three decades of the nineteenth century.[10]

Reading all the Waverley novels, often in order of composition (and even, in extreme cases, on an annual basis) was a known habit of pre-World War I enthusiasts (like the Victorian Lord Carnarvon); this completist approach has its merits. Working through Scott's novels in sequence suggests something of what it must have been like to have discovered them as they appeared on the scene, one by one, over some eighteen years. The serial reader of the Waverley novels is charmed into playing overlapping, often tricky, games of place, time, and person. By (improvised) stages, the novels create a version of history linked to geography, its necessary prerequisite; to chronology, its inevitable armature; and to transmission through an author or chain of authors, its claim to truth.

Geography: Throughout the eighteenth century, elementary history manuals argued that the study of geography should precede the study of history. Scott agrees; in effect, his historical novels begin geographically. Waverley experiences his initial journey to the Highlands as a trip into the past (which, over the course of the narrative, seems to self-destruct before his eyes). In later works, the novelist generalizes this method by repeating and refining a certain narrative gesture; he begins stories with the sighting of a mysterious traveler who moves through an expressive yet unfamiliar landscape. Going on a journey turns out to be a way of making history visible, or even, on the level of plot, of setting it in motion. Over the long run, the Waverley novels expand in geographical scope, claiming increasingly distant swaths of the globe as their rightful material. Scott's books themselves become mysterious travelers to distant lands. The geographical fantasies of the long romantic poem, such a dominant feature of this period, are thus reappropriated for prose fiction.[11]

Chronology: Scott uses a range of techniques for situating his narratives in the realm of historical time. *Waverley; or, 'Tis Sixty Years Since* is already slightly elusive as a title; we have to take literally Scott's invitation to subtract sixty from the year of publication to infer that the tale is going to treat the charged date of 1745. The sensation of working for this knowledge is important to the book's effect; like Waverley himself, the reader is lured into a historical event, rather than attracted towards it. History comes as a surprise. Later novels try out further methods for integrating fiction with historical chronology, or keeping fiction and chronology at a tantalizing distance from one another. A date can go into a title – so the reader can't miss it – or a title can specify a day while making the year in which it appears impossible to determine (*St. Valentine's Day; or, The Fair Maid of Perth*).[12] Scott consistently and consciously uses anachronisms to make the past less foreign, more sympathetic to his readers, but he also supplements this illusionary device with devices of alienation, like antiquarian footnotes, designed to remind us how different the past was from the present. Historical timelines – a recent invention – become intriguingly problematic, a process of complication integral to the impact of these books.[13] History can be sighted, but only in glimpses.

Authorship: The Waverley novels became a practical encyclopedia of methods for attaching a written narrative to the name of an author or authors; Scott steadily invents and reinvents fictions of authorship. The first and predominating means of authorial self-presentation is anonymity – a standard feature of fiction in the Romantic era, but one that Scott manages to present as problematic and mysterious: a way to highlight identity even while masking it. We are invited to ask just who "the Author of Waverley," "the Great Unknown," might be. And then "the Great Unknown" starts to seem not a discreet absence but a character in himself – a blank that must be filled in, a mystique to be conjured with. As time goes by, a further method supplements or replaces this one; often elaborate prefaces claim that Scott's novels are communicated to the reader through elaborate networks of eccentric, vividly characterized intermediaries. Finally, after his bankruptcy in 1826, Scott's public, almost ritualized acknowledgment of his own fiction (to private acquaintances, at a banquet, in print) constitutes a further feint in the endless project of authorship.

When they played these games with chronology, geography, and authorship, the Waverley novels cast everyday readers as learned inquirers into traces of the past. Moreover, once such readers accepted this role (which was, in most cases, a fiction), they also began to feel not only eager but able to travel through history. As apprentices to "The Wizard of the North" (yet another of Scott's semi-mythical alternate identities), they can defy, indeed reverse, the "inundations of time" – and with much greater success than an explicitly supernatural character like Godwin's St. Leon. Outside of Charles Darwin's great books, a generation later, this approach to synthesizing novelistic and historiographical modes of thinking constitutes the nineteenth century's most effective act of popularization; Scott's novels preserve both the aura and the substance of philology and antiquarianism, yet they also communicate to a mass audience a sense of collective human experience over many generations.

In the field of prose fiction, Scott was the dominant author of his time; looking further ahead, he became the foundational novelist of the nineteenth century. Over the short run, at least, the most interesting of the historical novelists who followed in his footsteps were also the most critical of his accomplishment, or the best able to rethink it. James Hogg was a shepherd who learned to write and became an author only in middle age. Scott patronized him in every sense; Hogg was grateful for the help but sometimes, productively, asserted his own independence. His *Three Perils of Man* (1822) appeared three years after *Ivanhoe*. Like Scott's novel, Hogg's narrates the retaking of a castle held by invaders. But if *Ivanhoe* uses its chivalric tale to contain and transform threatening images of mass mobilization, *Perils* makes nonsense of this accomplishment; despite Hogg's political sympathies with his friend, his admiring upside-down Scott tribute is more disturbing than most direct attacks would have been. There is a grand chivalric beginning: "The days of the Stuarts, kings of Scotland, were the days of chivalry and romance."[14] Then the narrative devolves into ever bloodier and more perverse byways, dominated by images of cannibalism (associated first with the specialized conditions of siege warfare, then with a supernatural extravaganza centered around the figure of Michael Scott, the fearsome sorcerer of "The Lay of the Last Minstrel"). Like the vast majority of his contemporaries, Scott himself was flustered by this performance.[15] In a memorable miscalculation, the errant protégé decided that he would include one of Sir

Walter's ancestors as a major character in *Perils*; his horrified patron had to demand revisions. The nightmare of Hogg's novel seems to have stayed with him, since his *Castle Dangerous* is an effort to reassimilate the same story into a more controllable narrative of progress and reconciliation – a reprise of *Ivanhoe* in the wake of Hogg's brilliantly out-of-control fantasy, acknowledging its power but trying to render it harmless.

Already censored by Scott, after Hogg's death, *Perils* reappeared in much more drastically gutted form as *The Siege of Roxburghe*; deprived of its Michael Scott episodes, the book must have seemed almost pointless. Other Hogg works had a similar fate; most of the author's novels, tales, and poems have thus been unavailable in satisfactory texts until recently. The new Stirling/South Carolina edition has brought back into circulation an astounding range of historical romances and other Hogg works largely unread since the early nineteenth century. The romances offer, simultaneously, a homage to the Waverley novels and a pointed critique of their frailties, hesitations, and evasions. At the end of *Old Mortality*, the hero, Henry Morton, evades his fanatical double and opponent, Burley, by leaping over an apparently impassible chasm. Morton is thus spared killing or being killed by a friend and rescuer of his father. Hogg would not have allowed this miraculous evasion. In Scott's novels, there is typically a presumption that we can, in effect, make the necessary leap; the reign of the Hanover kings (seen as stolid, workable replacements for the glamorous and unreliable Stuarts) often seems to constitute the End of History, where all political differences can be reconciled. In Hogg's novels, there is a stronger and more explicit emphasis on the possibility that history is never at an end. The exhumation scene at the end of his best-known tale, *The Private Memoirs and Confessions of a Justified Sinner* (1824), suggests the way that the past keeps coming back, even after it is buried. So, in a larger manner, books like *Perils*, *Winter Evening Tales* (1820), and *Tales of the Wars of Montrose* (1835) evoke the problematic life-in-death of history.

Thomas Love Peacock is mainly remembered as the author of "conversation novels," like *Nightmare Abbey* (1818) and *Crotchet Castle* (1831), the latter featuring his major critical treatment of Scott's novels, which are compared to the eclectic spectacle of the pantomime. However, to borrow a phrase from Nicholas Joukovsky, he also produced a group of "satiric romances."[16] *Maid Marian*, the first of these, was written mostly in 1818, a year before the appearance of *Ivanhoe*, but not published until 1822. An epicurean and utilitarian thinker, Peacock uses the Robin Hood legend to mock poaching-laws, along with other dubious features of class privilege. *Ivanhoe's* agenda is substantially different. Here Robin and his Merry Men are the loyal yeoman supporters of Richard I; bandits prove to be monarchists at heart. Nonetheless, insofar as Scott really did produce novels as fantastic as pantomimes, he was a writer whom Peacock could admire. Neither *Maid Marian* nor *Ivanhoe* could have influenced one another, but in crucial respects they manifest the same extravagant, spectacle-oriented aesthetic. They even share a sense of humor: Athelstane, Scott's Anglo-Saxon pretender, is resurrected after three days in the tomb, only, when he staggers out like a slightly addled Messiah, to be rejected by his potential subjects. Peacock novels feature similar reversals. History, or historical legend, becomes a plaything for authorly wit; form, in effect, trumps politics.

The Misfortunes of Elphin (1829), the second satiric romance, is another, more ambitious *jeux d'esprit*. Peacock's wife, Jane Gryffydh, knew Welsh. By the time he wrote *Misfortunes*, he too both spoke it and read it, gaining by this means a good working knowledge of the archaeology, history, and literature of the country. Well before *The Mabinogion* (the great collection of medieval Welsh stories) appeared in English translation (1838–49), Peacock was conversant with its contents. His studies spill over into *Misfortunes*, which highlights the early exploits of the bard Taliessin. At first it seems that there is more satire than either romance, or history, or romantic history, in the novel, one of whose central characters (Seithenyn ap Seithen Saidi) is drunk from beginning to end, and none of whose major occurrences (the collapse of a castle into the sea; the kidnapping of Guinevere) is taken with any great seriousness. But *Misfortunes's* lightness of tone and treatment is itself an argument. In the much-admired "Song of Dinas Vawr," Peacock evokes just the kind of raid on livestock featured at the start of *Waverley*, introducing its hero to Highland manners. He does not so much parody Scott's argument about the historical development of customs as push it to an absurd, though disturbing, conclusion. The Author of Waverley (and of the "Essay on Chivalry") contends that archaic social arrangements persist, softened and subtilized, in a modern guise. Peacock suggests, more bluntly, that the cattle raid is the model for many subsequent assertions of national power by means of military force.

In some ways, *Misfortunes* strips down Scott-ish historicism to a bare and thus expressive minimum; in other ways, it elaborates upon it. A novel set in the time of Uther Pendragon can hardly adhere to Enlightenment standards of factuality. Nonetheless, Peacock manifests the synchronic historical sense of the born antiquary. His flair for marshaling erudition in the service of romance comes out most vividly when he evokes localities and the buildings that dominate them, in the description of Caer Lleon (chapter 12) or the abbey of Glastonbury (chapter 13). Peacock imagines the abbey as it might have been in Taliessin's time; he then evokes it as it was in his own day (a picturesque ruin); he then reconstructs the intermediary stages, suggesting how the abbey got from alpha to omega. The book's sense of history emerges from just this sort of intricately layered account. Peacock's scholarly explorations of spots – or more precisely, layers – of time, are the frequent, if not inevitable, prelude, to his terse retellings of Welsh myth. At their best, these canny appropriations are both accurate and ironic.

Hogg is a Scott disciple in rebellion against his master and putative model, Peacock a political opponent of Scott but his rival's secret sharer. Frederick Marryat defined for himself a third order of succession from the Great Unknown; he helped invent the military novel, a once-popular offshoot of historical fiction. The military novel was usually written by a military man. It was typically bursting with anecdotes, favoring the rambling, obsessive war-story mode of the demobilized veteran at a loose end, but it admitted just enough plot to give all this talk a discernible overall shape. The military novel's most striking period is the 1820s and 30s, when a whole generation, home from the fight against Napoleon, found itself at a loose end, and a scattering of old soldiers decided to take up writing. During the 1820s, the two great successes in the field of the fictionalized memoir of war, both serialized in *Blackwood's Magazine*, were George Gleig's *The Subaltern* (1825) and Michael Scott's *Tom Cringle's Log* (1829). Marryat took a little longer to get started. In 1806, at the age of fourteen, he had joined the crew of the frigate *Impérieuse*, which harassed French forces up and down the coast of Spain. Later he helped guard Napoleon on St. Helena, and later yet sailed and fought all over the world, while ascending to the rank of Captain (in 1826). Marryat not only perfected an important signalling system, but also wrote a controversial pamphlet against impressment. In the late 1820s, he produced his first novel, *The King's Own* (published 1830).

The King's Own is a lost-heir story with a difference. The action begins with the great naval mutinies of 1797; a ringleader, the son of an admiral, is hung for his part in one of these affairs, but before he dies he binds his own son to naval service. This action is supposed to test and restore the honor of the family. Willy, the boy, is literally named, and literally branded as, "the King's Own" (i.e., he is in the navy as an expendable servant of the Crown); by the time he inherits his grandfather's wealth, he himself is thought dead (and, like Scott's Harry Bertram in *Guy Mannering*, doesn't quite know who he is anymore). The novel alternately traces Willy's maritime adventures around the world and the sordid scandals that engulf his estate back home (which has fallen into the hands of a vicious rake). The whole narrative seems to be set up to culminate in a grand homecoming and recovery of memory, like that in *Guy Mannering*. Instead, there is a double grand catastrophe. First, in the maritime plot, the frigate on which Willy serves pursues a French ship to its doom, in a kind of collective suicide mission (articulated as such by the inhumanly selfless captain, who simply won't listen to the sensible protests of his officers); the two ships go down almost simultaneously, leaving our hero, along with a few others, clinging to some wrecked planks on a reef, in the middle of an annihilating storm. And it is at this moment, the moment of mass death and its aftermath, where the scene of memory-recovery occurs, only it is not Willy's memory-recovery but that of a minor character who has been trying unsuccessfully to quote Shakespeare all through the story and suddenly, devastatingly, remembers *King Lear* and *The Tempest* virtually *in toto*, then jumps, delusively, to his death: "Poor Tom's a-cold." Willy survives, returns to the family estate, and is about to marry the rake's daughter (that classic, genealogically elegant solution to property disputes) when her father surreptitiously poisons him. Thus, as the last chapter winds up, our hero lies dying in agony. He is one of the king's own to the end; and to be marked as such, physically or legally, is to accept the inevitability of violent, meaningless death, even if your grandfather is an admiral.

Not in the least an anti-war screed, *The King's Own* is nonetheless frank about what it means to be cannon-fodder. No wonder, either: the author still had his day-job. "Whilst I write I am holding on by the table, my legs entwined in the lashings underneath, and I can barely manage to keep my position before my manuscript."[17] As he notes elsewhere, he wasn't sure whether he would survive long enough to finish the book. In a late chapter, a prelude to the fatal storm (widely acknowledged as a great set-piece of the age), Marryat observes that he is not quite pleased with his work. All the same, "I've one comfort left – Sir Walter Scott has never succeeded in making a hero." (p. 378) For Marryat, the problem with Scott's heroes is insipidity. One powerful later reading identifies the blandness and sluggishness of Waverley and most of his successors with the idea of property.[18] This is a useful clue for understanding the conclusion of *The King's Own*. Lost to the Napoleonic Wars, Willy is not only will-less (despite occasional appearances to the contrary), but also incapable of a substantive return to land. Land is no longer his business; the heir cannot inherit. The heir is at sea, disabled like a Scott hero but for different reasons and with different consequences. If Willy is like any of Scott's protagonists, he is a shadow of the singular figure of Lammermoor (whose formative meeting with his life's great love, mediated by a mad bull, is oddly parodied in *The King's Own*). In sum, the military novel, as Marryat sets its ground-rules, proposes its own peculiar contract with history. Produced by an author who has been in a battle, and shot at with intent to kill, it grasps the difficulties of exiting an exciting historical scene gracefully and intact. The punchline of the veteran's anecdotes is death, a topic on which he tends to be relentlessly cheerful, though the cheer is all in the telling.

During the early 1830s, Marryat edited the liberal *Metropolitan Magazine*, producing for it in rapid succession a series of his naval tales. His work was often linked to eighteenth-century fiction. (Hogg called him a "Sea-Fielding," others saw him as a successor to Tobias Smollet.) But his raggedness, literalness, and broad knowledge of sea warfare make his literary pretensions – his accessions to metaphor and form – stand out distinctively. In time, Marryat would make a plausible Victorian. It was, however, a fourth successor to Scott who bridged most aptly the gap between the Romantic and the mid-nineteenth-century historical novel. When Edward Bulwer-Lytton published *The Last Days of Pompeii* (1834), he was known mainly as the author of *Pelham* (1828), the best novel of Regency dandyism. *Last Days* replaced *Pelham* as his most popular work. A pioneering essay in the field of ancient historical fiction, it both carried on the tradition of Scott and effected its own synthesis of a wide range of fictional and historical trends.

Not everyone registered Scott's mainly unsentimental attitude towards social obsolescence. The Waverley novels are largely an argument for modernity, but they can be misread as a celebration of a nobler past, for which the author yearns. Bulwer often favors such a misreading; his titles (and novels) harp incessantly on lastness. The dandyism of *Pelham* is a purposeful parading of archaic, out-of-date elegance – masquerading, rebelliously, as the latest thing; correspondingly, the historicism of *Last Days* is the dandyism of a committed antiquary. Bulwer goes to Pompeii and wanders around obsessively. The broken dandy on his travels confronts the shattered remnants of a society that must have been at one time what he himself is today – an elegant, walking corpse, doomed (it would seem) to quick annihilation. He determines to resurrect this society, to bring it back – a tribute, narcissistic at root, to his own superb irrelevance.

If *Last Days* is a Waverley novel filtered through the Regency ethos of the dandy, it is also a tribute to a peculiar sort of London guidebook. Pierce Egan's *Life in London* (1821, with many sequels and imitations over the next decade) follows the anecdotal adventures of a man about town (a rake more than a dandy) who roams from one scene of diversion to another. Egan provides jolly songs, local color, and thinly disguised portraits of well-known characters. We hardly realize that we are reading anything more than paragraphs in the newspaper, yet we absorb, gradually, an idea of the city. The lighter-than-air exploits of Egan's revellers prepare a new, totalizing urban realism (high and low life, with middle life soon to be added by Charles Dickens). Bulwer takes all this over. *Last Days* is arranged so that, as its characters circulate from locale to locale, from Eganesque gambling dens to aristocratic villas, he builds up a broad, almost inclusive model of the ancient town. We map it with him, step by step, as one picture, one sketch, succeeds another.

Last Days was also influenced by recent trends in Naples itself. During the early 1830s, Neapolitans were newly fascinated by the popular life of their city; a range of journals, albums, and anthologies recorded folk customs and everyday scenes of the region. Andrea de Jorio, a local archaeologist and cleric, found a particularly ingenious use for this kind of material. His *Gestural Expression of the Ancients in Light of Neapolitan Gesturing* (1832) linked the postures and hand gestures of figures on vases and frescoes excavated at Pompeii and related sites to the behavior of people whom the author had observed in the streets, or studied in this new ethnographic literature.[19] Jorio's book not only helped Bulwer envision the physical movements of his characters, but strengthened his sense of an unusually palpable continuity between past and present. The Pompeiian ruins acquired an eerie presentness; the historical novel's effort to envision the past as though it were happening now, in front of our eyes, acquired a particularly powerful validation.

A final side of *Last Days* is French. Working from the example of Scott, Victor Hugo's *Notre-Dame* (1831–2) had decisively reintegrated historical with Gothic fiction, while subordinating both to an architectural and topographical theme. Like many English writers of the 1830s, Bulwer studied *Notre-Dame* closely, and profitably. Hugo's novel features a gloomy priest, Claude Frollo; his deaf protégé, Quasimodo the Hunchback; and the beautiful gypsy Esmeralda with whom they are both (quite differently) obsessed. Bulwer adapts Frollo and Quasimodo to his own artistic and ideological purposes. His version of Frollo is the Egyptian sorcerer, Arbaces, another sallow, conniving, and murderous intellectual. His version of Quasimodo (with assistance from Goethe's Mignon) is the pathetically disabled Nydia, a blind slave whose self-sacrificial love embodies the pathos of a city forever gone – whether through volcanic eruption or drastic modernization. In seeking across the Channel for its basic narrative structure, *Last Days* bears witness to the French celebration of Scott, whose influence is evident in the extraordinarily popular and ambitious prose fiction of Alexandre Dumas and Victor Hugo; if the historical novel had begun in France, to France it would return, as the nineteenth century went on, in the work of Hugo, Dumas, and many others.

Pelham, Life in London, Gestural Expression, Notre-Dame: Bulwer derives from his models a powerful governing principle. His Pompeii is literally a city stopped in time and by this means preserved for our own, much later moment. Originally, the volcano stopped it; in the course of *Last Days*, we are seldom allowed to forget the spatial disposition of Pompeiian remains, skeletons marked by the heat of lava, the traces of lost bodies in the earth. In the medium of words, the novel both opposes and repeats the

3 *Nydia, the Blind Flower Girl of Pompeii,* detail from sculpture by Randolph Rogers (modeled 1855–6, carved 1858).

volcano's act. It reanimates Pompeii, even while preserving it forever. This equivocal tribute to movement and immobilization fascinated Bulwer's nineteenth-century audience. Randolph Rogers's famous mid-nineteenth-century sculpture depicts "Nydia, the Blind Flower Girl of Pompeii" in the hour of her city's doom. Her body bent forward, Nydia cups her ear, listening intently for the voices of Glaucus and Ione, the couple that she was leading to the beach (see Figure 3). The blind girl is the only Pompeiian who can navigate the storm of dust and ash. Glaucus needs Nydia's help, yet she needs his even more; emotionally, she cannot live without him. It's Quasimodo's Esmeralda problem all over again. Quasimodo, however, resolves his difficulties by immuring himself in a mass grave, where he can embrace the corpse of his own impossible love-interest; their interlocked remains are recovered many years later, an enigmatic monument to love, a riddle for the ages. Nydia, by contrast, escapes from the beach on a rescue ship, then, the next morning, slips overboard, the victim of erotic despair. The sculptor brings her back; no less than Hugo's hunchback, Nydia must retain her trace on earth. It was not until 1863 that the hollows left by Pompeiian bodies would be used as molds for a crude and eerie sort of statuary. In his much more virtuoso mode, Rogers seems to anticipate this practice; he re-embodies Nydia, as though she had been caught in the eruption rather than escaping fleetly (and futilely). Her presence in the flesh, or the marble, is startling; at the same time she inhabits a conspicuously different, more narra-tivized dimension than the one from which the viewer regards her. A fallen Corinthian capital at Nydia's feet marks out the ruins of a city that is just on the verge of disappearing. But there's no dust; we can spot Nydia without any strain at all, even if Glaucus, somewhere nearby, remains utterly disoriented. Thus, Rogers's *Nydia* reconstructs the lure of Bulwer's *Last Days*, and perhaps of most other historical fiction: We've travelled through time to a dangerous moment, even if we're still at home, where life is (perhaps) safer.

NOTES

1 Antoine Prévost, *Oeuvres choisies de Prévost*, 38 vols., Vol. XXVIII (Paris: Leblanc, 1810), pp. i–ii (author's translation).

2 See John Stephen's survey of the conventional wisdom on this subject in his edition of *Longsword* (New York: New York University Press, 1957), pp. vii–viii.

3 Horace Walpole, *The Castle of Otranto* in *Three Gothic Novels*, ed. E. F. Bleiler (New York: Dover Books, 1966), p. 18.

4 As J. M. S. Tompkins notes, this element of nostalgia comes out even more strongly in Reeves's other historical novel, the *Memoirs of Roger de Clarendon*.

5 I have used the text "Of History and Romance" in Maurice Hindle's edition of *Things as They Are or The Adventures of Caleb Williams* (London: Penguin Books, 1988), pp. 359–73.

6 William Godwin, *St. Leon* (1797), p. 4.

7 Its most famous exemplification, Goethe's *Faust, Part One*, would not be published until 1808.

8 See the discussions of the Seringapatam panorama in Anne Buddle, *The Tiger and the Thistle* (Edinburgh: National Gallery of Scotland, 1999); Dibdin is quoted on p. 52.

9 J. G. Lockhart, *Memoirs of the Life of Sir Walter Scott, Bart*, Illustrated Library Edition, nine volumes in three (Boston: Houghton, Mifflin, and Co., n.d.), Vol. I, p. 74.

10 See Katie Trumpener, *Bardic Nationalism: The Romantic Novel and the British Empire* (Princeton: Princeton University Press, 1997).

11 On the popularity of geographic poems and their relevance for the Waverley novels, see William St Clair, *The Reading Nation in the Romantic Period* (Cambridge: Cambridge University Press, 2004).

12 The "historical notes" in the new Edinburgh edition of the Waverley novels provide exemplary instances of how intricate and involving the effort to date these books can become.

13 On the invention of timelines, see Daniel Rosenberg, "The Trouble with Timelines," *Cabinet* 13 (Spring 2004).

14 James Hogg, *The Three Perils of Man: War, Women, and Witchcraft*, ed. Douglas Gifford (Edinburgh: Scottish Academic Press, 1972).

15 On Hogg's critiques of Scott, see Douglas S. Mack, "James Hogg in 2000 and Beyond," *Romanticism on the Net*, August 19, 2000.

16 See Joukovsky's *Dictionary of National Biography* essay on Peacock.

17 Frederick Marryat, *The King's Own*, Everyman's Library (London: J. M. Dent, n.d.), p. 161.

18 Alexander Welsh, *The Hero of the Waverley Novels* (New York: Atheneum, 1968).

19 Andrea de Jorio, *Gesture in Naples and Gesture in Classical Antiquity*, translated by Adam Kendon (Bloomington: Indiana University Press, 2000). See Kendon's introduction, esp. p. lxix, for the contemporary cultural and intellectual context.

5

MARTHA BOHRER

Thinking locally: novelistic worlds
in provincial fiction

Of all situations for a constant residence, that which appears to me most delightful is a little village far in the country; a small neighbourhood, not of fine mansions finely peopled, but of cottages and cottage-like houses. . . . Even in books I like a confined locality. . . . Nothing is so tiresome as to be whirled half over Europe at the chariot wheels of a hero, to go to sleep at Vienna, and awaken at Madrid; it produces a real fatigue, a weariness of spirit. On the other hand, nothing is so delightful as to sit down in a country village in one of Miss Austen's delicious novels, quite sure before we leave it to become intimate with every spot and every person it contains; or to ramble with Mr White over his own parish of Selborne, and form a friendship with the fields and coppices, as well as with the birds, mice, and squirrels, who inhabit them.

(Mary Russell Mitford, *Our Village*)

In the first chapter of *Our Village*, her collection of rural sketches (published as a collection 1824–34), Mary Russell Mitford stages her taste for a confined rural locality through three points of divergence from eighteenth-century aesthetic tastes. First, she shifts attention from the finer classes and their country estates to the village and its inhabitants. Second, she esteems residence over travel. And third, she prefers a detailed, specific, and intimate knowledge of a single place to a broad cosmopolitan knowledge of many places, achieved by propertied aristocratic gentlemen through extensive travel, education, and leisure.[1] Mitford gently mocks this cosmopolitan knowledge gained from a whirl "half over Europe" and subscribes instead to a competing model of knowledge espoused by Gilbert White in *The Natural History and Antiquities of Selborne* (1789): "Men that undertake only one district are much more likely to advance natural knowledge than those that grasp at more than they can possibly be acquainted with: every kingdom, every province, should have its own monographer."[2] Here "monographer" means someone researching and writing about a particular place; in this chapter I use the term monograph to refer to both factual and fictional studies of rural places, such as White's *Selborne* and Mitford's *Our Village*.

White and Mitford privilege the paradigm of a resident's specialized perspective gained by industrious observation over many years. As resident monographers they find a worthy and complex subject in their immediate neighborhood.

White marks an early stage and Mitford a later (and more sentimental) stage of a major shift in epistemological and aesthetic values during the Romantic period that brings various kinds of rural locales (villages, towns, coasts, marshes, and other waste places) and a new conception of place as a specific kind of locality, into the literary landscape. The very term "locality," instead of the more ancient British term "parish," has empirical connotations designating specific material conditions that usefully differentiate it from the place as determined by church and state.[3] In natural-historical writings from the late eighteenth to the end of the nineteenth century, locality is synonymous with the less commonly used scientific term "habitat," derived from the Latin *habitus* or *habitatio*, which arrives in English in the 1790s as botanical guides shift from scholarly Latin to vernacular English.[4] Both terms designate the kind of environment where a species commonly thrives.

Mitford's suggestion that natural history played a central role in the development of the taste for new forms of representations of village life as localities is demonstrated by three provincial authors' reliance on the empirical discursive forms of natural history to achieve the major change in rural perspective and taste outlined above. This chapter examines Maria Edgeworth's *Castle Rackrent* (1800), George Crabbe's *The Borough* (1810), and John Galt's *Annals of the Parish* (written 1813, published 1821) which adopt the scholarly paradigm of the local parson–scholar and take a provincial locale as their main subject. These exemplary fictional monographs experiment with form, combining non-fiction conventions from local histories such as White's with fictional inhabitants or specimens. The texts illustrate how natural history's quest for comprehensive knowledge of all forms of life and their economies, its method of habitual *in situ* observation, and even its forms for reporting its findings structured representations of provincial novelistic worlds in provincial fiction by initiating changes in narrative perspective, persona, and form. Calling themselves, respectively, a domestic biography, a local history, and a theoretical history, they imagine a new kind of British rural world, not chorographic, topographic, or pastoral, but one consisting of diverse provincial localities, each worthy of study because of their unique environment and local society. The imagined localities of Edgeworth, Crabbe, and Galt represent historically situated environments constituted by a particular assemblage of inhabitants. Their tales all exhibit a deep interest in the economy of the locale and in the individual domestic economies of the various inhabitants.

The segregation of Crabbe's work from discussions of fiction because it is verse, and the usual categorization of Edgeworth's and Galt's earliest fictions as national tales of the Celtic periphery, have isolated all three texts from critical analysis within the larger context of rural fiction throughout Britain. Local tales and village anecdotes are not merely a product of the Celtic periphery, they are part of a very broad range of variously flavored, but distinctively rural literature in the Romantic period: didactic tales on the domestic economies of cottage life by Hannah More, Mary Leadbeater, Elizabeth Hamilton, and Alexander and John Bethune, didactic morality tales of provincial middle-class and gentry life by Maria Edgeworth, George Crabbe, and Amelia Opie, folkloric tales by Robert Bloomfield and James Hogg, and tales for children by Harriet Martineau. Cross-fertilization between natural history and fiction, as between rural Ireland, Scotland, and England, produced more complete and complex descriptions and analyses of rural localities and their socio-economic systems than are found in eighteenth-century fiction.

The emergence of these provincial perspectives was due in part to the new economic power of industrializing provincial towns and the concurrent growth of provincial intellectual communities that included the Lunar Society near Birmingham and circles in Bristol, Edinburgh, and around Manchester near the Warrington Academy for dissenters. These circles of entrepreneurs, teachers, doctors, and clergy with shared scientific interests reflect the increased economic and cultural capital of the rapidly industrializing rural periphery, and begin to diffuse the intellectual dominance of the southern Oxbridge–London center.

Amidst the variety of rural fiction, Edgeworth's, Crabbe's, and Galt's rural tales stand out. Like scientific monographs, they are narrowly focused and clearly exhibit the well-researched basis for the information that they deliver to a national and largely metropolitan audience, which, presumably, does not understand the diversity and difficulties of provincial life in Britain. Their anecdotal narratives capture the reader's interest through the characteristic idiosyncrasies and life cycles of specimen inhabitants instead of the mysteries of plot and complications of romance. *Castle Rackrent* and *Annals of the Parish* are widely recognized as the comedic masterpieces in their authors' œuvre. Together with Crabbe's unjustly forgotten satiric verse monograph *The Borough*, they must be understood as leading examples of a particular kind of British realism that is rooted in the ability of early nineteenth-century provincial writers to imagine their local novelistic worlds with the help of the practice and discourse of natural history.

Rural perspectives

Perhaps the most striking difference between the rural tales and eighteenth-century fiction is the switch in perspective from a view of the countryside from the country house to a view of the countryside from the village. In much eighteenth-century fiction, London and the country house constitute the dominant axis of action. Although characters in Gothic and picaresque novels roam between these two axes, down turnpikes and into country inns, the particularities of specific rural locales are rarely described. The major locus of country fiction, the landscaped country house, was artfully insulated from surrounding arable lands, villages, and provincial towns by various landscaped territories such as outer parks of meadows and woodland, more formal inner gardens and terraces, and distinct boundaries such as hedges, terraces, walls, and ha-has, famously evoked in Jane Austen's 1814 *Mansfield Park*.

The ha-ha (as the name indicates) perpetrates a visual joke on the viewer inside a country house garden. In the mid-eighteenth century, Lancelot "Capability" Brown created serpentine landscapes with a central grazed park that demonstrated the productive use of a rich owner's vast spaces. An invisible ditch was required to keep the livestock out of the surrounding woods.[5] The ha-ha, a ditch with a steep wall on the country-house side and a gently sloping rise on the pasture side, invisibly separates livestock in the park from adjacent areas. Standing within the garden a few feet from the unseen ha-ha, the viewer believes it possible to walk right up to the grazing sheep and wonders why they aren't cropping flowers. Depending upon its position within the landscape, a ha-ha makes a "natural" meadow seem continuous with either the inner formal gardens or the outer wilderness, until one stands at its very edge or approaches from the opposite side. The ha-ha creates and conceals the division between spaces of leisure, agriculture, and nature so that the upper classes can enjoy the pleasurable aesthetics of agricultural life without destructive encroachment from livestock or the discomfiting activities of real farming.

Like other tricks in the sister arts, such as elevated prospects in topographic poetry and shadows in chiaroscuro painting, ha-has construct an imaginary, "green" England from and for the point-of-view of the upper classes by disguising or distancing less pleasing aspects of rural life and labor.[6] They performed simultaneous exclusionary and appropriative functions. They enabled the urban and upper-class eye to overlook the grayer, grimmer scenes of rural British life, to appropriate the land and the landscape for aesthetic pleasure, and to ignore the condition of the laborers who work the agricultural landscape and live in the neighboring village, so carefully kept from sight. So long as the viewpoint remained unidirectional from the estate to the working land, from the city to the country, from the space of the upper class to the space of the lower – these visual and verbal ha-has performed their aesthetic and hegemonizing functions. But Edgeworth's, Crabbe's, and Galt's monographs suggest the demise of the country house and the reversal of perspective, a new "change in literary bearings" from country house to village, from aristocratic and gentry classes to middle and working classes.[7]

The Borough offers the most direct refutation of the limited perspective from the country house in its first letter, "General Description," addressed to an imaginary gentleman correspondent who resides in a tranquil country house securely bounded by hedges and a bubbling brook. From his library he sees the paddocks and pastures of the sleepy pastoral upland, but the dirty, vigorous, vital town hovers beyond his view behind a smoky veil. Crabbe compares this country house landscape to town gardens, guarded by spikes, ditches, traps, and guns designed to keep poor poachers at bay.[8] The country gentleman's perspective is out of touch with important aspects of provincial reality and requires the burgher's corrective point of view from within the smoky coastal town.

In *Castle Rackrent* and *The Annals of the Parish*, the country house literally falls into ruin. Castle Rackrent disintegrates slowly as three generations exploit it by the practices designated in its name. Its slow ruin illustrates the end of a semi-feudal era of colonial exploitation and a country ripe for improving landlords like Maria Edgeworth's father, Richard Lovell Edgeworth. The perspective outward from the country house is subverted by the servant narrator's inside perspective. In *Annals*, Breadland, the local estate which serves as the primary source of subsistence (and therefore power) within a simple, undiversified, grain-based agrarian economy, is rented out after the death of the last Scottish laird and burns to the ground only four years later. The power and patronage of the local laird eventually pass to an absent, occasionally attentive, English landowner, Lord Eaglesham, and an emigrant American entrepreneur, Mr. Cayenne. The narrator Rev. Balwhidder becomes the primary mediator between the villagers and the new capitalists, while a succession of industrious Mrs. Balwhidders lead the way toward a diversified agricultural economy. The perspective on rural life from the country house is replaced by the parson–narrator's view from within the village.

The perspectives of the provincial burgher, the servant insider, and the parish parson contest the country house perspective on rural life and the socio-economic dominance of the landed classes. The tales demonstrate the threatened obsolescence or irrelevance of the country house in the face of

4 Thomas Bewick, Tailpiece to Oliver Goldsmith's "The Deserted Village," in *Poems by Goldsmith and Parnell* (London: W. Bulmer, Shakespeare Printing Office, 1795), p. 51.

the increasing importance of provincial villages and towns. If, in the view of these provincial authors, the country house no longer dominates the community, then what scenes and perspectives take its place?

Thomas Bewick, the foremost wood engraver of the late eighteenth and early nineteenth centuries, and the first provincially located engraver (in Newcastle on Tyne) to develop nationwide repute, visually represents the new perspective of provincial authors. In 1795 Bewick engraved a headpiece and tailpiece for Oliver Goldsmith's poem *The Deserted Village*, itself a critique of the artificial landscape of the country house and its threat to traditional village life.[9] In both pieces the point of view is from a low point outside the village and upward toward distant hills. In the headpiece, villagers and livestock occupy the foreground; the cottages of the village are spread across the middle ground; and a church is elevated in the background at the center. In the tailpiece (see Figure 4), the overgrown foreground is devoid of people; thatch is missing from the neglected cottage roofs in the middle ground; and just above the village, separated from it by a sweeping park, sits the new neoclassical country house. In the tailpiece's background, the church is displaced from the highest spot in the center to a lower hill on the right, and on the left ships leave a harbor. The irony is clear: the moral foci of the scene, villagers and church, have been replaced by the false stewardship of the ostentatious neoclassical country house. Crabbe's introductory descriptive letter to his upland correspondent in *The Borough* enacts the same view upward toward the elevated country house, but replaces Auburn's weedy foreground with the smoky, bustling coastal town. In both cases, the moral authority and knowledge of the gentry in their emblematic country houses proves hollow.

The perspective that takes the place of the view from the country house over a pastoral landscape is best illustrated by Bewick's most famous later

5 Headpiece to the Introduction of Thomas Bewick's *History of British Birds*, Vol. I: *Land Birds* (Newcastle: Beilby & Bewick, 1797), p. vii.

work, *History of British Birds* (Vol. I, 1797; Vol. II, 1804), the book that fires the imagination of young Jane Eyre on a rainy day. Bewick revolutionized the art of animal and bird illustration by drawing upon his own observation of live birds, drawing from dead specimens only when absolutely necessary. He is noted for being the first to illustrate species with indications of their natural habitats. In addition to the beautifully detailed wood-engravings of individual birds, chapters end with remarkably detailed vignettes of rural life that are bereft of country houses and picturesque landscapes, but instead depict wildlife, travel, and the comedy and struggle, the sports and travails of the lower rural classes. In Volume I, *Land Birds*, the Introduction's headpiece (see Figure 5) sets forth the full range of his avian subjects: domestic fowl in the foreground, wild swallows soaring overhead, and dead specimens of large birds adorning the gable end of the barn, with farm labor, the winnowing and bagging of grain taking center stage. It announces a new intent to represent birds and laborers in the immediacy and totality of their shared rural environment. The natural-historical values of detailed and comprehensive representation of all types of inhabitants determine the composition of the scene instead of picturesque aesthetics. Wild and domesticated animal life encompass the seasonal work of the rural inhabitant. The level, egalitarian representation depicted from a pedestrian point of view, the essential perspective for investigating the life and conversation of humans and animals, supersedes the upward gaze in the engravings for *The Deserted Village*, where elevations emphasize the power structure within the social strata. In Bewick's illustrations for *British Birds*, Crabbe's *The Borough*, and Galt's *Annals*, the lower levels of these strata assume a new importance and centrality in rural life. The new representations reveal that Britain is not as seamlessly green, idyllic, prosperous, or stable as the limited and false view from inside the ha-ha and the country estate would lead the reader to believe.

Borrowed forms

The discursive forms of the earliest fictional monographs by Edgeworth and Crabbe provide the most direct evidence for the powerful effect of natural history on fictional representations of provincial worlds and mutual influences between British provincial authors. Form gives the clearest indication that provincial novelists borrowed the accumulating cultural capital of the discourse of natural history to support their representation of provincial worlds previously marginalized or nondescript in literature.[10]

Footnotes and appendixes are the most obvious markers of empiricist discourse in *Castle Rackrent* and *The Borough*. They are reminiscent of the explanatory footnotes found, for example, in Erasmus Darwin's verse popularizations of natural history, with which both authors were familiar. With the exception of the first footnote, most footnotes in *Castle Rackrent* are natural historical in style instead of antiquarian, like the glossary notes that speculate on origins or cite other authorities. The natural-historical footnotes focus on small details of appearance and behavior gleaned from direct observation, such as Thady's characteristic wig worn atop grown-out hair and frequently used as a duster.[11] Edgeworth's habitual collection of vivid physical and behavioral descriptions may be partly indebted to her familiarity with White's empiricist descriptions of animal behavior.[12]

Of all three monographs, *The Borough* most closely approximates a specific empiricist genre, the local county history. Like White's *Selborne*, it is written in epistolary form (albeit in heroic couplets). The genre of the local history was devised by Robert Plot in the early seventeenth century to offer a comprehensive account of a county's topography, flora and fauna, great homes and churches, economic products, and parish statistics. *The Borough* adapts the general categories of local history to Crabbe's specific interest in the lives of the middle and lower classes. During the 1790s, Crabbe contributed "A Natural History of the Vale of Belvoir" and several parish descriptions to John Nichols's eight-volume, folio size, antiquarian *magnum opus, The History and Antiquities of the County of Leicester* (1795–1815), whose title-page purports to offer "an account of its Religious Foundations, Public Institutions, and Parochial History, With Annals of that Antient Borough."[13] The twenty-four letters in *The Borough* certainly fit under these categories, with letters on religion ("The Church," "The Vicar – The Curate, &c," and "Sects and Professions in Religion"), on public institutions, a category Crabbe expands to cover informal social activities ("Amusements," "Clubs and Social Meetings," "Inns," and "Players,") and formal public institutions ("The Alms-House and Trustees," "The Hospital and Governors," "The Prisons," and "The School"). In place of parochial annals, which usually consist of lists of past clerics and population statistics, he substitutes descriptions of particular inhabitants.

The most memorable characters in *The Borough* are found in the series of letters on the lower classes, "Inhabitants of the Alms-House" and "The Poor of the Borough". In these letters, Crabbe arrives at the subject that interests him most, the imagined lives of various specimens of the lower class of inhabitants: Celia, a silly flirt, falls from the middle class to the almshouse; the Parish Clerk steals from the collection plate and is ostracized; misled by profligate young men, the young clerk Abel Keene finally commits suicide; the blind teacher Ellen Orford is the sole exemplar of blameless poverty; and Peter Grimes, a fisherman and murderer of apprentices, is the most depraved inhabitant of the borough (and the only character still famous, through Benjamin Britten's 1945 eponymous opera). Like Edgeworth's generations of Rackrents, the lives of Crabbe's characters are tales of moral failure and economic decline. His tales sketch the psychology of their moral choices and the environmental and socio-economic contexts for their behaviors. Like Bewick and any good natural historian, he includes all classes. However, as a satirist, he depicts their behaviors with less sympathy and humor than Bewick, Edgeworth, or Galt.

By drawing on the standard epistolary forms of scientific communication, by using the annotative apparatus common to literature drawing on scientific knowledge, and adapting the categorical structure of a local history, Crabbe transforms the eighteenth-century, moral-philosophical verse epistle into a natural-historical, moral verse epistle concerned with exactly the kind of detail that Alexander Pope avoided – the specific relations, manners, and situation of the inhabitants of a provincial port. *The Borough* complicates the simplistic dichotomy between city and pastoral countryside with a more complex, less idealistic representation of another kind of provincial locale. It slyly subverts the genre of local antiquarian history that focused on the property and institutions of the landed classes by borrowing the structure and categories of the gentry's genre of local history and then filling it with the tales of the middle, laboring, and indigent classes that were mere statistics in local antiquarian histories.

Another form of local history was the annal or annals, yearly records of events, a form turned into fiction by both Crabbe and John Galt. In 1807, Crabbe's poem "The Parish Register" provides an early instance of the fictionalization of this form, taking its epigraph from "Elegy Written in a Country Churchyard":

> Let not Ambition mock their useful toil,
> Their homely joys, and destiny obscure;
> Nor Grandeur hear with a disdainful smile
> The short and simple annals of the poor.[14]

Crabbe's poem is ostensibly the result of a country parson's reflections on the lives of his parishioners as he reviews his parish register's births, marriages, and deaths. Gray's phrase, "annals of the poor," is repeated throughout Crabbe's poem. John Galt's *Annals of the Parish* also echoes Gray's phrase in its title, and Galt's narrative persona is a close cousin to Crabbe's parson–narrator. Rev. Micah Balwhidder's fifty-year memoir recounts the yearly events in his parish in the west of Scotland between 1760, when he arrives as a young pastor, and 1810, when he retires.

Both Crabbe's and Galt's texts construct themselves as answers to Gray's call for "short and simple annals of the poor" that more fully and realistically describe the lives of the lower classes in rural society than his elegiac homage to stereotypical cottage life. The provincial pastor as narrative persona draws upon such figures as Gilbert White, George Crabbe, and many other rural clergy who contributed to empiricist projects that document rural locales. In the 1790s as Crabbe was contributing statistical and antiquarian descriptions of parishes within Leicestershire to John Nichol's county history, parish ministers all across Scotland, "locality by locality," were completing their local surveys of population, local topography, natural history, and economy for the *Old Statistical Accounts of Scotland* (published 1791–9). Galt's novel legitimates the fictional rural world of western Scotland by linking its annalistic title and form with Gray's poetic stature (and perhaps Crabbe's, which was much higher in the early nineteenth century than it is now), and from the well-known empiricist activities of country parsons.

In their formal intertextual referentiality, the works of natural history and local history by Darwin, White, Nichols, and others and the fictions of

Edgeworth, Crabbe, and Galt share forms of provincial literary discourse that circulate across rural Britain and not merely around the Celtic periphery. This distinctive provincial literary discourse indicates the writers' shared concern for the visibility of provincial life and the social and moral problems of the rural poor within an increasingly metropolitan and industrializing nation. The overt empiricist forms of Edgeworth's and Crabbe's monographs and Galt's later, indirect allusion to natural-historical and antiquarian activities of local pastors also suggest early nineteenth-century provincial authors' need to legitimate the factual basis of their fictions for readers whom they imagine as sceptical or ignorant of the interest, merits, and problems of their provincial subject. Thus the preface to *Castle Rackrent* justifies the editorial apparatus as a solution to the problem that Thady's "Memoirs will perhaps be scarcely intelligible, or probably they may appear perfectly incredible. For the information of the *ignorant* English reader, a few notes have been subjoined by the editor" (author's emphasis).[15] To combat these anticipated problems with readers' scepticism and ignorance, early provincial writers used tactics that drew on the discursive power of natural history and important poetic predecessors such as Gray in order to present a new subject of fiction, the diversity of life in a rural locale. In so doing, of course, they in turn impose a new set of power relations on rural places in which the resident, educated, middle-class intellectual, the man or woman of science, has a dominant role as a translator of local dialect and custom, or an onsite empiricist gathering raw data on behaviors, customs, and the economy. Fictional monographs about locales do not represent a Romantic reaction against empiricism; they deliberately draw upon the widely popular discipline of natural history in order to imagine neglected and marginalized rural societies.

Persona tactics

And yet throughout the works of early provincial monographers, a common anxiety betrays itself about being identified solely as an inhabitant of marginalized and misunderstood rural culture. White, Edgeworth, and Crabbe feel compelled to defend the importance of their subject to a reading audience that they imagine as ignorant or unappreciative. This defensiveness is first visible in White's seminal monograph on place addressed to two different correspondents, in which he positions himself and his project relative to the tension between the localist and the generalist and their two forms of knowledge, the monograph and the national survey.

Edgeworth and Crabbe also exhibit the anxiety of the provincial monographer with respect to a readership of metropolitan outsiders more accustomed to the "whirl half over Europe" than to the particulars of a "confined locality." Their anxieties about "belonging and not belonging" to the broad republic of letters find direct expression not only in their empiricist forms, but in the mutual constructions of narrative persona and reader persona. The use of a narrative persona is a distinctive tactic in the early fictional monographs to relieve the tension between the author and his/her audience. By deploying narrative personae and natural-historical forms, provincial authors situate themselves, Janus-like, as both direct observers within a particular locale and as knowledgable participants in wider empirical circles.[16] These formal tactics are, in Michel de Certeau's words, "an art of being between," whereby they define themselves and their world against metropolitan chauvinism and idealizing nationalistic constructions of rural life.[17]

In *Castle Rackrent*, Edgeworth creates personae who are both insiders and outsiders to the locale. Thady Quirk, cunning servant and steward to generations of Rackrents, provides the quintessential inside, secret family history, "pour[ing] forth anecdotes, and retail[ing] conversations, with all the minute prolixity of a gossip in a country town."[18] An Anglo-Irish resident, Edgeworth uses an Editor's annotation both to address a presumably uninformed English audience and to substantiate the ethnographic facts of Thady's ostensibly oral and definitely self-interested account. This Editor carefully elides identification as an Anglo-Irishman (or woman) by shifting between first person and third person sources of anecdotal evidence, but the erudite footnotes lead the English reader to identify him as a cosmopolitan participant in the gentlemanly Republic of Letters.[19] The Editor is both a local empiricist and a cosmopolitan antiquarian.

George Crabbe confronts a different insider–outsider dichotomy by imagining his monograph, *The Borough*, as a correspondence from a provincial burgher to a country gentleman. By using a country gentleman as his foil and stand-in for the reader, he avoids alienating his metropolitan readership with charges of ignorance like those found in Edgeworth's preface while asserting the diversity of provincial situations to metropolitan readers who would idealize country life as that pastoral perspective visible from the grounds of a country house. Already his first description of the town gardens contrasts the placid pastoral scene from the country house with the visible class tensions manifest in a marshy coastal town:

> We scent the Vapours of the sea-born Gale;
> Broad-beaten Paths lead on from Stile to Stile,
> And Sewers from Streets, the Road-side Banks defile;
> Our guarded Fields a sense of danger show,
> Where Garden-crops with Corn and Clover grow;

Fences are form'd of Wreck and plac'd around,
(With tenters tipp'd) a strong repulsive bound;
Wide and deep Ditches by the Gardens run,
And there in ambush lie the Trap and Gun[20]

In the borough, a highly visible ditch filled with man-traps separates upper and lower classes. The noxious urban ditch of mingled brine and sewage is the antithesis of the ha-ha that seamlessly incorporates the sanitized pastoral scene into the garden view (and the bubbling stream surrounding his correspondent's country house). In Crabbe's imagined rural world, upper and lower classes and nature and society cannot be either invisibly or painlessly separated or intentionally oblivious of each other.

Writing in 1813 only three years after *The Borough* was published, Galt, like Crabbe, also creates an imaginary village in a very specific part of Britain – Dalmailing in western Scotland. Like Edgeworth, Galt publishes anonymously and, like both predecessors, he too utilizes a local inhabitant as a narrative persona: Reverend Micah Balwhidder, originally shunned as an unwanted outsider to the town that he describes, has earned his right to narrate its history by fifty years of service as its resident pastor. Unlike the cunning insider Thady Quirk, whom the reader suspects of withholding crucial information about his own role in the fall of the Rackrents, Balwhidder is a mild reactionary, adapting unwillingly to local socio-economic pressures, whose account reveals the relations between his locality and the British economy and empire. Galt offers no editorial apparatus to create a truth effect. Instead he aligns his authorial point-of-view with his audience: both are assumed to be more knowledgable and cosmopolitan than the narrator and therefore able to interpret events (and Balwhidder) within a broader explanatory historical context than his simplistic providential explanations provide. By 1813, when *Annals* was written, Galt no longer needs personae to function as Janus-like characters facing both the city and the country, or center and periphery, because the readership for provincial monographs, didactic tales, and memoirs has been thoroughly developed by White, Edgeworth, Crabbe, and other provincial authors. In addition, Galt's social location as an established London writer is quite different from the provincially located Edgeworth and Crabbe.

Without an editorial apparatus like Edgeworth's, Galt turns this seemingly naive account into a sophisticated analysis of a small community's progress from a subsistence agricultural economy to a diversified economy based upon commercial agriculture, mining, and textile manufacture. This Whiggish history, told through the eyes of a conservative Tory, imagines the development, not of the wealth of a nation, but of the wealth of a parish gained through increasing intercourse with the larger world. Although initially the parson's means are limited and his knowledge of the world is quite circumscribed, over the course of fifty years both his income and his knowledge are enlarged through the influx of energetic entrepreneurial strangers (including his two wives) and by the export of inhabitants into the merchant marine, the navy, and the army and their periodic returns. Balwhidder's strong Christian beliefs enable an occasional critique of the moral and social ills that accompany economic development. Except when facing sectarian competition, Balwhidder has, by the annals' end, become a conciliatory, mediating figure between the social classes, helping to ease the transition to a cash economy for the poor and mediating the rise of impoverished families such as the Malcolms into the middle class through his contacts with the aristocracy.[21] Galt's stance with respect to Dalmailing is clearly that of an outsider casting an affectionate backward glance toward an earlier time, but ultimately supporting the industrial and social advancements from the face-to-face village community to a modern socially heterogeneous industrial town.

Thinking locally

Do these long-vanished local worlds matter as more than a source of nostalgic laughter and sighs? They offer ways to think locally in a world increasingly enmeshed in a global economy and culture. In *Annals of the Parish*, local worlds do not persist in unchanging isolation from the global; economic development and social change are intimately tied to exchanges with the broader world. Dalmailing's youth leave as sailors and soldiers and return with the goods of the world: parrots, limes for the pastor's tropical punch, and tea, the commodity so vital to the impoverished Malcolm family's return to middle-class standing. Emigrants from America and Ireland threaten the hegemonic church and gentry power structure with their entrepreneurial and radical activism, but they also enrich the community with their books and newspapers. *Castle Rackrent* demonstrates that a class's refusal to change old exploitative ways that failed to consider the land and all its inhabitants leads eventually to its own demise.

In Crabbe's borough, where the sea's water, sound, and smell penetrate every corner, poorer inhabitants are constantly reminded of their human vulnerability to nature's powerful forces and to the power of the richer classes. *The Borough* insists upon the brutalizing influence of a poor and polluted environment where "reformers come not" and "Infant-Sailors" pretend to be Nelsons in the ponds of effluent between cottage "ash heaps."[22] In *Annals* such middens are the signs of present squalor and instruments of future improvement when Lord Eaglesham is unceremoniously overturned in his carriage into the middens that crowd the village street, an incident that incites him to initiate road construction that is vital to economic development of the nearby mines.[23] *Castle Rackrent* offers few details of habitat and exterior description, except the images of a barren bog with puny planted trees and a gentry midden, a broken carriage abandoned at the estate's gate. Middens and ditches are the persistent signs of provincial poverty that none of these tales allow the reader to overlook. What these texts render invisible are the farms, arable land, and pastures. The fictional monographs have undone the work of the invisible ha-has. Pastoral images are excluded in favor of beaches and bogs, the barren environments that are one cause of uneven development. As each monograph makes evident, none of the locales they describe, including Selborne, were naturally fruitful, easy places to live. The fortified gardens of the borough imply that if the situation of all is not improved, then inhabitants become locked in a ruthless battle for resources.

These texts lay the essential groundwork for thinking of locality as a combination of a natural and social environment. Like Bewick's headpiece, they represent social nature and thereby nudge the reader beyond the aesthetic appreciation of a landscape or wildlife and into the harder questions of the economic relations between an environment and its local society. Thinking locally about the economies of social nature poses questions of environmental justice instead of simply fostering an aesthetic appreciation for landscapes and nature. These texts move away from overly simplistic dichotomies – country/city or nature/metropolis – toward the complexities of provincial life. British localities are not pure sources of pleasure as Mitford's introduction suggests; as her own anecdotes also prove, a confined locality makes social and economic tensions manifest.

The opening epigraph from Mitford and my analysis of imagined rural localities' indebtedness to the empirical naturalist tradition of White suggest one last line of inquiry: What is the relationship between the imagined rural worlds of anecdotal fictional monographs and Jane Austen's imagined novelistic worlds? Her novels use third-person omniscient narrators instead of clerical or empiricist personae. They do not attempt comprehensive accounts of all classes of inhabitants, but restrict themselves mostly to the lower gentry and middle class. Austen's novels absorb imagined rural localities, which appear in the best rural tales as entities with their own socio-economic character capable of either development or deterioration, into the terrain of the *Bildungsroman* that focuses on the maturation of individual heroes or heroines instead of places. However, like the rural tales, Austen's narrative perspective is largely displaced from the country house. With the exception of Emma, her heroines are alienated from the country house in various ways.

Catherine Morland is a stranger at the Gothic house of Northanger Abbey. The Bennet girls face future alienation from their small estate through an entail. Upon their brother's inheritance, the Dashwood sisters must leave Norland Park for a modest, distant country cottage. Fanny Price is a poor relation, dependent on the charity of her aunt at Mansfield Park, and Anne Elliot becomes virtually homeless when her father economizes by renting Kellynch Hall.

Important differences between Austen's later fiction (written after 1811) and her earlier novels may be due in part to the imagined worlds of British village literature published in such quantities in the first fifteen years of the nineteenth century. Her admiration for Crabbe, whose most popular works were published between 1807 and 1819, is well known. She publicly acknowledges his influence by transforming his character Fanny Price, a "Damsel, meekly firm" who refuses a womanizer in *The Parish Register* into her own "meekly firm" heroine in *Mansfield Park*.[24] Although she shows little of Crabbe's moral didacticism or his comprehensive representations of classes, *Mansfield Park*, *Emma*, and *Persuasion* exhibit a more marked concern with the representation of a locality, its economy, and its relations between classes than the earlier novels.

Provincial tales open up the range of rural life and rural worlds beyond the ha-ha, so that when Austen represents the country house in her later fiction, it is with a different vision of its relationship to a locality. Fanny Price recognizes immediately that local wagons should not be requisitioned to deliver Mary Crawford's harp while the grain is being harvested. Mr. Knightley eschews an improvement that would lengthen a long-established path and inconvenience the village laborers. Emma Woodhouse must learn her proper role within local society and understand the serious repercussions of her mockery and neglect of impoverished Miss Bates and her inappropriate mentoring of illegitimate Harriet Smith. Although Fanny and Emma may still regard the village from the country house, and the ha-ha still marks moral boundaries that should not be crossed, in these later novels the country house perspective no longer limits Austen's novelistic worlds, which now extend to include villages, farms, and other classes.

NOTES

1 John Barrell, *English Literature in History, 1730–80: An Equal, Wide Survey* (New York: St. Martin's Press, 1983), pp. 36–8.

2 Gilbert White, *The Natural History of Selborne*, ed. Richard Mabey (London: Everyman, 1993), p. 106.

3 Despite the fact that surveys were given to parish ministers for completion, Sir John Sinclair explains that the Statistical Accounts of Scotland provide "a unique survey

of the state of the whole country, locality by locality." Quoted by Charles J. Withers in "Statistical Accounts of Scotland," www.electricscotland.com/webclans/statistical_accounts.htm, par. 9.

4 The *OED* cites the first English usage and definition of habitat in William Withering's 1796 edition of *British Plants*. In 1810 George Crabbe defined it in a footnote in Letter VIII as the "favourite soil or situation of the more scarce species" in *The Borough, George Crabbe: The Complete Poetical Works*, eds. Norma Dalrymple-Champneys and Arthur Pollard, 3 vols., Vol. I (Oxford: Clarendon Press, 1988), p. 436.

5 For an excellent schematic representation of the history of landscape gardening see "Garden History Style Guide," www.gardenvisit.com/s/estyle2/estyle.htm.

6 See John Barrell, *The Dark Side of the Landscape: The Rural Poor in English Painting 1730–1840* (Cambridge: Cambridge University Press, 1980) on the apparently aesthetic, but actually moral and social constraints, that governed representations of the poor in landscape and genre painting and pastoral and georgic poetry.

7 Raymond Williams, *The Country and the City* (New York: Oxford University Press, 1973), pp. 166–8. Williams dates this change in bearings and the emergence of knowable rural communities to George Eliot's fiction and attributes its emergence to Eliot's knowledge of economic power and her social location outside the gentry.

8 Crabbe, *The Borough*, Letter I.115–34, p. 364.

9 Goldsmith, Oliver, *The Deserted Village, Poems by Goldsmith and Parnell* (London: Shakespeare Printing Office, 1795), pp. 29 and 51.

10 Since at least the eighteenth century, nondescript has been a scientific term for species not yet recognized through description in the scientific literature. The discovery and classification of nondescript species was the central focus of eighteenth-century natural history. However, as White argues in *Selborne*, the domestic economies and behavior of fauna should also be an important part of a naturalist's mission. These two goals of providing a complete taxonomy of local life and accurate descriptions of their behaviors and domestic economies also motivate the fictional monographs and justify writers' efforts to describe lesser known places, and the behaviors of the lower classes.

11 Maria Edgeworth, *Castle Rackrent, Novels and Selected Works*, 12 vols., (London: Pickering & Chatto, 1999–2003), Vol. I, eds. Jane Desmarais, Tim McLoughlin, and Marilyn Butler, p. 40.

12 Edgeworth refers to White's *A Naturalist's Calendar* (John Aikin's 1795 posthumous compilation of White's journal notes into a calendar of flora and birds) in *Practical Education* by Edgeworth and her father Richard Lovell Edgeworth, 2nd edn. (London: J. Johnston, 1798).

13 John Nichols, *The History and Antiquities of the County of Leicestershire*, 4 vols. (London: John Nichols, 1795–1815).

14 Thomas Gray, "Elegy Written in a Country Churchyard," *The Longman Anthology of British Literature: The Restoration and the Eighteenth Century*, 3rd edn., Vol. I C (New York: Pearson Longman, 2006), ll. 28–32, p. 2855.

15 Edgeworth, *Castle Rackrent*, p. 6.

16 On the issue of an author's "divided consciousness" see Williams, *The Country and the City*, p. 174.

17 Michel De Certeau, *The Practice of Everyday Life*, trans. Steven Rendall (Berkeley: University of California Press, 1984), p. 30.

18 Edgeworth, *Castle Rackrent*, p. 6.

19 For a fuller discussion of the liminal narrative personae in *Castle Rackrent* see my "Tales of Locales: The Natural History of *Selborne* and *Castle Rackrent*," *Modern Philology* 100 (2003), pp. 407–10.

20 Crabbe, *The Borough*, Letter I.124–32, p. 364.

21 On Galt's empiricism and Balwhidder's mediating role see Keith M. Costain, "The Community of Man: Galt and Eighteenth-Century Scottish Realism," *Scottish Literary Journal*, 8 (May 1981), pp. 10–29.

22 Crabbe, *The Borough*, Letter VIII.274–9, p. 529.

23 John Galt, *Annals of the Parish and the Ayreshire Legatees* (Edinburgh: Blackwood, 1895), Vol. I, pp. 60–1.

24 Crabbe, *The Parish Register*, p. 251, ll. 558–9.

6

MARSHALL BROWN

Poetry and the novel

Rhymesters fail when they try to write prose. In prose there are no empty
syllables to fill up; something absolutely has to be said.
— But, Monsieur, Walter Scott also wrote poems ...
(Balzac, *Illusions perdues*)

Tell me but this — is there poetry in it?
(Scott, *The Pirate*)

The oil of poetry and the water of prose do not mix easily. There have
indeed been exceptions: the carnivalesque mode of Menippean satire; the
self-designated (and isolated) medieval "chantefable" (tale with inserted
poems) *Aucassin et Nicolette*; the Renaissance pastoral romance and its
parody in *Don Quixote*. And then there is the genre at the center of this
chapter, which I shall designate the "Romantic novel." Adapted from
German, this term will include not just novels with poems in them, but also
short prose narratives (stories and novellas) that include poems as well as
verse narratives with incorporated lyrics. The first "Romantic novel" in this
sense is perhaps Oliver Goldsmith's *Vicar of Wakefield* (1766), with its
famous ballad "Edwin and Angelina," its "Ode on the Death of a Mad
Dog," and its sentimental lyric "When lovely woman stoops to folly"; in
English the last major examples are some tales of Edgar Allan Poe and the
familiar twin peaks are Ann Radcliffe and Walter Scott (though instead of
Radcliffe I shall discuss the slightly earlier instance of Charlotte Smith, a
more productive author and a better poet).

The theorist of the "Romantic novel" was the early German Romantic
critic Friedrich Schlegel. Playing on the German word for novel, a famous
passage of Schlegel's "Dialogue on Poetry" (1800) takes the novel to represent the essence of Romanticism: "A novel [ein Roman] is a romantic book."
And his collection of aphorisms and mini-essays known as the Athenaeum
Fragments defines the genre:

> Romantic poetry is a progressive, universal poetry ... It tries to and should mix
> and fuse poetry and prose, inspiration and criticism, the poetry of art and the
> poetry of nature ... It embraces everything that is purely poetic, from the

greatest systems of art, containing within themselves still further systems, to the sigh, the kiss that the poetizing child breathes forth in artless song.[1]

To be sure, many difficulties confront the impulse to read Schlegel's quicksilvery utterances normatively, even for German fiction, let alone for that of other countries. He changes his perspective continuously and uses the term "Roman" for many kinds of composition beyond prose (or mixed) fiction, and his principal reference points – Goethe's *Wilhelm Meister's Apprenticeship*, early works by Ludwig Tieck, and perhaps the never-finished projects soon to be undertaken by his friend Novalis (Friedrich von Hardenberg) and himself – were known abroad, if at all, only decades later. On the other hand, his own culture was broadly international, with Cervantes as central to him as to British novelists, and his strength as a critic is more intuitive and projective than either descriptive or prescriptive. To the extent that "Romantic novels" are experiments, Schlegel's formulations can help assess their intention or what in the tradition of Benjamin and the early Lukács might be called their formal ideal. To that end, I will also cite an unpublished fragment of 1797: "The opinion that the novel is no poem is founded on the thesis: All poetry should be metric. But an exception from this thesis can be made for the sake of progressivity, if only for that. The novel is a yet incomparably more mixed mixed poem than idyll or satire, which follow a definite law of mixture."[2] Despite their bewildering diversity, Schlegel's comments on the mixed forms he calls novels leave no doubt that they should aim at the reflective fusion he repeatedly calls "poetry squared" or "the poetry of poetry." The "Romantic novel" was intended to be the incomparable apotheosis of the literary expression of the age.

No one has written more penetratingly on the interaction of verse and prose than Georg Lukács, in scattered segments of his early *Theory of the Novel*. Epic verse, he writes, "creates distances, but in the sphere of the epic (which is the sphere of life) distance means happiness and lightness ... abolishing triviality and coming closer to the essence." And in mixed forms, where "the artist's personality ... proclaims its own interpretation of the meaning of the universe ... [w]hat is given form ... is not the totality of life but the artist's relationship with that totality, his approving or condemnatory attitude towards it."[3] The most highly wrought examples are surely to be found in German writing. They include Goethe's *Wilhelm Meister's Apprenticeship* (1795–6, trans. Thomas Carlyle, 1824) and its eccentric continuation, *Wilhelm Meister's Travels* (incomplete version, 1821, trans. Carlyle, 1827; final version 1829), haunting fantastic tales and mostly rather less haunting novels by Tieck, Novalis, Clemens Brentano, Achim von

Arnim, and especially Joseph von Eichendorff. Paul Neuburger has detailed the trajectory leading from the mixed forms of antiquity and arriving, by way of Richardson and others, at German Romanticism: eventually verse proliferates to the extent that even narrative passages are sometimes versified, and songs express feelings that may be generic (typical of earlier instances) or character-specific or may entirely overflow the situation. Indeed, late in the game, Eduard Mörike's intricately neurotic novel *Nolen the Painter* (1832) contains not only a variety of poems, but an entire play. Goethe is Neuburger's hero on account of his infinite variety, and Goethe's *Faust* (1790, 1808, 1832) conforms to Schlegel's precepts fully enough to count as the masterpiece of the entire genre. In their exuberance, that is, these transgeneric German works often leave behind the novel as it is known in other national traditions. Yet they form an important context for the seldom examined generic mixing in the tamer, more conventionally novelistic, more broadly accessible worlds of British Romantic fiction.

If German Romantic fiction forms a crucial context to genre mixing in British writing of the period, then earlier and later prose narrative serves as an illuminating foil. For both before and after the Romantic decades authors conspicuously avoided mixing prose and verse. The novels of sensibility are often lyrically effusive, but in prose. G. Gabrielle Starr has discussed the powerful impress of both hymn writers and metaphysical and Cavalier poets on Richardson, but she notes only two original poems that appear in Pamela's letters: a parody of Psalm 137 (accompanied by three psalm translations) and a flowery love lyric from Mr. B. (There is one other, the prosy "Verses on My Going Away.") One further poem, Clarissa's "Ode to Wisdom," was stolen from Elizabeth Carter; by way of recompense Richardson added a musical setting that turns the phrase "Of intellectual light" into a most unlyrical refrain.[1] Prosaic as they are, Richardson's attempts at verse appear exceptional in the eighteenth century; more revealing (and unmentioned by Starr) is the disruptive force of Uncle Toby's Lillabulero in Laurence Sterne's *Tristram Shandy*, along with the comic ode stanza in "Slawkenbergius's Tale" with which the lovesick Diego "eased his mind against the wall," though, as Slawkenbergius says, "The lines were very natural – for they were nothing at all to the purpose." And while eighteenth-century insertions are a distraction or a disruption, after the Romantic decades it becomes almost axiomatic that poems signal danger. Thus, for instance, in Charles Dickens's *Martin Chuzzlewit*, the pawnbroker David Crimple attributes "the inventive and poetical department" to the sleazy swindler Tigg Montague, and the poetic Silas Wegg is one of the more villainous characters in Dickens's *Our Mutual Friend*.[5] Although many nineteenth-century novelists also wrote poetry, Emily Brontë, George

Eliot, Meredith, Hardy, and Wilde generally avoided inserting verses into their narratives except as disturbances. (*Adam Bede* and *The Mayor of Casterbridge* include some hymns, and there are a very few verses scattered in other Hardy novels and in Kipling.) Similar strategies are followed by Herman Melville and Stephen Crane in the United States, and Victor Hugo, Théophile Gautier, Gottfried Keller, Theodor Fontane, and Theodor Storm on the Continent. On its rare appearances in Realist novels, poetry usually strikes a sour note. The beautiful, feminized Lucien de Rubempré in Balzac's *Illusions perdues* is a brilliant but doomed opportunist, equally lacking in morals and in ruthlessness (a number of his poems are quoted, including a drinking song he writes for money while grieving over his dead mistress); Canalis in *Modeste Mignon* is a social climber (one poem, with music); the comically named Athanase in *La Vieille Fille* a pale youth. Thus, Henry James's *The Portrait of a Lady* repeatedly characterizes the odious Gilbert Osmond as the son of "the American Corinne," unceremoniously termed "a defunct poetess" (the allusion is to the eponymous heroine of Mme de Staël's best-known novel), and he prefaces his profession of love for Isabel Archer with "a little sonnet" entitled "Rome Revisited," in "correct and ingenious verse."[6] In Fontane's *Effi Briest* allusions to poems by Heinrich Heine and Clemens Brentano frame the heroine's adultery, and some children's doggerel, absurdly critiqued by a maid and a teacher, prefaces the moment of Effi's return to her husband when her love letters are accidentally discovered.[7] Such juxtapositions are telling precisely for being so very casual in appearance. At the other extreme is the systematic poetry-hatred in the remarkable *Max Havelaar* by the Dutch novelist Multatuli (E. D. Dekker).[8]

Nor are "Romantic novels" universal even in the Romantic decades. The poet Wordsworth attacked "sickly and stupid German novels" in the Preface to *Lyrical Ballads* (1800). And while Jane Austen frequently alludes to and echoes Cowper and other favorite poets, she retains a clear sense of decorum when it comes to the separate spheres of prose and verse. "I wonder who first discovered the efficacy of poetry in driving away love," exclaims Elizabeth Bennet, and the turning point in her love comes as a result of the substitution of a trip to Derbyshire for a planned voyage to Wordsworth's Lake District.[9] " 'I have read several of Burns' Poems with great delight', said Charlotte as soon as she had time to speak, 'but I am not poetic enough to separate a Man's Poetry entirely from his Character; – and poor Burns's known Irregularities, greatly interrupt my enjoyment of his lines. – I have difficulty in depending on the *Truth* of his Feelings as a Lover.'"[10] There is an unstated implication here that a ragged right margin reflects a ragged, or at least overly emotional life. *Poetry and Truth* was to be the paradoxical title of Goethe's autobiography; in Austen the collocation is not just a paradox but a scandal.

Trafalgar House, on the most elevated spot on the Down was a light elegant Building, standing in a small Lawn with a very young plantation round it, about an hundred yards from the brow of a steep, but not very lofty Cliff . . . Charlotte having received possession of her apartment, found amusement enough in standing at her ample Venetian window, and looking over the miscellaneous foreground of unfinished Buildings, waving Linen, and tops of Houses, to the Sea, dancing and sparkling in Sunshine and Freshness.[11]

With a genuinely lofty cliff in view, Wordsworth gained sight of the immortal sea; the novel's humbler perspective is filled instead with the intervening litter of life, the "trivialities" of which Lukács writes. Poetry appears as doggerel alongside the charades in Chapter 9 of *Emma*, and in *Persuasion* Captain Benwick's fondness for poetry is a character flaw: the heroine Anne Elliot warns him that "it was the misfortune of poetry, to be seldom safely enjoyed by those who enjoy it completely."[12] Benwick and the flighty Louisa "of course . . . had fallen in love over poetry," whereas the hero Wentworth mistrusts poems, not least because they are "all written by men."[13] Despite many affinities with her contemporaries that recent critics have highlighted, Austen stands apart from the authors I will discuss in taking for granted the mutual repulsion of poetry and reality.[14]

To be sure, even in the anti-poetic times before and after Romanticism, things are not so neat. Tonally lyrical interludes of meditation and idyll recur in Enlightenment fiction and, with greater prominence, in Victorian novels. Though poetry envy can mean hostility, it can also mean jealous emulation: there is a reason why Gilbert Osmond is so fascinating. And the verse excluded from the text sneaks back in the epigrams of Stendhal and Eliot. Thomas Gradgrind's hatred of imagination in Dickens's *Hard Times* is self-defeating; real life rarely succeeds at banishing romance.

Still, the Romantic movement remained distinctive in the way it welcomed the merging of romance and real life (on which Michael Gamer has written[15]). Indeed, despite the tendency still found in some criticism to regard the "Romantic novel" as a mongrel, prose seeps into the poetry of the Romantic period just as poetry barges into the prose. Wordsworth opposed poetic diction and sought "the real language of men," Goethe indulged in verse his penchant for aphorism, Hölderlin's parataxis (as characterized in an essay of that name by Adorno) replaces the idealist intricacy of classic verse with a distinctively modern kind of difficulty, Shelley is as often urbane as he is sublime, and Keats – yes, even Keats – interrupts "Isabella, or the Pot of Basil" (derived from a prose tale) with ironic asides and frames his Nightingale Ode – yes, even the nightingale – with monosyllabic gestures straight out of the epistolary tradition: "My heart aches . . . Do I wake or sleep?" When Gogol subtitled *Dead Souls* "Poem" or when Pushkin labeled

Eugene Onegin "Novel in Verse," they were envisioning a fusion of types, as was the great translator Vasily Zhukovsky when he turned Friedrich de la Motte Fouqué's German prose tale "Undine" into a classic of Russian Romantic versifying. During the brief Romantic hiatus in the long-running quarrel between prose and verse, novel and poem do not face off but greet one another.

The earliest regular practitioner of the "Romantic novel" was probably Charlotte Smith. She began publishing poems in 1784, and over the course of a decade she incorporated poems into seven of her ten novels, beginning in 1788 with *Emmeline*. The greatest number of poems (six) is found in *Celestina* (1791); the focus here will be rather on Smith's best-known novel, *The Old Manor House* (1793).

The Old Manor House contains three original poems: "Hymn to Love and Hope" at the end of Vol. III, ch. 7 (entitled "Hymn to Love and Life" in *Poems*), the sonnet "Ill omen'd bird" concluding Vol. III, and a second sonnet, "While thus I wander," in Vol. IV, ch. 7. Yet while the quantity of actual verse is limited, the novel is in fact pervaded by poetry and poeticisms. The first three volumes carry labeled epigraphs by Ariosto, Shakespeare, and Cowper. (The epigraph to Vol. IV, unlabeled, comes from Rousseau's *Julie*.) Shakespeare's plays are quoted at intervals, along with dramatic lines of Otway and Addison, once each in the latter volumes, and there are some echoes of Milton, not always marked. Late in Vol. II, lines from "the ballad of Hardyknute" (1719) come to the mind of the hero Orlando, "who was passionately fond of poetry," and two lines from "Chevy Chase" are adapted (by replacing "hunting" with "taxing") early in Vol. III to initiate Smith's bitter critique of the attempt to suppress the American Revolution, in which her hero is involved and nearly dies. A line from the mid-century sentimental poet Langhorne is quoted in Vol. II, ch. 1, "The child of misery, baptized in tears," initiating a theme that pervades this very weepy book. And there are several further quotes from Thomson, Gray, Goldsmith, and Cowper in Vols. III and IV.

While the poems and quotations in *The Old Manor House* do not bulk larger than in *Clarissa*, their function is far more pointed. In Richardson's novel, verse appears as an almost routine part of the general culture of a decadent society, and indeed a random assemblage of quotes written crooked forms the climax of Clarissa's "mad papers" (Letter 261). Smith's novel, by contrast, moves toward and into poetry. The hero Orlando (poetically named after Ariosto) learns to love poetry and shares his passion with his beloved cousin (Monimia – whose name comes from the Otway play that is quoted – who "dwelt on the pages where he had with a pencil marked some peculiar beauty in the poetry").[16] Orlando begins as companion to another beautiful youth, his good-natured eventual brother-in-law Warwick, but they grow apart: Warwick merely trifles in verse and eventually recognizes his inferiority to Orlando: "You, Orlando, who are yourself a poet, would you be tasteless enough to check a man inspired?" (III.9; p. 327). The attorney's clerk Carr, a lesser character who becomes Orlando's savior, also has "a taste for poetry" and admires the "natural turn to poetry" in Orlando's (unquoted) ode to Poverty (IV.11; p. 506); thereupon, he brings Orlando to a fashionable but degraded poetic salon (a satire on Hannah Cowley), where Orlando re-encounters Warwick, long thought dead en route to America. The happy denouement, restoring all to fortune, ensues rapidly after this meeting, though not directly as a result. Good fortune is linked associatively even if not by any plot mechanism with the proper definition of a poetic sphere.

Smith's fiction is thoroughly anti-theatrical, predicated on the primacy of atmosphere over plot. The intrigue is complicated rather than complex, with many incidental characters and digressive ramifications. Hair-raising incidents, especially Orlando's American adventure and Indian captivity, are but briefly summarized, and only one minor character, Lt. Fleming, has a death scene (a quick one, in the heat of battle, no time for tears); Orlando's father, brother, and aunt-protector all die offstage, as does the dissolute villain Stockton. The elopement of Orlando and Monimia likewise takes place between sentences (IV.10). Large stretches of the long novel are occupied with the fears and hopes of the characters, who reason at length about their confusions, often in long, intricately articulated sentences. The characters are concerned not with the presence of passions, but with their ungraspability. The first extended nature description emphasizes its poetic potential, inspiring erotic thoughts: "Orlando had hardly ever felt himself so impressed with those feelings which inspire poetic effusions 'Oh, Monimia!' sighed he ..." (II.5; p. 160). Surely following the example of Werther calling out the name of the greatest German poet of the day, Friedrich Georg Klopstock, at a storm-inspired erotic high point of Goethe's *Sorrows of Young Werther* (Book 1, end of the long letter dated June 16), poetry appears here as the telos of nature, the great mother, the heart's home. Amid the turbulent flux of emotions, nature appeals to and poetry addresses the core of the soul. Later, as Orlando is about to be drawn off into the navy, nature turns bleak, with a "chill and hollow ... wind," and an "owl's cry ... dull and melancholy." There is a conflict between feeling and thinking: "he endeavoured to reason himself out of these comfortless presages," but suffers instead a "blank that strikes on the heart" – and remembers the ballad of Hardyknute (II.13; pp. 235–7). Yet another thrust from nature into lyric closes the third book. The scenery of the St. Lawrence (as Smith fantasized it) transmutes the Gothic notes that had begun the novel into a bookish fantasy "where the dark knots of cypress seemed … to represent groups of supernatural beings in funereal habits." Once again, landscape leads to poetry:

> Orlando endeavoured to shake off the uncomfortable sensations, which, in despite of his reason, hung about him; but he rather indulged than checked them, in throwing upon paper the following

SONNET   (III.14; pp. 385–6)

In its separate publication, the sonnet, a Gothic address to the nocturnal whippoorwill, ends gloomily: "Ah! Reason little o'er the soul prevails, / When, from ideal ill, the enfeebled spirit fails." The version in the novel, however, is far more hopeful: "But aid me, Heaven! my real ills to bear, / Nor let my spirit yield to phantoms of despair." Plot is the problem, indeed the threat; poetry is the solution. Poetry offers an image of control and pensive depth to characters whose destinies appear to be in the hands of more or less ill-intentioned others; its apparent lifelessness becomes a critique of things as they are.[17]

The interiority of the genuine poetic impulse explains why the superficial Warwick spouts verse in fashionable banter, whereas Orlando and Monimia read it, remember it, or write it. Poetic composition begins for Smith, exactly as it was to do for Wordsworth, in a state of renewed agitation, and it both exercises and composes the mind. The last of the original poems in *The Old Manor House* achieves its aim most fully.

> All around was dreary and silent; and blank, he thought, as his destiny. Yet he wished the torpid sensation that being long exposed to the cold had given to his limbs could reach his heart, which was too acutely sensible! … Orlando … passed on; his thoughts (as he compared their peaceful slumbers with the state of his own troubled mind) assuming a poetical form, in the following

SONNET

> While thus I wander, cheerless and unblest,
> And find in change of place but change of pain;
> In tranquil sleep the village labourers rest,
> And taste repose, that I pursue in vain.
> Hush'd is the hamlet now; and faintly gleam
> The dying embers from the casement low
> Of the thatch'd cottage; while the moon's wan beam
> Lends a new lustre to the dazzling snow.
> – O'er the cold waste, amid the freezing night,
> Scarce heeding whither, desolate I stray.
> For me! pale eye of evening! thy soft light

Leads to no happy home; my weary way
Ends but in dark vicissitudes of care:
I only fly from doubt – to meet despair.   (IV.7; pp. 453–4)

What does the "poetical form" accomplish here? By itself the sonnet skirts incoherence. The moonlight is "wan," "pale," "soft," lustrous; the earthly lights, faint, "dying," and "dazzling." The present tenses and definite articles lend an aura of emblematic placelessness that Smith reinforced by using mythologizing capitals for "Moon's" and "Eye of Evening" when she republished the sonnet among her poems. As a result, the "I" also seems diffused, generalized, and aggrandized. It certainly can't be identified with the female poet, and the italicized "my" in the separate publication prepares the way for the cleverly pointed, alliterative aphorism in the closing line.

By itself, in short, the poem is a display piece. The context of the novel sets the accents differently. Here the symmetries of the first quatrain – "I wander . . . / And find"; the "labourers rest, / And taste repose" – reflect the effort to find form in suffering, while the asymmetrical clause lengths in the second quatrain (where the sequence "now," "and," "while," "new" intimates the flux of time) reflect Orlando's particular disquiet. The closing aphorism seems less gratuitous, particularly to the careful reader who has noted an earlier appearance of the sonnet's longest word ("he could not help reflecting on the strange vicissitudes of fortune," IV.4; p. 422); consequently, here it does serve the function of objectifying Orlando's unfathomable feelings. By itself Smith's poetry wittily, even showily indulges emotions; in narrative context, it allows them to be formed, confronted, and thought.

Through its bifold nature, the "Romantic novel" gives privileged access to the unplumbed and unthought. But for Smith and those in her tradition, the poem (as Goethe says about the poem in his "Novelle") is like a flower: "the leafy green [of the prose] was there only for it and would not have been worth the trouble without it" (conversation with Eckermann, January 18, 1827). It is the realized potential (a philosopher would call it the entelechy) that fulfills the ramified form of the prose. In this guise, the poem comes not from an alien realm but from a concealed one. Here is an example from Radcliffe:

Unseen I move – unknown am feared
Fancy's wildest dreams I weave:
And oft by bards my voice is heard
To die along the gales of eve.[18]

In the Gothic tradition with which Smith's gloom is allied, inserted poems typically refract the turbulent, dark psychology haunting the protagonists. For "dark vicissitudes," the version of Smith's sonnet published with her poems has "sad vicissitudes": the poem by itself is in touch with the surface of feelings, whereas the poem in the novel burrows beneath the moonlit lustre. Such inserted poems may prolong experience into reverie; a number of the lyrics in Radcliffe's *Romance of the Forest* continue mysterious music or are continued by it, and ballads like "The Mariner" (in *The Mysteries of Udolpho* III.9) tell stories without transition (line 6: "How swift the moments fly!") that dissolve into persisting resonances:

> Oft...
> A melancholy voice is heard to pour
> Its lonely sweetness o'er poor Henry's grave!
> And oft, at midnight, airy strains are heard
> Around the grove ...   (Lines 45–50)

Not infrequently, too, the poems register the beloved's unseen proximity in a time of trial. In these various forms, the poems constitute a world beyond the interactions of the characters and the ordinary causal order of empirical existence. They resemble the Freudian unconscious in their ethereal timelessness, though they are rarely appetitive like Freud's drives. Yet they must be seen as the fulfillment, not the displacement, of the prose of the world.[19]

If in the "Romantic novel," poetry fulfills prose, then it cannot be the case that the Victorian, all-prose novel is the telos of Romantic narrative. Such is, however, the thesis of the only extended investigation of my topic in English letters before Starr's, Karl Kroeber's *Romantic Narrative Art*.[20] Kroeber's thesis (generally followed in the genetic account of C. I. Rothery and in the more generic one by Ruth Eller[21]) is that Romantic verse narrative developed toward the Victorian novel. Ballad narrative was too simple and linear for Byron and Scott in particular. As their art matured, they – and to a lesser degree other poets as well – developed complexities in point of view and causal understanding of events that transformed fictional narration from the Augustans' "simple, orderly, and rational" manner to the Victorians' "wonderfully diverse and complex achievements."[22] But the facts of literary history suggest that Kroeber's movement from naive poetic simplicity to sophisticated prose intricacy is not the real story. The itinerary he predicates is anything but typical. Quite the contrary, in fact, for while many authors separated verse from prose (see for instance Jurij Striedter's essay on genre in Pushkin[23]), Walter Scott is the only major poet then or later who might be said to have abandoned verse for prose. (Hardy moved the other way; Gottfried Keller confined himself to occasional ceremonial verse after his early years, when he included some half dozen poems in his novel *Green Henry*; Hofmannsthal abandoned lyric but chiefly for drama; Gogol, Joyce, and Beckett merely flirted with verse before dedicating themselves to narrative and dramatic prose; Pasternak wrote a novel late in life but its best part is the appendix to which the poems are relegated, and he can hardly be said to have changed his allegiance. Others including Hugo, Meredith, Fontane, D. H. Lawrence, and Borges wrote lyrics throughout their careers.) As Scott's career shows, the frequent original and quoted poems in his novels do not represent "a tendency toward the unusual and the exotic for its own sake";[24] the eventual subordination of poetry is to be understood as sacrifice, not enrichment.

Scott began as the author of supernatural and uncanny ballads. The mode links immediacy of sensation with remoteness of underlying explanation. Affect trumps knowledge: speakers are caught in the midst of mysterious events, and narrators withhold the reassurance of an overview. Excited openings often dissolve in abrupt conclusions. Time moves fast and jerkily if it moves at all, avoiding the smooth unfolding of cause and consequence. Even when nominally historical, the past carries an aura of legend; events arising out of unpredictable fatality cast a shadow over troubled present and indistinct future. Scott's original impulse toward verse in this spirit lies in his early translations from the German. But the voice is uncertain. Emil Staiger's influential phenomenology of lyric on the Romantic model punningly joins lyric memory ("Erinnerung") with inward-ness, making lyric the most rooted of his three fundamental genres.[25] But that is exactly what the Romantic ballad calls into question. How can there be a unified, Kantian, inward self in a world where "Half seen by fits, by fits half heard, / Pale spectres fleet along" (Scott, "William and Helen," 1795, a translation of Gottfried August Bürger's "Lenore")? Scott's narrative career starts with a lack, not with the "simple, orderly, and rational" foundation Kroeber presupposes.

Scott quickly moved to extended narrative poems that aim to ground the lyric aura in the realm of experience and comprehension. The earliest of these poems, *The Lay of the Last Minstrel*, is set in a shadowy past only tenuously transmitted by the title figure, whereas the ensuing poems move toward the historical sphere or, in the experimental *Bridal of Triermain*, toward an interesting combination of the near-contemporary, the vaguely historical, and the magically legendary. The diction of the magic-infused *Lay* is heavily Spenserian, which for Scott implies a "rich, luxuriant glow / Of fancy" (*Rokeby* 2.6). Poetry is associated in *Lay* 3.9 with "glamour," a Scots word for magic that Scott is responsible for popularizing in English. (The line is cited in the *OED* and is glossed by Scott in one of his copious annotations.) But even as early as the *Lay*, high style and mystery periodically yield to a prosiness that can only be understood as a rationalizing impulse mostly kept under wraps. Thus lines of sudden confrontation – "The speaker issued from the wood, / And checked his fellow's surly mood, / And quelled the ban dog's ire" – rhyme abruptly and imperfectly with dog-trot certificates of citizenship and birth, "He was an English yeoman good, / And born in Lancashire" (*Lay* 3.16). And a few stanzas earlier comes a couplet where common-sense explanation upends uncanny authority as well, again, as decent rhyme: "But his awful mother he had in dread, / And also his power was limited" (3.13). The clash of values is evident from the clash of styles: Scott's early verse narration serves two masters.

The ensuing verse tales take different approaches to accommodating prose and verse, surface and depth, immediacy and endurance, sensation and sentiment. But none finds a stable balance. The second tale, *Marmion*, is described in Scott's "Advertisement" as "a romantic tale" that includes "an attempt to paint the manners of feudal times" without aspiring to be a "historical narrative," and the verse reiterates: "Mine is a tale of Flodden field, / And not a history" (5.34). The bard who appears briefly in 1.13 sings a "barbarous lay," and the famous ballad of Lochinvar in 5.12 is a legend whose relevance to the main narrative is tenuous and never explicated. Neither fish nor fowl, the narrative this time falls between its two stools:

> Some love-lorn fay she might have been,
> Or, in romance, some spell-bound queen;
> For ne'er, in work-day world, was seen
> A form so witching fair.   (6.3)

The third and best tale, *The Lady of the Lake*, perfuses its narrative with the charms of verse, at the cost of confusing its aims. It has a watery surface, touching on historical events only to smooth their edges with "bright uncertainty" (a phrase from the exquisite landscape that opens Canto 3). The climactic battle happens by mistake and is described after the fact by the bard while the Highland chief's life is ebbing away. An abundance of similes infiltrate the rough and ready tetrameter couplets that Scott applied to extended narrative for the first time here (after using them for the long canto introductions of *Marmion*):

> As wreath of snow, on mountain breast,
> Slides from the rock that gave it rest,
> Poor Ellen glided from her stay,
> And at the monarch's feet she lay . . .   (6.27)

The inserted lyrics form an anthology of (mostly) labeled types including lullaby, barcarolle, dirge, hymn, ballad, and a rollicking soldier's song;

several of Ellen's songs were given appropriately haunting settings by Schubert. But the profiles of prose and lyric, reality and romance, are not yet sufficiently distinguished. In *Rokeby*, the next verse tale and the last before *Waverley*, a complicated narrative tends to bog down in circumstance (1.18: "Tis honour bids me now relate / Each circumstance of Mortham's fate," delaying the action), and Scott overcompensates by stressing startling turns of fortune. This time, the bard is a spy who penetrates Rokeby Castle and lets in marauders to destroy it. Glamour has become enchantment, in lines that echo Dryden's *Alexander's Feast* (Scott had edited a complete, multivolume, annotated Dryden):

> I've seen a ring of rugged kerne...
> Shift from wild rage to wilder glee,
> To love, to grief, to ecstasy,
> And feel each varied change of soul
> Obedient to the bard's control. (5.10)

Here, however, the harper repents his treacherous power (5.26), as, indeed, the villainous Bertram finally renounces his own treachery (6.20) to bring about a happy resolution. Poetry is commandeered by drama.

The turn to prose narrative enabled Scott to clarify dramatic roles more clearly and to accommodate the multiple perspectives that his fiction always strives to balance. Like much else in Scott's self-portrayals, the General Preface to the Waverley Novels accounts for his turn to prose in ways that appear disingenuous, even obfuscatory. "It is enough to say, that I had assumed the latter character [of a follower of literature] for several years before I seriously thought of attempting a work of imagination in prose, although one or two of my poetical attempts did not differ from romances otherwise than by being written in verse." This bland, belated claim for a merging of prose and verse obscures the fact that Scott's poems wrestled for years with the tension between bard and historian. Rather than a fusion, the inserted verse reflects the novels' ongoing effort to balance the polar allegiances to truth and to interest.[26] In addition to the frequent verse epigraphs, most of Scott's prose fictions contain at least snatches of quoted or original verse, or the occasional hymn or ballad purportedly translated from Gaelic or some medieval tongue. The most extensive collections are found in *Waverley* (1814), *The Heart of Midlothian* (1818), and *The Pirate* (1821, but conceived in 1814 in conjunction with the 1815 verse narrative *The Lord of the Isles*).

The characteristic poems in Scott's novels are of three types: associated with the primitive past, with the popular present, or with the voice of individual feeling. On the face of it, these are incompatible origins, being respectively remote and diffused to the point of impersonality, immediate and collective, or intimate and personal. Yet they share the essential quality of poetry, in this context, which is its impalpable transcendence. Edward Waverley's verse compositions "serve, at least, better than narrative of any kind, to acquaint [the reader] with the wild and irregular spirit of our hero." The poem in this instance is about reflections and is itself one, for it projects Waverley's character onto the landscape:

> In wild and broken eddies whirled,
> Flitted that fond ideal world,
> And, to the shore in tumult tost,
> The realms of fairy bliss were lost. (ch. 5)

The forty-four-line poem is immediately followed by a translation: "In sober prose, as perhaps these verses intimate less decidedly, the transient idea of Miss Cecilia Stubbs passed from Captain Waverley's heart amid the turmoil which his new destinies excited." Although less informative, the poem is still more revealing than the prose. As such it corresponds to the narrator's mission announced three paragraphs later in the same chapter: "My plan requires that I should explain the motives on which its action proceeded; and these motives necessarily arose from the feelings, prejudices, and parties of the times." The prejudices and parties will be the subject of analytical narration, but the feelings exist in the turmoil of interior monologue and in the evocations of verse. As the verse remains mistier than the sober prose of the objective narrator, so the feelings remain beyond even the verse in which they are recorded, as is made explicit when Flora McIvor later sings: "The following verses convey but little idea of the feelings with which, so sung and accompanied, they were heard by Waverley" (ch. 22, entitled "Highland Minstrelsy"). Remoteness and relevance are inextricable, as in the songs of mad Madge Wildfire in *The Heart of Midlothian*: "He then began to hum . . . the first stanza of a favorite ballad of Wildfire's, the words of which bore some distant analogy with the situation of Robertson" (ch. 17); "it was remarkable, that there could always be traced in her songs something appropriate, though perhaps only obliquely or collaterally so, to her present situation" (ch. 40).

In *Wilhelm Meister* poetry goes hand in hand with mental alienation, and so it does in Madge, as also in Davie Gellatley in *Waverley*. But the prophetic or mysterious figures who abound in Scott's fiction do not necessarily sing much and are not normative. In *Redgauntlet* the blind fiddler Wandering Willie Swenson communicates essential secrets by playing tunes whose words are revealing (ch. 10 as a motif, ch. 23 as a climactic revelation when he plays "The Campbells are coming"). Elsewhere poetry is posited as an alternative to magic. Thus, in *A Legend of Montrose* the mysterious heroine Annot Lyle, who "far exceeds the best performers in this country in playing on the clairshach, or harp" (ch.6, where she later sings "a lively air … from some court masque"), is juxtaposed to the grim madman Allan M'Aulay. She temporarily sings him back to his senses. Supposedly a Gaelic air, her song "The rising sun," "although submitted to the fetters of English rhythm, we trust will be found nearly as genuine as the version of Ossian" by Macpherson (ch. 6). The joke is that neither original Gaelic nor acknowledged new English verse would work: accuracy would destroy aura, which remains the preeminent characteristic of Scott's inserted verse. Throughout, the style of Scott's verse suits the purpose, for verse that is too precise or too personal would be serving insight, whereas intuition is the value that is sought. Madness approximates lyric inspiration, but finally misses the beat.

Folk refrain, modernized translation, individually attributed composition, and old or recent poetic epigraph thus all contribute similarly to the Romanticism of Scott's fiction. They offer a better alternative than the Gothic with which Scott always nervously flirts. When the ghost of the blind old Alice appears to Edgar Ravenswood at the Mermaiden's Well in *The Bride of Lammermoor*, the narrator discounts the apparition: "We are bound to tell the tale as we have received it; and, considering the distance of the time, and propensity of those through whose mouths it has passed to the marvelous, this could not be called a Scottish story, unless it manifested a tinge of Scottish superstition" (ch. 22). The problem with the Gothic is that it is too perfect: "the torment of romance-writers, those necessary evils, the concluding chapters" that explain everything are an even greater improbability than the supernatural itself.[27] Perfect knowledge in Scott's fiction is always deluded, whether it be the terrifying mad preacher Habbakuk Mucklewrath in *Old Mortality*, or the more affecting Norna of the Fitful Head in *The Pirate*, who appears to command the winds and foretell the future in precise detail until she is revealed as a fraud and her world and her identity come crashing around her. Meanwhile, poetic knowledge, while approximate, is enduring. Hence poets of all eras can be called to witness, including Scott's contemporaries (Burns, Wordsworth, Coleridge, Southey, etc.), whose words ring true even when centuries posterior to the events they are used to explain. That is why it is more than a figure of speech when Scott says that the words of "our immortal Joanna Baillie" beautifully express Edgar Ravenswood's feelings (*Bride*, ch. 20). "Beautifully," of course, does not mean flawlessly. As Scott imagines and uses it, verse communicates not perfect knowledge but the limits of the knowable. It becomes immortal when, insofar as humans can, it grasps feelings that transcend situation, circumstance, and moment.

Whereas the realistic novel aims to tell stories that are at once self-contained and resonant – if always, in one way or another, haunted by the irrational or transcendent aspects of romance – the "Romantic novel" overlays disparate and imperfect explanatory frameworks.[28] Scott particularly specialized in the detailed accounting of complicated and mixed motivations arising from personal, social, and historical factors that render his narration expansive and his plots intricate. But they also recognize compromise, imperfection, whim (for whom the models are Cervantes and Sterne), and inexplicable irrationality. Not all loose ends are tied up, no narrator can gain full faith and credit, and motives lie beyond comprehension. Fergus McIvor's fanaticism, for instance, "was a mixture of feeling which he did not avow even to himself, but it existed, nevertheless, in a powerful degree" (*Waverley*, ch. 22).

One name for the eccentric workings of romance that gradually emerges in Scott's writing is "unconscious." Lucy Ashton, the tragic, romantic, ultimately insane heroine of *The Bride of Lammermoor*, entangles herself at one point in compromising behavior: "holding fast by the stranger's arm, though unconscious of anything save the support which it gave, and without which she could not have moved, mixed with a vague feeling of preventing his escape from her, she was urging, almost dragging him forward" (ch. 4). This is not quite yet the Freudian unconscious, since it fails to offer itself as a symptom subject to clinical investigation. Yet passion, if not exactly what Freud would call a "drive," pushes her forward even when her body is reported to be totally passive, in a moment of heightened eroticism: "her eloquent blood, flushing over neck and brow, spoke how much she was ashamed of the freedom with which she had craved, and even compelled, his assistance." Body and soul here live in different worlds, speak different languages, measure different pulses.

Scott's fiction lives by the disconnect between matter and spirit, between consecutive event and permanent or eddying feelings. The poetic aura that swathes his composition breaks out in various ways and in different quantities of actual verse. But it doesn't take many lines of force from a second world to supplant the accounting of the causes of action with a recognition of the opening left for breaking or sustaining waves of passion. Regulated in their own way, they will develop into the formal unconscious of the realist novel and of the mental topographies that grew out of it. But in the "Romantic novel," the elements of verse bear in from a world not lower than the earth but higher, not traumatic but transcendent, not driven but inspiring. The vital fluids here are "eloquent"; the life-blood of the form is poetic.

For Scott, in other words, poetry does not find its fulfillment in prose complexity (as Kroeber argues); rather, prose finds its fulfillment as poetic intensity. The prosaic turn reflects an exhaustion of the "Romantic novel." I will conclude with three forms of generic collapse.

Perhaps the most poem-filled British fictions of the era were the seven novels (if one should call them that) by Thomas Love Peacock, six of them published between 1816 and 1831, the last in 1864. Along with quantity comes normalization, socialization, and levity. Peacock follows in the mode of Scott (with Lochinvar, misquoted presumably from memory, providing the epigraph for the Robin Hood novel *Maid Marian*); his poems are festive songs and bardic ballads, sometimes delicately evocative but more often comic or even raucous. The best-known is "The War-song of Dinas Vawr" in chapter 11 of *The Misfortunes of Elphin*, beginning "The mountain sheep are sweeter, / But the valley sheep are fatter; / We therefore deemed it meeter / To carry off the latter." Even jollier is the glee "The Ghosts" in chapter 16 of *Melincourt*, with a refrain beginning "Three merry ghosts – three merry ghosts – three merry ghosts are we." But though Peacock was not above travestying Wordsworth's "Resolution and Independence" (five lines, signaled by a footnote, in *Maid Marian*, ch. 5), it would be too quick to conclude that he intended a send-up of either poetry or romance. For the works hover charmingly between parody and homage, and they appeal to a cultivated taste that can recognize the allusions. Bonhomie is reflected not just in the easy original verse but even more in the frequent quotations in chapter epigraphs and in the text, rarely from English authors other than Shakespeare, but frequently in Greek, Latin, Italian, French, Middle English, and Welsh. Only the Welsh is always translated. These are cultured comedies for cultivated souls; their aspirations are social rather than psychological, and they turn Romantic poetry into refined display.

In Scott himself poetic aspiration takes a darker turn toward a forlorn nostalgia. The second epigraph to this chapter comes from late in *The Pirate* (ch. 39) and can be taken as an epitaph over the whole project of the "Romantic novel." The speaker is Claud Halcro, the bard of the Shetlands where the novel is set. The islands are, so to speak, the Scotland of Scotland, a realm in the far north, still living in an Edda-haunted primitivism and looking with resentful suspicion on both Highlanders and Lowlanders in the land to the south. Pirates sometimes land in this lost world but are more often shipwrecked on it; the economy appears to function mainly on flotsam and jetsam. Scott spins his plot thin and becomes a painter of super-exotic local color. The bard might be expected to loom large in a world barely touched by history, but almost the reverse is the case. While closely associated with the domineering and ultimately mistaken Norna, Halcro is

English-identified from having once met Dryden, whom he cannot stop talking about. Halcro proves virtually irrelevant to the plot; Scott's norm is for minor characters at some point to play a role in the action, but Halcro does so only via an unexplained friendship with an assistant pirate to whom he provides very incidental and inconsequential aid. In a world out of time, out of history, and almost out of Britain, poetry is no better than an oddity. There is a lot of it, all lifeless, for there can be no meaningful encounters on such desolate, depopulated shores. The triumph of prose in the fiction of realism is reflected here dialectically, not ideologically, as the shipwreck of a mode devoted to truths beyond experience.

Edward Bulwer-Lytton's *Last Days of Pompeii* offers one last end point of the "Romantic novel," for its abundant poetry is associated throughout with magic and decadence. "It seemed the melodies of invisible spirits, such as the shepherd might have heard in the golden age, floating through the vales of Thessaly, or in the noontide glades of Paphos" (Bk. 1, ch. 8). Such, we are told, is "The Hymn of Eros," but the description really characterizes all the pseudo-antique poetry of Bulwer's overwrought, oversexed, fake historical novel, complete with documentary notes (albeit themselves far sparser and less informative than Scott's). The novel's world is no more historical than that of *The Pirate*; rather, it's a prehistoric world. The poetry here is no longer a technology of depth (as Siskin characterizes Romantic poetry), but a shallow entertainment buried by the explosion that symbolically represents the downfall of paganism.[29] When poetry is privatized, sequestered, or sublimated, it loses contact with history, society, and reality. Even the more exotic novels of German Romanticism have tentacles that cling to the experiences of revolution, dispossession, and industrialization. When the "Romantic novel" loses its roots, as it does in Bulwer, it also loses its bearings, and a new form is born, the realist, the merely prosaic novel.[30]

Like Austen's ambivalence toward poetry, then, the dead ends in *The Pirate* and *The Last Days of Pompeii* signal a real rupture. A Romantic world permeated by poetry is not like the prose of the world that constitutes the novel of realism. The realistic novel rejects verse as a false world: "How prosaic our novel is! First meeting – and soup, heads spin from the first kiss – and healthy appetite, such is the scene of love!"[31] Here poetry represents illusion; prose, truth. The *Künstlerroman* or artist novel is often regarded as a subtype of the *Bildungsroman*, but these genres – both were designated ex post facto, moreover – are really opposites: Smith's Orlando learns to poetize his world, whereas the disenchanted heroes of realism grow out of their Romantic illusions. Goethe's Wilhelm Meister is their prototype: he dreams himself becoming an artist in a world inhabited by exotic and poetic creatures, and he must be guided back into the path of maturity. Apart from a few comic lines from the still childish Friedrich in the last chapter of *Wilhelm Meister's Apprenticeship*, the only verses in *Apprenticeship*'s last two books are Mignon's self-elegy in 8.2 ("So laßt mich scheinen, bis ich werde"), ending with the refusal to grow up, "Macht mich auf ewig wieder jung!" (Make me eternally young again); even her choral exequies (8.8) are in prose. And in the sequel, *Wilhelm Meister's Journeyman Years: or, The Renunciants*, in which Wilhelm becomes not a poet or an actor but a humble surgeon, the poetry is all either gnomic or light and sociable, apart from a line and a half of nostalgic reminiscence of Mignon's "Kennst du das Land" in 2.7. The novel of realism is shot through with rejected or tragic Romanticism, of course; Goethe's strange paired novels spanning the traditional decades of British Romanticism (complete versions 1795–6 and 1829 respectively) are merely the most programmatic instance of the generic transformation I have been discussing.

The realistic world is horizontal; even mountains like the Alps in Dickens's *Little Dorrit* are crossed on roads, and the protagonists must find a way to chart their course through life. Gothic and Romantic heroes and heroines also traverse large distances, but through trackless wildernesses symbolizing what Goethe and Eichendorff famously called "the labyrinth of the breast" (originally in Goethe's early poem "Mailied," another moonlit vision). The crucial dimension is vertical, whether in Radcliffe's Apennine fastnesses, Scott's Highlands, Lowlands, cliffs, and quicksands, the mines of Tieck and Hoffmann, or the falling down and rising up repeatedly experienced by Byron's Don Juan. There are many overlaps and later relapses, of course, as when Eliot's Silas Marner and Dickens's Stephen Blackpool die by falling into pits, but Realistic mastery consists in managing the ongoing course of events, whereas the "Romantic novel" focuses on the depths of the spirit and on enduring and enveloping temporalities. Poems are by no means uniquely determining, but they do define the ideal type of the "Romantic novel."

NOTES

1 Friedrich Schlegel, *Kritische Schriften*, ed. Wolfdietrich Rasch (Munich: Carl Hanser Verlag, 1958), pp. 37–8.
2 *Literary Notebooks*, Number 4. My translation ignores typographical features. Also pertinent is a posthumous fragment of 1808 published in the commentary to LN 1569: "Lyrical poems should not be a genre apart but rather should only be used alongside and interwoven with mystical works, dramatic, novel, etc."
3 Georg Lukács, *The Theory of the Novel*, trans. Anna Bostock (Cambridge, Mass.: The MIT Press, 1971), pp. 57, 52–3. Lukács presents his discussion as a general typology, but it is better understood as an account of Romantic genres; in other eras, verse and prose genres and lyric and narrative tones may interface in countless

other ways, as Heather Dubrow shows in great detail (*The Challenges of Orpheus: Lyric Poetry and Early Modern England* (Baltimore: Johns Hopkins University Press, 2007)).

4 G. Gabrielle Starr, *Lyric Generations: Poetry and the Novel in the Long Eighteenth Century* (Baltimore: Johns Hopkins University Press, 2004), p. 168. The omission of Carter is noted in Deirdre Lynch's review of Starr's book, *Modern Language Quarterly* 67(2006), p. 277.

5 Charles Dickens, *Martin Chuzzlewit*, ed. P. N. Furbank (Harmondsworth: Penguin Books, 1968), p. 499 (ch. 27).

6 Henry James, *The Portrait of a Lady*, ed. Robert Bamberg (New York: W. W. Norton, 1975), p. 376 (ch. 44); p. 259 (ch. 29). James's Robert Browning complex has been studied by Ross Posnock in *Henry James and the Problem of Robert Browning* (Athens, Georgia: University of Georgia Press, 1985), but of genre issues we learn only that novelists skirt the "danger of concussion" because poets "elegantly walk" on the other side of the street (p. 36, quoting James's essay "The Novel in *The Ring and the Book*"), and that James appreciated the "prosiness" of Browning's "creation of a novelistic intimacy in verse" (p. 139).

7 *Effi Briest*, chs. 17–19; see the discussion by Peter Pütz, "Wenn Effi läse, was Crampas empfiehlt …: Offene und verdeckte Zitaten im Roman," in *Theodor Fontane*, ed. Heinz Ludwig Arnold (Munich, Text & Kritik, 1989), pp. 174–84.

8 Sample discussions (none very comprehensive) are Catherine Robson's allusion to poetry envy in Victorian novels in "Standing on the Burning Deck: Poetry, Performance, History," *PMLA* 120 (2005), pp. 156–7; Dino Felluga's examination of the image of Byron in "Novel Poetry: Transgressing the Law of Genre," *Victorian Poetry* 41 (2003), pp. 90–9; and Jay Clayton's reflections on lyric transcendence in Dickens, where, Clayton says, "the mode of lyric always appears as the vanishing point of narrative" (*Romantic Vision and the Novel* (Cambridge: Cambridge University Press, 1987) p. 139) – I would query the "always." I owe the example from Multatuli to my wife, Jane K. Brown.

9 Jane Austen, *Pride and Prejudice*, ed. Frank Kinsley and James Bradbrook (Oxford: Oxford University Press, 1970), p. 38 (Vol. I, ch. 9).

10 Jane Austen, *Sanditon*, in *Northanger Abbey, Lady Susan, The Watsons, and Sanditon*, ed. John Davie (Oxford: Oxford University Press, 1990), p. 352 (ch. 7).

11 *Sanditon*, pp. 339–40 (ch. 4).

12 Jane Austen, *Persuasion*, ed. D. W. Harding (Harmondsworth: Penguin Books, 1965), p. 122 (Vol. I, ch. 11).

13 *Persuasion*, p. 178 (Vol. II, ch. 6); p. 237 (Vol. II, ch. 11).

14 As William Deresiewicz notes (*Jane Austen and the Romantic Poets* (New York: Columbia University Press, 2004), p. 5), *Sanditon* contains the only mention of Wordsworth in Austen's fiction, as one favorite of a fool. Deresiewicz's account of tonal affinities between the later Austen and contemporary poets is not interested in questions of genre.

15 Michael Gamer, "Maria Edgeworth and the Romance of Real Life," *Novel: A Forum on Fiction* 34 (2001), pp. 232–66.

16 Charlotte Smith, *The Old Manor House*, ed. Anne Henry Ehrenpreis (Oxford: Oxford University Press, 1989), p. 289 (Vol. III, ch. 5).

17 Starr compares Smith's poems (confined, quotational, and self-denying) with her novels (expansive and "successfully unit[ing] description of inner and outer

worlds in terms both of a single subject," *Lyric Generations*, p. 153); she does not discuss the uses of the poems within the novels. Stuart Curran surveys Smith's use of poems in the novels up through *The Old Manor House*: "General Introduction," *The Works of Charlotte Smith*, Vol. I, ed. Michael Gamer (London: Pickering and Chatto, 2005).

18 Ann Radcliffe, *The Romance of the Forest* (London, Routledge, n.d.), p. 192 (ch. 11; end of "Song of a Spirit"). On Radcliffe's inserted poems see Gary Kelly, *English Fiction of the Romantic Period, 1789–1830* (London: Longman, 1989), pp. 55–6.

19 Dubrow's discussion of Desdemona's willow song links "songwork" to Freudian dreamwork and jokework (*The Challenges of Orpheus*, pp. 221–6). Favret's "Telling Tales about Genre: Poetry in the Romantic Novel," (*Studies in the Novel* 26 (1994), pp. 281–300; detailed and informative about poems in the novels of Smith, Radcliffe, Mary Robinson, and Matthew G. Lewis), argues that the poetry is indiscriminate, "practiced by nearly anyone upon nearly any premise" (p. 290), but omits the kind of close reading that would test this – to my mind, mistaken – claim. She also associates verse with the feminine (as does Curran, "General Introduction," p. xxi). It is true that the poems in *Celestina*, for instance, are all composed by the heroine, but her love for poetry is a mixture of her own "natural turn" with the "passionate fondness" of the hero Willoughby (p. 190), who read poems to her in childhood, and the figure most insistently presented as a lover and composer of poetry is the co-principal Montague Thorold, who finally has to make do with Celestina's cousin. The novel contains thirty-six marked quotations by male writers (mostly poets and dramatists), three not securely identified (two of them attributed to men by the editor), and one by Anna Barbauld. The quotations are frequently inexact or intentionally varied; in one case Othello's "even from my boyish days" becomes Mrs. Elphinstone's "even from my girlish days." Everything in Smith's life, works, and liberal beliefs militates against gender stereotyping.

20 Karl Kroeber, *Romantic Narrative Art* (Madison: University of Wisconsin Press, 1960).

21 C. I. Rothery, "Scott's Narrative Poetry and the Classical Form of the Historical Novel," in *Scott and His Influence: The Papers of the Aberdeen Scott Conference, 1982*, ed. J. H. Alexander and David Hewitt (Aberdeen, Association for Scottish Literary Studies, 1983), pp. 63–74. Ruth Eller, "The Poetic Theme in Scott's Novels," in *Scott and his Influence*, pp. 75–86.

22 Kroeber, *Romantic Narrative Art*, p. 185.

23 Jurij Striedter, "Poetic Genre and the Sense of History in Pushkin," *New Literary History* 8 (1977), pp. 295–309.

24 Kroeber, *Romantic Narrative Art*, p. 185.

25 Emil Staiger, *Basic Concepts of Poetics*, trans. Janette C. Hudson and Luanne T. Frank (University Park: Pennsylvania State University Press, 1991).

26 See my "Theory of the Novel," in *The Cambridge History of Literary Criticism*, Vol. V: *Romanticism*, ed. Marshall Brown (Cambridge: Cambridge University Press, 2000), pp. 250–71.

27 Scott, Walter, "Ann Radcliffe," *Sir Walter Scott on Novelists and Fiction*, ed. Ioan Williams (New York: Barnes and Noble, 1968), p. 115, echoed at the end of the introduction to *The Pirate*.

28 See my *Shape of German Romanticism* (Ithaca: Cornell University Press, 1979), pp. 199–214, on the image of poems and prose as coordinate centers (or foci) of the "eccentric" form of German Romantic novels.

29 Clifford Siskin, "William Wordsworth," in *Oxford Encyclopedia of British Literature*, ed. David Kastan (Oxford: Oxford University Press, 2006), pp. 332–3.

30 On the transition to Realism see also my "Theory of the Novel."

31 N. K. Chernishevskii, *Chto delat'*? (What Is to Be Done?) (Moscow: Russkii Yazyk, 1987), p. 292 (Vol. IV, ch. 5), my translation. This is a particularly interesting moment because shortly thereafter the protagonists quote an idyll by the Romantic poet Nekrasov, as the implausible lead-in to a discussion of the superiority of women over men. Much later, the novel's bizarrely utopian denouement is introduced by a riot of quotations from the romantic poetry of Lermontov in the last section of ch. 5 (followed only by the one-page ch. 6 and the concluding "Appendix"). My thanks to Richard Maxwell and Katie Trumpener for their meticulous editing in general, and in particular for pointing me to Peacock and Bulwer.

7

JAMES WATT

Orientalism and empire

In a 1762 review of John Langhorne's *Solyman and Almena*, the *Monthly*'s critic stated that there was so little of "invention or originality" in the work that "a reader, who is but moderately acquainted with this modish kind of literature, may anticipate most of the incidents"; "in truth," he went on to add, "few of the Oriental Novels differ very essentially from each other."[1] Even as reviewers sometimes complained that moral tales such as Langhorne's bore few signs of the properly Eastern style of the *Arabian Nights* (first translated as *Les Mille et une nuits* by Antoine Galland in 1704), works of this kind represented perhaps the dominant if by no means the only form of "oriental" narrative published in English, for most of the eighteenth century. Well-known works such as Samuel Johnson's *Rasselas* (1759) and John Hawkesworth's *Almoran and Hamet* (1761) conceived of the East at the level of neoclassical generality, without much interest in accuracy or specificity of detail, and – although they reflected on topical issues – employed a broadly applicable language of abstract morality, so that one critic noted that the insight into the human condition in *Rasselas* might be acquired "without going to Ethiopia."[2] The contemporary sense of what the oriental amounted to in this context was capacious enough for "Igluka and Sibbersik," subtitled "A Greenland Tale," to be included in *The Orientalist: A Volume of Tales after the Eastern Taste* (1764). Charles Johnstone presented *The History of Arsaces* (1774) as a fiction concerned with "the universal manners of Nature," and stated that "greater particularity would only have been pedantry," insisting that the reader would excuse him "not having paid more minute attention to the manners of the times and countries, in which the various scenes of the work are laid."[3]

William Beckford's *Vathek* (1786) was an oriental tale with a difference in large part because of its unprecedented attention to detail, a feature emphasized by one reviewer's claim that "perhaps there is no other work of the same extent, from which so much knowledge can be derived of the peculiar manners and customs of the East."[4] *Vathek* assumes the form of a didactic oriental tale, in punishing the Caliph for his overreaching ambition, but it also confronts the reader with the weight of its specific reference: the work's opening lines announce Vathek's status as a historical figure, "ninth Caliph of the race of the Abassides ... the son of Motassem, and the grandson of Haroun al Raschid," while Samuel Henley's endnotes to the first edition, making use of the new professional scholarship sponsored by the East India Company, take up a third of its total length.[5] Initially written in French, and displaying a fictional extravagance and tonal instability more characteristic of French than English literary orientalism, Vathek has commonly been understood in biographical terms, so that for Hester Lynch Thrale, for example, it was in the final analysis "a mad Book ... written by a mad author."[6] At the same time, however, the bizarre conjunction of this narrative excess with historical reference and scholarly annotation also served to elevate the text as a possible source of evidence about the East, providing what might be thought of as a "last days"-type focus on Arabian decadence, with a wider application to Eastern empires more generally. Numerous later Romantic-period works, most famously perhaps P. B. Shelley's "Ozymandias" (1817), went on to follow Beckford's example, and to frame in ironic terms the self-delusion of impotent oriental despots. But Beckford's tale also provides a useful perspective on the slipperiness of so much of the fiction dealing with the East in this period, not only because the eccentricity of its detail (banquets of vulture and wolf, and so on) sometimes takes the language of orientalist fantasy almost to a point of collapse, but also since the work hints at the wider resonance and adaptability of "oriental despotism" itself. The Giaour who tempts Vathek to embark on his quest has persuasively been read as a monstrous embodiment of the slave economy on which Beckford's vast fortune depended, and – as a purveyor of "extraordinary ... merchandise" from "a region of India which is wholly unknown" (Vathek, pp. 5 and 14) – the Giaour more clearly still alludes to the potentially destructive allure of Britain's own rapidly growing Eastern empire.

A range of other fictions published in the 1780s referred to Britain's overseas interests in more direct terms, further crowding out those oriental tales that sought to draw "universal manners." The figure of the vulgar and newly rich "nabob" emerged as a stock object of satire in poetry and drama from about the early 1770s onwards, and a number of later novels such as Agnes Maria Bennett's Anna; or Memoirs of a Welch Heiress (1785) also made villains out of "Asiatic plunderers," now harassing young heroines in Britain rather than terrorizing "the inhabitants of the East."[7] Those works that were set (or partly set) in India tended to be less schematic than this, however, and several interestingly disjointed fictions from the period engaged, albeit at times obliquely, with the intense debates that were taking place about the proper business of the East India Company, increasingly a sovereign as well as merchant power following the establishment of its bridgehead in Bengal. *The Indian Adventurer; or, History of Mr Vanneck* (1780), for example, set in the late 1750s, is a picaresque work that details the exploits of its title character, a trained surgeon who at different points styles himself as a liberator, saving a high-caste widow from immolation, and as a libertine, declaring his indulgence in "unlawful pleasures" with "obliging" Indian women.[8] As its subtitle suggests, Helenus Scott's *The Adventures of a Rupee: Wherein are Interspersed Various Anecdotes Asiatic and European* (1782) is an even more difficult work to categorize. Ostensibly in the tradition of the circulation novel, Scott's fiction frames the "mercantile spirit" and energy of the Company by making its "rupee" narrator, at the close, describe the experience of being removed from the process of exchange, and "laid up in the storehouse of a society of antiquarians." But the rupee also briefly refers to a speech against corruption by "Cato," which emanates from this company of medals and busts, and the work employs a similar language in one of its many episodes, when the Scottish Mr. Melvil – while underlining the distinction between trade and settlement – reminds his India-bound son that others have "cursed our rapacity." The novel further offers a brief captivity narrative, telling the story of Melvil's daughter, who is captured by Hyder Ali in attempting to join up with her enlisted lover, and her brother; Hyder's seraglio predictably serves to define the blessings of "English" civility and sociability, but any sense that he is a stereotypical oriental despot is qualified by the fact that he protects Miss Melvil with what she describes as "fatherly affection," and restores her to her betrothed "in her native innocence."[9]

Written at the end of the same decade, Phebe Gibbes's epistolary novel *Hartly House, Calcutta* (1789) indirectly but intriguingly engages with the scholarly research into Hinduism being undertaken by Sir William Jones, and other members of the recently founded Asiatic Society of Bengal. "The pursuit of knowledge in the service of power is translated ... into the feminized discourse of sentimentality," Kate Teltscher has argued, as the work's narrator, having followed her father to Calcutta, declares herself to be "a convert to the Gentoo faith," and describes her infatuation with the young Brahmin who educates her in the principles of his religion.[10] In abiding by the generic norms of "colonial romance," and killing off the love-object of the European protagonist, *Hartly House* finally retreats from its exploration of the possibilities of cross-cultural encounter, and frames the relationship between Sophia and the Brahmin in circumscribed terms: the Brahmin remains an idealized figure throughout, indeed, and he is not individuated, or even named. For Sophia, nonetheless, India is still a space of relative freedom from the constraints and expectations that apply at home, and the man with whom she is to "domesticate" in Britain (the "little winning Mr Doyly") seems wanting not only in comparison with the Brahmin, but also with the Indian prince described a few pages from the end, a man whose gaze prompts "ambitious throbs" in her heart. Sophia's penultimate letter also complicates the rhetorical movement of the novel by briefly referring to an army officer's rape of an Indian woman, and subsequent murder of her father. Although the work is unable to articulate the obvious symbolic potential of this story, such an episode exceeds the conventions of the colonial romance plot, and, albeit minimally, acknowledges acts of violence that Sophia suspects are "much oftener perpetrated than detected."[11]

In attempting to make sense of the ways in which Britain was becoming increasingly interconnected with India, generically and tonally unstable works such as these reflect larger ideological contradictions. One feature that distinguishes Elizabeth Hamilton's *Translation of the Letters of a Hindoo Rajah* (1796) from most fictions of the 1780s is that it sides with the recently acquitted Warren Hastings, and as a result far more clearly argues for the potentially beneficial impact of the British presence in India. After a preliminary dissertation that pays tribute to the oriental scholarship of her brother Charles (and at the same time asserts her own right to engage with such material), Hamilton's work begins with a rewriting of the story of Old Edwards in Henry Mackenzie's *The Man of Feeling* (1771), and describes the title character's sentimental encounter with the wounded English officer Captain Percy, presented as one of the British protectors of "amiable and benevolent" Hindus from the aggression of the Muslim Rohilla Afghans. Following in the footsteps of a number of previous imaginary oriental travellers, the Rajah is then taken on a tour of Britain, a land that his conversations with Percy initially lead him to believe is "highly favoured."[12] The morally serious exposure of domestic corruption unwittingly provided by the Rajah in his letters home effects a transformation of this popular eighteenth-century genre that ultimately helped to take the device of the specifically *oriental* commentator out of service for subsequent British writers. Hamilton's work nonetheless legitimizes the social criticism implicit in the Rajah's misunderstanding of British customs and manners by making him endorse the civilizing mission of the British in India: whereas a range of earlier writers focused on the corrupting impact of returning nabobs, *Letters of a Hindoo Rajah* inverts the terms of this polemic by suggesting that Britons at home have to live up to the ideals by which people like Captain Percy, and also the virtuous Rajah, conduct themselves abroad.

Despite its nuanced engagement with contemporary debates about the education of women, *Letters of a Hindoo Rajah* has often been classified as an anti-Jacobin work as a result of episodes such as the elopement of the free-thinking Miss Ardent and Mr. Axiom. The novels of Robert Bage, by contrast, take a number of strikingly progressive positions on the question of sexual morality: in *Mount Henneth* (1782), for example, the hero Mr. Foston relates his experiences in India during the late 1750s, describing how he fell in love with and eventually married a Persian merchant's daughter who had been raped by soldiers serving the defeated Nawab of Bengal; Bage neatly draws attention to the exceptional nature of this outcome by making the novel-reading Caralia state that "No author has yet been so bold as to permit a lady to live and marry, and be a woman after this stain."[13] What is also striking about Bage's novels, however, is the manner in which they so confidently appeal to the idea of a more or less homogeneous "Orient." *The Fair Syrian* (1787) incorporates the "true romance" of its title character, Honoria Warren, born to English parents in Tripoli, and imprisoned with her father in Damascus after falling victim to "a violent stroke of despotism." Honoria's narrative names specific people and places (just as the work as a whole evidences a larger geopolitical awareness), but it also at times refers much more generally to "Asia" as a monolithic entity, invoking a common knowledge of a vast region that is said to be "fruitful . . . in insurrections and rebellions," since "avarice and despotism, their productive causes, are never wanting." Like all of Bage's fiction, *The Fair Syrian* is an urbane work that incorporates a diverse range of characters, such as the French aristocrat the Marquis de St. Claur, who tells a story about buying and selling "Mingrelian girls" in Istanbul. For all the novel's dialogism, though, the casual remarks that different figures make about "the Asiatics" and their treatment of women are never qualified or rebutted, so that when – on hearing Honoria's story – Lady Bembridge proclaims her "aversion" to "that horrid bear, Mahomet, with his lock-up houses for women," Honoria's response is to declare: "You certainly would not have been his."[14]

While treating harem life or the idea of polygamy in a largely comic manner, a work such as *The Fair Syrian* contributed towards what Saree Makdisi has identified as "the fabrication of a new Orient," which was not much more specifically drawn than the Orient of earlier eighteenth-century tales, but that was now the object of a much more assertive generalization. This imaginary conception of the East was defined with particular reference to the condition of women in Islamic societies, and in Makdisi's terms served above all as a "surrogate target" for radical or reformist critique, such that the seraglio in the work of Mary Wollstonecraft, for example, functions as a potent symbol of *ancien régime* despotism and excess.[15] The idea of an undifferentiated Orient was also brought into being in this period as a foil against which to define an exceptional "Gothic" femininity, the legacy of which was widely claimed to mark the distinctiveness of Anglo-British modernity: "With us, the two sexes associate together, and mutually improve and polish one another," James Beattie wrote in 1783, "but in Rome and Greece they lived separate; and the condition of the female was little better than slavery; as it still is, and has been from very early times, in many parts of Asia, and in European and African Turkey." In the same essay, "On Fable and Romance," Beattie additionally offered a quasi-sociological account of oriental narrative, taken en bloc, contextualizing the role of "inchantment and prodigy" as the only likely means of rousing Eastern despots from their luxurious indolence.[16] If a range of Romantic-period writers nostalgically looked back to their first encounter with the *Arabian Nights*, the exotic content of such tales was increasingly subject to critical regulation in the late eighteenth century, with collections such as *The Oriental Moralist* (1790), for example, likening Galland's pioneering translation to "a once rich and luxurious garden, neglected and run to waste, where scarce anything strikes the common observer but the weeds and briars with which it is overgrown."[17] As in Jonathan Scott's preface to his translation of the Persian romance *Bahar-Danush* (1799), oriental narratives were often presented in this period in such a way as to tell a specific story about the customs and manners of "the East": seizing on the treatment of women, like so many other writers, Scott contrasted "the cruel tyranny of the haram, and the shameful ignorance in which women are kept in Asia" with "the superiority which liberty, education, and well merited confidence give to the fair sex of this happy island and other unrevolutionized parts of Europe."[18]

Beckford's *Vathek* stages the possible tension between a regulatory editorial "containment" and an undisciplined readerly "absorption," as Nigel Leask has argued, and Beckford's comic novel *Azemia* (1797) disrupts the use of woman as an index of cultural comparison (and offers a reworking of the captivity narrative tradition), by opening with an episode in which a fair Turkish heroine is taken as a prize by an English man of war, named "The Amputator."[19] James Lawrence also challenged the established consensus about the condition of Eastern women in his "utopian romance" *The Empire of the Nairs* (1811), which focuses on the matrilineal system of inheritance, and the sexual customs, of a Hindu caste on the Malabar Coast. Probably more representative of the fiction published around the turn of the century, however, is Mary Pilkington's novel *The Asiatic Princess* (1800), which deals with the education of the title character by Sir Charles Corbet and his wife, as the three of them undertake the journey from Siam to "Britannia's favoured shore," being shown (or reminded) along the way of "the advantages which an English woman enjoys."[20]

The stories and tracts published by evangelicals in this period also tended to consider the relations between Britain and India (in particular) in abstract and familial terms, and a number of fictions by the prolific Mary Martha Sherwood, for example, similarly attribute moral agency to English characters, especially (as in the case of *Little Henry and his Bearer*, 1814) to foster children, who convert and "improve" their native caretakers. If epic poems such as Robert Southey's *Thalaba the Destroyer* (1801) and *The Curse of Kehama* (1810) still sought to filter or mediate oriental otherness for their readers, a range of different works of fiction more emphatically distanced themselves from such exoticism, in a manner that was in keeping with their often explicitly pedagogical ends. Maria Edgeworth's short work "Murad the Unlucky," for example, one of her *Popular Tales* (1804) written for children, tells the story of two brothers living in modern-day Constantinople, Murad and Saladin, who are respectively presented, in schematic terms, as an opium-addicted fatalist and an industrious merchant. Murad's failure to take the chances that come his way – his failure to make his own luck – initially seems to be a subject for comedy, and generates a series of pantomime-like episodes, but the tale's uncompromising conclusion later informs the reader that while Saladin went on to reap the rewards of his prudence, Murad eventually "died a martyr to the immoderate use of opium."

An attached footnote to the final page of Edgeworth's tale quotes from the Memoirs of Baron de Tott, and presents the "curious spectacle" of real opium addicts in Constantinople as a "most ludicrous and laughable picture."[21] In appealing to recent accounts of life on the ground, and at the same time emphasizing the gulf between the present and the past status of a particular Eastern culture, Ottoman Turkey, "Murad the Unlucky" in many ways anticipated the direction in which much later fiction would develop. Although formulaic oriental tales continued to be produced in the early nineteenth century, along with narratives published by scholarly orientalists such as Terrick Hamilton (translator of the "Bedoueen" romance *Antar*, 1819), many writers now began to explore the possibilities that were offered by the figure of a first-person narrator, as a kind of plain-speaking indigenous informant. The title character of Thomas Hope's three-volume picaresque novel *Anastasius, or Memoirs of a Greek* (1819), for example, decides to throw in his lot with Turkish rule and pass for a Muslim, only to be frustrated in his quest for upward mobility, and disappointed by what he sees of the celebrated cities of the Levant. Hope's work, which itself rode the tails of Byron's comic epics, was followed by several similar fictions including, most famously, James Morier's *The Adventures of Hajji Baba of Ispahan* (1824), and William Browne Hockley's *Pandurang*

Hari, or Memoirs of a Hindoo (1826). While alluding to the "off-stage" role of European powers – to the British, French, and Russian interests attempting to exert their influence over Persia, for example, or to the apparently inexorable spread of British dominion in India – these novels are primarily concerned to detail the ups and downs of their narrators' lives. The oriental picaro of the 1820s and 1830s intermittently acknowledges the corruption of the system of government under which he lives, but also recognizes the futility of any efforts to reform it from within, and – for the most part separated from family or other social networks – attempts to play the system as far as he can; as Hajji Baba says during his brief stint as one of the Shah's executioners, "formerly I was one of the beaten, now I am one of the beaters."[22]

Many readers of *Anastasius*, especially, complained about the repetitiveness and the generic lowness of this new style of picaresque narrative: whereas "Mahometans, in a poet's hands, are poetical personages," the *Edinburgh Monthly Review* stated, "an analysis, in a novel, of the *everyday* of the dull Moslemin ... is insupportable."[23] Emphasizing his first-hand experience of Persia as a diplomat and traveler, however, Morier for his part signed up to the "anti-orientalist" backlash that had been given renewed impetus by James Mill's *The History of British India* (1817), offering his fiction as a necessary corrective to the delightful illusions fostered by previous oriental tales, and most immediately by Thomas Moore's best-selling oriental romance *Lalla Rookh* (1817). Both Morier and Hockley stressed the evidential value of their works, furthermore, with Hockley stating in his introduction to *Pandurang Hari* that his time as a judge in the Bombay Presidency "undeceived" him about the true Hindu character: "From the rajah to the ryot, with the intermediate grades, they are ungrateful, insidious, cowardly, unfaithful, and revengeful."[24] The imperial administrator Sir Henry Bartle Frere later wrote that novels by Morier, Hockley, and James Bailie Fraser provided him with a unique insight into "the inner life of orientals," and this appeal to the testimonial authority of fiction in many ways substantiates Edward Said's influential claims about the circularity and the pervasiveness of orientalist discourse.[25] But these tales of oriental scoundrelism also have much in common with the "Newgate novels" of the period, since both kinds of work often elicit sympathy for their protagonists by presenting them as victims of a repressive social environment. The culmination of the oriental picaresque tradition, Philip Meadows Taylor's *The Confessions of a Thug* (1839), moreover, stages a prevalent anxiety about the reach of colonial authority, and reflects on the limits of the knowledge that readers might distil from such a source. Although the Thug informant Ameer Ali appears to pay tribute to the hold of British power by giving an unprompted confession to an almost silent sahib, the novel is unable to suppress the sense of ignorance (or in C. A. Bayly's terms, "information panic") that drives its efforts to systematize oriental criminality.[26]

From about the end of the eighteenth century onwards, it is fair to say that most works of fiction rejected any idea of imaginative sympathy for Eastern cultures, and eschewed the defining features of Romantic orientalist poetry, such as the quest narrative or the treatment of transcultural desire. In drawing on the conventions of colonial romance, however, Sydney Owenson's remarkable novel *The Missionary* (1811) itself exerted an important influence on the work of poets such as Thomas Moore and P. B. Shelley. Owenson's work, set in the 1630s, was published just before the revision of the Company's charter that cleared the way for missionaries to operate in India, and it takes the project of Christianization as the basis for an ambitious historical perspective on colonial oppression, describing the Portuguese priest Hilarion's growing obsession with the woman that he had been challenged to convert, Luxima, the "Prophetess of Cashmire." The novel upholds a clichéd gendering of East and West (Luxima is said to be "lovely and luxuriant," while Hilarion is "lofty and commanding"), and it indicts Brahminical bigotry in its account of the excommunication of Luxima for her contact with the European.[27] But Hilarion also comes to interrogate his initial endeavor, to the extent that he falls foul of the Spanish Inquisition in Goa, and the "conversion" of Luxima remains incomplete, as is made clear in the novel's climactic scene where she commits an act of sati on Hilarion's pyre, prompting a popular insurrection against Jesuit authority. Rather than just project colonial violence onto seventeenth-century Spanish Catholics, *The Missionary* suggests analogies between Spain's ascendancy over Portugal and Britain's domination of Ireland, and further refers in a brief footnote to the Vellore mutiny of 1806, a rising of Indian troops that was in many ways proleptic of the rebellion of 1857; one index of how Owenson understood the larger resonance of her novel is that she published a revised version of it, now titled *Luxima, the Prophetess*, in 1859.

Whereas "oriental picaresque" fictions sometimes engaged with specific questions about the daily business of empire (if also acknowledging the tension between writing to expose and writing to amuse), *The Missionary* might be read as a pioneering instance of "imperial Gothic," with Hilarion's eventual fate, the solitary death of a recluse gone native in the hills of Srinigar, emphasizing how he had lost sight of the ideals that once inspired him. "The Tale of the Indians" in Charles Maturin's *Melmoth the Wanderer* (1820) offers a rewriting of *The Missionary*, in which Melmoth tries to seduce the innocent castaway Immalee, and Gothic romances such as Charlotte Dacre's *Zofloya* (1806) and Lady Caroline Lamb's *Ada Reis*

(1823) similarly engage with themes of illicit desire as well as demonic temptation. But the work of fiction that does most to develop the possibilities of imperial Gothic in this period is Sir Walter Scott's *The Surgeon's Daughter* (1827). Although it takes the British presence in India as a given, and acknowledges the commercial appeal of sending the Muse of Fiction to the East, *The Surgeon's Daughter* also adds a new level of pathos, as well as sensation, to the emergent novel of Anglo-Indian life. Returning to the 1770s, Scott's work accentuates the gulf between the myths of romance and the realities of life on the ground, as it contrasts the experiences of Richard Middlemas, who is drawn to India by the prospect of "lacs and crores of rupees," and Adam Hartley, who travels to India as a surgeon's mate on a Company ship, sublimating his unrequited love for the title character, Menie Gray. Middlemas tries to remake himself in India, and to throw off his murky past, but his attempts to maneuver between Madras and Mysore as a double agent eventually bring about his demise, in a remarkable scene where he is crushed to death by an elephant, on the orders of Hyder Ali. While Scott presents this archetypally despotic act of summary execution as an instance of "just punishment," the novel offers Hartley no reward for his selfless endeavor, and refuses to unite him with the woman that he still loves, describing instead how he died of fever, "a victim to his professional courage." The function of Scott's historical perspective remains ambivalent throughout, since the novel both suggests that a "superior class of people" now serves in India *and* provides a distinctly non-celebratory focus on an earlier phase of Company affairs; if the work's final chapter recognizes the ongoing domestication of empire at the level of commodity culture, in its reference to "the imitation shawls now made at Paisley, out of real Thibet wool," it is nonetheless striking that *The Surgeon's Daughter* does very little to locate the British role in India within any larger framework of military domination or administrative and economic "improvement."[28]

Scott's earlier novel *The Talisman* (1825), the best known of his *Tales of the Crusaders*, is a similarly playful work, which displays its familiarity with the contemporary market for fiction while at the same time confounding the expectations of its readers. Although the opening contest of arms between Sir Kenneth and Sheerkohf (Saladin in disguise) initially seems to establish an essential antagonism between Christianity and Islam, Scott omitted such scenes of combat from the rest of the novel, as reviewers sometimes complained: "here we are altogether among the Crusaders," the *Monthly Magazine* stated, "in the very heart of the camp, and yet without a battle."[29] Rather than pitting Crusader against Saracen in violent conflict, *The Talisman* seems much more interested in the dynamics of contact and encounter between East and West, drawing attention at one point, for example, to the "motley concourse" of merchants in the Christian tents: "the caftan and the turban, though to drive them from the Holy Land was the professed object of the expedition, were nevertheless neither an uncommon nor an alarming sight in the camp of the Crusaders." The intimacy of this contact is most clearly figured in the implicitly homoerotic relationship between King Richard and Saladin, and the gradual shifting of alliances depicted by the novel culminates in a scene where the latter, the main adversary of the Third Crusade, beheads the Grand Master of the Templars, a conspirator against the joint Christian enterprise; Richard applauds this punishment as "a great act of justice."[30] If Scott was largely ignorant about Islam, and made little effort to depict Saladin in realistic terms, he cast a sceptical eye on the ways in which many of his contemporaries sought to recuperate the idealism of the Crusades so as to draw analogies between past and present conflicts. Other novels by Scott, such as *Ivanhoe* (1819) and *The Betrothed* (1825), likewise undermine any sense of the Crusades as a national endeavor, and focus on the lack of common purpose among the disunited (and also ethnically heterogeneous) English, instead of on the inevitability of the opposition between Christians and Muslims.

Mary Shelley's futuristic novel *The Last Man* (1826) makes a crusader of the self-aggrandizing Lord Raymond (an unflattering portrait of Byron), who declares his ambition to "subdue all Asia," and vows "to plant the cross on yonder mosque" in Constantinople, while leading the Greeks during their conflict – still alive in the 2070s – with the Turks.[31] The plague that goes on to wipe out the human race begins to spread when Raymond is about to enter Constantinople, and Raymond receives his comeuppance shortly afterwards, when he is thrown from his horse by falling ruins, and crushed to death. Despite this framing of Raymond's hubris, however, *The Last Man* is by no means a straightforwardly anti-imperialist work, since both Adrian (Mary Shelley's far more generous figuring of her brother, Percy) and Lionel (the Cumbrian shepherd who is civilized by Adrian) also see the Greek cause as an essential struggle between liberty and slavery, Hellenism and oriental despotism. In its retrospect on Enlightenment perfectibility and revolutionary optimism, *The Last Man* demonstrates how the critique of despotism, even if it continued to have a strong domestic resonance, could easily be compatible with ideologies of liberal imperialism. Rather than directly contesting the idea of empire, therefore, the novel rehearses long-standing concerns about the Asiatic corruption of the British body politic, along with more immediate fears about the potentially global ramifications of "colonial disease," especially fraught following the outbreak of epidemic cholera in India in 1817. Britain itself becomes a colonial contact zone in

The Last Man, as Alan Bewell has pointed out, and fantasies of island exceptionalism are shown no longer to provide any reassuring sense of splendid isolation from the outside world.[32]

One important story to tell about "Orientalism and empire" in the Romantic period concerns the growth of an ethnocentric confidence in Britain's essential superiority over its Eastern others, perhaps most infamously expressed in T. B. Macaulay's "Minute on Indian Education" (1835). Whereas Macaulay stated in his 1840 essay on Clive that the reader of any novel published sixty years previously would find its villain to be "a savage old Nabob, with an immense fortune, a tawny complexion, a bad liver, and a worse heart," in other words the embodiment of *Company* despotism, numerous works of fiction published around the time that Macaulay was writing instead offered comic portraits of life under distant and almost interchangeable oriental despotisms, as if to substantiate William Thackeray's later remark that "The much-maligned Orient ... has not been maligned nearly enough."[33] A discussion of *The Last Man* provides a useful point at which to conclude, however, since Mary Shelley's novel was one of a number of works written towards the end of this period that also began to probe the imperial unconscious, by imagining the uncanny domestication of the colonial encounter. Any more extensive survey would need to attend to the rich variety of nineteenth-century orientalisms, and to consider, among other issues, the complex and distinctive engagement with the *Arabian Nights* in the work of, for example, Dickens and Wilkie Collins. But a particularly telling development over the course of our period is that as the formulaic oriental tale gave way to the different novels addressed in this chapter, which directly or indirectly engaged with the eastward expansion of British imperial power, so the eighteenth-century figure of the imaginary oriental traveler gave way to a range of more threatening outsiders, such as Mary Shelley's Evadne and Thomas De Quincey's Grasmere Malay. The figure of the sinister, racially marked intruder went on to become a significant presence in Victorian fiction, and many later novels alternate between the casual denigration of different racial others and the uneasy acknowledgment of their presence in Britain itself.

NOTES

1 *Monthly Review* 26 (March 1762), p. 254.
2 *Monthly Review* 20 (May 1759), in James T. Boulton, ed., *Samuel Johnson: The Critical Heritage* (London: Routledge and Kegan Paul, 1971), pp. 141–6.
3 Charles Johnstone, *The History of Arsaces, Prince of Betlis*, 2 vols. (1774), Vol. I, p. vii.
4 *A New Review* 9 (June 1786), p. 412.

5 William Beckford, *Vathek*, ed. Roger Lonsdale (Oxford: Oxford University Press, 1970), p. 1.

6 *Thraliana: The Diary of Hester Lynch Thrale (Later Mrs Piozzi), 1776–1809*, ed. Katherine C. Balderston, 2 vols. (Oxford: Clarendon Press, 1942), Vol. II, p. 799.

7 Agnes Maria Bennett, *Anna; or Memoirs of a Welch Heiress. Interspersed with Anecdotes of a Nabob*, 4 vols. (1785), Vol. I, pp. 91–2.

8 *The Indian Adventurer; or, History of Mr Vanneck, A Novel, Founded on Facts* (1780), pp. 221–2.

9 Helenus Scott, *The Adventures of a Rupee: Wherein are Interspersed Various Anecdotes Asiatic and European* (1782), pp. 244, 260, 60, 91.

10 Kate Teltscher, *India Inscribed: European and British Writing on India 1600–1800* (Oxford: Oxford University Press, 1995), p. 135.

11 *Hartly House, Calcutta*, ed. Monica Clough (London: Pluto Press, 1989), pp. 191, 259, 255, 271, 279.

12 Elizabeth Hamilton, *Translation of Letters of a Hindoo Rajah* (1796), ed. Pamela Perkins and Shannon Russell (Peterborough, Ontario: Broadview, 1999), pp. 57, 84.

13 Robert Bage, *Mount Henneth*, 2 vols. (1782), Vol. I, p. 233.

14 Robert Bage, *The Fair Syrian*, 2 vols. (1787), Vol. I, p. 119; Vol. II, p. 44; Vol. II, p. 282; Vol. II, p. 36.

15 Saree Makdisi, *William Blake and the Impossible History of the 1790s* (Chicago: University of Chicago Press, 2003), pp. 219, 206.

16 James Beattie, "On Fable and Romance," in *Dissertations Moral and Critical* (1783), pp. 525–7, 509.

17 J. Cooper, *The Oriental Moralist, or the Beauties of the Arabian Nights' Entertainments* (1790), p. 2.

18 *Bahar-Danush; or, Garden of Knowledge. An Oriental Romance Translated from the Persic of Einaiut Oollah*, 3 vols. (1799), Vol. I, p. v.

19 See Nigel Leask, "'Wandering through Eblis': Absorption and Containment in Romantic Exoticism," in Tim Fulford and Peter Kitson, eds., *Romanticism and Colonialism: Writing and Empire, 1780–1830* (Cambridge: Cambridge University Press, 1998), pp. 164–88.

20 Mary Pilkington, *The Asiatic Princess*, 2 vols. (1800), Vol. II, p. 138; Vol. I, p. 60.

21 Maria Edgeworth, "Murad the Unlucky," in Robert L. Mack, ed., *Oriental Tales* (Oxford: Oxford University Press, 1992), pp. 215–56 (p. 256).

22 James Morier, *The Adventures of Hajji Baba of Ispahan* (1824), intro. C. W. Stewart (London: Oxford University Press, 1970), p. 177.

23 *Edinburgh Monthly Review* 4 (October 1820), p. 444.

24 William Browne Hockley, *Pandurang Hari, or Memoirs of a Hindoo*, 3 vols. (1826), Vol. I, p. xiv.

25 William Browne Hockley, *Pandurang Hari, or Memoirs of a Hindoo*, intro. Sir Henry E. Bartle Frere, 2 vols. (1873), Vol. I, p. v.

26 C. A. Bayly, *Empire and Information: Intelligence Gathering and Social Communication in British India, 1780–1870* (Cambridge: Cambridge University Press, 1996), pp. 171–4.

27 Sydney Owenson (Lady Morgan), *The Missionary*, ed. Julia M. Wright (Peterborough, Ont.: Broadview, 2002), p. 109.

28 Sir Walter Scott, *Chronicles of the Canongate*, ed. Claire Lamont (Harmondsworth: Penguin, 2003), pp. 199, 285, 204, 287.
29 *Monthly Magazine* 59 (July 1825), p. 552.
30 Sir Walter Scott, *The Talisman* (London: J. M. Dent, 1991), pp. 219, 311.
31 Mary Shelley, *The Last Man*, ed. Morton D. Paley (Oxford: Oxford University Press, 1994), pp. 57, 193.
32 Alan Bewell, *Romanticism and Colonial Disease* (Baltimore: Johns Hopkins University Press, 1999), pp. 296–314.
33 Thomas Babington Macaulay, "Lord Clive," in *Critical and Historical Essays contributed to the Edinburgh Review* (1877), p. 535; William Thackeray, *Notes of a Journey from Cornhill to Cairo, by Way of Lisbon, Athens, Constantinople, and Jerusalem* (1846), p. 264.

8

PAUL KEEN

Intellectual history and political theory

'Useful books': The use and abuse of novels in the Romantic age

In his autobiography, the London Corresponding Society activist Francis Place reflected on the ways that "a love for reading, and a desire for information" which had been "implanted" by his "good schoolmaster" encouraged him to embark on a program of self-education which was as relentless as it was serious: "even while I was an apprentice, I always found some time for reading, and I almost always found the means to procure books, useful books, not Novels." Eager to establish his credentials for political enfranchisement in the service of a broader vision of democratic republicanism in which the status of citizenship rested on the sure ground of individual merit rather than the idle privilege of landed wealth, Place was understandably anxious to demonstrate the intellectual rigor of his reading habits:

> I had read in English the only language in which I could read, the histories of Greece and Rome, and some translated works of Greek and Roman writers. Hume Smollett, Fieldings novels and Robertsons works, some Hume Essays, some Translations from french writers, and much on geography – some books on Anatomy and Surgery, some relating to Science and the Arts, and many Magazines. I had worked all the Problems in the Introduction to Guthries Geography, and had made some small progress in Geometry. I now read Blackstone, Hale's Common Law, several other Law Books, and much Biography.[1]

Place's disclaimer – "useful books, not Novels" despite his inclusion of "Fieldings novel's" and Smollett (if he was referring to Smollett's novels rather than to other writings such as his *History of England*) – suggests just how deeply rooted was this suspicion of novels. Novels were "useful" primarily so that one could declare that one had had nothing to do with them, and so, by implication, had spent one's time productively. They were inherently political, not so much because of their content, but because they served as a kind of shorthand for the dissipated world of fashionable excess that threatened to undermine Place's insistence (faithful to his reading of Hume's essays) that "the progress made in refinement of manners and morals seems to have gone on simultaneously with the improvements in Arts Manufactures and Commerce" (p. 82). It was not enough to rehearse a reading list which did not include novels (one or two authors excepted); novels, if they were to be truly useful, needed to be highlighted in order that their omission – and all that that omission stood for – might be properly noted.

Place's politically motivated resistance to novels was a widely shared one that ranged across the ideological spectrum. In her 1788 review of Charlotte Smith's *Emmeline* in the *Analytical Review*, Mary Wollstonecraft warned that "[f]ew of the numerous productions termed novels, claim any attention; and while we distinguish this one, we cannot help lamenting that it has the same tendency as the generality, whose preposterous sentiments our young females imbibe with such avidity." Like Place, Wollstonecraft worried that the cause of rational enlightenment which underpinned hopes for political reform was threatened by novels' tendency to arouse "false expectations" for "wild scenes" which diminished readers' capacity to embrace "the moderate and rational prospects of life."[2] Reformers may have been eager to denounce these problems as symptoms of a debauched world of leisured wealth in need of a revolution (in manners if not in government), but their conservative counterparts were equally judgmental. In *Strictures on the Modern System of Female Education* (1799), Hannah More complained in strikingly similar terms about the plague of "novel writers" who, "with unparalleled fecundity are overstocking the world with their quick succeeding progeny," and who, in doing so, effectively undermined their readers' capacity and inclination for the sorts of "dry tough reading" that would "lift [...] the reader from sensation to intellect."[3] Not that this emphasis on fostering readers' intellect was to be automatically equated with a sympathy for the campaign for political reform, though. On the contrary, for More a course of "dry tough reading" (I.165) was valuable because it would give readers the sort of intellectual "ballast" that would protect them from the romantic temptations of radicalism's overblown appeal to the imagination (I.167).

Whether critics' disavowal of novels was informed by an underlying desire to prepare readers to participate in the project of radical reform or to know enough to resist it, they coincided in their disgust with the degrading effects of novels' contribution to "[t]he glutted imagination" of readers who ought to have been devoting their time to other, more edifying genres (I.170). But ironically, it was in some ways precisely because of these perceived weaknesses that novels were so well adapted to support the cause of popular radicalism as political debate intensified in the wake of the outbreak of the French Revolution. The endless sycophantic clergymen, hypocritical bishops, corrupt lawyers, dissolute husbands, callous nouveaux riches businessmen, and predatory aristocrats who played leading roles in melodramatic plots of victimization drove home in strikingly personal terms reformers' sense of the human cost of the many interwoven forms of political oppression in contemporary British society. In doing so these novels closed the gap between sensation and intellect by depicting "wild scenes" of persecution in ways that were intended to bring their readers' attention to bear on the very question of what might constitute a "moderate and rational ... life" and, just as importantly, of the sorts of barriers that society placed in the way of those who genuinely wished to pursue a virtuous life.

For audiences that were already well versed in the agonies of tales of sensibility, these narratives of heart-wrenching struggle and noble resistance made for compelling fiction. In the conclusion to her anti-Jacobin novel, *A Tale of the Times* (1799), Jane West warned that "the novel," because it was "calculated, by its insinuating narrative and interesting description to fascinate the imagination without rousing the stronger energies of the mind," was, of all the literary genres, the one which was most easily and dangerously "converted into an offensive weapon, directed against our religion, our morals, or our government."[4] It was precisely this sense of the dangerous power of this "offensive weapon," West explained, which inspired her to "repel the enemy's insidious attacks with similar weapons" (III.387). In *Strictures on the Modern System of Female Education*, which appeared in the same year, More offered a similar warning. "Novels, which used chiefly to be dangerous in one respect, are now become mischievous in a thousand. They are continually shifting their ground, and enlarging their sphere, and are daily becoming vehicles of wider mischief. Sometimes they concentrate their force, and are at once employed to diffuse destructive politics, deplorable profligacy, and impudent infidelity" (I.31). Far from contributing to an enlightening and therefore liberating exchange of ideas, novels (this sort, at least) amounted to "a net ... spread to entangle innocence and ensnare inexperience." The association of reading with education implied the promise of self-knowledge and, with it, rational self-government, but one of the most dangerous aspects of the "net" which these novels spread over unsuspecting readers was the fact that "unhappily, the victim does not even struggle in the toils, because part of the delusion consists in imagining that he is set at liberty" (I.33–4). Warming to her subject, More insisted that "the principal evil arising from [these sorts of novels] is, that the virtues they exhibit are almost more dangerous than the vices" (I.34).

Equally dangerous, as More and West were both well aware, was the popularity of many of these novels, especially with "persons whom books of philosophy and science are never likely to reach," as William Godwin had insisted in his Preface to *Things As They Are; or, the Adventures of Caleb Williams* (1794).[5] Novels offered reformers a means of extending debates about government to a set of readers who would have been unlikely to seek out political pamphlets. In its review of Thomas Holcroft's *The Adventures of Hugh Trevor* (1794–7), which immediately followed its review of Godwin's *Things As They Are*, the ultra-loyalist (and government-funded) *British Critic* acknowledged that "it has often been said, that the best writers are apt to range themselves on the side of Opposition in politics. At present we are sorry to remark, that the opposition to revealed religion and to civil society can boast of two very amusing novelists among its advocates."[6] Few readers would have been inclined to describe Godwin's and Holcroft's gloomy delineation of things as they were as "very amusing," but these novels' unrelentingly bleak tone did little to dampen their appeal. "[N]o one ever began *Caleb Williams* that did not read it through," William Hazlitt famously recalled. "[N]o one that ever read it could possibly forget it, or speak of it after any length of time, but with an impression as if the events and feelings had been personal to himself."[7] Mindful of the political dangers inherent in this sort of impact, especially given novels' ability to appeal to a wider and more susceptible audience unused to "books of philosophy and science," the *British Critic* took predictable exception to what it regarded as the distorted picture which both novels conveyed of the ills of their age. In *Things As They Are*, "every gentleman is a hard-hearted assassin, or a prejudiced tyrant; every Judge is unjust, every Justice corrupt and blind" (IV.70). Holcroft's novel followed the agonizing struggles of "Hugh Trevor, who, like the ill-fated Caleb Williams, meets with brutality and insolence in every Clergyman, from the Curate to the Bishop, and injustice, coupled with want of humanity, in every person whose station is superior to his own" (IV.71).

Narratives of the "brutality and insolence" of the ruling classes were often spiced with dramatic allusions to contemporary events and to leading political figures of the day. In one of Charlotte Smith's most overtly political novels, *Desmond* (1792), the protagonist arrives in Paris in time to witness the *Fête de Fédération*, the enormous celebration held in Paris to mark the first anniversary of the fall of the Bastille, at which 400,000 people gathered to watch Louis XVI take the national oath. Robert Bage's *Hermsprong* (1796) included references to the Birmingham riots in which Church-and-King loyalists burnt the houses of radical sympathizers such as William Hutton (Bage's business associate) and Joseph Priestley. More to the point, *Hermsprong* also included a parodic example of a sermon (by the scrupulously sycophantic Reverend Doctor Blick) condoning and even tacitly encouraging this sort of intolerance and violence.[8] Mary Robinson's *The Natural Daughter* (1799) treated readers to scintillating cameo appearances by two of the most notorious French revolutionaries, the "monster" and "despot" Jean-Paul Marat, who threatens to execute the imprisoned but virtuous Mrs Sedgely unless she "consent to become his wife," and Maximilian Robespierre, who turns out to have been the lover of the decidedly unvirtuous Julia Bradford.[9]

These sensational allusions to topical events and individuals were complemented by intertextual references which effectively bridged the divide between fiction and more "useful" genres by participating in the broader debate ignited by Edmund Burke's notorious *Reflections on the Revolution in France* (1790). *Desmond* carried on a running critique of the "virulence, as well as the misrepresentation with which [Burke's *Reflections*] abounds," adopting the radical line that "far from finally injuring the cause of truth and reason, against which Mr Burke is so inveterate, it will awaken every advocate in their defence."[10] Later in the novel Smith (or Smith's protagonist, Lionel Desmond) hailed "the calmness and magnanimity shewn by the French people, on the re-entrance of the King into Paris" as certain proof that "the bloody democracy of Mr Burke, is not a combination of the swinish multitude, for the purposes of anarchy, but the association of reasonable beings, who determine to be, and deserve to be, free" (p. 310). Deriding the "mob" of people whose "affectation of the manners of upper life ... overbears all retiring and simple virtues" in *The Young Philosopher* (1798), Smith again invoked and revised Burke in her insistence that "it is not the swinish multitude – the "plebs et infima multitudo," that disgust one with the species. It is such people as these; people who hold the honest labourer and the industrious mechanic in contempt, yet are indeed poor in intellect and vulgar in all they do or say."[11] *Hermsprong's* reflection on the "absurd ... boast of cherishing prejudices, because they are prejudices" (pp. 90–1) would have been instantly recognizable as a sardonic allusion to Burke's infamous comment that "instead of casting away all our old prejudices, we cherish them to a very considerable degree, and, to take more shame to ourselves, we cherish them because they are prejudices."[12]

However much the *British Critic* may have sniffed at Godwin's and Holcroft's overblown portraits of injustice, conservative novelists proved to be just as adept at all of these strategies, countering images of petty tyrants with their own depictions of opportunistic posers who mobilized a seemingly noble Enlightenment rhetoric of liberation in order to pursue their own cynical interests – usually, as in novels such as Charles Lloyd's *Edmund Oliver* (1798), Elizabeth Hamilton's *Memoirs of Modern Philosophers*, (1799) Charles Lucas's *The Infernal Quixote* (1801), and West's *A Tale of the Times*, for illicit sexual relationships. Depictions of these sorts of sexual predators were complemented by images of radicals who were too foolish to be dangerous: dim-witted pseudo-intellectuals whose faith in jargon betrayed their obvious ignorance. However indebted it may have been to a message of Christian piety and resignation, Hamilton's *Memoirs of Modern Philosophers* contained a vicious caricature of Mary Hays in the pathetic Brigetina Botherim. George Walker's *The Vagabond* (1799) relied on slightly more charitable send-ups of Godwin ("the divine Stupeo") and Joseph Priestley (Doctor Alogos) for much of its satirical humour.[13] Following Godwin's lead by exploiting novels' widespread appeal for political gain, Walker's dedication to the Bishop of Landaff described his own efforts as "an attempt to parry the Enemy with their own weapons," a strategy that was all the more urgent, he suggested, because "a Novel may gain attention, when arguments of the soundest sense and most perfect eloquence shall fail to arrest the feet of the Trifler from the specious paths of the new Philosophy" (p. 53).

If reformist novels celebrated revolutionary high points such as the Fête de Fédération, anti-Jacobin authors countered with equally biased references to more dubious events (depending on one's politics) such as the 1798 Irish Uprising in *The Infernal Quixote* and the Gordon Riots in *The Vagabond*, and to damning accounts of the inner workings of radical associations such as the London Corresponding Society and the United Irishmen in both novels. These demonized versions of radical associations may have had little to do with any sort of demonstrable reality, but their fictional excesses were arguably just the inverse of the sorts of excesses that the *British Critic* complained of in Jacobin novels such as *Things as They Are* or *Hugh Trevor*. More to the point, perhaps, these lurid accounts of the shadowy world of popular radicalism were well suited to counter-revolutionary tastes in a decade when conspiracy theories such as the ones propounded in Abbé Barruel's *Memoirs, Illustrating the History of Jacobinism* (1797) and John Robison's *Proofs of a Conspiracy against all the Religions and Governments of Europe, Carried On in the Secret Meetings of Free Masons, Illuminati, and Reading Societies* (1798) were widely embraced as historical fact.

Where radical authors integrated a running critique of Burke's *Reflections* into the novels, their conservative counterparts offered a matching denunciation of a pantheon of reformers such as Godwin, Mary Wollstonecraft, and Thomas Paine. Godwin's *Enquiry Concerning Political Justice* (1793) was a favourite target. *Memoirs of Modern Philosophers*, *The Vagabond*, and *The Infernal Quixote* incorporated ongoing references, often using footnotes, which cited and implicitly countered Godwin's more notorious claims, especially his rejection of the domestic sphere as the site of one's prime affections.

Hamilton's attribution of Godwin's suggestion that *"[i]n a state of equality, it will be a question of no importance to know who is the parent of each individual child"* (which she placed in italics and identified in a footnote) to the philandering revolutionary poser, Vallanton, as part of a seduction strategy, highlighted her sense of the ease with which a seemingly principled rejection of inherited rules and prohibitions could collapse into cynical opportunism.[14] Lucas chose a similar scene (Marauder's seduction of Emily) to break from the narrative in order to reject Godwin's insistence that "nothing can be so ridiculous upon the face of it, or so contrary to *the genuine march of sentiment*, as to require the overflowings of the soul to wait upon a ceremony."[15] *The Vagabond* offered a slight revision on the theme. When Doctor Alogos asks Stupeo how "the great and powerful opponent of matrimony, should be married to *three* at once," Stupeo responds, "with a look of superiority," that Alogos's bewilderment suggests how "little versed [he is] in the sublime doctrine of political justice. Sir, you would there find that contradictions are nothing in the way of truth" (p. 171). Radicals may have frequently aligned themselves with the cause of virtue as a counterweight to the pressures of custom but the point of the seduction narrative that was a hallmark of anti-Jacobin novels was that the more radicals talked of virtue, the more sinister were their real intentions (p. 48). "Can we wonder at the prevailance [sic] of adultery, when doctrines such as these men hold out in *fascinating language*, are tolerated?," Walker demanded in his Preface (p. 54).

These seduction plots (and their polygamous variations), which linked radicals' derision of "the tedious forms and ceremonies" (*The Vagabond* p. 71) of marriage to their attacks on innocent but unsuspecting heroines, were ultimately a personalized form of more straightforwardly political denunciations of reformers such as "Mr. Payne [sic] and his faction" as a "wretched banditti of revolutionarists, who are ever greedy of political hurricanes, that they may live on the wrecks of ruined states."[16] Burke himself had blamed the French Revolution on the work of a "cabal, calling itself philosophic" which "pretended to a great zeal for the poor, and the lower orders" in order to advance their own selfish ambitions (pp. 185, 213). The warning implicit in these novels' seduction plots was that the customs and laws which radicals liked to blame for "the faults, and the miseries of mankind" constituted a necessary foundation for personal agency rather than a threat to it.[17] To be "freed" from these sanctions was to be abandoned to an ethical vacuum in which sound judgment (based on the reliable distinction of virtue and vice) was impossible. Even more ominously, this supposed liberation left unsuspecting individuals vulnerable to the destructive machinations of schemers who, because they "live[d] on the wrecks of ruined [lives] and states," were, after all, the only people who felt at home in this sort of moral abyss.

'Mingled virtue and vice': Textual complexity and moral ambiguity

If these novels' explicit allusions to intellectual antagonists – whether Burke or Godwin – were part of a tendency to bolster narratives with references to notorious individuals and events, they also suggested a more profound engagement with some of the most pressing issues of a highly polemical age. Beyond the clamor for and against democracy (for men, at least), the revolutionary debate ultimately turned on the epistemological question of the form of knowledge that was best suited to the demands of national government. Burke's denunciation of the sorts of professionals who comprised France's Third Estate had recycled the civic humanist stress on the unique benefit of landed wealth as a possession which conferred general rather than particular forms of knowledge because of its supposed distance from the division of labor:

> It cannot escape observation, that when men are too much confined to professional and faculty habits, and, as it were, inveterate in the recurrent employment of that narrow circle, they are rather disabled than qualified for whatever depends on the knowledge of mankind, on experience in mixed affairs, on a comprehensive connected view of the various complicated external and internal interests which go to the formation of that multifarious thing called a state.
>
> (p. 133)

Burke's celebration of landed wealth as a transcendent perspective enabling the sort of "comprehensive connected view" which these professionals were incapable of was easily countered in the Jacobin novels by a parade of startlingly unperceptive and petty aristocrats, all demonstrating what Eliza Fenwick's novel *Secresy* (1795) had decried as the "impenetrable selfishness of high birth."[18] Their estates, which formed the Gothic contexts for so many Jacobin novels, seemed to leave them isolated and, as a result, profoundly ignorant about the world around them – "rather disabled than qualified for whatever depends on the knowledge of mankind."

But Burke's defence of the monarchy and aristocracy was grounded in a more fundamental and in many ways more ambitious point: the importance of a widely embraced mystification of power. Social order required that people accept an aestheticized set of "pleasing illusions, which made power gentle, and obedience liberal," dressing hierarchical relations and the forms of obedience which they required up in the "decent drapery" of "superadded ideas, furnished from the wardrobe of a moral imagination"

(p. 171). The problem was that these "pleasing illusions" could only flourish as long as they remained sheltered from the corrosive effects of what Burke scathingly dismissed as the "new conquering empire of light and reason" (p. 171). However confident Enlightenment thinkers may have been of the liberating power of critical debate, Burke insisted that "it has been the misfortune of this age, that every thing is to be discussed" (p. 188). The question of the relative worth of any particular idea was dwarfed by the larger issue of the dubious wisdom of encouraging a robust discussion of any ideas.

As Burke was well aware, it was an audacious position that flew in the face of an Enlightenment emphasis on the importance of unrestrained critical debate with its implicit faith in the sound judgment of ordinary individuals. As Hays put it in the Preface to *The Memoirs of Emma Courtney* (1796), "free thinking, and free speaking, are the virtue and the characteristics of a rational being" (p. 3). In *The Proper Objects of Education* (1791), Joseph Priestley had mocked those who resisted the idea of a society which was distinguished by the free thinking and free speaking of its citizens:

> The late writings in favour of liberty, civil and religious, have been like a beam of light suddenly thrown among owls, bats, or moles, who, incapable of receiving any pleasure or benefit from it, can only cry out, and hide themselves, when the light approaches, and disturbs them. But may this light increase, and let all who are offended by it retire into whatever holes they think proper.[19]

Thomas Paine's "Letter Addressed to the Addressers on the Late Proclamation" (1792), which responded to his arrest (in absentia) for seditious libel for *Rights of Man* Part Two (1792), warned that "[i]t is a dangerous attempt in any government to say to a nation, *'thou shalt not read'* ... because *thought* by some means or other, is got abroad in the world, and cannot be restrained, though reading may."[20] One year later, Godwin insisted in *Enquiry Concerning Political Justice* that the ubiquity of "prejudice and mistake" which continued to distort people's thinking placed a premium on the ability of robust debate or "the collision of mind with mind" to generate and disseminate a new appreciation of important truths, all of which would have an inevitably reformist influence (he offered the ideas of Newton and Locke as examples).[21]

Radical novelists were quick to embrace this position. Hays foregrounded her own inscription within this process in her comment, again in the Preface to *Emma Courtney*, that "[e]very writer who advances principles, whether true or false, that have a tendency to set the mind in motion, does good" (p. 3). Holcroft's insistence in *Hugh Trevor* that the "nation that remarks, discusses, and complains of its wrongs, will finally have them redressed," was

rooted in a broader historical sense of the transformative power of developments in "the art of printing":

> When knowledge was locked up in Egyptian temples, or secreted by Indian
> Bramins [sic] for their own selfish traffic, it was indeed difficult to increase this
> imaginary circle of yours: but no sooner was it diffused among mankind, by the
> discovery of the alphabet, than, in a short period, it was succeeded by the
> wonders of Greece and Rome. And now, that its circulation is facilitated in so
> incalculable a degree, who shall be daring enough to assert his puny standard is
> the measure of all possible futurity?[22]

In *Desmond*, Smith implicitly aligned her writing with the spectacle of what
Montfleuri, the benevolent French aristocrat-turned-revolutionary, hailed as
"the light of reason thus rapidly advancing, which has shewn us how to
overturn the massy and cumbrous edifice of despotism" (p. 101). Not only
was this "rapidly advancing" process inevitable, Smith suggested, its omnipo-
tence was assured because "the progress of letters ... was insensibly dispelling
that ignorance which alone could secure this blind obedience" (p. 105). *The
Young Philosopher* offered a dramatic version of what had quickly become a
central radical argument about the violent excesses that had marred the
revolution in its depiction of a one-sided debate (another staple of these novels)
in which Delmont easily gets the better of Dr. Winslow's charge that "those
who call themselves philosophers ... have occasioned all the bloodshed and
misery ... in a neighbouring kingdom." Delmont responds by distinguishing
those who "endeavoured to emancipate the people from the fetters which
galled and crushed them" from the deeper sources of the revolutionary violence which, like many radicals, Smith traced back to the morally crippling
effects of the *ancien régime*. "The truth is, that the gloomy and absurd
structures, raised on the basis of prejudice and superstition, have toppled
down headlong; many are crushed in their fall" (p. 45).

Conservatives turned these arguments back against reformers by dismissing this vision of unending debate as a new and potentially dangerous
alienation from the steady moral guidance of history rather than a new
freedom. In *The Infernal Quixote*, Lucas countered Smith's picture of "the
massy and cumbrous edifice of despotism" with what he described as the
"dark and gloomy ... prospect of the human mind left to itself" (p. 225). If, as
Lucas insisted in terms that were borrowed straight from Burke, "the wisdom
of man, unlike all other animals, seems to be the collection of former ages,"
then it followed that the true mark of individual wisdom was a respect for
this process of accumulation, rather than the kind of disdain that was implied
by shallow celebrations of the usefulness of unbridled skepticism (p. 225). In
Memoirs of Modern Philosophers, the ill-fated Julia's tragic end is sealed by

her willingness to accept the idea that "by combatting her [own] arguments, she might herself become more enlightened. She had been told by the philosophers, that views ought to be for ever changing, and that there was nothing so pernicious as *fixed principle*" (p. 182).

Burke's rejection of free and open debate as a recipe for disaster because it would inevitably lead to this kind of repudiation of "*fixed principle*" received its most articulate defence in novel form in Charles Lloyd's *Edmund Oliver* (1798). Lloyd's novel enjoyed a certain notoriety as a roman-à-clef written from within the heart of the Coleridge–Wordsworth circle during the two poets' *annus mirabilis*, but it also offered one of the most thoughtful articulations of Burke's critique of the intellectual bankruptcy of the public sphere. "You will hear," Charles (the novel's moral centre) warns Edmund, whose life has been thrown into near fatal upheaval by the siren call of radical reform,

> in the circles of London, that the society and frequent intercourse of fellow beings which towns only admit of, are necessary to the growth of mind; to calling forth the activities of the intellect: that men of genius are found in clusters, and that frequent collision is the only means of eliciting truth.[23]

Far from this being the case, however, this sort of "intellectual gladiatorship, adopted in literary and argumentative circles," only tends to "fritter away genius, and level down the sublimity of original thought" (I.53). Echoing Burke, Charles warns Edmund that "by attempting a great deal we often do nothing: it is not loose declamations, or an harangue of general and popular application" that will reform people's prejudices (I.127).

Truly "unlimited communication of ideas" turns out to depend on precisely the sort of close personal contact that print had rendered unnecessary (I.53). Debate, if it was ever to "eradicate habits, disentangle the foldings of prejudice, and regenerate the mind," must be founded on "a strict intimacy ... between two persons" that was inconsistent with current ideas about the public sphere: "We must have gained the confidence of the person we wish to reform; cultivated sympathies with him; and twined ourselves round his heart. ... We must be sentient before we can be rational beings" (I.127–30). The rural utopia with which the novel concludes, in which three couples "meet every evening at each other's house, and by means of reading or conversation endeavor to approximate to a common identity," was a slightly enlarged version of the idealized domestic sphere that novels such as More's *Coelebs in Search of a Wife* (1808) embraced as the truly liberating focus of mature individuals in an age of upheaval and distraction (II.292). Conservatives did not surrender the high ground of "rational liberty" – a term which Burke embraced in the *Reflections* (p. 183) – to their radical counterparts; they insisted that it was to be found in the inherited understandings which made up the sum total of a community's customs. But this required that people possess the humility and wisdom to value it properly. Those who did, these novels implied, also recognized that it was the sort of knowledge that was best directed at what Burke had called "the little platoon" of one's domestic circle (p. 135).

These celebrations of the private sphere provided conservatives with a positive alternative to radicals' enthusiasm for the democratizing effects of public debate, in part because they implied that radicals failed to appreciate the importance of this affective level of personal experience. But however compelling this strategy may have been, it overlooked the extent to which radicals such as Wollstonecraft and Hays rooted their oppositional stances in a similar priority; they simply tended to emphasize the degree to which genuinely meaningful conceptions of the domestic sphere had been distorted by the inherited weight of mistaken values and chauvinistic laws. Framing larger political issues in terms of the quotidian world of everyday life was one of the most significant achievements of both conservative and radical novelists. For radicals, this focus on people's private relations meant a chance to demonstrate the extent to which "the spirit and character of the government intrudes itself into every rank of society," as Godwin had insisted in the Preface to *Things as They Are* (p. 3), by tracing the degree to which tyrannical structures of government had extended themselves to the ultimately more oppressive web of beliefs and behavior that Wollstonecraft denounced in *Wrongs of Woman* (1798) as "civilized depravity."[24] The bleak endings of many of these novels dramatized Hays's depiction of life as a state of "warfare" in which "we have too frequently but a choice of evils."[25]

But this orientation towards people's private relations also resonated with a broader shift throughout the eighteenth century towards an emphasis on the primary significance of everyday life and personal interiority in a modern commercial nation. Novels' inherently dialogic character made them ideally suited to probe the ways that the effects of the French Revolution were compounded by this broader commercial revolution which tended to hybridize various levels of private and public experience, and which put a premium on the realm of personal relations. To this extent novels were part of a much broader philosophical shift towards the importance of quotidian concerns. In *The Idler*, Samuel Johnson countered traditional claims for the instructive power of histories of illustrious men who had contributed to great events by insisting that however appealing these narratives may be, "they are oftener employed for show than use, and rather diversify conversation than regulate life."[26] This was inevitably the case, he suggested, because, ironically, their dramatic impact ensured their broader irrelevance. "Few are engaged in such scenes as give them opportunities of growing wiser by the downfall of statesmen or the defeat of generals. The stratagems of war, and the intrigues of courts, are read by far the greater part of mankind with the same indifference as the adventures of fabled heroes, or the revolutions of a fairy region" (pp. 629–30). Inverting the usual hierarchy of importance, Isaac D'Israeli similarly argued that for modern readers, "a parish register might prove more interesting" than "a dull chronicle of the reigns of monarchs."[27]

As critics frequently argued, this broader turn towards everyday life had also implied a shift toward the sort of moral complexity that More feared in novels' dangerous tendency to confuse virtue and vice. In a discussion of the history of drama, the Edinburgh periodical, *The Lounger*, argued that in primitive societies, "[V]irtue and vice were strongly and distinctly marked, [and] wisdom and weakness were easily discriminated ... But in the modern drama there is an uncertain sort of outline, a blended colouring, by which the distinction of these objects is frequently lost."[28] The novel had long been a target for these sorts of concerns. Samuel Johnson had famously protested against the tendency of novels to promote this moral ambivalence or "blended colouring" in *The Rambler* No. 4, which decried modern novelists' inclination to "so mingle good and bad qualities in their principal personages, that ... we lose the abhorrence of their faults, because they do not hinder our pleasure, or perhaps, regard them with some kindness, for being united with so much merit" (I.18). The June 18, 1785 edition of *The Lounger* warned that the dangerous "moral tendency" of the "mingled virtue and vice which is to be found in" novels was more extreme in the best novels "which are frequently put into the hands of youth, for imitation as well as amusement" than in "that common herd of Novels (the wretched offspring of circulating libraries)" (p. 80).

The tendency of the political pressures of the 1790s to throw these issues into stark relief highlighted for many observers both the strengths and the dangers of the Jacobin novels. But however unprecedented the spectacle of the French Revolution may have been, the debate about novels was not new. It had emerged out of an already existing set of questions about ideological complexities inherent in Britain's experience of commercial modernity. In the 1790s these debates were animated by an increasingly raw sense of their possible consequences – an issue which, ironically, received some of its most sustained and nuanced consideration within the pages of the Jacobin and anti-Jacobin novels themselves.

NOTES

1 Francis Place, *Autobiography of Francis Place* (1824), ed. Mary Thale (Cambridge: Cambridge University Press, 1972), p. 109.

2 Mary Wollstonecraft, *The Works of Mary Wollstonecraft*, ed. Janet Todd and Marilyn Butler (London: William Pickering, 1989), Vol. VII, p. 26.

3 Hannah More, *Strictures on the Modern System of Female Education* (London: T. Cadell Junior and W. Davies, 1799), Vol. I, pp. 169, 165.

4 Jane West, *A Tale of the Times*, ed. Gina Luria, Vol. III (New York and London: Garland Publishing, 1974), p. 388.

5 William Godwin, *Things As They Are; or, the Adventures of Caleb Williams*, ed. Maurice Hindle (London: Penguin Books, 1988), p. 3.

6 *British Critic: A New Review* 4, (1793), p. 71.

7 William Hazlitt, *Selected Writings*, ed. Duncan Wu, Vol. VII (London: Pickering and Chatto, 1998), p. 94.

8 Robert Bage, *Hermsprong*, ed. Pamel Perkins (Peterborough: Broadview, 2002), p. 164.

9 Mary Robinson, *A Letter to the Women of England* and *The Natural Daughter*, ed. Sharon M. Setzer (Peterborough: Broadview, 2003), pp. 165, 167, 165.

10 Charlotte Smith, *Desmond*, ed. Antje Blank and Janet Todd (Peterborough: Broadview, 2001), pp. 182, 183.

11 Charlotte Smith, *The Young Philosopher*, ed. Elizabeth Kraft (University Press of Kentucky, 1999), p. 197.

12 Edmund Burke, *Reflections on the Revolution in France* (1790), ed. Conor Cruise O'Brien (Harmondsworth: Penguin Books, 1968), p. 183.

13 George Walker, *The Vagabond*, ed. W. M. Verhoeven (Peterborough: Broadview, 2004), p. 65.

14 Elizabeth Hamilton, *Memoirs of Modern Philosophers*, ed. Claire Grogan (Peterborough: Broadview, 2004), p. 92.

15 Charles Lucas, *The Infernal Quixote*, ed. M. O. Grenby (Peterborough: Broadview, 2004), p. 84.

16 Frederick Hervey, *A New Friend on an Old Subject* (London: J. F. and C. Rivington, 1791), p. 27.

17 Mary Hays, *Memoirs of Emma Courtney*, ed. Eleanor Ty (Oxford University Press, 1996), p. 49.

18 Eliza Fenwick, *Secresy*, ed. Isobel Grundy (Peterborough: Broadview, 1994), p. 63.

19 Joseph Priestley, *The Proper Objects of Education* (London: Johnson, 1791), pp. 36–7.

20 Thomas Paine, "Letter Addressed to the Addressers on the Late Proclamation," *The Thomas Paine Reader*, ed. Michael Foot and Isaac Kramnick (Harmondsworth: Penguin Books, 1987), p. 368.

21 William Godwin, *Political and Philosophical Writings*, Vol. III, ed. Mark Philp (London: Pickering and Chatto, 1993), pp. 14–15.

22 Thomas Holcroft, *Hugh Trevor*, ed. Seamus Deane (Oxford: Oxford University Press, 1983), pp. 364, 352.

23 Charles Lloyd, *Edmund Oliver*, Vol. I (Oxford: Woodstock Books, 1990), p. 52.

24 Mary Wollstonecraft, *Wrongs of Woman or, Maria*, ed. Janet Todd (Harmondsworth: Penguin Books, 1991), p. 62.

25 Mary Hays, *Victim of Prejudice* (1799), ed. Eleanor Ty (Peterborough: Broadview, 1998), p. 37.

26 Samuel Johnson, *The Idler*, (1758–60), *The Works of Samuel Johnson, L.L.D.*, ed. Robert Lynam (London: George Cowie, 1825), Vol. II, pp. 629–30.
27 Isaac D'Israeli, *Literary Miscellanies: A New Edition* (London: Murray and Highley, 1801), pp. 6–7.
28 *The Lounger: A Periodical Paper. Published at Edinburgh, in the Years 1785 and 1786* (Edinburgh: W. Creech, 1786), p. 108.

9

JILL CAMPBELL

Women writers and the woman's novel: the trope of maternal transmission

When Catherine Morland of Austen's *Northanger Abbey* explains to her more experienced and rather arch new friend, Henry Tilney, that she is acquainted with the landscape of southern France only through the pages of Radcliffe's *Mysteries of Udolpho*, she hastens to add, "But you never read novels, I dare say?" Although she has herself become deeply absorbed in the reading of novels, and of Gothic novels in particular, Catherine anxiously acknowledges to Henry her awareness that such books "are not clever enough for you – gentlemen read better books." Henry quickly corrects Catherine's assumption; but Catherine's generalization, deprecating both to women and to novels, is founded not only on an earlier conversational rebuff by the rude John Thorpe but also on a commonplace of eighteenth-century culture: novel-reading is for women.[1] The first literary history of the genre, published in 1785 by a woman novelist, Clara Reeve, reflects this commonplace, presenting its history of "the progress of romance" and of its offspring, the novel, through a debate between a female defender, Euphrasia, and a male opponent, Hortensius, who explains that it is in fact for women's sake that he wishes to ban such books: members of the female sex "are most concerned in my remonstrance for they read more of these books than ours, and consequently are most hurt by them."[2] From Hortensius's point of view, the phrase "the woman's novel" is redundant, with that redundancy convey-ing a special suitability and therefore susceptibility and therefore danger.

Hortensius's apprehension of novels' special dangers for female readers was nothing new in 1785: in 1712, Addison and Steele had warned women against consuming "Romances, Chocolate, and the like Inflamers"; in 1766, when James Fordyce declared in his *Sermons for Young Women* that "we consider the general run of Novels as utterly unfit for you ... They paint scenes of pleasure and passion altogether improper for you to behold, even with the mind's eye," he was summarizing a familiar view.[3] As this pair of brief quotations makes evident, from the time of the novel's emergence in England, moral monitors particularly feared its potential to rouse women's sensual appetites, often likening women's novel-reading to the ingestion of rich foods or stimulating drinks and warning that it was likely to incite sexual desires.[4]

These longstanding terms of attack, however, took on new resonances and applications in the Romantic period. Beginning in the middle of the eighteenth century and coming to a height in the 1760s and 1770s, the cult of sensibility (and its close cousin, sentimentalism) made the experience of strong feelings for others' suffering a defining human event, and the susceptibility to such feelings a standard of human value and distinction. As G. J. Barker-Benfield, Ann Jessie Van Sant, and others have chronicled, this movement was always ambivalent, calling attention to the potential dangers as well as the transcendent selflessness of such empathic responses; evoking their overlap with feelings of a sexual kind; and treating the novel as a literary form that could manipulate such susceptibilities to particularly noble or dire effect. By the 1790s, this broad cultural movement had become the backdrop for topics of urgent, overtly political debate: both what has been called the feminist controversy of 1788 to 1810 (contesting women's claims to equality and the proper nature of their education) and the fierce struggle between Jacobins and anti-Jacobins about the 1789 revolution in France hinged to a surprising extent on questions of feeling, and even, at times, specifically on the moral status of women's feeling responses to novel-reading.[5] At the same time, women themselves had become increasingly prominent in this period as the creators as well as consumers of popular novels.[6]

In fact, a century earlier, women writers had in many ways pioneered the novel form in England. In the late seventeenth and early eighteenth centuries, Aphra Behn, Delariviere Manley, Eliza Haywood, and other women experimented with prose fiction forms that are now recognized as important predecessors to those works of Daniel Defoe, Samuel Richardson, and Henry Fielding that were long taken to be the first English novels. By the turn of the nineteenth century, however, as Ina Ferris has shown, reviewers had already begun to establish a canon of the English novel that erased its origins among largely women writers, so that the contemporary prominence of women novelists was understood – and often decried – as a new development.[7] Some of the women novelists of the late eighteenth and early nineteenth centuries built on the novelistic tradition established by Richardson's *Pamela* (1740), accepting his purportedly moral redefinition of the novel form as a structurally unified narrative of courtship and of virtue's triumph, as opposed to the episodic tales of amorous intrigue typically offered by Behn, Manley, and Haywood. Ian Watt's vastly influential account of "the rise of the novel" posed Jane Austen as the first major woman novelist in

English, and as the dialectic inheritor of two male mid-eighteenth-century novelists, Richardson and Fielding.[8]

More recent critics, such as Marilyn Butler and Claudia L. Johnson, have debated the extent to which Austen's domestic, seemingly apolitical novels implicitly engage in the controversies of her own time about women's place and about revolution and national governance that I have mentioned. Other women novelists of the period indisputably took on those debates, adapting the novel form to explore questions of men's superior rights and powers and the proper basis of human social and political relations in reason or in feeling. All of these novels, whether apparently conservative novels of court-ship and social manners or polemical novels of social critique, focus largely on "women's issues" of sexuality and marriage; they also characteristically link those issues to questions about representation, communication, and instruction. These two seemingly disparate areas come together in an insis-tent concern with reproduction, in its various senses, and with the question of what it takes, and what it means, to conceive of individual women as parts of a unified body of "women." Critiques of the novel form in the period, although written from a range of viewpoints, hone in alike on the faulty ways that novels do or do not go about constituting a collectivity of women – or even an entity so homogenous, for better or worse, as to warrant the singular collective noun, "Woman" – out of their depictions of individual imaginary women.

For moralists warning against women's novel-reading, the form danger-ously entails mechanisms of automatic replication and recapitulation: the fascinated woman reading of the seduction and fall of a fictitious female character is drawn inexorably to repeat the fate of that character in her own real life. In *Letters for Literary Ladies* (1795), Maria Edgeworth portrayed the dire consequences of this kind of passive reading: although Julia's pru-dent friend warns her against the dangers of novel-reading, Julia defends her absorption in the feelings aroused by tales of passion and eventually dies in disgrace, having engaged in an adulterous affair.[9] Although Edgeworth would herself later publish a number of what we call novels, she continued to raise grave doubts about novels' effects from a didacticist's point of view; she insisted on terming her *Belinda* (1800), for instance, a "moral tale" rather than a novel and depicted within it (in the subplot involving Virginia) the imaginative dangers for women of passively receptive reading, whether of novels or of romances. Like that of other women novelists considered here, Edgeworth's work as a writer was not confined to the genre of the novel: she was particularly renowned in her own time for her writings on education and for her many didactic tales for children. Writing about and for young people, Edgeworth emphasized again and again that narrative's influence must be used to persuade readers of their power to shape their own lives through moral actions, rather than to suggest the inexorability of certain patterns. In one of her children's tales, for instance, a kindly mentor assures a little boy that, although he is "the son of a man of infamous character," he may through good behavior "make himself whatever he pleased."[10] A certain kind of novel reading, Edgeworth warns, surrenders that power, submerging the individual woman's unfinished story in the foreclosed generic fate of "Woman."

Although she too published a collection of didactic tales for young people, Mary Wollstonecraft is best remembered for her remarkable works of social and political critique, *Vindication of the Rights of Men* (1790) and *Vindication of the Rights of Woman* (1792). She is also the author of one novella and a longer, more ambitious novel left unfinished at her death. In the former, as Edgeworth did in *Belinda*, Wollstonecraft resisted the generic categorization of her work as a novel, pointedly titling it *Mary, A Fiction* (1788). She also included in *Mary* a derisive portrait of the novel-reading woman in the character of her protagonist's mother, who allows her eyes to "r[u]n over those most delightful substitutes for bodily dissipation, novels," in intervals between gazing at herself in the mirror while her hair is dressed, and whose neglect of her daughter lays the early basis for Mary's tragic end. Mary's mother not only neglects her real maternal relationship as she reads about fictional characters but also reads only to indulge her appetite for love-scenes that would have "contaminated" her mind and potentially led her into adultery, had she in fact read with any mental attention.[11] The title of Wollstonecraft's second work of fiction proclaimed her intention to use narrative as a means to address women's situation in the real world rather than to provide a diversionary and "dissipating" escape: *The Wrongs of Woman: Or, Maria. A Fragment* (1798) harks back bitterly to the key phrase – "the rights of woman" – in the title of Wollstonecraft's radical analysis of those customs of English society that doom women to trivial and useless lives.

In the draft of her preface to *The Wrongs of Woman*, published by her husband, William Godwin, after her death, Wollstonecraft explained that her "main object" in composing it was "the desire of exhibiting the misery and oppression, peculiar to women, that arise out of the partial laws and customs of society." Her narrative of the fictional Maria, however engagingly novelistic, is intended to serve a representative and polemical function: Wollstonecraft declares that "it ought rather to be considered, as of woman, than of an individual."[12] As Gary Kelly puts it, Wollstonecraft's purpose in *The Wrongs of Woman* was "to fictionalize the arguments of *A Vindication of the Rights of Woman*."[13] Similarly, in discussing *The Victim of Prejudice* (1799), the second novel of Mary Hays (a friend of Wollstonecraft and Godwin as well as of Southey and Coleridge), critics describe the novel as an effort to "illustrate," "dramatize," or "exhibit" the conditions in which English women in general suffered, which Hays had vehemently condemned in her *Appeal to the Men of Great Britain in Behalf of Women* (1798), through the compelling story of a fictional individual. Between the time Wollstonecraft composed her first prose fiction narrative in 1788 and her second work of fiction ten years later, English Jacobin novelists, including Godwin, Thomas Holcroft, Robert Bage, Elizabeth Inchbald, and Hays herself in *Emma Courtney* (1796), had energetically experimented with political uses of the novel form. In their novels, the psychological interest and emotional power of the stories of individual characters are coordinated with the objective of making a general case – of conveying the force of prevailing general circumstances, and the oppression and suffering of a collectively defined group. Patricia Meyer Spacks argues that this coordination is rarely successful. "Fiction and political argument are not coterminous ... A novel may show ... the evil of political oppression, but the effects of such oppression on imagined individual persons will necessarily focus a reader's interest more insistently than generalized conclusions can do. . . The eighteenth-century novel, with its stress on the individual, does not readily lend itself to political purpose."[14]

How might a novel bridge the gap between the individual experience related in its fictional narrative and the depiction of general wrongs to a social group such as "woman"? In the two overtly political novels that we will consider below, *The Wrongs of Woman* and *The Victim of Prejudice*, Wollstonecraft and Hays both address the potential disjunction observed by Spacks by structuring their works around the inexorable repetition of individual women's experiences across two generations. The trope of generational transmission and recapitulation also appears in many novels of the period with no interest in the systemic analysis and argument that motivate Wollstonecraft and Hays. Edgeworth uses that trope to warn the reader of the dangers of passively receptive reading and of imitative behavior, while insisting that individual moral exertion can promise real change. More pessimistically, Sophia Lee's pseudo-historical *The Recess; or, A Tale of Other Times* (1783–5), which traces the tragic life-courses of the twin daughters and grand-daughter of Mary, Queen of Scots, uses a generational structure to convey the inexorability of historical forces beyond the individual's ken. The notion of an inheritance of experience from generation to generation, especially from mother to daughter – and especially as transmitted in the form of a text penned by a dead or missing mother – is a powerful and pervasive one in the late eighteenth-century and Romantic-era novel.[15] In the hands of

Wollstonecraft and Hays, mother–daughter plots become a means to extend the implications of novelistic narrative beyond the individual case, making it the bearer of rational, social, or political critique; at the same time, the mother–daughter relationship in their novels is the site of intense, irrational, even uncanny emotional power.

Briefly considering novels by several women writers from the period – Burney, Inchbald, Wollstonecraft, Hays, Austen, and Shelley – this chapter will use a focus on mother–daughter plots to explore the range of ways in which some novels by women writers merit the appellation "the woman's novel" in a more specific sense than the one evoked at this chapter's opening. In the great inaugural work of women's literary history, *A Room of One's Own* (1929), Virginia Woolf hailed women writers of the past as the "foremothers" of women readers and writers of the present; feminist literary criticism has worked with the resonances and the limitations of Woolf's metaphor ever since.[16] The survey below can offer neither a full-blown investigation of the metaphorical function of one woman writer as "mother" to another outside the narratives of novels, as those novels circulate among readers, nor a general account of the psychological character or thematic importance of mother–daughter relations within novels' narratives. Rather, we will trace suggestive intersections between the two, as novels by women frequently include books, memoirs, or letters that "mother" women within their narratives, for better and for worse. Focusing on this recurrent formal device provides one way to think about the categories of the woman writer and of the woman reader, and of texts especially intended for women, as figured within novels themselves. In the final example we will consider, Shelley's *Frankenstein* (1818), it is not a daughter but a male and uniquely motherless monster who finds in books a painfully ambivalent parenting. The experience Shelley imagined for her creature – encountering the story of his horrific origins in a manuscript journal – is closely modeled, however, on the treatment of a daughter's textual inheritance both in Hays's *The Victim of Prejudice* and in *The Wrongs of Woman*, by Shelley's own mother. The latter novel, of course, was part of the body of words that offered the only means for the young Mary Wollstonecraft Godwin to know the mother who had died giving birth to her.

At the close of Wollstonecraft's didactic fiction for girls, *Original Stories from Real Life* (1788), Mrs. Mason, the near relation "of tenderness and discernment" who has undertaken the tuition of two ill-educated and motherless girls, bids the girls farewell, urging them not to forget the lessons they have learned in their months of conversing with her. Trembling with concern for their future good, Mrs. Mason does not, however, leave the girls entirely on their own: as she parts with her charges, she places in their hands a "last present," "a book, in which I have written the subjects that we have discussed." "Recur frequently to it," she urges them, "for the stories illustrating the instruction it contains, you will not feel in such a great degree the want of my personal advice."[17] The reader learns, then, as *Original Stories* comes to a close, that what she has been reading should be imagined as a version of a manuscript book prepared by the wise educator for the girls who have flourished and been enlightened in her personal care: the didactic instruction offered in the print text of the book the reader holds is an extension of the loving but stern instruction provided by a present human individual, which has first been transcribed to take the woman's place in her absence.[18]

The idea of a book as a surrogate for a human instructor or parent is a frequent feature of the didactic literature of the eighteenth century and Romantic period, although that idea is not often folded so explicitly into the work's narrative itself: it is implied by the title of Edgeworth's influential volume of tales, *The Parent's Assistant* (1800), and it undergirds the dialogue and illustrations of Anna Laetitia Barbauld's immensely popular *Lessons for Children* (1778–88), which opens with a picture of a mother and with her words addressing her child, as if the book addresses its young reader through her person. Wollstonecraft's works, however, give special force to the linkage of books and the emotional claims of close human contact. The narrator of *The Wrongs of Woman*, describing her imprisoned protagonist's eager anticipation of the return of an unkind and uncouth attendant, comments, "It is so cheering to see a human face" but the protagonist is soon seeking that cheer in books rather than faces, poring over books loaned to her through an intermediary by another prisoner, scanning them with particularly anxious longing for the marks of his marginalia, and regarding them as "a mine of treasure" (pp. 79–86). The channeling of Maria's yearning for human connection into a desperate appetite for books has an uncertain and destabilizing effect in the narrative, however, rather than an effectively didactic one. The mediation through reading of mother–daughter bonds, in particular, takes a number of forms in the novels of the period, with a range of consoling, redemptive, instructive, diversionary, and dangerous effects.

The title character of *Evelina*, Frances Burney's 1778 novel of courtship and social manners, famously brings the last letter of her mother to her first meeting with her father, who, having denied his secret marriage to Evelina's mother, has left in doubt Evelina's legitimacy, her social standing, and even her proper name. Writing on her deathbed, Caroline Belmont composed her letter "in behalf of the child, who, if it survives its mother, will hereafter be the bearer of this letter" – its bearer, but not its addressee. It was "the feelings of a mother, a mother agonizing for the fate of her child," that gave the dying

Caroline Belmont the courage and determination to write, but her last words are addressed not to that child but rather to the man who must belatedly own his marriage and "receive as [his] lawful successor the child who will present [him] this [her] dying request" in order to earn Caroline's posthumous forgiveness.[19] Indeed, Evelina has never read the letter that constitutes her one legacy from her mother; until her father opens it, it "has never been unsealed" (III, xix, p. 385).[20] Instead, Evelina, the carrier of her mother's letter, is herself another version of it: the letter remains unopened until Evelina's second meeting with her father because in the first he is overwhelmed to the point of near madness by Evelina's appearance as a living "image" of the dead Caroline. Racked with remorse at the sight of Evelina's face, "the representative of the most injured of women" and the "dear resemblance of thy murdered mother," Sir John oscillates between impulses to embrace her as the vehicle of his atonement and to send her away angrily in a repetition of his injustice to her mother (III.xix, pp. 384–5; III.xvii, p. 372).

Evelina's mother had fearfully anticipated the latter response as she penned her letter, awaiting death: "Should'st thou, in the features of this deserted innocent, trace the resemblance of the wretched Caroline, – should its face bear the marks of its birth, and revive in thy memory the image of its mother, wilt thou not, Belmont, wilt thou not therefore renounce it?" (III.xiii, p. 339). Evelina briefly seems in danger of meeting this fate, but then her uncanny resemblance to her mother, coordinated with the delivery of the mother's letter, becomes the means of her father's repentance, forgiveness, and atonement: expressing the wish that her father could "but read [her] heart" as well as her face, Evelina delivers her mother's letter; and the double act of reading that follows, as Sir John refers back and forth between the figure of his kneeling daughter and the text of his wife's letter, leads to his full embrace of his daughter (III.xvii, pp. 372–3; III.xix, p. 384). Appropriately in a novel centered on a variety of fathers – biological, adoptive, and spiritual, or paternalistically spousal – Evelina's relation to her mother insures the happy outcome of her story only through an act of reading by her father in which Evelina herself plays a passive role.

The more fully developed two-generational structure of Elizabeth Inchbald's *A Simple Story* (1791) also revolves around a deathbed letter written to a father by an anguished mother on behalf of her child. In this case, the letter cannot demand justice, as Caroline Belmont's does, but instead begs for mercy for the child left behind: the former Miss Milner of the novel's first half, married at the end of Volume II to Lord Elmwood, has committed adultery before Volume III opens and dies in a state of penance in a remote and austere retreat. The now "implacabl[y] rigor[ous]" Elmwood accepts his wife's claim on him from beyond the grave but only "in the strictest sense of the word": he agrees to receive their daughter, Matilda, into his household on the condition that he never see or hear her. The moment that his daughter is seen or heard, he warns, "my compliance to her mother's supplication ceases, and I abandon her once more."[21] Installed in one of her father's "magnificent seats" but required to remain out of his sight, Matilda thus leads an isolated, anxious, and intensely inhibited existence, inhabiting the spaces of her parents' marriage, even trapped within those spaces as the product of their unhappy story, but forced to hide herself at all times from her father's direct observation. In close proximity with her father but required, at all costs, never to appear before him, Matilda seeks indirect contact with him by touching the furniture and objects he has touched, looking particularly "with the most curious attention into those books that were laid upon his reading desk" (III.x, pp. 229–30). Reciprocally, the first hint of an opening in the heart of the implacable Elmwood comes as he begins indirectly to recommend books for Matilda, with selections painstakingly suggested to her attendant, "as the most cautious preceptor culls for his pupil, or a fond father for his darling child" (III.xiv, pp. 254–5). Matilda considers the volumes thus selected "almost like presents from her father," but the peculiar "as" of Inchbald's formulation – describing the care of Elmwood for his daughter as *like* that of a father – insists on the thwarting mediation of their relation through books as well as through the unforgiven guilt of Matilda's mother. As a result, Matilda and her father's movement towards reconciliation by the close of *A Simple Story* is circuitous, vexed, and incomplete. Nonetheless, although Inchbald, as a Jacobin, would also employ a two-generational plot in *Nature and Art* (1796) to offer a powerful critique of the corrupting force of social custom, her *Simple Story* retains the basic plot trajectory of the courtship novel, twice repeated.

Perhaps the most radical feature of Wollstonecraft's first work of prose fiction, *Mary* (1788), is its absolute refusal of the literary and social convention of marriage as the essential ingredient of a comic resolution. As the novel concludes, its protagonist, who has married a man she does not love to please her dying mother, looks towards her own death as a release from those embraces that make her wish "the earth would open and swallow her": "In moments of solitary sadness, a gleam of joy would dart across her mind – She thought she was hastening to that world *where there is neither marrying, nor giving in marriage*" (pp. 14–15, 67–8). In *The Wrongs of Woman*, Wollstonecraft offers a much more fully developed and systematic critique of marriage in fictional form.

The Wrongs of Woman opens with the dramatic revelation that Maria has been imprisoned in a madhouse by her own husband, who angles to extract from his wife control over the fortune that her uncle has bequeathed to their infant child; this central plot scenario provides both the imagery and the main analytic focus of Wollstonecraft's general critique of a woman's position in marriage. Throughout the novel, the imagery of imprisonment – and relatedly, of slavery – is used metaphorically to express all women's loss of freedom in marriage: in a moment of despair, Maria wonders why she exerts herself to plot an escape, for "Was not the world a vast prison, and women born slaves?"; even before her imprisonment, she has concluded that "Marriage had bastilled me for life" (pp. 79, 154–5).[22] The control over property in marriage granted to men by English law, which forms the crux of the struggle between Maria and her husband and which leads to her imprisonment, is at the center of Wollstonecraft's searing critique. This control, as Maria bitterly complains, allows a married woman "nothing she can call her own," making a woman herself "as much a man's property as his horse, or his ass" (p. 158).

Wollstonecraft effectively uses a web of subplots to widen out her treatment of marriage in English society from the particular melodramatic situation of her protagonist: in the course of her trials, Maria comes into contact with women from a range of economic classes who share the oppression attendant upon their sex. Most notably, Maria's fate becomes intertwined with that of Jemima, her illegitimate, working-class prison attendant; but she also encounters a series of minor characters, including several landladies, suffering in marriages to husbands who abuse them and who appropriate all of their hard-earned savings. Maria herself formulates the generalizations about women's situation that Wollstonecraft's plot juxtapositions suggest, and she applies those generalizations with horror to the prospects of her own infant child, a daughter: "Thinking of Jemima's peculiar fate and her own, she was led to consider the oppressed state of women, and to lament that she had given birth to a daughter" (p. 120). Most horrifically, because of her husband's tyranny and Maria's lack of legal recourse as a woman, this girl-child had been removed from Maria's care – torn forcibly from her arms and breast – at the age of four months; and the worst "agony" caused by Maria's imprisonment is that it entails a forced separation from her child, whose fate is unknown to her. Haunted nearly to the point of madness by her infant's image but prevented from providing her in the flesh with a mother's care, Maria decides to write down the events of her past life as well as "the sentiments that experience, and more matured reason, would naturally suggest" in the hopes that "they might perhaps instruct her daughter, and shield her from the misery, the tyranny, her mother knew not how to avoid" (p. 82). The memoirs Maria composes are addressed to her daughter and motivated by a fervent desire to care for, educate, and protect her; that desire can be pursued in no other, more immediate way because of Maria's unnatural separation from her child by an abusive husband and an unjust society.

As Susan C. Greenfield observes, the memoirs that Maria therefore creates for her daughter's eyes are "a poor substitute for maternal connection."[23] Indeed, although the reader of *The Wrongs of Woman* gains access to those first-person memoirs in the novel's seventh chapter, and they make up about one-half of Wollstonecraft's novel, there is no indication of any likelihood that Maria's daughter will ever read them. In fact, though we learn early on of Maria's work composing them, the memoirs are not presented to us as a text until Maria learns of her daughter's at least apparent death. We read Maria's memoirs, then, "over the shoulder" not of their addressee and intended reader, Maria's unnamed daughter, but of a male fellow-prisoner, Henry Darnford, who asks to read the memoirs while Maria grieves for her child. The text of *The Wrongs of Woman*, composed during her pregnancy with the future Mary Shelley, was left incomplete at Wollstonecraft's death in childbed; and manuscript notes suggest several alternative endings to its narrative. In the most extended draft fragment, a pregnant and despairing Maria swallows laudanum to take her own life, only to find that the incidents of her past life, the substance of her written memoirs, now return involuntarily in a nightmarish sequence of rapid memories – interrupted by "a new vision" of Jemima entering with a little child, who has not died but rather been hidden by Maria's husband and brother. Met by this vision, Maria decides after an "agonizing struggle of her soul" to "live for my child!" – a mother in the anguished flesh, though of a child only tentatively asserted as living and real (pp. 201–3).[24]

While Maria of *The Wrongs of Woman* is haunted by phantasmagoric images of her lost child, Mary, the protagonist of Mary Hays's *The Victim of Prejudice* (1799), is haunted by "the visionary form of [her] wretched mother," who has been seduced, abandoned, exploited by a series of men, barred from re-entry to society, and ultimately executed for murder.[25] Like Burney's *Evelina*, the Mary of *The Victim of Prejudice* has been raised by a wise and benevolent male guardian in ignorance of the circumstances of her birth; those circumstances, however, when they come out, are far more sordid than those of Evelina's. Mary's mother (also named Mary) has in fact erred, although it is the unscrupulousness of male appetites, the sexual double standard, and the prejudices of society that have prevented her from recovering her lost way; when the daughter's guardian reveals her mother's story, he addresses her as the "child of infamy and calamity!" (p. 69). *The Victim of Prejudice* takes the form of a first-person narrative written by the daughter in a two-generational story of women's ruination by social forces, but that narrative contains a Chinese-box structure which holds, at its center, the brief but entirely formative memoirs of her long-dead mother.

Those memoirs were written in prison, as Mary's mother calmly awaited her execution. They thus follow in the tradition of the criminal autobiography that had inspired earlier novelists such as Defoe; but they take the specific form of a letter to Mr. Raymond, a former admirer and friend, with the purpose not only of pouring out the mother's story of guilt and penance but, most important, of pleading that he undertake the care and proper education of the child she will leave behind (p. 69). Mary's mother worries about the effects on her child of eventually reading these memoirs: "Why should I stain the youthful purity of my unfortunate offspring, into whose hands these sheets may hereafter fall, with the delineation of scenes remembered with soul-sickening abhorrence?" (p. 66). And indeed, Mr. Raymond withholds them, and any knowledge of her mother's story, from the girl whom he raises in the ways of the utmost virtue, fortitude, and mental rigor. When Mary falls in love with a young man whose haughty family will surely scorn her on the basis of her parentage, however, Mr. Raymond feels compelled to reveal her mother's story to her, enclosing it in a letter retailing his own life-story and relations with Mary's mother to make up what Mary refers to repeatedly as a "fatal packet," a "fatal narrative" (pp. 73, 71). Later her own history of abuse will in turn become a "fatal tale" (p. 140). For although Mr. Raymond on his deathbed treats Mary's mother's memoirs as a morally instructive legacy of great value (p. 102), and although a delirious Mary is later haunted by visions of her mother, "all pallid and ghastly, with clasped hands, streaming eyes, and agonizing earnestness, [seeming] to urge me to take example from her fate!" (p. 123), Hays's novel ultimately insists on the inexorability of a pattern, enforced by social prejudice and injustice, of generational recapitulation.

The sense in which Mary the daughter may "take example" from the story of her mother proves only to be that of psychological identification and literal re-enactment. Despite her own extraordinary education in virtue and mental vigor, and despite the powerful monitory precedent of her mother's mistakes, Mary is destined ultimately to repeat the sensational and tragically doomed life of that mother. Unlike her mother, she never falters in the ways of virtue; and unlike her mother, she has an intellectual grasp of the forces that surround her. Such differences, however, do not avert Mary's fate as the victim of sexual exploitation, of the exclusion of women from economic opportunities, and of social prejudice: like her mother, Mary the second is destined to compose her own memoirs in the confinement of a prison cell. Eerily, a brief introduction that precedes Mary's narrative directly addresses the novel's reader herself as the next "victim of despotism, oppression, or error, and successor to its present devoted inhabitant" – that is, as the next "tenant" of the dungeon cell in which the sheets of the memoir have been written and will be left "when the hand that wrote them moulders in the dust, and the spirit that dictated ceases to throb with indignant agony" (p. 3). Social forces are not altered by the recognitions afforded by either direct or vicarious experience; it is possible, Hays even seems to suggest, that our absorption in stories of other women's inexorable ruination only seals our fate.

In novels written around the same time as Wollstonecraft's and Hays's, but with a very different touch and tone, Jane Austen seems to warn the reader away from the magnetic power of collective identification with the plight of women, or "Woman." In *Sense and Sensibility* (composed *c.* 1797; revised and published 1811), the name of Marianne, the representative of that sensibility which forms half of the title's pairing, sounds a variation on the names of Wollstonecraft's Mary and Maria and of Hays's two Mary's; like each of them, Marianne is dangerously dominated by feeling – and more specifically, by the force of a mother–daughter bond and by the influence of books. In the course of the experiences related in *Sense and Sensibility*, Marianne must learn not to be, like her own mother and like Wollstonecraft's Mary, "in love with misery," and not to use shared books and music to dwell on lost intimacies with a beloved person.[26] Most important, perhaps, she learns indirectly from the story of sexual weakness, infamy, and ruin of Colonel Brandon's first love, Eliza, and its repetition in the story of her daughter, the second Eliza, who has been seduced by Marianne's own beloved Willoughby (II.9, pp. 196–8). Marianne stands blessedly outside the line of generational recapitulation constituted by the two Elizas, and their story comes to her safely, as transmitted orally by Brandon to Marianne's sister and thence to her. The closest thing to written memoirs that circulates in *Sense and Sensibility* is Marianne's own unguarded and imprudent correspondence with Willoughby, which Willoughby returns to her when he jilts her for the wealthier Miss Grey; the story of dangerous feelings these letters contain thus travels in a painful but ultimately harmless loop, as the letters return to their writer to be wept over and seen in a new light, but then put aside. In Austen's *Northanger Abbey* (drafted 1798–1803; published 1817), Catherine Morland, having unreflectingly internalized what she has encountered in novels, searches the Tilneys' abbey home with eager anxiety for the memoirs of her friends' dead mother – only to be painfully chastised that she has been wrongly directing her investigation. Instead, as Henry urges her, she should be looking within, as Marianne eventually learns to do: a woman's "investigation" is rightly turned to her own individual feelings, mind, and conduct (II.9–10, pp. 179–94).

A growing body of critical work traces aspects of Mary Shelley's *Frankenstein* (1818) – a strikingly unprecedented work in many ways – to the writings of her parents, William Godwin and Mary Wollstonecraft, and of their friends, such as Mary Hays.[27] The character who tells his own story at the center of the Chinese-box structure that forms this novel is neither a mother nor a daughter, but a male creature whose distinction and great deprivation is to be without any parents at all. He does have a creator, however; and readers have long recognized the mirroring relation between the identities of the creature and his creator, Victor Frankenstein. At the same time, mothers haunt the interlocking stories of Frankenstein and his creature in a number of disturbing ways: fleeing in horror from the scene of the creature's long-awaited animation, Frankenstein falls into a restless sleep, in which he dreams of encountering his beloved Elizabeth, only to find her transformed into the corpse of his mother at the touch of his kiss; his mother has in fact died as a result of the maternal care she provided Elizabeth when she was suffering with scarlet fever; and her maternal image, in the form of a miniature portrait, itself circulates like a fatal contagion in the episode involving Justine's false condemnation for murder. Justine's imprisonment and calm anticipation of her execution for murder recall those of Mary's mother in *The Victim of Prejudice*; while Mary's mother felt the circumstances of her life and crimes made her sentence an injustice, Justine's verdict is simply wrong, as it results from the evidence of Mrs. Frankenstein's portrait planted in her pocket by the vengeful and motherless creature. In both cases, the imposition of masculine law and the circulation of a mother's story or image make a fatal combination with potential to spread destruction.

The creature has no parents, but he does become (through an implausible but essential series of turns of plot) a reader, and he uses his hard-won literacy to try to make sense of his own obscure and anomalous origins. "No father had watched my infant days, no mother had blessed me with smiles and caresses ... What was I? The question again recurred, to be answered only with groans" (II.5, p. 149). The parentless and friendless creature learns to read almost literally over the shoulder of a young woman, Safie, in the cottage that he peers into, where she has joined her French friends and is instructed in "the science of letters" (II.5, pp. 146–7).[28] The creature then happens upon a leather portmanteau that contains some books, including *Paradise Lost*, a volume of *Plutarch's Lives*, and *The Sorrows of Werther*; and as he reads, he "applie[s] much personally to [his] own feelings and condition" – still left wondering "Who was I? What was I? Whence did I come?" *Paradise Lost* provides the creature with some possible versions of himself: he likens himself to the parentless Adam; but then also to Satan. It is another sort of reading material – a manuscript of more peculiar personal interest to himself – that confirms for him, finally, his "accursed origins" and outcast state. Having discovered some papers in the pocket of the dress he took with him from Victor's laboratory, he now can decipher them as his creator's "journal of the four months that preceded my creation." Like the unnamed and possibly already dead daughter of Wollstonecraft's Maria, were she ever to read her mother's memoirs; or like Hays's Mary, who does; the creature discovers from his creator's journal that his own life emerged from horror: in the journal, he laments, "every thing is related ... which bears reference to my accursed origin; the whole detail of that series of disgusting circumstances which produced it is set in view" (II.7, pp. 154–8).

Maria's daughter and Mary's Mary were not created through Promethean manipulation of body parts garnered from crypts, but rather conceived by sexual acts between a man and a woman. What their mothers' memoirs reveal is not only how horrifying that act was to them, but also how unnatural its circumstances were: how their own lives, and the very fact of their daughters' physical beings, have been shaped by a monstrous assemblage of socially constructed customs and laws. And yet those mothers yearn to communicate with their beloved offspring – to educate them, to care for them even through a body of words – in a way that Shelley's creature could only envy. Shelley's novel joins a tradition of women's novels that explore the power of bonds forged by reading, and that liken those bonds to the life-giving and constraining bonds of mother and child.

NOTES

1 Jane Austen, *Northanger Abbey*, ed. Marilyn Butler (New York: Penguin Books, 2003), pp. 102–3 (Vol. I, ch. 14).
2 Clara Reeve, *The Progress of Romance, and The History of Charoba, Queen of Aegypt*, with a bibliographical note by Esther M. McGill, Vol. II (New York: The Facsimile Text Society, 1930), pp. 80–1.
3 *Spectator* 365 (April 29, 1712) and Fordyce, Sermon IV, both quoted in Sabine Augustin, *Eighteenth-Century Female Voices: Education and the Novel* (New York: Peter Lang, 2005), pp. 26, 12.
4 For a particularly interesting account of this tradition of anti-novel discourse, see Ina Ferris, *The Achievement of Literary Authority: Gender, History and the Waverley Novels* (Ithaca: Cornell University Press, 1991), pp. 32–59.
5 On these connections, see especially Claudia L. Johnson, *Equivocal Beings: Politics, Gender, and Sentimentality in the 1790s: Wollstonecraft, Radcliffe, Burney, Austen* (Chicago: University of Chicago Press, 1995).
6 For a statistical account of the sharp rise in the production of novels by women at the end of the eighteenth century, see Cheryl Turner, *Living by the Pen: Women Writers in the Eighteenth Century* (New York: Routledge, 1992).
7 Ferris, *Achievement of Literary Authority*, pp. 71–8. See also William B. Warner's *Licensing Entertainment: The Elevation of Novel Reading in Britain, 1684–1750* (Berkeley: University of California Press, 1998), for a stimulating argument about

male novelists' often-concealed incorporation of aspects of the more disreputable writings of the women novelists they succeeded and displaced.

8 Ian Watt, *The Rise of the Novel: Studies in Defoe, Richardson, and Fielding* (Berkeley: University of California Press, 1957), pp. 296–9.

9 *Letters of Julia and Caroline* in *Letters for Literary Ladies* (facsimile edition (New York: Garland Publishing, 1974)); see especially pp. 5–7 and 24–5.

10 "The False Key," in *The Parent's Assistant* (New York: Routledge & Co., 1857; first published 1800), p. 49.

11 *Mary, A Fiction*, in *Mary, A Fiction*, and *The Wrongs of Woman*, ed. Gary Kelly (New York: Oxford, 1976), pp. 2–3.

12 Author's Preface to *The Wrongs of Woman*, p. 73.

13 Introduction, *Mary, A Fiction*, and *The Wrongs of Woman*, p. xvi.

14 *Novel Beginnings: Experiments in Eighteenth-Century English Fiction* (New Haven: Yale University Press, 2006), pp. 230, 253.

15 Within her study of the epistolary subgenre of "novels of women's correspondence," which may include letters between friends, between mother and daughter, or between a mother-substitute and a young woman, April Alliston considers "the problematic relation between the transmission of example and the transmission of inheritance from mother to daughter, which generated the plots of so many eighteenth-century novels in both France and England"; she is interested in the possibilities that some novels offer for daughters "to read a mother's letter *across* the lines of descent, rather than being compelled to repeat her unhappy narrative" (*Virtue's Faults: Corrrespondences in Eighteenth-Century British and French Women's Fiction* (Stanford, Calif.: Stanford University Press, 1996), pp. 18, 34, 9–10).

16 *A Room of One's Own* (New York: Harcourt, 1989). As an instance of this prevailing metaphor among classic studies of novels by women, note the title of Dale Spender's *Mothers of the Novel: 100 Good Women Writers Before Jane Austen* (New York: Routledge/Methuen, 1986). Charlotte Sussman's "Daughter of the Revolution: Mary Shelley in Our Times," *JEMCS* 4 (2004), pp. 158–86, observes a recent turn towards examining Shelley's works as, most significantly, those of a daughter rather than as those of a mother; she argues that this shift reflects the evolving state of feminist studies (p. 180).

17 *Original Stories from Real Life; with Conversations Calculated to Regulate the Affections and Form the Mind to Truth and Goodness*, 3rd edn. (1796), in *The Works of Mary Wollstonecraft*, ed. Janet Todd and Marilyn Butler, Vol. IV (New York: New York University Press, 1989), pp. 449–50.

18 In Chapter 10 in this volume, Katie Trumpener notes a fascinating extension of the linkage Wollstonecraft thus creates among fictional characters, books, and instructive relationships between individual people: in her own didactic writing for children as an adult, the girl for whom Wollstonecraft had served as a governess, Margaret King Moore, took on the pen-name of "Mrs. Mason" in tribute to Wollstonecraft's influence.

19 Frances Burney, *Evelina, or, The History of a Young Lady's Entrance into the World*, ed. Edward A. Bloom (New York: Oxford University Press, 1968), Vol. III, Letter xiii, pp. 338–9. Citations will hereafter be given by volume and letter number, and by page.

20 The reader of the novel, however, has been presented with and read the text of Caroline's letter some thirty-five pages and six letters before Evelina's father

breaks its seal. Note also that in 1767 the young Frances Burney wrote and then destroyed a novel entitled *The History of Caroline Evelyn* – in some sense a "mother" text to her first published novel, *Evelina*.

21 Elizabeth Inchbald, *A Simple Story*, ed. Pamela Clemit (New York: Penguin, 1996), pp. 198–201 (Vol. III, chs. 3–4).

22 For related imagery of married women as slaves, see, for example, p. 171, on Maria's landlord and landlady ("he, forsooth, was her master; no slave in the West Indies had one more despotic"). The comparison of women's situation in marriage to that of the enslaved Africans in British colonies was a common and politically powerful – and vexed – one in the period.

23 *Mothering Daughters: Novels and the Politics of Family Romance, Frances Burney to Jane Austen* (Detroit: Wayne State University Press, 2002), p. 98.

24 As Kelly notes, this draft conclusion to the novel draws on Wollstonecraft's own two suicide attempts. He comments, "Since M. W. did decide to live for her child Fanny, the scene that follows, perhaps drawn from life, may not be mere tear-jerking" (p. 231).

25 *The Victim of Prejudice*, ed. Eleanor Ty (Peterborough, Ontario: Broadview Press, 1994), p. 123.

26 *Mary*, pp. 34, 57, 60. See *Sense and Sensibility*, ed. Ros Ballaster (New York: Penguin Books, 2003), pp. 8–10 (Vol. I, chs. 1–2); pp. 83–4 (Vol. III, ch. 6); pp. 283–4 (Vol. I, ch. 16).

27 See, for instance, the Broadview edition of *Frankenstein; or The Modern Prometheus*, ed. D. L. Macdonald and Kathleen Scherf (Peterborough, Ontario: Broadview, 1994), which reproduces selections from both Godwin's and Wollstonecraft's writings in an appendix and emphasizes their influence on Shelley in its introduction (pp. 12–17). On Wollstonecraft's presence in *Frankenstein*, see two fine recent articles, both of which also review relevant critical studies: Syndy M. Conger, "Prophecy and Sensibility: Mary Wollstonecraft in *Frankenstein*," *1650–1850: Ideas, Aesthetics, and Inquiries in the Early Modern Era* 3 (1997), pp. 301–28, and Carolyn Williams, "'Inhumanly Brought Back to Life and Misery': Mary Wollstonecraft, *Frankenstein*, and the Royal Humane Society," *Women's Writing* 8 (2001), pp. 212–34.

28 On the centrality of Safie's letters, and on the connection Safie's story suggests between Shelley's novel and her mother's works, see Joyce Zonana, "'They Will Prove the Truth of My Tale': Safie's Letters as the Feminist Core of Mary Shelley's *Frankenstein*," *Journal of Narrative Technique* 21 (1991), pp. 170–84.

10

KATIE TRUMPENER

Tales for child readers

No sooner had George Crabbe learned to read than he "devoured without restraint whatever came into his hands, but especially works of fiction – those little stories and ballads about ghosts, witches, and fairies, which were then almost exclusively the literature of youth, and which, whatever else might be thought of them, served, no doubt, to strike out the first sparks of imagination in the mind of many a youthful poet."[1] The child Samuel Taylor Coleridge became so haunted by chapbook stories that his father burned his chapbooks.[2] John Clare's childhood "stock of learning" was all "gleaned from the Sixpenny Romances of 'Cinderella', 'Little Red Riding Hood', 'Jack and the Bean Stalk' ... etc and great was the pleasure, pain, or surprise [sic] increased by allowing them authenticity, for I firmly believed every page I read and considerd I possesd [sic] in these the chief learning and literature of the country." Clare spent all his money on such chapbooks. And since "it is common in villages to pass judgment on a lover of books as a sure indication of laziness," he was forced to "hide in woods and dingles of thorns in the fields on Sunday" to read them.[3]

Around 1800, London schoolboys at Christ's Hospital would offer to exchange the matron's library book, speed-read it on the way back to school, then recount it to each other in bed at night. Such stories and their miscellaneous chapbook reading seemed to them far more interesting than the Greek and Roman classics they spent their schooldays translating.[4] A generation earlier, precocious children just as happily immersed themselves in classical works of drama, poetry, and historiography. Walter Scott records both an early obsession with his grandmother's Robin Hood-style stories and voracious early reading of *Pilgrim's Progress*, *As You Like It*, Allan Ramsay's *Evergreen*, and Josephus' *Jewish Wars*. Although such works were in some ways too difficult and complex for a child reader, Scott believed this made them all the more stimulating.[5] Jane Austen, too, spent her early reading years immersed in history books and courtship novels. Yet far from impressed by their difficulty, she travestied their generic cliches in her own juvenile writings.[6]

Romantic novels frequently suggest the life-long impact of early reading materials. Inflamed by oral retellings of the *Arabian Nights, Turkish Tales*, and "other works of like marvellous import" the assertive and impulsive heroine of Mary Hays's *Memoirs of Emma Courtney* (1796) learns to read early. By the age of six, she is reading her uncle's favorites – Pope's *Homer*, Thomson's *Seasons* – aloud to admiring adults, although she comprehends little. This early literary training, indeed, feeds her vanity and her ignorance.[7] Raised in great social and psychic isolation, the sensitive orphan in Mary Shelley's *Mathilda* (1819), on the other hand, finds that books "in some degree supplied the place of human intercourse." Her aunt's small library yielded "strangely assorted" volumes ranging from Shakespeare, Milton, Pope, and Cowper to Livy.[8]

Such influences are recounted partly to chronicle a major historical and cultural shift. For by the time these Romantic novels were written, many contemporary children were being introduced to recreational reading using a new set of reading materials. During the Romantic period, for the first time, a critical mass of British writers begin to address their work primarily or exclusively to juvenile readers. The development of a separate juvenile book market, begun in the mid-eighteenth century by publishing impresario John Newbery and institutionalized around 1805, inaugurated a new and lasting split in the reading public. And as some commentators worried, it threatened to transform the texture of childhood – not least for young readers who would grow up to become writers themselves.

Romantic polemics about the future of children's fiction – and hence the future of childhood itself – can be read as a protest against the commercialization of the children's book market and against a didactic (and evangelical) turn in children's fiction, against the way moral and moralizing children's fiction threatens to supplant more traditional – and more fantasy-oriented – reading material, and against the feminization of children's writing (given the growing number of women who began to write children's fiction).[9] The new fiction, they predict, will be all too successful in inculcating piety, inwardness, or empathy (depending on whether the authors are Evangelicals, secular rationalists, or political reformers). What will be lost as this fiction takes hold, they prophesy, is the possibility of a richer, less fettered fantasy life. "Think what you would have been now," Charles Lamb famously writes to Coleridge in 1802, "if instead of being fed with tales and old wives' fables in childhood, you had been crammed with geography and natural history!"[10] In a letter of 1823, Scott, too, argues that fairy tales are "better adapted to awaken the imagination and soften the heart of childhood than the good-boy stories which have been in later years composed for them."[11]

As such critics perceive it, a plot-driven mode of fiction is being replaced by a more character-centered one, the adventure stories of the chapbook tradition giving way to moral or spiritual *Bildungsromane*. Late eighteenth-century juvenile authors like Mary Ann and Dorothy Kilner often wrote both episodic adventure stories and domestic tales, stories tracking the adventures of inanimate objects and stories tracking social and moral development. Most early nineteenth-century writers, in contrast, presented their children's fiction as explicitly or implicitly "improving."

From the mid-eighteenth century onward, the children's and the adult novel might be seen as developing in tandem, and in some respects, they continue to do so long after they appear to occupy separate publishing and marketing categories. It seems no coincidence, in retrospect, that the volumes which, from the 1740s onward, laid the foundation for Newbery's juvenile publishing empire – and in many respects inaugurated the modern conception of children's literature – were published during a period of renewed excitement and debate over the novel itself. Newbery's most celebrated volumes, *The History of Giles Gingerbread, A Little Boy Who Lived Upon Learning* (1764) and *The History of Little Goody Two-Shoes ... With the Means by which she acquired her Learning and Wisdom, and in consequence thereof her Estate* (1765), indeed, are often attributed to novelist and poet Oliver Goldsmith (one of Newbery's stable of writers, who also published *A History of England, in a Series of Letters from a Nobleman to his Son* with Newbery in 1764).

As their subtitles suggest, *Goody* and *Giles* are amusing didactic narratives, advocating literacy as a means not only of self-improvement but of gaining a fortune. Yet most of Newbery's other books are miscellanies, derived from popular chapbook materials. The physical presentation of Newbery's books (from their crisp woodcuts to their marbled endpapers and decorative bindings) lent new middle-class respectability to once-humble materials.[12] Yet Newbery's choice of chapbook-style names for some of his materials – his short-lived, pioneering children's journal, the 1751 *Lilleputean Magazine*, whose miscellany included a travel narrative echoing *Robinson Crusoe* and *Gulliver's Travels*; his *Food for the Mind, or a New Riddle Book ... By John-the-Giant-Killer, Esq.*; his *Fables in Verse by Abraham Aesop, Esq.* (both 1757) – deliberately linked these new books to long-popular children's and chapbook reading, from Aesop's fables to *Jack-the-Giant-Killer* and abridgments of *Crusoe* and *Gulliver*.

Towards the end of the eighteenth century, children's stories began to model themselves explicitly on contemporary adult novels, adopting existing fictional genres to the situations and fantasies of (middle-class) childhood. In Mary Ann Kilner, Dorothy Kilner, and Thomas Day's juvenile picaresque and circulation novels, children, animals, or toys are moved through the world, encountering adventures as they go.[13] In Dorothy Kilner's juvenile epistolary novel, *First Going to School, or the Story of Tom Brown and His Sisters* (1804), a boy's sojourn at boarding school provides the occasion and material for an exchange of letters with distant family members. The omnipresent grandmother in "Arabella Argus's" *Juvenile Spectator* (1810) proffers advice on how to reform naughty children. Sixty years earlier, famously, Samuel Richardson's *Pamela* had evolved from a book of model letters, intended to give advice in a variety of situations, including amorous and employment. *The Juvenile Spectator*, too, develops fictionalized situations, sometimes dramatic or humorous, out of the potentially dry material of the conduct book.

Yet the early nineteenth-century boom in children's publishing was spurred not by didactic literature but by the runaway 1805 success of Sarah Catherine Martin's *The Comic Adventures of Old Mother Hubbard and her Dog* (John Harris, 1805), which sold 10,000 copies within a few months, going through twenty editions within a year. *Old Mother Hubbard* reached adult and child readers in equal measure (and quickly passed into the public domain and the realm of popular lore). Yet its success spurred fierce new competition over the children's book market. Publishers commissioned many new "Novelties for the Nursery," illustrated fantasy, nonsense, or satirical texts, frequently based on nursery rhyme or fairy tale material.[14] Although the new "nursery novelties" remained popular for decades, moral and didactic writers faulted them for lacking deeper education value. The child protagonist of *Lucy, or the Little Enquirer: being the Conversation of a Mother with her Infant Daughter* (1815) thus comes to regret her choice to buy *Old Mother Hubbard* over a more improving volume, for soon she grows "tired of … that silly book: it says a great deal that I am sure is not true."[15]

Old Mother Hubbard's success boosted every aspect of the children's book market. Children's books proliferated and so did children's bookstores, so-called "juvenile libraries" run by a particular publisher, and showcasing his or her particular list. From Newbery onward, didactic fiction was often motivated by commercial as well as religious, political, or pedagogic considerations. During the initial 1805 juvenile literature boom, children's fiction focused repeated attention on the book market, usually extolling the superiority of one particular publisher, list, and juvenile library over all others. In extreme cases like Eliza Fenwick's 1805 *Visits to the Juvenile Library*, the story itself is shaped completely by the exigencies of product placement: Fenwick's child protagonists visit and dream about the juvenile library run by Fenwick's own publisher, and enthusiastically endorse a long list of his recent offerings.[16]

Many of the Romantic period's ostensibly "fictional" stories are at core expository, using a thin fictional frame story to lighten their potentially dry pedagogical presentation. Yet these narratives often remain playful and imaginative. They are didactic mainly in their attempts to help children understand their own motivations and hence achieve emotional self-control. For some latter-day commentators (influenced by social theorists like Louis Althusser and Michel Foucault), this mode of self-control appears particularly coercive. Yet if children are to interact successfully with others they must learn to control their own impulses and conduct themselves with some understanding of those around them. Many assumptions of Romantic juvenile novelists still inform current pedagogical practice: fantasy literature (especially that involving violence) can potentially lead children to develop inappropriate beliefs or social responses; children stand to gain from more realistic fiction, which can teach them not only about the larger world but about their own mental and emotional processes, helping them to learn or deepen their sense of empathy, and improve interactions with their own teachers, families, and peers.

Many Romantic stories, moreover, attempt various forms of consciousness-raising, working to supplant children's innate selfishness with social or moral conscience. Socially critical works like Maria Edgeworth's *History of Poor Bob, the Chimney Sweeper* (1819), for instance, stir compassion for child laborers and outrage at their brutalization. Some juvenile city guidebooks try to inculcate a politicized form of urban curiosity, pleasure in novelty and variety leavened by awareness of the economic and social cross-connections between apparently disparate social spheres. As they show, moreover, children's struggles to understand the division of labor and social stratification, their impulsive empathy for the poor and their consequent inability to assent to the existing social order represent an important potential for social change.[17]

In practice, didactic fiction covered a very large range of subjects, from Christian catechism to scientific method to facts about history, agriculture, and city life. It also demonstrated a broad spectrum of modes and approaches, from evangelical to Rousseauian to utilitarian. Influential textbook series like Pinnock's Catechisms (published from 1817 onward, eventually encompassing eighty-three volumes and many fields, from *A Catechism of Modern History* and *A Catechism of Music* to *A Catechism of Mineralogy*) seemed determined to collapse any remaining genre distinctions between the catechism and the encyclopedia, between sacred and secular education, between received truth and educational investigation.

Edgeworth's influential *Early Lessons* (1801) has different pedagogical aims, modeling how the daily activities of young protagonists like Harry,

Lucy, and Frank – gathering different kinds of plants, observing milking, trying to make bricks – help them develop inquiring minds, give them contact with the natural and social world, provide them with information, and help them to begin developing artisanal skills.

Children thus educated begin to understand the different forms of labor which make up economic life, and develop an empathetic sense of the difficulties and social value of manual work. When authors decided to give fictional flesh to their presentations of fact, they implicitly acknowledged subjective and moral dimensions to the educational process. And at times, they explicitly underscored the intellectual autonomy of child learners – and the possibility that children's naive questions and intuitive perceptions might yield new insights into complex social phenomena.

Romantic polemics against didactic fiction are thus implicitly countered within children's fiction itself. Together, these interventions and fictional ripostes might be seen as constituting a debate roughly parallel to the repeated eighteenth-century debates about whether novel-reading (and more rarely, novel-writing) would have a deleterious effect on women's morals, presence of mind, and anchoring in the external world. Eighteenth-century accounts of the novel's effects often took the form of Quixotic satires: dedicated novel-readers, usually female, read so obsessively they begin to project fictional situations and conventions onto everyday life. For women readers the ostensible danger of fiction reading was titillation, their imaginations (and perhaps even their bodies) inflamed until they lost touch with reality. Romantic critics see a corresponding yet opposite danger for child readers: the overloading and dessication of their brains. The new children's fiction comes under fire for its putative tendency to promote inwardness and stern intellectuality at the expense of physical exploration, fantasy, and imaginative play. Yet as some writers insist, juvenile fiction thereby minimizes the danger of a Quixotic response, since children can now be given books about their own life circumstances rather than chapbook-style adventures. In Jeffrey Taylor's *Harry's Holidays: or the Doings of One, Who Had Nothing to Do* (1819), a boy's excited immersion in *Robinson Crusoe* almost results in serious injury, as he tries to recreate aspects of Crusoe's adventures. (Children, don't try this at home!) The fable suggests the need for a new children's literature which addresses the adventures of everyday life, absorbing in a very different way.

In an era when most novels for adults ran to three volumes, Romantic children's fiction tended to be much shorter, presumably in part because its inexperienced young readers were uncertain in their reading abilities, hence easily daunted or wearied by longer narratives. Yet this disparity in length and complexity does raise the question of whether children's fiction was commensurate with the adult novel, or read rather in relationship to the tale or short story.

Adult novelists pondered the relationship between tale and novel throughout the Romantic period. Around 1805, some fiction-writers and publishers began designating novels with Irish, Scottish, or other forms of local color as "national tales"; by the 1820s and 30s, Scottish and Irish writers from James Hogg to Gerald Griffin had begun publishing collections of traditional, legendary, and local color stories (sometimes linked by a frame narrative, sometimes not) under the nomenclature of "tales." A few writers had also embarked on ambitious novel cycles. The most famous and most influential series, Walter Scott's many coordinated volumes of historical fiction, was known as the Waverley Novels, a title which stressed the novel as the organizing generic unit. Yet John Galt's equally ambitious Tales of the West of Scotland and John and Michael Banim's Tales by the O'Hara Family, cycles of similar length and complexity as Scott's, billed themselves as extended and interlocking "tales." Under either generic designation, such cycles were experiments with shifts of scale and perspective, with the ability of individual tales to stand on their own, and with the additional meaning they gained from juxtaposition and from their subsumption to overall frame structures.[18]

The designation of "tale" appears frequently in Romantic children's literature as well, and here, too, it remains an elastic term, covering very different kinds of writing. It might simply designate a brief, often didactic story. Following the influential model of late eighteenth-century French moral and historical tales like Arnaud Berquin's *L'Ami des enfants* (1782) or Mme. de Genlis's *Les Veillées du château* (1784, translated in 1785 as *Tales of the Castle*), British reformers of various stripes begin composing tale collections, from Hannah More's "Cheap Repository Tracts" (1795-8) to Mary Wollstonecraft's *Original Stories from Real Life* (1788) and Edgeworth's *Moral Tales* (1801). But the term "tale" could equally well designate a traditional or pseudo-traditional narrative: a fairy story, whether of oral or courtly provenance, a chapbook legend, or an "Oriental tale," whether faithfully translated from the Persian or Arabic or newly invented in Orientalist style. Some tales, moreover, were actually renarrated and simplified pieces of an established, indeed fundamental, literary heritage. William and Mary Jane Godwin thus published Charles and Mary Lamb's famous *Tales from Shakespear* (1807) as part of a highly ambitious, experimental juvenile publishing list that also included Charles Lamb's *Adventures of Ulysses* (1808), based on Homeric epic, and William Godwin's own *Fables Ancient and Modern* (1805) and *The Pantheon* (1806), redactions of Greek myth published under the pseudonym of "Edward Baldwin," and a major influence on the young Keats.[19]

In practice, Romantic children's tales and tale collections often reflect the confluence and overlap of apparently opposed narrative traditions. One particularly influential Romantic-era fairy tale, *The Story of the Three Bears*, thus slides between a potential cautionary narrative (girl learns not to trespass) and a fantasy story, with its talking, anthropomorphized beasts, pleasure in oral repetition, and final sense of inconsequence for naughty behavior. (The tale's own genesis is equally slippery: published by Robert Southey in 1837, and attributed to oral tradition, it was subsequently found in an 1831 version written by Eleanore Mure; controversy continues whether this is primarily a traditional or a literary fairy tale.)[20]

In many other cases, too, the didactic moral tale is barely distinguishable from juvenile versions or imitations of the *Thousand and One Nights*. Edgeworth's *Moral Tales* (1801) thus includes "Murad the Unlikely," a newly composed moral parable couched in pseudo-Oriental style; Jane Porter's *The Two Princes of Persia, Addressed to Youth* (1801) uses an Oriental framework to develop moral lessons. The same children's publisher, Elizabeth Newbery, brought out *The Looking Glass of the Mind* (1787), the most influential English translation of Berquin's *L'Ami des enfants* (selling 20,000 copies by 1800), and the equally popular *The Oriental Moralist or the Beauties of the Arabian Nights Entertainment* (1791), the first English-language edition of the *Thousand and One Nights* aimed at children.

As assimilated into the children's literary tradition, to be sure, *The Thousand and One Nights* typically lacks several of its usual hallmarks: sexual explicitness, formal complexity, and tacit meditations on the status of women. Antoine Galland's influential French translation of the *Thousand and One Nights* had shaped, excised, and added additional stories to the *Nights*, blunting the original's sexual explicitness and turning a carefully sequenced, and thematically coherent story collection into a miscellany. *The Oriental Moralist* expunged further: as its title announces, it alters the tales to moralize them, and promote virtue. What remains of the *Arabian Nights* framework is primarily the intricate relationship between narrative sequencing and intermittently reappearing frame story. In English juvenile narratives, more generally, frame stories are used to explore varieties of life-experience and to trace children's moral and emotional maturation. In John Aikin and Anna Letitia Barbauld's influential miscellany *Evenings at Home* (1792–6), a domestic framework and frame story thus serves to anchor, harmonize, and moralize a disparate range of stories. And the boarding school students in Charles and Mary Lamb's *Mrs. Leicester's School* (1808) tell a sequence of life-stories, some of them tales of neglect, loss, or domestic tragedy, even as the frame-narrative tracks the school's curative influence.

Like the *Arabian Nights*, Romantic children's collections demonstrate the gradual, but transformative effect of storytelling on youthful auditors. In Thomas Day's *History of Sanford and Merton* (1783), a mixture of Oriental and cautionary stories help a Jamaica planter's son assimilate more egalitarian British values and win the friendship of a stalwart farmer's son. Mrs. Mason, the strict but loving governess in Wollstonecraft's *Original Stories*, uses vivid cautionary stories to educate her charges in the principles of virtue. Wollstonecraft herself was governess to Margaret King Moore (later Lady Mountcashel). As an adult, Moore would adopt the pseudonym Mrs. Mason, in explicit tribute to Wollstonecraft's influence. Moore's own *Stories of Old Daniel, or Tales of Wonder and Delight* (1807) follows the narrative framing of Wollstonecraft's *Original Stories*, its main narrator an old man whose succession of adventure stories indirectly guide neighborhood youth, by heightening their moral consciousness.

In the preface of *Two Princes of Persia*, Jane Porter honors her grandfather's elderly retainer, in whose lap Porter sat as a girl, listening to his fairy-tales. Yet if Porter's book is in some ways a memorial to this "man of the people," as a simultaneously popular and antique source of oral lore and narrative fascination, she also deplores the way traditional fantastic stories can inculcate lifelong superstititions and fears in their auditors. Her own Orientalist tale collection thus seeks to replicate the intensity and absorption of this early listening experience, yet with tales that are explicitly didactic.[21]

Walter Scott's writing about childhood and for children contains a related paradox. Remembering his own childhood reading, he argues that children have much to gain by an early exposure to texts too difficult for them to comprehend completely – and which push them to puzzle out meaning on their own. Yet his own *Tales of a Grandfather* (1828–30) arranges its tales of Scottish history not only chronologically but in narratives of graduated difficulty; young readers are meant to mature developmentally alongside Scotland itself.

Romantic children's fiction is most didactic, perhaps, where it models this stadial approach to education in its form as well as content. Galland's redaction of his *Arabian Nights* source virtually dissolved the frame story, turning the tale collection back into a set of randomly assembled pieces. Romantic children's literature moves in the opposite direction. Indeed, because its authors are so frequently preoccupied with the process of moral education, juvenile *Nights* adaptations underscore the cumulative force of apparently miscellaneous tales; frame narratives are where where the tales' impact is demonstrated and modeled most fully. And this emphasis on larger, longer narrative and development time-spans in turn begins to move children's fiction away from the short story collection towards a novelistic sensibility, its characters developing increasing descriptive depth and complexity as tracked over time.

The development of Romantic children's literature is hence finally towards characters marked by complex interiority, and an increasingly nuanced relationship to the social world around them. Those who lamented the didactic turn within Romantic children's literature were too hasty to announce the end of imagination. But they were undoubtedly right in underscoring the long-term, incalculable consequences of this shift for British fiction, juvenile and adult.

Key Victorian works shape themselves alternately in direct imitation or in reaction to Romantic children's writing. In title as in plot situation, Thomas Hughes's 1857 *Tom Brown's Schooldays* alludes to Dorothy Kilner's *First Going to School, or the Story of Tom Brown and His Sisters*. Edgeworth's shrewdly observed domestic stories inspire not only Jane Austen but later children's novelists including Louisa May Alcott, Mrs. Ewing, Annie Keary, and Charlotte Yonge. Lewis Carroll's *Alice in Wonderland*, conversely, travesties not only cautionary tales and didactic poetry, but the didactic frame of mind they mean to inculcate. Charles Dickens's satirical essay "Mr. Barlow" (published in *All the Year Round* in 1868–9) describes a life blighted by reading Thomas Day's *Sandford and Merton* (1783); forced thereafter to experience the world through the eyes of Day's didactic tutor, the narrator finds all pleasure in entertainments like the *Arabian Nights* tainted by doubts about its veracity – even as fear of further didactic explanation makes him shun all further information and knowledge.

In E. Nesbit's *Wet Magic* (1913), likewise, children who adore Charles Kingsley, *Little Women*, *David Copperfield*, and Scott's *Quentin Durward* experience the Romantic tradition of juvenile didactic fiction as unmitigated terror:

> You hear that cold squeak? That's Fairchild ... that icy voice is Rosamond's mother, the one who was so hateful about the purple jar.[22]

Nesbit's children show equal distrust of Mrs. Sherwood's evangelical *History of the Fairchild Family* (1818) and of "The Purple Jar," the famous episode from Edgeworth's *Early Lessons*. What these tales share is their earnestness and the rigidly didactic model of parental behavior they seem to endorse. *The Fairchild Family* is now best remembered for the ghoulish scene in which parents show their children a hanged man, to force them to accept human transience. Edgeworth's mother is equally pitiless in making Rosamond live with – and learn from – her mistakes.

In other respects, however, their fiction is extremely various. Sherwood's works for children express deep distrust not only in the distractions but even in the things of this world. It is thus the poor, downtrodden, and destitute who may be closest to salvation. In the venerable tradition of James Janeway's *A Token for Children* (1672), Sherwood's famous colonial story, *Little Henry and his Bearer* (1814) tells of infant sanctity and happy, if early death. Here the deep mutual affection between Anglo-Indian waif Henry and his faithful native servant Boosy inadvertently mirrors divine love – the Christian belief which Henry discovers first and, before dying, manages to impart, as a kind of Holy Child, to his Indian bearer and St. Christopher. The only possession worth owning, Sherwood stresses, is a Bible; other worldly baubles merely distract from the pressing issue of salvation. In Sherwood's *A Drive in the Coach, Through the Streets of London. A Story Founded on Fact* (1818), even more insistently, a child lured into window-shopping in London's glittering shopping district is checked by her mother's exhortations to focus instead on death and resurrection. The tale spells out this message with morbid literalism: the girl may have something from every shop on Regent Street, her mother promises, provided she is also willing to buy herself a coffin – and face her own mortality, including the immanent dissolution of all flesh.

Other didactic authors are equally concerned with the pitfalls of children's window-shopping. Yet in *Memory* (1824), by Sherwood's sister and fellow evangelical Mrs. Cameron, as in Edgeworth's much earlier "Purple Jar," the pedagogical approach and the ultimate moral are strikingly different. The elderly frame-narrator of *Memory* tells a child a series of autobiographical stories amounting cumulatively to a spiritual autobiography. Some are vignettes of regret, episodes of moral failure about which the narrator still feels shame and chagrin, decades later; others describe moments of ethical insight or timely rapprochement with family members, soon to die unexpectedly. Cameron's fiction is simultaneously moralistic and psychological. Like Sherwood, she urges the anxious consciousness of mortality. Yet she also offers delicate insights into the complex calculus of childish desire. As a small girl, the narrator is transfixed by the shop-window of the local corner-shop, enchanted particularly by a toy fireplace, whose realistic details – including "a spit with a joint of meat roasting and a kettle hanging to boil" – she still recalls vividly, many decades later on.[23] For Cameron, the girl's attraction to this miniature world appears not only excusable but inescapable. Yet the girl's temptation to buy this toy is problematic, for it would take money she has saved for a more charitable purpose: to buy fabric so she could sew a dress for an impoverished neighborhood child. Her mother, in whom she confides, reminds her "so sweetly of the reality of heavenly things, and of the emptiness of earthly things" that she determines to forego the fireplace after all, although for a time it remains hard to pass the window where it is displayed. The reward for her altruism is not only the other girl's gratefulness for the dress, but her own receipt, soon after, of a similar, less elaborate but equally wonderful toy fireplace, a present from distant friends, perhaps inspired by her mother's hint. As in Sherwood's tale, the mother–child relationship is explicitly pedagogical, yet here the mode of teaching is tender and understanding. And the attractions of the world are palpable, paralleling those of fiction itself. The virtuous apparently deserve a guiltless enjoyment of both. Fiction successful in inculcating empathy and moral vision can also afford to show readers what is delightful about the temporal realm, and risk heightening their earthly attachments.

Edgeworth's secular tale is equally complex. Her window-shopping Rosamond mistakes an apothecary's bottle for a gleaming treasure, and sacrifices a new pair of shoes to obtain this bauble, only to find that neither the unctuous purple ointment the bottle contains nor the bottle itself, quite ordinary once emptied, can be worth the pain of wearing outgrown shoes. The tale offers a finely detailed account of the child's over-investment, consumer disillusionment and dawning scepticism. Edgeworth's empiricist attention to the materiality of the world's things, Jill Campbell argues, links her children's fiction to earlier modes of novelistic realism. Moreover, Campbell demonstrates, the obsessions Edgeworth's children sometimes develop towards particular fetish objects may come under local criticism, from parents and narrative commentors – only, later in the story, to provide the stories' denouement, even their happy ending.[24] On one level, Edgeworth shows her young protagonists outgrowing their immature obsession with surfaces and appearances. On another level, these attachments are what bind them into the physical and social world – and thus prepare them for intellectual and psychic development.

If Romantic children's fiction develops beyond some of its generic prototypes – the circulation novel, the sentimental novel, the chapbook, the tract – it also works to reconcile their apparently divergent preoccupations. In Edgeworth's tales, at least, the circulation novel, with its stress on the autonomous life and socially revelatory vantage point of mere "things," is grafted onto the sentimental novel. Edgeworth's world is manifest in its details, as experienced by a developing psyche and finely attuned observer. What Edgeworth's juvenile fiction underscores, indeed, is the dialectical alternation and interpenetration between inwardness and exteriority. This dialectic comes to define the nineteenth-century realist novel – even as Edgeworth's child readers grow up to become the readers and writers of Victorian fiction.

NOTES

1 George Crabbe, *The Life of George Crabbe by his Son* (London: The Cresset Press, 1947), p. 13.

2 Letter to Thomas Poole, October 9, 1797, *Collected Letters of Samuel Taylor Coleridge*, ed. Earl Leslie Griggs, 10 vols. (Oxford: Clarendon Press, 1956), Vol. I, pp. 207–9.

3 John Clare, "Sketches in the Life of John Clare" (1821), *John Clare's Autobiographical Writings*, ed. Eric Robinson. (Oxford: Oxford University Press, 1983), pp. 1–26, here p. 5.

4 William Pitt Scargill, *Recollections of a Blue-Coat Boy or, A View of Christ's Hospital* (1829; rpt. Wakefield: S. R. Publishers and New York: Johnson Reprint Corporation, 1968). For a fuller account of Scargill's memoir, Newbery's juvenile publishing empire and Romantic children's publishing, see my "The Making of Child Readers," forthcoming in James Chandler, ed., *Cambridge History of British Romanticism* (Cambridge University Press).

5 Walter Scott, *Autobiographical Fragment*, in John Lockhart, *Memoirs of the Life of Sir Walter Scott*, 9 vols., Vol. I (Boston: Houghton, Mifflin, n.d.), pp. 53 ff.

6 See Margaret Anne Doody, "Jane Austen, that disconcerting 'child,'" in Christine Alexander and Juliet McMaster, eds., *The Child Writer from Austen to Woolf* (Cambridge: Cambridge University Press, 2005), pp. 101–21.

7 Mary Hays, *Memoirs of Emma Courtney*, 2 vols., Vol. I (London: G. G. and J. Robinson, 1796), p. 16.

8 Mary Shelley, "Mathilda," in *The Mary Shelley Reader*, ed. Betty T. Bennett and Charles E. Robinson (Oxford: Oxford University Press, 1990), pp. 175–246, 184.

9 See for instance Geoffrey Summerfield, *Fantasy and Reason: Children's Literature in the Eighteenth Century* (Athens: University of Georgia Press, 1984) and Samuel Pickering, *Moral Instruction and Fiction for Children, 1749–1820* (Athens: University of Georgia Press, 1995).

10 Letter to Samuel Taylor Coleridge, October 23, 1802, *The Complete Works and Letters of Charles Lamb* (New York: Modern Library, 1935), pp. 726–8, 727. For fuller contextualization, see my "Visits."

11 Cited by Iona and Peter Opie, *The Classic Fairy Tales* (London: Oxford University Press, 1974), p. 8.

12 F. J. Harvey Darton, *Children's Books in England: Five Centuries of Social Life* (1932; Cambridge: Cambridge University Press, 2nd edn., 1970), p. 137 and John Rowe Townsend, ed., *John Newbery and His Books: Trade and Plumb-cake for Ever, Huzza!* (Metuchen, N. J.: Scarecrow Press, 1994). On the chapbooks' centrality for early modern (child) readers, see Victor E. Neuburg, *The Penny Histories. A Study of Chapbooks for Young Readers over Two Centuries* (New York: Harcourt, Brace and World, 1968) and Margaret Spufford, *Small Books and Pleasant Histories: Popular Fiction and its Readership in Seventeenth-Century England* (Athens: University of Georgia Press, 1981); on early modern children's reading, see Warren W. Wooden, *Children's Literature of the English Renaissance*, ed. Jeanie Watson (Lexington: University Press of Kentucky, 1986).

13 Mary Ann Kilner's *Adventures of a Pincushion* (London: John Marshall, c. 1780) and *Memoirs of a Peg-Top* (London: John Marshall, 1783); Thomas Day's

History of Little Jack (London: John Stockdale, 1788); Dorothy Kilner's *Life and Perambulations of a Mouse* (London: John Marshall, *c.* 1790).

14 Iona and Peter Opie, *The Nursery Companion* (Oxford: Oxford University Press, 1980), p. 5.

15 *Lucy, or the Little Enquirer: being the Conversation of a Mother with her Infant Daughter* (London: William Darton, 1815?), p. 53.

16 Eliza Fenwick, *Visits to the Juvenile Library; or, Knowledge Proved to be the Source of Happiness* (1805; rpt. New York: Garland, 1977). Self-promotional fiction for children dates back at least to Newbery's mid-eighteenth-century books; see my "The Making."

17 See my "City Scenes: Commerce, Modernity, and the Birth of the Picture Book," Richard Maxwell, ed., *The Victorian Illustrated Book: New Explorations* (University of Virginia Press, 2002), pp. 332–84.

18 See my "The Peripheral Rise of the Novel: Scotland, Ireland, and the Politics of Form" in Liam MacInvernay and Raymond Ryan, eds., *Ireland and Scotland: Culture and Society 1707–2000* (Dublin: Four Courts, 2004), pp. 164–82, esp. pp. 181–2.

19 William St Clair, "William Godwin as Children's Bookseller," in Gillian Avery and Julia Briggs, eds., *Children and Their Books. A Celebration of the Work of Iona and Peter Opie* (Oxford: Oxford University Press, 1989), pp. 165–79.

20 Opie and Opie, *The Classic Fairy Tales*, pp. 199–200.

21 Jane Porter, *The Two Princes of Persia. Addressed to Youth* (London: Crosby and Letterman, 1801), p. xii. On servants as agents of transmission, see my *Bardic Nationalism: The Romantic Novel and the British Empire* (Princeton: Princeton University Press, 1997), ch. 4.

22 E. Nesbit, *Wet Magic* (1913; rpt. New York: North-South Books, 2001), p. 118.

23 Mrs. Cameron, *Memory* (Wellington: F. Houlston and Songs, 1824), p. 18.

24 Jill Campbell, "Everlasting Whipcords and Homing Pigeons: Formal Realism in Edgeworth's Children's Tales," unpublished manuscript.

I I

ANN WIERDA ROWLAND

Sentimental fiction

Walter Scott's introductory chapter to *Waverley: 'Tis Sixty Years Since* (1814), with its brief and breezy survey of the possible titles Scott has *not* chosen for his novel, offers itself as a clearing of the decks for nineteenth-century fiction. Choosing a supposedly unknown and therefore "uncontaminated name" for his hero rather easily, Scott lingers on the "second or supplemental title," well aware that it will announce the book's generic allegiances and be "held as pledging the author to some special mode of laying his scene." Scott rejects both "a Tale of Other Days" and "a Romance from the German" because of the Gothic expectations they raise: "would not the owl have shrieked and the cricket cried in my very title-page?" "A Tale of the Times" is also passed over for promising "a dashing sketch of the fashionable world ... a heroine from Grosvenor Square, and a hero from the Barouche Club or the Four-in-hand." Scott likewise rejects a "Sentimental Tale" for its promise of a "heroine with a profusion of auburn hair, and a harp, the soft solace of her solitary hours, which she fortunately finds always the means of transporting from castle to cottage."[1]

Ina Ferris and Katie Trumpener have alerted us to the many ways Scott obscures his debts to other novels in this opening gambit.[2] Dismissing the "sentimental" along with the other major novelistic genres of the day, for example, Scott will proceed to write a novel that shamelessly exploits sentimental conventions and assumptions. Edward Waverley has all the "powers of apprehension," "brilliancy of fancy," and "love of literature" that any sentimental heroine could ever desire; Scott persistently places him before picturesque landscapes or outside the main scenes of action, giving Waverley the role of reporting on what he sees and on how it makes him feel; and then there is Flora, a heroine with a harp easily hauled from castle to grotto. Scott often reminds his "fair readers" that he's not writing a "romance" or that Waverley's troubles do not all arise from "sentimental source[s]." This heroine also worries about history and politics, but he tends to do so after scenes which read as sentimental set pieces. Scott thus establishes the distinction and novelty of his type of tale – neither sentimental, nor Gothic;

neither a romance, nor a novel of manners – not by shunning the conventions of the dominant fictional genres, but by using them at the same time that he delimits them, incorporating them into his text often through the very gesture of dismissal.

Many major Romantic authors staked their claims to distinction by disclaiming the conventions of sentimentality. Jane Austen makes the critique of sensibility central to her fiction both early and late: in *Northanger Abbey* (1818), *Sense and Sensibility* (1811), as well as in the manuscript of *Sanditon* left unfinished at her death. William Wordsworth's invective against "frantic novels" and the "degrading thirst after outrageous stimulation" they encourage sets up his experimental poetry of the *Lyrical Ballads* as an antidote to the sensationalism of popular literature so often blamed on the sentimental novel.[3] For many years, literary historians followed the cues of such writers and described a literary Romanticism – exemplified in the psychological and interiorized mode of the "greater Romantic lyric," or the "lyrical" achievements, of Austen's novels – that had progressed beyond the superficial, clichéd, or excessive gestures of sensibility. More recently, however, renewed attention to the generic varieties of Romantic fiction – long verse romances, Gothic novels, national tales, abolitionist narratives, and women's literature – has renewed and altered our narratives of literary history. What was once described as an age when the novel stuttered and the lyric soared has now come into focus as a period fascinated with the cultural work of fictional narratives in prose and verse, novel and ballad, tale and romance.

These shifts in our generic picture of the period have, on the one hand, brought back into focus critiques of sentimentality other than the lyrical: William Godwin's scrutiny of sentimental masculinity in *Fleetwood: or the New Man of Feeling* (1805), Maria Edgeworth's moral and rational tales, Thomas Love Peacock's satire of sentimental morbidity in *Nightmare Abbey* (1818), Byron's early verse romances with their anti-sentimental yet formulaic heroes. But our expanded literary field has also made evident the continuing relevance of sentimental modes, even to the most critical writing, and the extent to which the rhetorical figures of sentimentality prove useful to emerging literary genres and social issues. Romantic writers continue to articulate their major concerns – whether subjectivity or history, social engagement or psychic retreat, domesticity or empire – within the discursive paradigms of sentimental culture, and they understand literary history as a history of sentiment and manners, well aware that theirs is a culture preoccupied with the workings of passion, the anatomy of feeling, and the communication of emotion.

"Sentimental" belongs to a group of words – including sentiment, sense, sensibility, sensitivity, and sympathy – which together form a crucial lexicon of both sentimental and Romantic literary culture. "Sentimental," however, was a term considered "newfangled," "modern," and difficult to define. As late as 1799, *Barclay's Dictionary* hesitates at the task: "sentimental: a word lately introduced into common use, but without any precise meaning. Those who use it appear to understand by it, that affecting turn of thought which is peculiar to works of fancy, or where there is a display of the pathetic as in the graver scenes of comedy, or of novels."[4] It is no coincidence that this late-century attempt at a definition gropes toward literary works and effects, particularly those of the novel. Many types of books in the late eighteenth century offered opportunities for "affecting thought" or "display[s] of the pathetic" and, accordingly, called themselves "sentimental": anthologies and literary extracts, volumes of verse, travel narratives, and histories.[5] But the burgeoning field of self-proclaimed "sentimental novels," particularly in the second half of the century, was at the forefront of sentimental culture, giving sentimentality its common currency and popularizing the major shifts in the understanding of human subjectivity and social experience that are also evident in the philosophical and historical writings of the time.

"Sensibility" in the eighteenth century suggested the capacity for highly refined and sensitive emotional response. Sentimental literature thus models "fine feeling," giving its characters opportunities to exhibit and valorize sympathetic and virtuous emotional expression, as well as giving its readers a chance to exercise their own sensibilities. Popular sentimental novels such as Laurence Sterne's *A Sentimental Journey* (1768) or Henry Mackenzie's *The Man of Feeling* (1771) repeatedly stage affective scenes of suffering, tears, and tender emotion, developing a theatrical narrative style in which plot is subordinated to the episodic presentation of sentimental spectacles and narrative propulsion gains more from the movement of emotions than the unfolding of incident or action.[6] Samuel Johnson's advice for reading Samuel Richardson – "you must read him for the sentiment, and consider the story as only giving occasion to the sentiment" – remains relevant at the close of the century to the larger sentimental reading culture that *Clarissa* (1748) helped to create.[7] Indeed, Wordsworth's directive to his own readers of the *Lyrical Ballads* – these are poems in which "feeling ... gives importance to the action and situation and not the action and situation to the feeling" – uses the rhetoric of sentimentality to explain ballads which almost entirely neglect their narrative obligations, ballads in which the feeling usually *is* the story.[8] Literature, of course, has always had recourse to pathos, affect, and sensation, but in the eighteenth century, literary culture developed an unprecedented emphasis on *feeling* as what determines character and subjective experience, as what shapes social life and relations, as what makes events or actions meaningful, and, by the end of the century in particular, as what ties both social and subjective experience into history and national culture.

Sentimental poetry and novels share this emphasis on feeling with the philosophical literature of the period. One can find in the moral sense philosophy of Shaftesbury, for example, ways of thinking about human affections that influence literary culture and fictional strategies well into the nineteenth century. Assuming man's fundamental benevolence and sociability – "there is naturally in every Man such a degree of social Affection as inclines him to seek the Familiarity and Friendship of his Fellows" – Shaftesbury describes the "Mind" of man as the "Spectator or Auditor of *other Minds*," always seeing in the world or picturing to itself the sentiments, thoughts, and moral actions of others.[9] He thus represents subjective experience as a condition of spectatorship in which one is irresistibly prompted into imaginative and emotional engagements: "in these vagrant Characters or Pictures of *Manners*, which the Mind of necessity figures to it-self, and carrys still about with it, the Heart cannot possibly remain neutral; but constantly takes part one way or other."[10] Shaftesbury also articulates the sense of disjunction between man's "natural" social state and the highly refined organization of modern society – "No wonder if in such Societys 'tis so hard to find a Man who lives NATURALLY, and as a Man" – that reverberates significantly in the primitivism of sentimental and romantic culture, informing its historical or stadial understanding of sentiment and manners.[11]

David Hume and Adam Smith provide the most important elaborations of Shaftesbury's sentimental philosophy for the British literary context. Hume's elevation of passion over reason makes emotion the currency of man's social life. Significantly, the work of sympathy – by which "inclinations and sentiments" are communicated and shared, and thus the way members of social groups, such as nations, cohere and resemble each other – can also, according to Hume, heighten emotional experience. Many passions are felt "more from communication than from [our] own natural temper and disposition."[12] In Hume's rhetoric, passions are "contagious" and "communicable"; "they pass with the greatest facility from one person to another, and produce correspondent movements in all human breasts."[13] Indeed, Hume emphasizes the movement of emotion between subjects to such a degree as to destabilize the relationship of persons to passions. Instead of an individual *having* feelings, feelings practically possess the individual, becoming impersonal entities that pass between and constitute individuals.[14]

Adam Smith's subsequent elaboration of sympathy in *The Theory of Moral Sentiments* (1759) can be seen as returning to Shaftesbury's structure and language of spectatorship precisely in order to re-establish some stability of distinction between individuals and the feelings they share. For Smith, sympathy works when the "spectator" of "the person principally concerned" tries to "put himself in the situation of the other."[15] Sympathy is a mirroring

relationship between individuals that encourages imaginative acts of identification which are, however, predicated on the separation and differentiation
of those individuals. In fact, Smith extends this specular structure into the
subject's interior life of introspection and self-approbation: "When I endeavour to examine my own conduct, when I endeavour to pass sentence upon
it, and either to approve or condemn it, it is evident that, in all such cases, I
divide myself, as it were, into two persons."[16] Smith's theory of sentiment
thus gives the late eighteenth century one of its dominant versions of subjectivity, in which identity is split or doubled between "spectator" and
"agent" and self-consciousness is staged in and through this doubled relationship. The specular structure of the social world enters the interior life of
the subject.

Such subjective and social structures prove uncannily suited to the work of
fiction, and the close alliance between sentimental philosophy and sentimental fiction reveals the extent to which new notions of subjectivity and literature emerged together. Hume and Smith both make the work of narrative
central to their understanding of emotional and social life. Smith, for example, is interested in how narrative supplements the spectacle of emotion to
produce imaginative, sympathetic exchange: "general lamentations," he
notes "express nothing but the anguish of the sufferer," and it is only when
the question "what has befallen you?" is both asked and answered that
sympathy begins to function.[17] Over the course of the eighteenth century,
literature largely becomes that category of writing which facilitates the
function and experience of this new sentimental subjectivity: one in which
the feeling self is open to and constituted through sympathetic and imaginative exchanges with other feeling selves. At the same time, literature's capacity to encourage and promote social bonds – and even, in fact, to manage or
script the movement of the impersonal and unpredictable feelings circulating
between subjects – was also stressed. Indeed, sentimentality's rather rapid
coherence into a set of conventional scenes and stock figures might be seen as
a sign of the social imperatives driving this literary culture. When Clara
Reeve complains in 1785 that sentiment is both over-exhibited and degraded
by writers who, by making a "Parade of sentiment, have brought even the
word itself into disgrace," we are beginning to see less a decline in the literary
status of the sentimental subject, than the consolidation of literary and cultural
hierarchies constructed around the style and economy of sentimental
representation.[18]

Reeve's complaint about the "parade of sentiment" in popular fiction is
not just that feelings have become cheap and easy to come by; it is also a
criticism of their excessive, bodily display. By the end of the eighteenth
century, worry about the excesses of sentimental fiction dominated its

critical discourse and were often focused on the overly sensitive, nervous, and unhealthy physical symptoms of sensibility. Sentimental literature and medical writing in the eighteenth century shared a vocabulary of sensibility and sensitivity, in addition to sharing a fascination with the body's capacity to feel and to display feeling. The 1797 edition of the *Encyclopedia Britannica* testifies to this shared set of concerns when it defines "sensibility" as "a nice and delicate perception of pleasure or pain, beauty or deformity" which "seems to depend upon the organization of the nervous system."[19] Scottish physicians such as Robert Whytt, William Cullen and Alexander Munro, as well as Continental physiologists such as Albrecht von Haller (an important early reviewer of Richardson's *Clarissa*) described and experimentally documented the degrees of physical sensibility in the animal and human organism.[20] Together, literary and scientific writing anatomized and scrutinized the feeling body, linking particular passions to specific gestures or somatic sites, and categorizing the male or female body, the child's body, the aristocratic or lower-class body as more or less physically sensitive. The *Encyclopedia Britannica* entry, for example, goes on to state that sensibility is "experienced in a much higher degree in civilized than in savage nations, and among persons liberally educated than among boors and illiterate mechanics." Here stadial categories of "savage" and "civilized," and an historical understanding of sentiment and manners, become the categories and framework for describing contemporary cultural difference.

When Edgar Allan Poe describes Roderick Usher as a hypochondriac suffering from a "morbid acuteness of the senses," he is, of course, parodying a figure familiar to his readers as the man of overly refined sensibilities which have mutated into disease and perversion. Poe, in fact, extends his description of Usher's disease to encompass a critique of Gothic fiction's reliance on affect and sensation. Usher's "nervous affection" leaves him bound to an "anomalous species of terror," one in which he dreads "the events of the future, not in themselves, but in their results"; Usher has "no abhorrence of danger, except in its absolute effect – in terror."[21] Here we have Johnson's notion of the story as simply giving occasion for the sentiment updated for the extremities of Gothic plots. Sentiments have routed events so completely as to be in themselves the objects of anticipation and dread, and Usher's terror of terror itself re-describes even the most plotted and eventful of narratives as privileging feeling over action.

Of course, Gothic must be seen as a significant branch of sentimental culture, one which explores its interest in the affective work of fiction as well as exposing its dubious fascination with scenes of suffering and forms of misery. Shaftesbury confidently proclaimed in the 1730s that "to feed, as it were, on Death, and be entertain'd with dying Agonys" is "wholly and absolutely unnatural, as it is horrid and miserable."[22] But by the 1790s, when Ann Radcliffe and Matthew Lewis are publishing their different brands of Gothic terror and horror, entertaining with agony had become fiction's forte. Radcliffe knows well that her sentimental heroines – always exhibiting beauty, youth, "apparent innocence," and an "artless energy" of manner – can "gain from distress an expression of captivating sweetness."[23] Matthew Lewis's monk is seduced into a life of libertinism and violence by Rosario/ Matilda, a figure whose initial charms are all the traditional sentimental virtues: "vivacity of genius," "simplicity of manners," and "rectitude of heart."[24] Charlotte Dacre writes poetry and fiction under the pen name of "Rosa Matilda" in homage to Lewis's demonic figure and its unmasking of sentimental pieties. Dacre's novels, in particular, extend Lewis's project of Gothic horror, making the critique of sentimentalism increasingly explicit. The libertine heroine of Dacre's Zofloya, or the Moor (1806), for example, acknowledges with relish that "there is certainly a pleasure ... in the infliction of prolonged torment"; her victim is that stock sentimental figure, the "poor and friendless orphan."[25] Later in the century, Swinburne will compare Zofloya to the novels of the Marquis de Sade, and in describing its denouement as "accomplishing the vivisection of virtue," he also very rightly diagnoses its relationship to sentimentality.[26]

Very few writers in the Romantic period go as far as Lewis or Dacre in cutting up and cutting down the figures and values of the sentimental tradition. The excesses and crises of the 1790s – in both sentimental literature and politics, and, as Claudia Johnson has demonstrated, in their urgent interconnections – can give one a sense of sentimental fiction operating solely at the extremities of its form and culture in these years.[27] In fact, the major modes of sentimentality continue to prove both useful and portable well throughout the Romantic period, helping a number of emerging genres and fictional strategies articulate themselves within literary culture's dominant framework. The national tale is one such emerging genre that uses the familiar conventions of sentimental fiction to package its less familiar geographical and cultural settings. Relying, as it so often does, on the basic courtship plot, the national tale also exploits sentimentality's interest in "primitive" manners and "natural" sensibility to offer the Scottish Highlands or the Irish countryside as an invigorating antidote to the malaise or ennui of English civilization. One need only look at the scene of Monimia sharing a song with her bird in the Highland wilderness in Christian Isobel Johnstone's Clan-Albin, a National Tale (1816) to see an example of how the genre generates conventional sentimental affect and then appropriates it for its national construction. The scene recalls Virginie amidst her birds in Paul et Virginie (1787), Bernardin de Saint Pierre's classic sentimental text translated for English readers by Helen Maria Williams. Monimia's natural sensibility and desirability as a love object are thereby established in a sort of sentimental shorthand, and Norman, the novel's hero, discovers "a new motive to love [his] country."[28]

Such scenes not only press sentimentality's "cult of the primitive" into national service; they also reveal the Romantic period's increasingly historicist understanding of sentiment, taste, and manners. Indeed, the national tale and the historical novel work together to convert historical narratives of literary genre and style – bird song and human song being understood as the earliest forms of poetry and language, for example – into a framework for cultural comparison and recovery. Here we might return briefly to *Waverley* and the "supplemental title" on which Scott ultimately lands: "'Tis Sixty Years Since." This subtitle specifies the date of his story, of course – "neither a romance of chivalry, nor a tale of modern manners," but one of "the last generation" – and yet it is also meant to imply that the novel will be "more a description of men than manners" and that Scott will primarily display "those passions common to all men in all stages of society, and which have alike agitated the human heart." Declaring dedication to "hearts" and "men" over "manners" is a standard gesture of sentimental fiction; here Scott recruits readers schooled in sentimentality, students of the "great book of Nature" who have been taught to analyze and appreciate the "deep-ruling impulses" of feeling and passion common to all "human hearts."[29] But neither Scott nor his sentimental readers ever completely dismiss "manners" or their interest in the different "stages of society." Manners are the texture and customs of social relationships, the conventions that govern the expression of passion, the standards of propriety and taste. They become the privileged object of historical study and analysis once man's fundamental sociability and inherently passionate nature are assumed. "Manners" are what happens when social and sentimental man enters history, and putting sentimental man into history is precisely what Scott does in the *Waverley* novels with so much success.

History, itself, is thus given to Scott by the sentimental tradition. It is a social field of manners, style, and emotional attachments and, as James Chandler has demonstrated, it operates both at the level of Scott's story and characters (in what he represents) and at the level of his text and readers (in how he represents it).[30] By negotiating different historical situations or social stages, by translating between the period of his story and the period of his writing, and by forging affective and identificatory ties between them in the "neutral ground" of "manners and sentiments which are common to us and to our ancestors," Scott participates in making the novel into a national form and exploits fiction's capacity to construct an affective or sentimental nation.[31]

The conventions of sentimentality also prove useful for representing and defining an affective humanity, and sentimental fiction thus remains a popular vehicle for abolitionist and anti-slavery opinion in these crucial years at the turn of the century. A number of sentimental texts – Sarah Scott's *The History of Sir George Ellison* (1766), Henry Mackenzie's *Julia de Roubigné* (1777), Thomas Day's *The History of Sandford and Merton* (1789), Anna Mackenzie's *Slavery, or the Times* (1792), and Elizabeth Helme's *The Farmer of Inglewood Forest* (1796) – feature accounts of plantation slavery or model the benevolent and humanitarian treatment of slaves. The sentimental slave owner becomes a stock character in his own right, a figure who embodies the conflicted political positions that the sentimental tradition can embrace and, even, seemingly resolve. This gentleman, as described by Maria Edgeworth in her tale "The Grateful Negro," (1802) wishes "that there was no such thing as slavery in the world," but convinced that the "sudden emancipation of the negroes would rather increase than diminish their miseries," exercises his benevolence "within the bounds of reason."[32] Edgeworth pairs her figure of the enlightened slave owner with the "grateful negro" of her title, and their first meeting adheres to Adam Smith's description of a sympathetic interaction like actors to stage directions or dancers to choreography. Smith, you recall, insists that "general lamentations" must be supplemented by narrative; spectator and sufferer must ask and answer the question: "what has befallen you?" In Edgeworth's tale, Edwards, the slave owner, hears loud "lamentation" and hastens "to inquire what misfortune had befallen" Caesar, the slave of his cruel and debauched neighbor. The key moment in this scene emphasizes symmetry and the exchange of glances between owner and slave: Caesar looks up and "fixing his eyes upon Mr. Edwards for a moment, advanced with an intrepid rather than an imploring countenance." Here the specular framework of sympathy both enables Caesar's "intrepid" gaze and ultimately mutes its threat: Caesar advances in order to ask, "Will you be my master?" The humanitarian sensibility emerging in such sentimental texts grants humanity to the slave but, like the slave owner's benevolence, only within bounds.[33]

Sentimental figures prove equally useful to more radical abolitionist literature. William Earle situates his novel about a Jamaican slave rebellion within the struggle for the "Rights of Man" and hopes for a reader "whose heart shall sympathize." *Obi or, The History of Three-Fingered Jack* (1800) capitalizes on the rhetorical connections between revolutionary politics and sensibility so often made in the 1790s, using a mixed or mock epistolary form, interspersed with sentimental poetry, to narrate the story of Jack, a slave raised and educated by his mother to revenge his father's enslavement and death. The narrative of his rebellion alternates between depicting the

European barbarity that extinguishes "all the remaining sparks of humanity" in the slave's heart – using, in effect, sentimentality's creeds of benevolence and education against the Europeans to reverse enlightenment categories of "savage" and "civilized" man – and reconstructing that humanity through sentimental set-pieces which testify to Jack's capacity to feel and call on the reader to feel as well.[34] Slave narratives in this period, such as *The Interesting Narrative of the Life of Olaudah Equiano* (1789), draw on Christian conversion narratives and the traditions of spiritual autobiography; but they rely equally on sentimental structures to stage scenes of sympathetic conversion and inversion. Equiano, for example, describes himself as the spectator at a sale in which brothers were separated: "and it was very moving on this occasion to see and hear their cries at parting." By addressing his readers in the next sentence, he insists that they, too, are spectators to these cruelties:

> O, ye nominal Christians! might not an African ask you, learned you this from your God, who says unto you, Do unto all men as you would men should do unto you? Is it not enough that we are torn from our country and friends to toil for your luxury and lust of gain? Must every tender feeling be likewise sacrificed to your avarice? ... Why are parents to lose their children, brothers their sisters, or husbands their wives? Surely this is a new refinement in cruelty, which, while it has no advantage to atone for it, thus aggravates distress, and adds fresh horrors even to the wretchedness of slavery.[35]

Proving his own sensibility by deploying the language of sentiment to describe and express "tender feeling," Equiano's narrative uses the structure of sympathy to move his European readers through a set of imaginative identifications: with the slave traders whose practice serves their "luxury and lust of gain," then with the slaves whose familial relationships and affections are normative and familiar. Sentimentality is made complicit with slavery – as the refinements of feeling encoded in "luxury" here produce "new refinement[s] in cruelty" – but continues to provide the fundamental language and structure of subjectivity that the narrative uses to establish Equiano's self and sensibility.

Sentimental subjectivity is also crucial to the workings of women's fiction in the Romantic period where heroines, as Deidre Lynch has observed, often "have nothing but their subjectivity to entitle them."[36] Wollstonecraft famously condemns sentimental novels and the culture of sensibility for producing women who are "weakened by false refinement" and neglect the "duties of life," and turn-of-the-century fiction abounds with women of excessive, unhealthy, false, or downright silly sensibility.[37] But such characters are often paired, as Austen famously does in *Sense and Sensibility*, with women of just and natural feeling, and the healthy and virtuous sensibility of that character often gives her claims to value and attention that her class and gender would otherwise deny her. Mary Robinson's *The Natural Daughter* (1799) pairs two such sisters. Julia, of a corrupt and artificial sensibility, spends the first half of the novel "exhausted from weeping" and ends as the mistress of Robespierre. Martha, of sincere and natural sensibility, is barred from her husband's household due to false accusations of infidelity, but turns her natural genius for feeling into successive careers as an actress, poet, and novelist. Robinson explicitly affirms that Martha's true sensibility and sincere expression are precisely what equip her to be an artist: she "was the thing she seemed, while even the perfection of her art was Nature."[38]

Robinson's two sisters have different temperaments, but they are also the products of different educations: Martha was "sent to a country boarding-school for education" while Julia, fatally, was tutored at home by a French governess. The Romantic era novel's interest in education and educational philosophy is one of its most sustained engagements with sentimental tradition. Eliza Fenwick's *Secresy* (1795), Elizabeth Inchbald's *Nature and Art* (1797), Mary Hays's *The Victim of Prejudice* (1799), Maria Edgeworth's *Belinda* (1801), and Amelia Opie's *Adeline Mowbray* (1805), for example, all feature characters who receive some sort of sentimental education in childhood: confined, by deliberate system, improbable circumstance, or neglect to rural seclusion and leading a natural, robust, sportive and even "wild" early life. These novels put their depiction of educational experiments to a variety of critical uses: they highlight the hypocrisies of a society that idolizes the "natural" but fails to nurture natural sensibility, or they expose the limitations of a sentimental education, arguing vehemently, for example, against Rousseau's dismissal of the rational capacities of girls and women. The heroines of *Secresy*, *The Victim of Prejudice*, and *Adeline Mowbray* either remain a type of naive primitive or adopt philosophies of virtue and conduct condemned by conventional society. As one might expect, the misfortunes and sufferings of these women are extreme: they are imprisoned, abandoned, betrayed, or raped by tyrannical fathers or libertine lovers. The cultural drama repeatedly enacted in this brand of fiction is the troubled emergence of a middle-class, feminine and sentimental subjectivity over and against the persecutions of a debauched and despotic aristocracy.[39]

While familial relationships and affections are often central to the sentimental norms of such novels, particularly to their recuperative conclusions, we would, nevertheless, be wrong to equate the sentimental and the domestic in these years. Innate sentimental virtue or a sensibility enlarged by a sentimental education often gives the women in these novels the ambition to pursue non-domestic work, and the exercise of their sentimental charity often refuses to confine itself to the bounds or interests of the husband's family. The rise of domesticity and the ideal of the domestic woman often work as checks on the more expansive possibilities offered to women by the exercise of their faculties for feeling. Frequently the tensions between the sentimental and the domestic threaten the capacity of either to offer full or satisfying fictional resolution. Amelia Opie's tremendously popular and influential novel, *The Father and Daughter* (1801), for example, begins with a classic sentimental spectacle and structure of address:

> The night was dark – the wind blew keenly over the frozen and rugged heath, when Agnes, pressing her moaning child to her bosom, was traveling on foot to her father's habitation.
> "Would to God I had never left it!" she exclaimed, as home and all its enjoyments rose in fancy to her view: – and I think my readers will be ready to join in the exclamation, when they hear the poor wanderer's history.[40]

That history, the narrator later insists, has little to do with either Agnes's seducer or with her illegitimate son: "the chief characters in it are the father and daughter."[41] When Agnes learns that her disobedience and disgrace have led to her father's insanity and made him the resident of the local madhouse, she works indefatigably to re-establish a home with him, to nurse him back to his senses and his knowledge of her. But her single-minded devotion to her father makes her an oddly inattentive mother, as she repeatedly drops, ignores or neglects her infant while exhibiting or brooding over her filial affections. Agnes's maternal deficiencies are relatively mild and benign, but the sentimental values of this novel ultimately produce only a retrograde and doomed domesticity that gives over quickly to the pathetic spectacle of a double funeral procession, as "at the same time, were borne to the same grave, the father and the daughter."[42]

Romantic writing has been described as moving the drama of feeling inward, as turning away from the spectacle of socially performed sentiments to the interior and private depths of the individual. In an 1814 review of Byron's Turkish tales, Francis Jeffrey accounts for that inward turn by drawing a history of sentiment, manners, and literary style. Describing "rude ages" when "men's passions are violent, and their sensibility dull" as a time when poetry deals in "strong emotions, and displays the agency of powerful passions," he next describes how, "as civilization advances" and "men begin to be ashamed of the undisguised vehemence of their primitive emotions," both manners and literature become "first pompous and stately – then affectedly refined and ingenious – and finally gay, witty, discursive and familiar." Byron's poetry is a product of the next stage in this "history of man and his inventions": a reaction against the high and artificial refinements of sentiment and literary style and, instead, an age of return and revival, when the "stronger and deeper passions" of earlier periods, along with their ancient and even vulgar literary forms (romances and ballads), again hold interest and value.[43]

Jeffrey's emphasis on his period's interest in "strong emotion" and "powerful passions" – in particular, the "fiery passions" of the Byronic hero – claims the primitive as a masculine antidote to the effeminate niceties of modern sensibility. In a similar vein, Hugh Blair had earlier praised the "vehemence" and "sublimity" of Ossian's poetry, and Wordsworth had embraced the "more emphatic language" of the rustic. But just as Blair can defend Ossian's poetry as both "manly" and *The Poetry of the Heart*," Jeffrey is well aware that the return to primitive passions evidenced in the literature of his day retains and exploits the assumptions and conventions of modern sentimental culture. The desire in such "a late stage of civilization" to find "beings capable of strong passions," according to Jeffrey, occasions the "revival" of both "the characters and adventures which animated the poetry of rude ages." But "it must not be thought that they are made to act and feel, on this resurrection, exactly as they did in their first natural presentation." Where early literature directs attention to what the hero "does – not to what he feels," the drama of the revival is in the feeling: "the passion itself must now be pourtrayed – and all its fearful workings displayed in detail before us." Minds must be "unmasked" and "throbbing bosoms laid open to our gaze," till "we can enter into all the motions of their hearts, and read, and shudder as we read, the secret characters which stamp the capacity of unlimited suffering on a nature which we feel to be our own." In short: "it is chiefly by these portraitures of the interior of human nature that the poetry of the present day is distinguished from all that preceded it."[44]

Jeffrey's interest in the exposure and display of secret, inner passions, and his faith in a social, sympathetic identification as what motivates that inter-est, betray the sentimental structure supporting this version of Romantic interiority. Such strong sentimental rhetoric in an account of what is sup-posed to distinguish the poetry of the day "from all that preceded it" is particularly striking for occurring in a review of Byron's verse romances. For the Byronic hero is a figure whose intensely private emotional drama and unrepentant criminality would seem to keep him outside the social and redemptive networks we expect to find in sentimental texts. The face of the Byronic hero, however, offers a "portraiture" of interiority that is, itself, a sentimental text, albeit one that inversely or perversely exploits sentimental conventions. Here the "outward signs of evil thought" may always be "slight," and the "lip's least curl" may "speak alone / Of deeper passions," but this inverted ratio of outward expression to inner depths relies no less than other sentimental displays of subjectivity on the calibration of gesture to

emotion, physical symptom to interior life. Less may be more in the sentimental economy of Romantic subjectivity, but Byron pushes this formula
even further, critically extending sentimental culture by pushing an underlying fascination with the personal and private toward a cult of the personality and a privacy more performed than guarded.

By tracking the continued relevance of sentimental modes to a variety of
Romantic writing, by enlisting both Scott and Byron as Romantic sentimentalists, this chapter works to extend our sense of the continuities between
sentimental and Romantic literary cultures. It is, perhaps, our own emphasis
on the performative and historical frames of subjectivity that has renewed
our interest in sentimentality and animated our growing sense of the sentimental grounds of British Romanticism. The conventions of sentimental
fiction no longer seem merely superficial gestures discarded by a deeper,
more authentic, or more ambitious Romantic writing. Rather, sentimentality
is a rhetorical tradition for the reading and representation of the self that
provides the terms in which depth, authenticity, and the high seriousness of
literature can be claimed and recognized.

NOTES

1 Walter Scott, *Waverley*, ed. Andrew Hook (London: Penguin, 1972), pp. 33–4.
2 Ina Ferris, *The Achievement of Literary Authority: Gender, History, and the
Waverley Novels* (Ithaca: Cornell University Press, 1991), p. 95; Katie
Trumpener, *Bardic Nationalism: The Romantic Novel and the British Empire*
(Princeton: Princeton University Press, 1997), p. 139.
3 William Wordsworth, *Lyrical Ballads and Other Poems, 1797–1800*, ed. James
Butler and Karen Green (Ithaca: Cornell University Press, 1992), p. 747.
4 Rev. James Barclay, *Barclay's Dictionary* (London: G. G. and J. Robinson, 1799).
5 John Mullan, "Sentimental Novels," in *The Cambridge Companion to the
Eighteenth-Century Novel*, ed. John Richetti (Cambridge: Cambridge
University Press, 1996), pp. 237–8.
6 James Chandler, "Moving Accidents: The Emergence of Sentimental
Probability," *The Age of Cultural Revolutions*, ed. Colin Jones and Dror
Wahrman (Berkeley: University of California Press, 2002), p. 146.
7 James Boswell, *Life of Johnson* (Oxford: Oxford University Press, 1980), p. 480.
8 Wordsworth, *Lyrical Ballads*, p. 746.
9 Anthony, Third Earl of Shaftesbury, *Characteristicks of Men, Manners,
Opinions, Times* (Indianapolis: Liberty Fund, 2001), Vol. II, p. 79.
10 *Ibid.*, Vol. II, p. 17.
11 *Ibid.*, Vol. II, p. 56.
12 David Hume, *A Treatise of Human Nature* (Oxford: Clarendon Press, 1978),
pp. 316–17.
13 *Ibid.*, p. 605.
14 Adela Pinch, *Strange Fits of Passion: Epistemologies of Emotion, Hume to Austen*
(Stanford: Stanford University Press, 1996), p. 19.

15 Adam Smith, *The Theory of Moral Sentiments*, ed. D. D. Raphael and A. L. Macfie (Indianapolis: Liberty Fund, 1982), p. 21.

16 *Ibid.*, p. 113.

17 *Ibid.*, p. 11.

18 Clara Reeve, *The Progress of Romance*, Vol. II (New York: Facsimile Text Society, 1930), p. 36.

19 *Encyclopedia Britannica* (Edinburgh: A. Bell and C. Macfarquhar, 1797), p. 272.

20 R. F. Brissenden, *Virtue in Distress: Studies in the Novel of Sentiment from Richardson to Sade* (New York: Harper & Row, 1974), pp. 39–43; John Mullan, *Sentiment and Sociability: The Language of Feeling in the Eighteenth Century* (Oxford: Clarendon Press, 1988), pp. 201–40.

21 Edgar Alan Poe, *Great Short Works*, ed. G. R. Thompson (New York: HarperCollins, 1970), p. 222.

22 Shaftesbury, *Characteristicks*, Vol. II, p. 94.

23 Ann Radcliffe, *The Romance of the Forest*, ed. Chloe Chard (Oxford: Oxford University Press, 1986), pp. 5–6.

24 Matthew Lewis, *The Monk*, ed. Christopher Maclachlan (London: Penguin Books, 1998), p. 41.

25 Charlotte Dacre, *Zofloya; or The Moor*, ed. Adriana Craciun (Peterborough, Ontario: Broadview Press, 1997), p. 205.

26 Quoted in *ibid.*, p. 9.

27 Claudia L. Johnson, *Equivocal Beings: Politics, Gender, and Sentimentality in the 1790s* (Chicago: University of Chicago Press, 1995).

28 Christian Isobel Johnstone, *Clan-Albin, A National Tale*, ed. Andrew Monnickendam (Glasgow: Association for Scottish Literary Studies, 2003), p. 101.

29 Scott, *Waverley*, pp. 34–6.

30 James Chandler, *England in 1819: The Politics of Literary Culture and the Case of Romantic Historicism* (Chicago: University of Chicago Press, 1998), pp. 141–7.

31 Walter Scott, *Ivanhoe*, ed. Graham Tulloch (Edinburgh: Edinburgh University Press, 1998), p. 9.

32 Maria Edgeworth, *Novels and Selected Works*, Vol. XII, *Popular Tales*, ed. Elizabeth Eger, Clíona Ó Gallchoir, and Marilyn Butler (London: Pickering & Chatto, 2003).

33 For discussions of slavery and sentimentality see Markman Ellis, *The Politics of Sensibility: Race, Gender and Commerce in the Sentimental Novel* (Cambridge: Cambridge University Press, 1996) and Lynn Festa, *The Sentimental Figures of Empire* (Baltimore: Johns Hopkins Press, 2006).

34 William Earle, *Obi; Or, the History of Three-Fingered Jack*, ed. Srinivas Aravamudan (Peterborough, Ontario: Broadview Press, 2005), p. 99.

35 Olaudah Equiano, *The Interesting Narrative of the Life of Olaudah Equiano*, ed. Angelo Costanzo (Peterborough, Ontario: Broadview Press, 2001), pp. 75–6.

36 Deidre Shauna Lynch, *The Economy of Character: Novels, Market Culture, and the Business of Inner Meaning* (Chicago: University of Chicago Press, 1998), p. 153.

37 Mary Wollstonecraft, *A Vindication of the Rights of Woman*, ed. Carol H. Poston (New York: W. W. Norton & Company, 1988), pp. 60 and 183.

38 Mary Robinson, *A Letter to the Women of England* and *The Natural Daughter*, ed. Sharon Setzer (Peterborough, Ontario: Broadview Press, 2003), p. 179.

39 See Nancy Armstrong, *Desire and Domestic Fiction: A Political History of the Novel* (Oxford: Oxford University Press, 1987) and Gillian Brown, *Domestic Individualism: Imagining Self in Nineteenth-Century America* (Berkeley: University of California Press, 1990).

40 Amelia Opie, *The Father and Daughter* with *Dangers of Coquetry*, ed. Shelley King and John B. Pierce (Peterborough, Ontario: Broadview Press, 2003), p. 65.

41 *Ibid*, p. 67.

42 *Ibid.*, p. 151.

43 Francis Jeffrey, unsigned review of *The Corsair* and *The Bride of Abydos*, *Edinburgh Review* (April 1814), reprinted in *Byron: The Critical Heritage*, ed. Andrew Rutherford (London: Routledge & Kegan Paul, 1970), pp. 54–5.

44 *Ibid.*, pp. 58–9.

12

GARY KELLY

Fiction and the working classes

This title could mean fiction that *interested* the working classes, in the related senses *engaged the attention of* and *addressed the material interests of*. It could also mean fiction that *represented* the working classes, in the overlapping senses *depicted* and *spoke for*. There were at least five kinds of fiction circulating during the Romantic period that interested or represented the working classes. There was fiction by and for them, fiction by but not particularly for them, fiction for but rarely by them, fiction by and for the middle classes but read by some working-class people, and fiction depicting the working classes but written by and for the middle classes. There was a little of the first and second, much of the third, some of the fourth, and a good deal of the fifth. Literature being mainly a middle-class cultural institution, the last has received most attention; in fact, some have argued that middle-class fiction, whether or not it represents/depicts the working classes, can nevertheless represent/speak for them. Most have also assumed that fiction read predominantly by the working classes could not represent their interests, being mere commercial entertainment with little artistic or intellectual value, drugging its "consumers" with escapist fantasy, concealing their exploitation from them, and distracting them from their real political interests. Such fiction may, however, have its own artistry, ideology, and politics. Investigating this possibility requires turning from the poetics of middle-class literature to those of working-class print culture, from authorship to reading, from "original" to recycled texts, from history of texts to history of books, from literary criticism as disciplined or "schooled" reading for professional purposes to unschooled but not unskilled reading for everyday life.

Literary studies usually understand fiction as invented, written (and printed), secular, prose narrative. But fiction may be in prose and verse, oral and written, pictorial and verbal, sacred and secular, and during the Romantic period working-class readers welcomed all of these indiscriminately. Literary studies usually distinguish between fiction and non-fiction, but during the Romantic period working-class readers relished both fiction

207

and non-fiction, from saints' lives to travelogues. Literary histories usually restrict themselves to "original" works produced in a particular period, but most fiction circulating during the Romantic period had been produced earlier, working-class readers enjoyed past and contemporary fiction equally, and most of the fiction they read had been first published before the Romantic period. Finally, literary studies usually deal with fiction considered to be of "serious" import, "artistic" merit, and "enduring value," variously defined. These assumptions reproduce Romantic ideologies of authorship, originality, and "literary" value serving middle-class culture and interests. Throughout the Romantic period most working-class readers ignored such distinctions and read what they could get and what interested them – they read what engaged their interest because it spoke to their material interests.

Who were these readers? The working classes have been defined variously in economic, social, political, and cultural terms, while some deny there is such a thing. The phrase "working(-)class" first appeared in print during the Romantic period, used by middle-class observers as a merely descriptive phrase. Only later did it come to indicate a social group with a particular ideology, culture, identity, and history grounded in their economic and social condition, mainly in the discourse of socialist theorists and historians. Others have preferred broader understandings of pluralized working "classes," "lower classes," "laboring classes," "plebeians," and "proletariat" or terms used at that time, such as "lower orders," "lower ranks," and "crowd." During the Romantic period these classes comprised a wide variety of skilled, semi-skilled, and unskilled laborers, from printers to farm laborers, blacksmiths to washerwomen, bookbinders to shepherds, tanners to cooks, coachmen to seamstresses. They included the occasionally, frequently, or normally unemployed; the independent artisan, the indentured apprentice, and the wage slave; the proudly prosperous, the constantly struggling, and the working poor. There were also pronounced regional, ethnic, and gender differences within the working classes. There was always movement between classes, too, as individuals and families moved back and forth from hired labor, or working-class status, to independent small-scale production and commerce, or lower middle-class status. Some conditions and events mainly affected a particular social class, others affected all classes, and all would participate in certain social and cultural practices, from festivals to reading, if not in the same way. People could also entertain identities and values other than those they normally inhabited in everyday life – in fact, fiction was one important way to do so.

What then was the relationship between fiction and these working classes during the Romantic period? Working-class autobiographies from the time give us clear indications.[1] Working-class culture retained much of the historic oral culture of folk song and folktale, and working-class readers assimilated printed fiction to this oral culture, or moved easily between them. Individual access to literacy depended on particular circumstances, especially personal or parental motivation, and availability of instruction by a parent, relative, or elderly woman at a local "dame school." Working-class readers were often regarded suspiciously by their peers, as idlers or aspirants above their community. The few autobiographies by working-class women from this period suggest that both sexes read what they could get, fiction and non-fiction, verse and prose fiction, sacred and secular narrative. Many who could not read, and many who could, were read to or had books retold to them; consequently, avid readers often became storytellers.

Working-class autobiographers recall five main fiction formats. Most common were chapbooks of a kind circulating for generations, usually bought from chapmen, or peddlers. Around 1800, chapbooks of a new kind began to appear, mainly much shorter versions of books read by the middle classes, and bought from publishers and small shops, or possibly borrowed from small circulating libraries and pubs. Books produced for the middle classes were expensive – a three-volume novel could cost two weeks' labourer's wages – but working-class readers did come by stray volumes. Middle-class readers usually rented books, especially fiction, from commercial circulating libraries, but working-class readers could rarely afford the subscription and rental fees. Increasingly available were cheap reprints and books published in weekly or monthly parts (or "numbers") and sold door-to-door, mainly for the burgeoning middle-class readership for both fashionable and "classic" literature. An increasing number and variety of periodicals aimed at working-class readers appeared by the 1810s and 1820s, mostly political or entertaining or both. Finally, there was much pseudo-popular print directed at the working classes by middle-class social reformers.

The fiction most often and fondly recalled in working-class autobiographies was the kind of chapbook that had been circulating for generations. These were small pamphlets costing from about one to sixpence, from eight to thirty-two pages long, badly printed on cheap paper, and decorated with woodblock images not always relevant to the story. Chapbook fiction constituted a large text comprising related categories of individual texts. There were tales featuring heroes and rogues, such as *Sir William Wallace* (an early eighteenth-century prose version of a Scots poem celebrating the medieval Scottish patriot warrior), *Robin Hood's Garland* (a collection of verse tales first published in the seventeenth century, about the legendary

6 *The History of Valentine and Orson* (early): One of the most perennially popular chapbooks in characteristic eighteenth-century format.

medieval outlaw), *Jack and the Giants* (anecdotes of a wisecracking strong-man who outwits and overcomes several giants and is rewarded with lands and genteel rank), *Doctor Faustus* (about the medieval scholar–magician who sells his soul to the Devil), *Fortunatus* (whose magic implements carry him through a succession of adventures), *Valentine and Orson* (originally published in the sixteenth century and based on a medieval French verse romance, recounting fabulous adventures of two noble brothers; see Figures 6 and 7), *The King and the Cobbler* (a tale originally published in the seventeenth century in which the king, usually Henry VIII, tours his capital incognito to learn his subjects' views and hears the truth from a merry cobbler, whom he subsequently rewards), and *Bamfylde Moore*

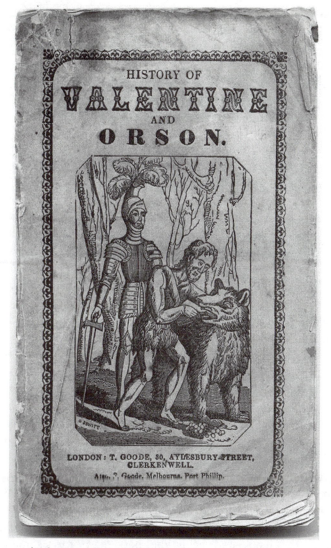

7 *The History of* Valentine and Orson (Goode): No "mass extinction": the historic chapbooks did not disappear but were reissued in formats similar to those of the new fashionable chapbooks that began to appear around 1800.

Carew, King of the Beggars, a late eighteenth-century addition to the chapbook repertory. There was a smaller body of tales featuring women, including *Fair Rosamond* (based on a historical figure whose beauty attracts the king and who is later murdered by the jealous queen), *Jane Shore* (based on another historical royal mistress), *Patient Grisel* (plebeian wife of a nobleman who cruelly tests her love and loyalty), and *Long Meg of Westminster* (a merry strongwoman who protects the weak from a succession of predatory and violent men). There were jestbooks such as *The Wise Men of Gotham* (a series of jokes first published in the sixteenth century about a village of fools) and *Joe Miller's Jests* (a jokebook). There were books of wonders, such as *Mandeville's Travels*. There were also "fairy tales," mainly folktales rewritten and published a century or more earlier for a genteel readership and then taken downmarket in collections such as "Mother Bunch's," a chapbook first published in 1773. These chapbooks were joined by a few longer works such as *Robinson Crusoe*, *The Pilgrim's Progress*, and parts of *Gulliver's Travels* that also could be read as sensational adventure stories.

Working-class readers seemed uninterested, however, in distinguishing such fiction from a larger body of cheap print, again comprising several related categories. There were prophecy books such as "Old Nixon's" and "Mother Shipton's," books of divination by dreams, portents, physiognomical traits, astrology, etc., and almanacs, which also contained prophecies, related to regular movements of the cosmos, earth, tides, seasons, weather, and animals (Figure 8). There were books of popular science that combined ideas of natural causation, craft, and magic, such as herbals and other books of practical health and living, and *Aristotle's Masterpiece*, a seventeenth-century guide to procreation and forecasting personal destiny by bodily features (physiognomy and palmistry). There were execution broadsides and "last dying words," supposedly uttered by condemned criminals and embodying an insistent fatalism, sold to crowds at public hangings, and going back to the origins of printing. There was popular song in ballad sheets and "garlands," or chapbooks containing a number of lyrics, similar in themes and narrative form to both the prose fiction chapbooks and folk ballads and tales. There were religious or "godly" chapbooks and books, usually more sensational than pious, featuring miraculous incidents, divine retributions, heroic sufferings of Protestant martyrs, and lives of saints such as Robert the hermit, who withdraws from the world in disgust at its injustices but defends and helps the poor (see, for example, *God's Judgment against Sinful Pride*, Figure 9).

The recurring themes of this fiction and its associated non-fiction are fortune and fate, chance and opportunity, destiny and personal gifts (cleverness, physical strength, beauty), innate character (fortitude, courage, loyalty, holiness) and its eccentricities and extremes, sensational events and extraordinary characters, and magical, prophetic, or clairvoyant powers. Working-class people also read these themes into earlier kinds of fiction otherwise associated with the middle classes, such as *Robinson Crusoe* and *Pamela* or religious texts such as *The Pilgrim's Progress*, and into fiction of

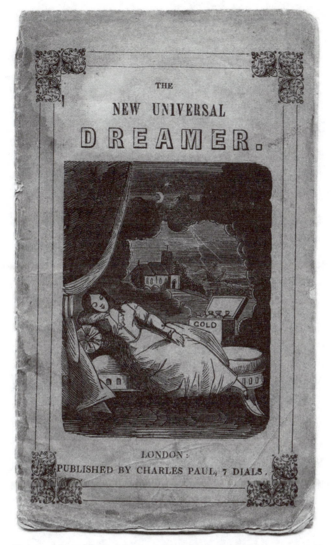

8 *The New Universal Dreamer*: For those with little prospect of improving their lives through hard work, self-improvement, or anything else, except winning the lottery or other strokes of luck, the ability to anticipate the future remained, as it had for centuries, a way of sustaining hope and imagining things otherwise.

the Romantic period produced for the middle classes, such as Gothic romances and Scott's historical novels, or non-fiction such as voyage and shipwreck narratives, criminal biography from execution broadsides to the *Newgate Calendar*, lives of religious heroes and martyrs, lives of extraordinary contemporary characters such as Nelson and Napoleon, historical

> # God's Judgment against Sinful Pride.
>
> Being a particular Account of one Lady Millwood, who refided near the Town of Brighton, and who was fo very proud, that fhe thought the Ground not good enough to fupport her Pomp. But, in the Beginning of Auguft laft, one Mary Willis afked her Charity, but was refufed in the moft fcornful Manner; on which the poor Woman called upon God to revenge her Caufe. When the Earth opened and fwallowed up Lady Millwood, who was foon after thrown up again, a confiderable Diftance from the Place where fhe firft funk, and being taken to her own Houfe, foon after expired in great Agonies.
>
> Alfo, the Sermon which was preached at her Funeral by the Reverend Mr. Gladding.

9 *God's Judgment against Sinful Pride*: Ostensibly religious, this kind of chapbook (here in characteristic eighteenth-century format) was in fact highly sensational.

narratives containing heroic, sensational, and horrific events, such as the translation of Josephus's *Jewish Wars*, and chapbook versions of ancient classical adventure narratives such as the *Iliad* (Figure 10).

In form, most of these texts are characterized by brevity, paratactic structure or string of similar episodes, third-person narration, presentation of events in chronological order, styles ranging from colloquial to elevated, desultory narrative structure, repetitive plot form, few literary or learned allusions, few direct references to contemporary social or political events, stereotypical characters and formulaic characterization, stylized dialogue,

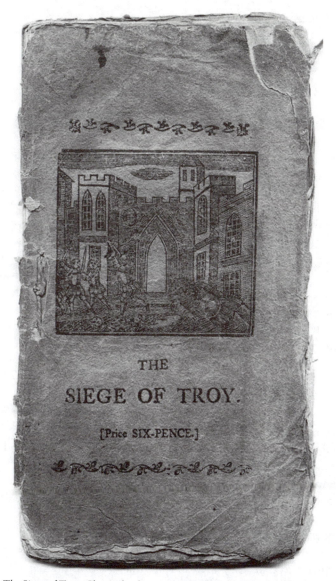

10 *The Siege of Troy*: Classical culture, again in characteristic eighteenth-century format, as a ripping yarn.

sparing description of settings, brief and formulaic representation of characters' subjectivity, little domestic realism, broad humor, proverbial expressions, and perfunctory or formulaic closure. These characteristics are also found in folktales, legends, and myths, which are less re-creations of a reality than stylized interpretations of it.

Such themes and forms interested working-class readers, listeners, and storytellers up to and through the Romantic period because they gave artistic embodiment to a culture and ideology formed in response to the realities of a subsistence economy. These realities included chronic scarcity of resources, numerous hazards of mortality, and cyclical patterns of work, social relations, life stages, church ritual and religious festivals, natural processes, and time. In this economy there was little prospect of saving for hard times, let alone of monetary or material accumulation, and little prospect of advancement in life. Just surviving required improvisation, opportunism, moral suppleness, indifference to the law, social agility, ingenuity and evasiveness before power and authority, and reliance on class solidarity and discipline, or working-class "moral economy" and "customs in common." The cyclical, repetitive form of chapbook fiction enacted for the working-class reader, on the level of narrative structure, the patterns of his or her experience from day to day, season to season, generation to generation. Reading and rereading chapbooks with this symbolic structure enacted the same patterns in the individual's reading practice over time, drawing readers into the kind of compulsive reading described in many of the working-class autobiographies, and still observable today. Chapbook fiction's open-ended structure, series of similar incidents, formulaic closure, and weak denouement enacted working-class experience of life and lives as diverse but repetitive rather than cumulative, inconclusive rather than "amounting to something" – let alone producing material accumulation or rise in social significance.

In a subsistence economy life seemed a lottery, with little prospect of improvement except through luck or magic. Luck could take various forms: inborn gifts such as physical strength, manual dexterity, and beauty; aptitudes such as cleverness and opportunism, or certain skills; and fortunate coincidences such as meeting a patron or lover. In chapbook fiction, magic is usually acquired by luck and could also take various forms – knowledge of the future, influence over forces normally beyond one's control (the weather, social superiors, the economy, love, one's physiognomy), or perhaps power to transform reality altogether, into paradise on earth. Magic is imagining things otherwise than they are, and approaches revolutionary politics or millenarian religion – both of which erupted during the Romantic period and incorporated elements of working-class fiction. For example, Tom Paine wrote in his working-class bestseller *Rights of Man* (1792) like a politicized Jack the Giant Killer, and Joanna Southcott couched her millenarian prophecies in a fusion of street-ballad verse and chapbook fantasy. Chapbook fiction itself contained little overt social protest, moralizing, or religious piety, but much transmuted protest. Printers and distributors had to avoid offending the powerful, and working-class readers might have found that overt protest or piety in fiction would have interfered with their use of fiction to negotiate through a difficult and uncertain world. For them, fiction registered their reality in objectified, abstract, semi-mythic form – the historic ideological and social function of popular fiction from oral folktales through chapbooks to modern romances.

The persistence of the chapbook repertory over generations indicates the continuity of working-class experience of subsistence economy. Of course, life had long been uncertain for people of all classes; the lottery mentality could appeal to rich and poor, leisured and laboring, comfortable and indigent, though not alike. Fiction and non-fiction embodying the lottery mentality was read and enjoyed by people of all ranks, though not necessarily in the same way; and much of the fiction read mainly by the middle and even upper classes through the seventeenth and eighteenth centuries, such as picaresque novels, romances, and adventure narratives, shared themes and formal traits with working-class fiction of the same period. The hardships of a subsistence economy fell mostly to the working classes, however, and remained their daily reality, sustaining the lottery mentality, social practices, and cultural forms created in response to it.

During this period, however, long-term structural transformations and particular events increasingly challenged historic formations of working-class ideology, social relations, and culture, including fiction. Modernization based on increasingly systematic application of capitalism introduced new technologies and wage relations, integration of local into national and international economies, urbanization and economic specialization, development of commercialized consumption based on novelty and social emulation, increased social surveillance and control of the lower classes by the upper and middle, and formation of a middle-class investment mentality emphasizing self-discipline and the accumulation of moral and intellectual capital. During the Romantic period, these larger changes were experienced through particular events, including the crisis of the American Revolution, the French Revolution panic and Napoleonic wars, resulting economic and social crisis, consequently accelerated politicization of middle and working classes, government repression of such movements, coalition of middle- and working-class elements for political reform, postwar economic downturn and social conflict, and the institutional and constitutional reform crises of the 1820s and 1830s.

Both long-term transformations and particular events were articulated through fiction – the form of print, apart from newspapers and magazines, most widely read by all classes. In the later eighteenth century new kinds of fiction were developed by and for the middle classes embodying their interests, characterized by most or all of the following: much greater length than the chapbook; hypotactic structure based on events connected as cause and effect; stories beginning *in medias res*; progressive plot form; much first-person narration and new hybrid third-person narration with free indirect discourse (or reported inward speech and thought of a character); representation of characteristic speech and of class and regional dialect; references to contemporary social and political events and conditions; highly individualized characters; detailed representation of subjective states; lengthy dialogues and detailed descriptions; detailed portrayal of everyday and domestic life; and emphatic closure resolving conflicts and assigning justice. Such fiction became increasingly popular, in the sense of widely read, among the middle classes because it embodied the investment mentality central to their developing class consciousness and identity. It did so by emphasizing the importance of disciplined subjectivity to a progressive life-plot in a world of comprehensible causes and consequences. Yet fiction in general retained its low status in middle-class culture because of fears that it stimulated dangerous desire and fantasy and so obstructed accumulation of moral and intellectual capital.

The commercialization of cultural consumption during the Romantic period created a world of material culture, including forms of fiction, adapted to different class interests and identities. A new kind of working-class chapbook fiction related to middle-class Romantic popular fiction began appearing around 1800, and rapidly marginalized the traditional chapbooks (see, for example, Figure 11). The new chapbooks were usually from thirty-two to seventy-four pages long and cost from sixpence to a shilling – the price of a meal or a cheap theatre seat. The majority comprised fiction of three main kinds: shortened versions of the three-volume Gothic romances, historical novels, and sentimental tales produced for the middle classes; original novelettes or stories from magazines, in the same genres; and novelettizations of popular plays, melodramas, and even poems (see, Figures 12, 13, and 14). These chapbooks purposely differed in appearance from the earlier kinds – more carefully printed, bound in attractively ornamented blue or yellow paper covers, and with hand-colored frontispieces depicting a sensational incident from the story (Figure 15). Such chapbooks were among the fashionable novelties, from clothing to entertainments, increasingly demanded by the working classes as cheaper versions of those purchased by the upper and middle classes in the expanding fashion system of consumption based on social emulation. The new chapbooks were more expensive than the earlier kind, indicating a readership spanning the working, lower-middle, and middle classes and corresponding to an emergent coalition of the same social elements for purposes of achieving political reform. This indication is reinforced by the new chapbooks' contents.

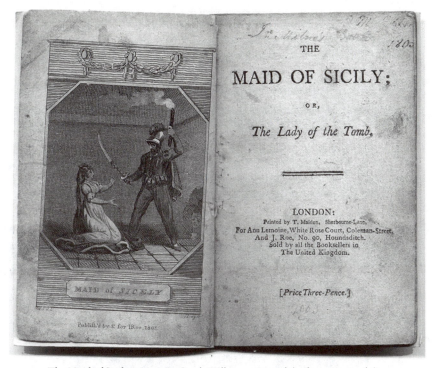

11 *The Maid of Sicily* (1805): By Sarah Wilkinson, one of the few writers of the new chapbooks who put her name on her work (on the next page of the chapbook) – she published scores of these.

For these chapbooks differed less from the old than they seemed to, containing elements of both traditional working-class fiction and fashionable middle-class fiction. Chapbook versions of three-volume novels retained such features as basic genre conventions (for example, of the Gothic), beginning *in medias res*, purple patches, hyperbole, and occasional moralizing, but lacked the detailed representations of subjectivity, extensive descriptive passages, lengthy social scenes, and literary allusions often found in their sources. Such reductions render the chapbook version a desultory, fast-paced, action-oriented, incident-packed narrative more like the traditional kind of chapbook and folk narrative. The original chapbook novelettes and novelettizations of melodramas have similar traits. Like the traditional kind of chapbooks, the new rarely have an author's name on the title-page, and rarely mention a source if there was one, except for the novelettizations of popular plays, where stating source and author could be a selling point. In style, the new chapbooks, like the old and like folk narrative, also rely on conventional language and formulaic phrases to stylize and

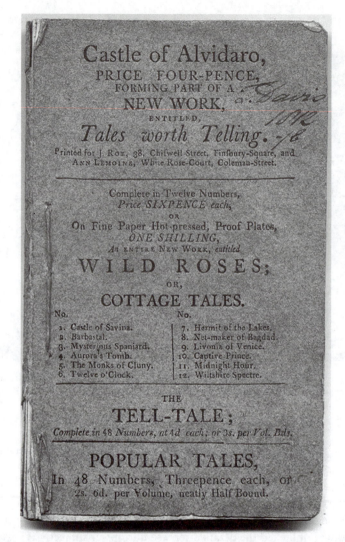

12 *Castle of Alvidaro*: The fashionable new chapbooks that began to appear around 1800, cut-down versions of Gothic triple-decker novels consumed by the middle classes, here in small format as part of a series and literally a "blue book." This publisher also issued historic chapbook titles in the new format.

generalize representations of characters, places, and events, giving them the quality of mythic narrative.

This approximation in form and style of the old and new chapbook fiction is affirmed by the presence of both kinds in publishers' lists. For example, the London firm of J. Bailey published long-familiar chapbook tales such as *Jane Shore, Blue Beard, Nixon's Prophecies, Friar Bacon, Jack Sheppard,*

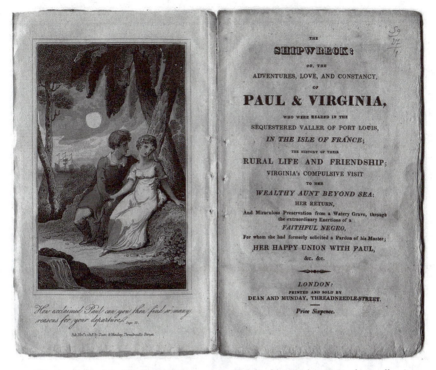

13 *Paul and Virginia*: The fashionable new chapbooks, like Harlequin Books swallowing Mills and Boon in the twentieth century, reached far and wide for titles to reissue – here Bernardin de St. Pierre's best-selling sentimental novella.

Bamfylde Moore Carew, *Sir William Wallace*, and *Ali Baba* and *Aladdin*. These were, however, given contemporary-sounding long titles, colored frontispieces, and a format uniform with that of Bailey's longer list of fashionable fiction, which included Gothic chapbooks such as *The Night Hag* and *The Tomb of Ferrados*, sentimental but sensational romances such as *Love in a Mad-house* and Goethe's *Sorrows of Werther*, and chapbook versions of bestselling Romantic novels, such as Scott's *Rob Roy* and *Ivanhoe*. For example, the old favorite *Sir William Wallace* reappears as *The Hero of Scotland; or, Battle of Dumbarton, an Historical Romance; in Which the Love of Liberty and Conjugal Affection Are Exemplified in the Characters of Sir William and Lady Wallace* (1825). Other London firms such as T. Hughes, Fairburn, Fisher, and Kemmish and provincial firms such as Richardson of Derby, Swindells of Manchester, Robertson of Glasgow, and Smyth of Belfast published similar lists.

Like the older chapbook fiction, the new also participated in a larger body of literature addressing the personal, social, commercial, and political

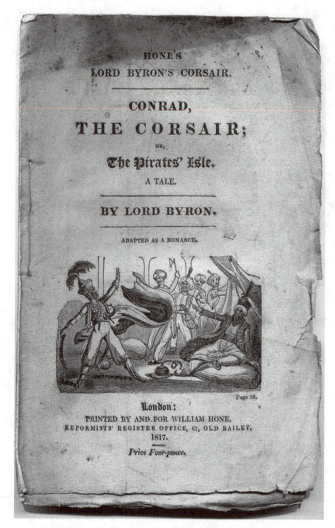

14 Title-page of Byron's "The Corsair" as novella (1817).

interests of its reading public. For example, J. Bailey's non-fiction publications comprised three broad groups. There were entertaining chapbooks,
including children's books, travels, songsters, true crime, divorce trials,
accounts of shipwrecks, an Indian captivity narrative, and a book of oddities
(Figure 16). There were chapbook manuals on diverse topics including
cookery, housekeeping, exterminating vermin, swindler's tricks, stowing
goods on shipboard, measuring and surveying, "gentlemen's" and "ladies'"
letter-writers, a Valentine writer, courtship, religious instruction, heathen
mythology, legerdemain, conjuring, Hoyle's rules of games, riding,

15 *The Watch Tower of Mazzara*: Characteristic larger format of the fashionable new chapbooks.

swimming, angling, use of the broadsword (a plebeian form of fencing), dog breeds, hunting small game, making fireworks, and Benjamin Franklin's *The Way to Wealth*. Finally, there were reform oriented chapbooks on public events including a life of Napoleon, the trials of the Cato Street conspirators, the trials of the popular Princess Caroline, the coronation of the unpopular George IV, a summary of the principles of Magna Carta, an address on liberties "by an independent friend to radical reform," and an edition of Robert Southey's early reformist poem, *Wat Tyler* (also republished to embarrass Southey, who was by the 1810s a conservative) (Figure 17). Linking the new chapbook fiction and reformist pamphlets were chapbooks such as Voltaire's account of the Calas affair, a true story of injustice, and an adaptation of the story of Jemima, a prostitute, from Mary Wollstonecraft's feminist novel *The Wrongs of Woman* (1798) – both given sensational Gothic-sounding titles by Bailey. Voltaire's work became *The Extraordinary Tragical Fate of Calas; or, Father & Son: Exhibiting an*

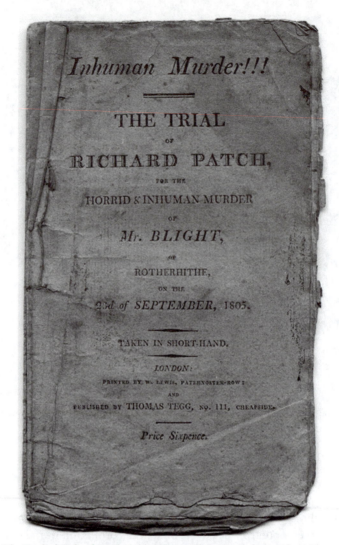

16 *The Trial of Richard Patch*: Publishers issued chapbook fiction alongside real-life trials and scandals that embodied similar elements.

Unparallelled Act of Human Butchery ... (1820) and Wollstonecraft's, the *Life of Jemima; or, The Confessions of an Unfortunate Bastard, Who, by the Antipathy of Her Parents, Was Driven to Every Scene of Vice and Prostitution!* ... (1800).

Such convergences occur elsewhere in working-class print of the period. An edition of *Joe Miller's Jests* included witticisms attributed to the pro-Revolutionary writer Tom Paine and *Tom Paine's Jests* appeared in 1793. In

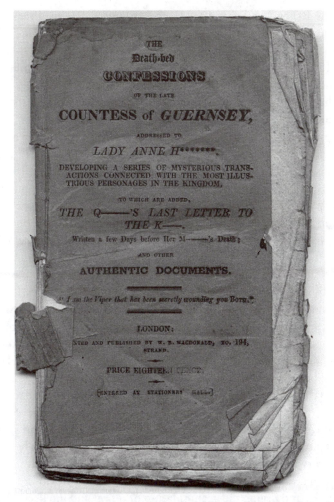

17 *The Death-Bed Confessions of the Late Countess of Guernsey*: Scandals in "high life" also paralleled the sensationalist new chapbook fiction.

allusion to *The Wise Men of Gotham*, the popular jestbook depicting a village of fools, the unpopular Prince Regent was satirized in political chapbooks as the "Prince of Gotham" and "Emperor of Gotham." Another satire on the Queen Caroline affair, *Jack and the Queen Killers* (1820), alludes to the well-known chapbook hero Jack the Giant Killer. The conflict between the Prince and Princess was transposed into a burlesque chapbook romance as *The Wife and Mistress; or, The Italian Spy: A Domestic Tale* (1820). The chapbook hero Tom Thumb, already appropriated by Henry Fielding in a theatrical satire on the government of his day, was so appropriated again to satirize the Regency government. Napoleon, self-proclaimed master of his own destiny, was assimilated to traditional popular print of fortune-telling in chapbooks purporting to disclose his secret knowledge of how to direct destiny. Regardless of genre or topic, the new chapbooks had similar format, appearance, and price range.

Together, working-class fiction and print culture in both old and new forms continued to serve their readers' interests through the Romantic period, giving artistic form to working-class ideology, registering and objectifying central features of working-class reality, and enabling readers to imagine things otherwise. This fiction and print culture participated in an emergent literary, theatrical, and musical culture that was popular in the sense of widely distributed, appealing not only to the working classes but also to the lower middle classes and many in the middle and upper classes, but also popular in the sense that it called its reading public into being as "the people" – the reformed political nation. Middle-class ideologues, cultural police, and moral reformers recognized these important functions and developments of working-class fiction and responded in several ways.

From the 1780s they increasingly urged middle-class parents to replace working-class fiction – the historic chapbook repertory – as reading matter for their own children with books embodying middle-class values and representing middle-class realities and interests. The result was an explosion in children's books, some by leading middle-class ideologues, intellectuals, political writers, and literary artists such as Anna Letitia Barbauld, Mary Wollstonecraft, Maria Edgeworth, William Godwin, and Walter Scott. The new middle-class children's literature used fiction reluctantly and insisted on its being factual and realistic, and opposed working-class fiction by denigrating the lottery mentality, showing the ill effects of succumbing to immediate gratification and the disastrous consequences of ethical flexibility and petty moral lapses, and urging the accumulation of moral and intellectual capital, or moral self-discipline and "solid and useful" knowledge for adult middle-class life.

These themes recur in the multitudinous pseudo-popular print produced in the Romantic period by middle-class social, moral, and religious reformers. During the 1790s, print's power to promote working-class interests was disclosed by huge sales of Paine's *Rights of Man*. Middle-class anti-Revolutionaries responded by attempting to supplant both reform literature and fiction read by the working classes with reading matter embodying middle-class values. The major initiative was the "Cheap Repository" (1795–8) organized and written by the Evangelical campaigner Hannah More and her sisters. More described traditional chapbook fiction as a "sans-culotte library," after Paris's *sans-culottes*, or working-class

Revolutionaries. A decade earlier, middle-class educators and parents had realized that working-class fiction obstructed the inculcation of middle-class values in their children. More, too, saw the connection between the attitude and style of fictions such as *Jack and the Giants* and those of Paine's *Rights of Man*, and saw that chapbook fiction, though usually lacking overt social protest, provided an ideological and cultural basis for working-class politicization and mobilization. Yet More and her supporters turned to fiction only reluctantly, recognizing that it enabled readers of any class to imagine things otherwise.

More's campaign was systematic and comprehensive. Cheap Repository included most genres of traditional chapbook fiction, imitated both their contents and style, and took up their central themes. But Cheap Repository relentlessly attacked the ideology and culture of traditional working-class print and the overt politics of pro-Revolutionary writers. *Tawny Rachel* attacks the historic plebeian culture of economic opportunism, indifference to the law, and belief in luck, fortune-telling, and magic (see Figure 18); *The History of Mr. Fantom* attacks Painite politics (Figure 19); *The Shepherd of Salisbury Plain* promotes submission to divine providence and social superiors and imitation of middle-class self-discipline and frugality. More also imitated the appearance of the traditional chapbooks, engaging an established publisher of such material, Marshall of Newcastle. She and her supporters used persuasion, threats, and bribery to get chapbook sellers to replace their traditional wares with Cheap Repository. She promoted use of Cheap Repository as work for welfare and training in small-scale capitalism: the indigent would be given a quantity of Cheap Repository material to sell, keep part of the proceeds for necessities, and put the rest into purchasing new stock for further sales. More also urged dispensers of charity to make it conditional on reading Cheap Repository.

There is no evidence these tactics worked. The huge sales of Cheap Repository probably depended on middle-class distributors – prices for bulk quantities appeared on the covers and More's middle-class correspondents called for editions of "superior" quality for their libraries. Cheap Repository's main readership was likely middle-class people receptive to a fantasy of the working classes as god- and employer-fearing, submissive, and quiescent. Nevertheless, middle-class social reformers, censors, and police continued to believe in the efficacy of pseudo-popular print. Cheap Repository was often imitated and was republished in times of working-class unrest, such as the late 1810s. After More and her sisters abandoned Cheap Repository in 1798 as too burdensome, its program was adopted in 1799 by a committee of clergymen as the Religious Tract Society and expanded enormously through the nineteenth century.

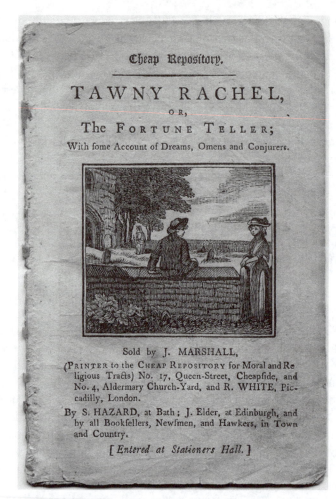

18 *Tawny Rachel*: Pseudo-popular print – Hannah More's Cheap Repository tracts, attempting to displace the historic street literature of the common people, here attacking fortune-tellers, central figures in the lottery mentality of the common people.

In the secular sphere, middle-class intellectuals, antiquarians, scholars, writers, and publishers attempted to disarm popular fiction and print as an ideological, cultural, and hence political force by subsuming it into middle-class literature in various ways. Antiquarians, local historians, clergymen, and literary amateurs collected lower-class oral and print culture, many predicting its imminent disappearance, some deploring it as vulgar "superstition" nevertheless showing how to reform the plebeians, others celebrating it as the simple and natural if childlike cultural expression of the common people, and some preserving and editing it as a primitive part of the

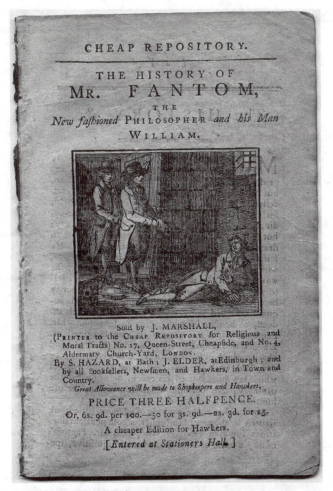

19 *The History of Mr. Fantom*: Pseudo-popular print – more Cheap Repository, here an attack on English Jacobin "new philosophy," sensationalized in attempted disguise as a crime chapbook.

"national" literature. Much of this material was later termed "folklore," a category isolating the plebeian within middle-class cultural, social, and academic discourse. Similarly, scholars edited various popular texts, from *Valentine and Orson* to *Robin Hood*, providing introductions, notes, and historical context, and pointing out sources in chivalric literature (Figure 20). Writers of middle-class children's books adapted many popular chapbooks, expurgating and altering when they thought it necessary. Even some working-class radicals condemned traditional chapbook fiction, or any fiction, for puerilizing its readers, and publishers of new fashionable chapbooks often grouped republished traditional chapbooks with their "juvenile"

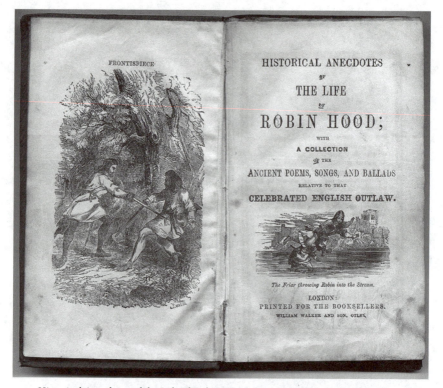

20 *Historical Anecdotes of the Life of Robin Hood*: Joseph Ritson's abduction of the most famous English folk and chapbook hero for an "English Jacobin" national literature.

publications. Historic working-class fiction, like the working classes themselves, was being categorized as childlike or childish. This movement corresponded to middle-class literary and political characterizations of the working classes. Middle-class novelists usually represented the lower classes as childlike – impulsive, undisciplined, feckless, unreliable. Conservative upper- and middle-class politicians similarly characterized the working classes in order to discredit a potential coalition of working and middle classes that threatened to effect radical reform, if not revolution, at various moments from the French Revolution debate of the 1790s to the Reform Bill debates of the late 1820s and early 1830s.

In response, during the 1820s middle-class reformers and publishers created pseudo-popular print projects to replace both old and new forms of working-class fiction with "solid and useful" reading. These projects were aimed at the "mechanics," or male artisans, perceived as most likely to become politicized and challenge the coalition of upper and upper middle classes for power, but also those most likely to respond to a discourse of

21 *The Portfolio of Amusement and Instruction* (1829): An example of the widely deplored – by middle-class do-gooders and proudly working-class activists alike – cheap magazines of sensational fiction, similar to the new format chapbooks.

meritocracy defined by middle-class ideology and culture. Many of these projects were serials, designed to engage working-class readers in disciplined self-education, and to displace both cheap political serials such as William Cobbett's *Weekly Political Register* (1802–35) and cheap fiction serials such as *The Tell-tale* (1810–?) and *The Portfolio* (see Figure 21). Pseudo-popular print included series of "libraries" of "useful" and "entertaining" knowledge, such as those edited by Charles Knight. More prominent were cheap periodicals such as Knight and Lacey's *Mechanics' Magazine* (1823–9), H. Fisher's *Mechanic's Oracle* (1824–5), and the *New London Mechanics' Register* (1824–8). The last was associated with the "Mechanics' Institutes" organized by well-to-do reformists to provide adult education to the working classes. The Society for the Diffusion of Useful Knowledge was founded in 1828 with similar leadership, motives, and publishing projects, such as Charles Knight's *Penny Magazine* (1832–5). These publications purposefully excluded both fiction and politics.

Finally, during the Romantic period certain writers countered both working-class and middle-class popular fiction by developing a specifically "literary" kind of fiction addressing the upper- and middle-class social coalition that would dominate state and empire through the nineteenth century. This fiction was diverse and written from differing ideological and political positions, representing various factions within the middle classes, by writers as different as John Moore, Ann Radcliffe, William Godwin, Mary Wollstonecraft, Maria Edgeworth, Sydney Owenson, Walter Scott, Jane Austen, Mary Shelley, John Galt, and Edward Bulwer-Lytton. Most of this fiction, despite differences, shared traits that could include some or all of the following: numerous literary allusions and quotations; incorporation of material from non-fiction and learned discourses such as travel literature, historiography, archeology, philosophy, the arts, and cultural studies, often supported by footnotes; extensive descriptions, often based on observation or research, again often footnoted; invocation of discourses of taste, discrimination, and distinction circulating among the upper and middle classes; detailed depiction of complex subjectivity; discrimination of social types and their speech, customs, and behavior; attention to the cause and effect relationship between character and incident; progressive plot leading to complex denouement and closure; and stylistic markers of the "literary," such as "poetic" language, elaborateness of construction, and effects that would be considered "original" rather than either formulaic or merely novel.

Literary fiction had several functions – to make money for its authors and publishers, to legitimize a genre widely regarded at the time as trivial and trivializing, to intervene ideologically and politically in the public sphere, to circulate among its readers a body of socially, culturally, and politically empowering knowledge, and especially to distinguish itself and thus its readers and writers from working-class fiction and middle-class popular fiction and their readers. In doing so, literary fiction helped constitute its authors and readers, in their own minds and in the public culture, as a vanguard and elite at a time when such status had important social, political, and professional benefits and made important claims for them in Britain's formation as a modern liberal state. Romantic literary fiction underwent various fates through the nineteenth century. Some had an impact at the time but dropped from sight or sustained a marginal fame. Some was immediately successful and influenced later novelists, but slid downmarket and became popular middle-class and "juvenile" literature. Some began obscurely but rose steadily in critical esteem and readership. In the twentieth century, professional critics, scholars, teachers, and publishers installed some of this fiction in a canon of texts they promoted as literature, or works supposedly of serious moral purpose, high artistic quality, and lasting value, embodying and reproducing, through compulsory reading in schools, both the "national" identity and culture and "universal" and "human" values, though Marxist, feminist, and post-colonialist critics have argued in recent decades that these values, if broadly liberal, were predominantly middle-class, patriarchal, Eurocentric, nationalistic, and colonialist.

Meanwhile, through the nineteenth and twentieth centuries the working classes continued to read kinds of fiction developed from those devised for them and the popular reading public during the Romantic period – adventure stories, crime fiction, the dime novel westerns and detective fiction created in the United States, romances, newspaper novels, pulp magazine fiction, pocket books. For about two-thirds of the nineteenth century, many in the working classes continued to read the traditional, centuries-old chapbook fiction, though mostly in the provinces. In the course of the next century and a half, huge and technologically innovative popular culture industries, including mass illustrated print, music recordings, film, radio, and television, cast fiction in new media. These kinds of fiction continued to be ignored by the increasingly well-organized and militant middle-class literary institution, which was steadily and more widely imposed on all classes through state education, and then higher education, state subsidies, literary prizes, arts councils, and so on. Many in the working classes did read literary fiction voluntarily, but probably did so, as they always had, from their own point of view. For in the end, working-class fiction is any fiction read in a working-class way. About that we still have much to learn.

NOTE

1 Here I draw on the autobiographies of Thomas Holcroft, John Binns, Thomas Carter, Eliza Fox, John Clare, William Lovett, William and Robert Chambers, Hugh Miller, Thomas Cooper, J. A. Leatherland, Mary Smith, Thomas Frost, Benjamin Brierly, Jesse Collings, and Ellen Johnston.

13

INA FERRIS

The Irish novel 1800–1829

Near the middle of Charles Robert Maturin's *Melmoth the Wanderer* (1820), the uncanny figure of Melmoth suddenly appears on the streets of seventeenth-century Madrid, prompting fearful but curious Spanish observers to wonder not only why he has not been seized by the Inquisition but if he has a known country of origin. "He is said to be a native of Ireland," reports one, "– (a country that no one knows, and which the natives are particularly reluctant to dwell in from various causes)."[1] In an important sense the Irish novel emerged in the early decades of the nineteenth century as an effort to remedy the strangely persistent situation defined in Maturin's throwaway parenthesis: to make familiar for both strangers and natives an unknown and unhomely land. "It is only with the last thirty years that the Irish have been very successfully represented," T. H. Lister wrote in 1831 in an essay on "Novels Descriptive of Irish Life" for the *Edinburgh Review*, going on to explain that earlier representations had concentrated on isolated single figures in primarily English settings. Thus English readers never saw the Irish as a people or Ireland as a native land: "we never saw them grouped – we never trod with them on Irish ground."[2] Like most of his contemporaries, Lister credits this shift in representation to Maria Edgeworth whose first novel, *Castle Rackrent* (1800), was widely identified in the period as the inaugural moment of a distinctive Irish line of English-language fiction. It has retained this status ever since. Not that *Castle Rackrent* was the first novel written either from or on Ireland but that Edgeworth's fictions, along with those of her compatriot Sydney Owenson (better known in the period by her married name of Lady Morgan), mark the emergence in the British literary field of what Terry Eagleton has called "a whole distinctive *object* known as Ireland," one that commanded attention in and for itself precisely because of its heightened "problematical" nature.[3]

Long a turbulent and irritating specter in English eyes, Ireland became newly "problematical" at the turn of the nineteenth century when it was formally incorporated into the political body of Great Britain under the terms of the Act of Union (1800). Motivated by England's desire to take direct political control after the explosion of republican–nationalist energies in the 1798 rebellion of the United Irishmen – an event that deeply shook the Irish populace as well as its colonial governors – the Act of Union abolished the quasi-autonomous Ascendancy Parliament to create the United Kingdom of Great Britain and Ireland. This new configuration, however, proved less consonant than dissonant, a spur to the recurring Irish agitation that was to unsettle British home space for most of the rest of the century. Ireland's new literary visibility on the British stage in the years after 1800 was a function of the fallout from this controversial Union, particularly from England's failure for almost three decades to act on the promise of Catholic emancipation, widely understood to follow upon Union but withheld until 1829. In particular, the Union debate was the crucible of the most important literary form to come out of Ireland in this period, the national tale, a female-authored genre launched by Edgeworth and Morgan, and named in the subtitle of the latter's highly successful *The Wild Irish Girl: A National Tale* (1806). Distinguished from the domestic novel of manners associated with women writers by its explicitly public and political orientation, the national tale sought to secure the insecure Union through reform of the Anglo-Irish landlord class on the one hand and the achievement of Catholic emancipation on the other. The genre's political charge, however, lay not so much in the particular agenda it espoused as in its dealing with the matter of Ireland in the first place. As Morgan put it in a retrospective preface, "every fictitious narrative that has had Ireland for its theme, has assumed a more or less decidedly political colouring."[4] English reviewers agreed, the *Athenaeum* declaring in 1828 that "not one able Irish romance" from Edgeworth's *The Absentee* (1812) to Michael Banim's *The Croppy* (1828) had been free from political ends, seeing this in itself as evidence of the fact that "Ireland and Irishmen are not what they ought to be."[5]

What unsettled such readers was less the political content of Irish novels (rarely threatening or exceptional) than their insistence on straying beyond the conventional borders of fiction, using the imagination "for supplements to the newspapers," as the *Athenaeum* put it.[6] Refusing to confine themselves to the moral and domestic matters proper to the realm of private life, the conventional realm of the novel, they placed themselves instead within the contentious sphere of public discourse where questions of national policy, national identity, and national history were debated. Thus the Irish national tale, targeting landlords and legislators rather than "fair readers" or idle youths, points to the wider ambitions of the novel itself in this period, when it both challenged and moved into closer proximity to higher-status genres such as historiography. This new ambition, especially when politically motivated, was regarded with some scepticism – "It must be the statistical man who will essentially benefit Ireland, and not the professed writer of fiction" declared a reviewer of Morgan's *Wild Irish Girl*[7] – but at the same time the critical attention accorded national and historical novels in powerful periodicals like the *Edinburgh Review* (which basically established Edgeworth as a major novelist) testifies to an increasing if reluctant recognition by men of letters that the novel was becoming an increasingly significant generic register of central intellectual and cultural currents.

As interventions in public debate, early nineteenth-century Irish novels are not only filled with specific debates but draw striking attention to themselves as performative and discursive acts (words engaged with other words in a thick multigeneric discourse) rather than representational "pictures."[8] It is no accident that the two inaugural texts, *Castle Rackrent* and *The Wild Irish Girl*, take the form of unblended or "seamed" texts rather than appearing as smoothly integrated narratives in the manner of Jane Austen. Not only do they set up different narrative registers but each has an elaborate quasi-scholarly paratext of notes offering authorial comment, recounting anecdotes, and citing or quarreling with other texts. Neither the pole of communication nor that of representation yields a single discourse. Characterized by hybridized narratives, national tales exploit a *mélange* of linguistic and stylistic modes, and they assume a diverse range of implied readers and readerly moods (e.g. Anglo-Irish/English, male/female, sentimental/hostile, indifferent/unknowing). The Preface to *Castle Rackrent*, for example, anticipates both insider readers familiar with "a certain class of the gentry of Ireland" and outsiders ("the *ignorant* English reader"), who will require help to make sense of the text's language.[9] Edgeworth's Irish novels as a whole exploit the doubleness of reference such a divided readership makes possible, allowing for quite divergent readings of the same sequences and words, so that in their own way they are quite as slippery as the famously slippery language of the Irish peasant. *Castle Rackrent*'s notes and glossary may, as often charged, seek to contain "the lower Irish," but they equally rebound on the inadequate "English reader" to make the point of the insufficiency of any single narrative frame.

Moreover, as a gesture of explanation and stabilization, Edgeworth's editorial frame, explicitly directed to "the English reader," is a spectacular failure given that the text it frames continues to elude definitive determination. The garrulous account of the decline of the Rackrent family by the old family servant Thady Quirk has puzzled readers from the start, and its precise tenor continues to be the subject of critical debate: is it a nostalgic lament for a lost feudal order or its ironic deconstruction? An affirmation of the upcoming Union or its bitter resentment? And how to place the voice of the rational editor, which seems at odds with itself in many of the notes constituting the quasi-anthropological Glossary added at the end? It does not help matters that the narrative itself ends with a literal question by the modern editor foregrounding Ireland's uncertain future under the upcoming Union. Declaring it "a problem of difficult solution to determine whether an Union will hasten or retard the amelioration of this country" (*Castle Rackrent*, p. 97), the editor abruptly switches to the odd and homely question of whether English drinking habits influenced those of the Irish or whether the latter influenced the former.

This apparently arbitrary swerve from the abstract language of politics to the homely idiom of the pub, however, underscores Edgeworth's identification of her novel with informal genres and the unofficial realm. *Castle Rackrent* aligns itself from the outset with the familiar modes of "secret memoirs and private anecdotes" in opposition to the narratives of "the professed historian," arguing that human truth and reality inhere in the details of private life to which a "behind the scenes" writing offers fuller access (*Castle Rackrent*, pp. 1–2). This argument in itself reflects the broad shift in the approach to the past among historical genres in the late eighteenth century, when the historical field was being extended to include cultural "manners" and everyday life under the impetus of a desire for a more intimate access to the past than traditional historical "distance" allowed.[10] Informed by a keen interest in manners, language, and anecdote, the Irish national tale clearly participates in this wider shift, but the tense political matrix of English–Irish relations in the period means that its "behind the scenes" move takes on a sharp critical charge, not simply a search for a more "authentic" ground of representation but a challenge to the official discourses that were the custodians of Ireland's history. The point is made most clearly by Morgan's *The Wild Irish Girl* with its clear targeting of received English histories of Ireland in both the main narrative and the extensive footnotes that frequently threaten to swallow it up. Acutely aware that "[m]anuscripts, annals, and records, are not the treasures of a colonized or conquered country,"[11] Morgan sets out to make visible an alternative, submerged history of Gaelic Ireland. As a source for this counter-history she turns to the Irish antiquaries of the late eighteenth-century Celtic Revival, liberally cited throughout the text.[12] Much of this antiquarian research was already suspect by the time of the novel's publication, and Morgan was soon to distance herself from its excesses, but the antiquarian turn itself was definitive, underscoring ways of investigating and reading the past outside the protocols of "the professed historian."

Transporting a young Englishman to an Ireland he has never visited, *The Wild Irish Girl* established the travel-and-education plot that would become a hallmark of nineteenth-century Irish fiction, structuring a whole range of narratives from Edgeworth's *Ennui* (1809) to Thomas Moore's *Memoirs of Captain Rock* (1824) and John Banim's *The Anglo-Irish of the Nineteenth Century* (1828). For its first readers, the novel was memorable primarily for the harp-playing Girl of the title, but its primary action is the destabilization of its callow aristocratic hero, Horatio. Arriving in Ireland, his mind stuffed with negative images garnered from various (named) travel texts and tales, he quite literally stumbles into a Gaelic enclave in the far west of the country, where he rapidly unlearns what he already "knows" under the tutelage of a trio of courtly native Irish, including Glorvina, whom he ultimately marries. Daughter of an impoverished Irish chief struggling to hold on to a remnant of the old order, the "wild Irish girl" turns out to be a ravishing young patriot – beautiful, accomplished, learned, virtuous – and she initiates the enchanted young Englishman into a very different history of Ireland and into the Irish language. His lessons provide ample opportunity for lengthy disquisitions on the Irish past, its poetry, and its customs, these in turn supplemented by the footnotes, crammed with references both formal and informal. In Morgan's passionate drive to counter the degraded standard image of barbaric and backward native Irish culture, the line between text and paratext repeatedly dissolves. It is crucial to her project that the alternative history be thus articulated out of a thicket of discussion and dispute, for it makes palpable the degree to which *struggle* characterizes the maintenance of historical and cultural memory in the face of the deliberate destruction of both under conditions of colonization. More flamboyantly than Edgeworth, Morgan positions her writing not just outside but against the English tradition. Both Irish writers looked to the Continent for generic models – Edgeworth to the philosophic tales of Voltaire and Marmontel, Morgan to Rousseau and French novels of sensibility – but Morgan's national tale consistently identifies itself as "not-English" in a way that Edgeworth's (for all its satire of English writing) does not. A liberal English reason remains clearly in play, but it is important to underline the degree to which the text approaches Englishness itself as a (necessarily bounded) nationality or culture rather than as the locus of a universal reason, for herein lies the key to the basic distinction between the two forms of national tale bequeathed by Edgeworth and Morgan to nineteenth-century Irish fiction.

Even as both writers deploy similar travel plots and turn cross-cultural encounter to similar conciliatory ends, their novels operate in the service of two very different models of the nation. Where Edgeworth understands the nation as an estate to be managed, Morgan sees it as a culture to be recognized. Neither does so in a simple fashion nor is the opposition as firm as this formulation suggests, but the distinction nonetheless holds. Profoundly shaped by late eighteenth-century Scottish political economy, Edgeworth's later Irish tales – *Ennui* (1809), *The Absentee* (1812), *Ormond* (1817) – make central the trope of contrasting estates to bring home their case for an enlightened landlordism dedicated to agricultural improvement, financial prudence, and the non-sectarian education of Irish tenants. Confronting disorderly and impoverished estates on the one hand and well-ordered and prosperous estates on the other, both irresponsible gentlemanly heroes like Glenthorn in *Ennui* and reformist ones like Lord Colambre of *The Absentee* absorb the lessons of a rational political economy, and dedicate themselves to living on their estates and bringing Ireland into modernity. It is thus no surprise that the whiggish *Edinburgh Review* should have proved so vigorous a champion of Edgeworth's novels. If they represent sophisticated forms of imperial romance in seeking to domesticate the Irish, as Seamus Deane has argued, they are also forms of gentry–professional romance, hence part of the more specific project of the middle-class British novel as a whole in the period.[13]

Ennui, included as part of Edgeworth's series of anti-fashion *Tales of Fashionable Life*, is exemplary, making the case for merit over inheritance as the grounds for legitimacy, and promulgating a modern virtue-based model of the gentleman over the old blood-based model of the 'born' gentleman. Its feckless English aristocratic hero in fact turns out to be an Irish peasant, changed at birth by his mother, and this discovery precipitates his self-transformation into a responsible, middle-class professional. Surrendering the estate to the heir-by-birth (currently a blacksmith), he uncharacteristically devotes himself to a disciplined pursuit of legal studies, acquiring virtue and earning the right to marry the worthy (and wealthy) heroine. Meanwhile, the peasant-turned-lord suffers the rapid disintegration of both his family and the estate, and, after suffering calamity, resigns the whole to return to his forge. The reformed Glenthorn now takes up the estate once again, this time by right of his wife's legal claim (she is the heir-at-law) and of his own fitness to manage the estate efficiently and equitably. But Edgeworth's schematic plots are never quite as transparent as they seem, and it is the volatile question of legitimacy and land on Irish soil that typically unsettles them. Glenthorn's return means that, as at the end of *Castle Rackrent*, ownership of an Anglo-Irish estate passes into the hands of a (technically) native Irishman.

Edgeworth's economic model of the nation may make it theoretically accountable only to rational economic laws, but her fictions continue to wrestle with the apparently irrelevant historical claim of native right. While firmly rooting the nation in the present as a project (rather than a history), her texts nonetheless keep bumping into the question of native right.

Suggestively, they do so largely through female figures, who skew (or threaten to skew) the prescriptive line of inheritance they should secure, as does the peasant nurse (Glenthorn's birth mother) when she changes babies at birth.[14] Certainly, a conventional femininity and a renovated domesticity ground the enlightened future nation Edgeworth's endings hopefully conjecture, but rarely without taking some peculiar swerve. So *The Absentee* worries questions of birth and belonging by blocking its courtship plot through an apparently perverse anxiety on the part of the hero over the legitimacy of the virtuous young heroine, Grace Nugent. Her legitimacy proves secure; her nationality less so. Possessing a resonant Irish name, she has lived up to it by demonstrating a warm Irish patriotism, but she turns out to have been born an Englishwoman named Reynolds. Strangely, this does not alter her status as a "native" Irishwoman, and the final pages of the novel acclaim her as "Gracey Nugent." Robert Tracy reads this odd ending as a product of Edgeworth's unwillingness either to adopt Morgan's "Glorvina solution" (whereby a native–landlord marriage conjoins traditional and legal claims) or to quite let it go.[15] In part her uneasiness is a class symptom, but it is also in part a function of a broader conceptual transition, as the older societal concept of the nation espoused by Edgeworth was becoming dislodged by an emergent cultural concept of nationality.

Predicated on precisely such a concept, Morgan's *The Wild Irish Girl* marks the influential entrance of cultural nationalism into the Irish novel. Despite this status, however, it sits uncomfortably in histories of Irish writing (e.g. "a work deficient in almost everything a novel should have, except success"[16]). Morgan herself came to regard its "misty" Celticism with a certain embarrassment, but she never repudiated the emotive "patriotism" that made her early book resonate so powerfully in its historical moment. Like Edgeworth, Morgan came out of the rational late eighteenth-century Patriot tradition associated with the liberal politics of Henry Grattan, but unlike Edgeworth she was attuned to the emergent energy of "national feeling," an affective category of national belonging rooted in a new concept of national "culture" as a distinctive way of life rooted in a particular history. In this model, a nation exists apart from political or territorial determinations, and this means that it can be preserved and perpetuated outside formal institutions of power. Such a model would have clear if complex attractions in a colonial space like Ireland, but it was not restricted to such spaces. Early nineteenth-century Europe witnessed an explosion of interest in local literatures, legends, songs, and languages across the entire continent.[17] Not all of these coalesced into "nations" nor did cultural nationalism necessarily converge with political nationalism, and Morgan herself wrote not simply Irish tales but national tales focusing on a range of places in Europe and beyond, including Greece (*Woman, or, Ida of Athens*, 1809), Belgium (*The Princess, or The Beguine*, 1835), and India (*The Missionary: An Indian Tale*, 1811). Her fiction thus presents Ireland less as a special case (although it is a case of special interest to British readers) than as symptomatic, an expression of wider modern cultural–political energies that sought to revise and reconfigure the understanding of the formation of nations.

Over the course of her four Irish novels, however, Morgan substantially revised the model of national culture informing the novel that made her reputation. Where *The Wild Irish Girl* posits a national culture rooted in an ancient historical origin, one that yields a coherent if precarious "heritage" secured by the national heroine, the three later Irish tales – *O'Donnel: A National Tale* (1814), *Florence Macarthy: An Irish Tale* (1818), *The O'Briens and the O'Flahertys: A National Tale* (1827) – abandon the pastoral enclave that governed the early novel to figure a complex, historical temporality out of which comes a new kind of national heroine and a less coherent national culture. Identifying the Irish nation with a tenuously preserved Gaelic nation whose pre-modern values cannot be sustained but must be somehow be incorporated if the modern nation is to be redeemed, *Wild Irish Girl* plays out its argument in allegorical terms through the romance of Horatio and Glorvina. As national heroine, Glorvina links her nation's past and future, both embodying and healing its troubled history. But novels like *Florence Macarthy* and *The O'Briens and the O'Flahertys* discard its Gaelocentric reading of Ireland, rewriting the Irish nation in terms of dispersal, disjunction, and complex stratifications (e.g. old English, new English, Presbyterian, Catholic). To this nation Morgan attaches her revised and innovative national heroine: an oddly mobile and hybrid figure who (in contrast to the rooted Glorvina) belongs to no particular place and answers to no single name. The Spanish–Irish Florence Macarthy, for instance, has at least three names, and travels about for much of the novel in what seems to be motiveless disguise; while Beavoin O'Flaherty (Irish–Italian) flits in and out of the narrative, confounding the hapless young liberal hero, and refusing to reveal her identity until very close to the end of the novel.

Living in parts (in various senses), these ambiguous female figures lie outside the wholeness of being conventionally linked to femininity in the period. Precisely because they do so, they can function as national heroines in fractured Irish space, for they emerge from a dissonant historical temporality that muddies the linear coherence allowing for clear lines of "inheritance" or "heritage." Incoherent and compromised, they belong to the impure matrix of the present as a sheltered figure like Glorvina does not. Thus Morgan's last Irish tale, the impressive *The O'Briens and the O'Flahertys*, foregrounds the heroine's immersion in the tangled temporalities and conflicting cultures that make up the tense compound of the colonial nation. Operating in its interstices and through informal associations, the deterritorialized Beavoin O'Flaherty works pragmatically with what lies at hand (teaching young girls, restoring a working mill), but her activities are necessarily contingent and limited. Enmeshed in the confused and conflicted scene of Ireland at the time of the 1798 rebellion, neither this heroine nor the United Irishman hero can find clarity or coherence, and the text itself is marked by proliferating narratives, intersecting temporalities, and historical dead-ends. Ultimately, patriotism itself can find no foothold, and in the final pages of her tale Morgan moves her national heroine out of Ireland altogether.

In the hands of Maturin this sense of historical impasse transforms itself into the trope of ruination that becomes the signature of the novelistic genre he developed out of the national tale, the one we now know as Irish or Protestant Gothic. Melodramatic and excessive, Maturin's strangely compelling narratives are at once the most derivative and the most original of early nineteenth-century Irish novels. Seeking commercial success, Maturin sought to capitalize on Morgan's fame by publishing *The Wild Irish Boy* (1808) under the pseudonym of Dennis Jasper Murphy, but it was his next novel, *The Milesian Chief: A Romance* (1812), published under the same pseudonym, that effectively translated Morgan's early novel into the "dark romance" of Irish Gothic. Rewriting the national tale's optimistic and conciliatory travel-and-education plot, *The Milesian Chief* sends a coddled English–Italian artist heroine modeled on Madame de Staël's Corinne (Armida Fitzalban) to a remote corner of Ireland, a country of which she has barely heard. There she falls in passionate love with a dispossessed young Irishman (Connal O'Morven), but cross-cultural encounter in this instance offers neither an erotic initiation into a pastoral Gaelic community nor helpful lessons in estate management. Rather it operates doubly as an entry into absolute devastation both within and without. Abandoning propriety to follow Connal as his "wandering companion" in the hopeless rebellion he mounts in the west (even as he knows its futility and doubts its premises), Armida finds herself in a ruined land and among a desolate people that lie outside both her understanding and any possibility of a future. Pursued by constant violence, betrayal, and madness throughout her sojourn, she experiences internal ruin and desolation as well, losing her talent, her bearings, and indeed her sense of identity under the dual pressures of Irish experience and romantic passion. In the novel's tragic conclusion, Connal suffers degradation and execution by the state, while Armida, threatened by forced marriage to another, takes poison to die a suicide beside his corpse.

So ruling out the sense of a national future, Maturin's novel removes contemporary Ireland from a progressive reading of history, and makes ruination its critical trope. His text not only continually invokes the actual ruins that are the traces of enduring historical violence (ruined towers, ruined abbeys, ruined houses) but renders disintegration the sign under which the present is lived out. It thus answers in an important way to the psycho-historical situation of the Anglo-Irish of Maturin's time, who increasingly felt themselves to be under siege and losing ground in the years following the Union, especially as the campaign for Catholic Emancipation gathered steam under Daniel O'Connell and began to consolidate a Catholic nation which, by contrast, grew increasingly confident. For the eccentric and deeply alienated Maturin, distrustful of both the Anglo-Irish establishment and Catholic majority, Ireland was impasse itself. Foregrounding its "strange existing oppositions,"[18] he sees it as well outside modern reason, eluding the rationalities of either political or historical understanding. Neither Armida's cosmpolitan humanist history nor Connal's radical nationalist history, for example, can sustain themselves in Irish space, for both (in their different ways) are premised on the coherence of historical time. The time of history on Irish soil, by contrast, is a time of discontinuity and dissolution, weirdly recursive and repetitive, so that Maturin's Irish novels turn on, rather than repudiate, the old negative trope of "wild" Ireland. Indeed a narrative like *The Milesian Chief* intensifies the trope through an almost obsessive reiteration of the "wild" land throughout the text, but in his hands this implicitly conservative move activates the trope's dissonant and critical charge. Repudiating the liberal national tale's attempt to bring Ireland within an enlightened political settlement, Maturin's dark romance makes enlightenment itself the subject of interrogation, challenging not simply particular "readings" of history but the very idea that history can be "read" at all.

Ireland's blocking of conventional political and historical reason, however, serves to release the speculative range of fiction, allowing Maturin to push to borders where he can explore and test the working of human passions with an intensity unusual in nineteenth-century English-language novels. *The Milesian Chief* casts Ireland as a land of curious and disquieting abstraction ("No sight of human habitation, no sound of human life ... nothing else above or below," *Milesian Chief*, Vol. I, pp. 61–2), implying that its troubled history has reduced it to an elemental space, one that both prompts and reflects a similar reduction of the human person on its ground. It is on the literal edge of Ireland that Armida endures mental collapse but also gains access to an authenticity of being unavailable to her in the civilized world of the European salon. The driving energy of Maturin's narrative is a quasi-experimental fascination with exploring the powers of passion in situations removed from regular civil and social constraints, as in his celebrated *Melmoth the Wanderer*, where it becomes the explicit project. Breaking down his characters, bringing them to ruination in this text, Maturin propels them to a moment of crisis, stripping them of their purchase on the conventions of "the human." At the same time, the notoriously disjointed and circuitous structure of the text breaks the novel itself (formally speaking) into pieces.

Even within the more realist and middle-class *Women; or, Pour et Contre* (1818), set in Dublin at the time of Napoleon's first defeat, Maturin pushes fiction into those regions of "intermediate existence" that border on the rational and everyday, blurring the boundaries upon which a stable subjectivity depends. Its solid setting is Gothicized from the outset in an arresting opening image of a sleeping golden-haired young girl over whom looms the dark figure of an old sibyl. Her rescue ensues, as does a strange love story that ends in destroying both the girl and her rescuer. Shot through with specters, dreams, abrupt disappearances, and reappearances (and characterized by an odd tonal mix of satiric undercutting and romantic rhapsody), *Women* narrates the fatal effects of erotic passion on a young Anglo-Irishman and the two women he loves, who turn out to be (unknowingly) mother and daughter. The ways of love in Maturin are rarely straight. What makes this a quintessentially Irish tale is that the personal story at its heart turns out to be inextricably entangled with the sectarian tensions of Irish history. Bringing about the original separation of mother and daughter, the eruption of these tensions in the past has produced the disconcerting collapse of generational order in the present, a collapse leading to the disastrous quasi-incestuous sexual rivalry. Over and over in his fiction, the murky processes of Irish history infect and skew the trajectory of private lives, and the past keeps bitterly returning. In the loss of horizons and distinctions represented by Ireland, there is for Maturin both anguish and a certain liberation of the imagination, but what there is not is release from history.

The advent of Catholic novelists in the 1820s with the publication of the pseudonymous first series of *Tales by the O'Hara Family* (1825) by John and Michael Banim at once stepped up the question of history and restored to the Irish novel the political and public ambitions renounced by Maturin's romance. Entering the literary scene during a heated decade that saw increased sectarian violence, renewed agrarian militancy, and the aggressive final stages of O'Connell's Emancipation campaign, the Banims pressed home the "unfinished business" of Irish history, urging that British peace depended on a thorough settling of Irish grievances. Writing from outside the Anglo-Irish gentry class inhabited (in different ways) by Edgeworth, Morgan, and Maturin, they brought into Irish fiction a rendition of small-town and rural Catholic Ireland unavailable to the earlier writers, extending the novel's representational range to include more familiar views of farmers, clerks, priests, and "the boys" of rural secret societies. But their tales too focus on personal lives disfigured by the inevitable slide of public into personal history on colonial ground: tales of failed interdenominational love, murder, abduction, burnings, and hangings. In their angular narratives, conciliatory moves repeatedly miscarry while violence depressingly carries its point. As Deane remarks, in their work the "malady of history" runs deep, and the key move to which the Banims bear witness is the summoning of this "malady" on the part of novels in the 1820s as a lever for present political purposes.[19]

In particular the decade witnessed the flourishing of the novel of insurgency, a modulation of the national tale by way of Scott's historical novel. Recollections of the 1798 United Irishmen's Rebellion were especially resonant, as in Michael Banim's *The Croppy: A Tale of the Irish Rebellion of 1798* (1828), James McHenry's *O'Halloran, or The Insurgent Chief: An Irish Historical Tale of 1798* (1828), and Morgan's *The O'Briens and the O'Flahertys* (1827). Departing crucially from the Scottish historical novel with which it overlaps, the Irish novel of insurgency conjures up the violence of Irish history less as a safely sublated energy in the past than as a potential volatility in the present. This is not to say that writers like the Banims supported a physical force revolution – they followed O'Connell on the constitutional path – but that with them a newly aggressive note enters the Irish novel. John Banim's rewriting of the national tale in *The Anglo-Irish of the Nineteenth Century* (1828) offers a telling example. Banim's talky novel (filled with long passages of debate on the Irish question) follows the generic travel-and-education plot, sending into Ireland the Anglo-Irish Gerald Blount, son of an absentee, who has not himself ever been to the country but despises it all the same. Subjected to various experiences (including capture by the militant Rockites), he learns the error of his views, marries the patriot heroine, and settles in Ireland. This conventional plot, however, is but the vehicle for an unusually scathing attack on the Anglo-Irish as an anachronistic and derelict cultural formation, one that must now banish itself out of existence, and cast its lot with the "real people" (i.e. the native Catholic population) of Ireland.[20] Enforcing this argument is the menace contained in the conjunction of Ireland's population-fact on the one hand (its huge population was a constant source of British anxiety) and its historical memories of insurrection on the other. As a local landlord reminds Banim's hero, Ireland now has the numbers and the will 'to form a great nation', and only physical force can stop its achieving this purpose. This step England will not take. To hammer home his point, he invokes the memory of the rising of the United Irishmen in 1798: "You did not, durst not, so take vengeance for the wild insurrection of ninety-eight; and what was out of the question thirty years ago, is now more remotely out of the question" (p. 130).

Bringing the "wild insurrection" to bear on the present, his remark illustrates the way in which the matter of 1798 repeatedly surfaces in the novels of the late 1820s as part of current political debate rather than a topic for a historical "understanding." Michael Banim's pioneering account of the Wexford rebellion in *The Croppy* may periodically remind the reader of the thirty years separating the time of representation from the time of the represented events, but the novel's jolting narrative shifts and sudden eruptions of graphic violence disrupt any attempt at a stabilized narrative distance. Moreover, the novel's epilogue fails to remove the event to the past, as is conventional in epilogues. On the contrary; it reaches directly into the present to link it to the ongoing problem of the Union (now reaching a crisis) with its "promise of advantages which have not yet been conceded."[21] Following Scott, James McHenry declares his intention to a "neutral" assessment of both sides of the rising in the preface to *O'Halloran*, but his attempt (like John Banim's similar attempt at a historical novel set in an earlier period in *The Boyne Water* (1826)) runs aground, defeated by Ireland's failure to enter the modernity that allows for the detachment of "understanding."

What was at stake in the novels of insurgency dealing with 1798 was indeed the question of how or if Ireland could move into modernity, and hence surmount its bitter past. What was equally at stake at the same time, however, was the question of national identity for which the past resonated in a rather different way. John Banim's turn in *The Anglo-Irish of the Nineteenth Century* to what Martin Thom calls "the tribe-nation" represents an attempt to resolve both questions: a native Catholic Ireland, rooted in the past, would now enter the future on its own terms.[22] As his novel replaces the tropes of mediation governing the early national tale with those of belonging, it points to an impatience with the aesthetics and politics of the intermediary and the intermediate that would have important implications for the writing of Irish fiction in the following decades. By the 1830s, Edgeworth's tales, while accorded pioneering status in the Irish canon now being established, would come to seem (in the words of the *Dublin Review*) as far from "*national*, in the fullest sense of the word" because there is "no warmth of indignant patriotism, no identification of self with the country, little more, in short, than the cold and half-contemptuous pity of a shrewd and right-minded stranger."[23] In these decades the Irish novel would draw closer to a realist aesthetic valorizing intimacy, familiarity, and transparency. In closing the gaps and erasing the seams foregrounded in the awkward and odd fictions of Edgeworth, Morgan, and Maturin, however, the mid-nineteenth-century Irish novel ironically moved itself closer to the mainstream British novel from which Romantic Irish fiction had effectively detached itself.

NOTES

1 Charles Robert Maturin, *Melmoth the Wanderer*, ed. Douglas Grant (Oxford: Oxford University Press, 1989), p. 326.

2 [T. H. Lister], "Novels Descriptive of Irish Life," *Edinburgh Review* 52 (1831), p. 411.

3 Terry Eagleton, *Heathcliff and the Great Hunger: Studies in Irish Culture* (London: Verso, 1995), p. 175.

4 *O'Donnel*, rev. edn. (London: Colburn, 1835), pp. ix–x.

5 Review of *The Anglo-Irish of the Nineteenth Century*, *Athenaeum*, October 8, 1828, p. 788.

6 *Ibid.*

7 Review of *The Wild Irish Girl*, *Monthly Review* NS 57 (1818), p. 381.

8 See Ina Ferris, *The Romantic National Tale and the Question of Ireland* (Cambridge: Cambridge University Press, 2002), ch. 2.

9 Maria Edgeworth, *Castle Rackrent*, ed. George Watson (Oxford: Oxford University Press, 1969), p. 4.

10 For the shift in historical genres, see Mark Phillips, *Society and Sentiment: Genres of Historical Writing in Britain, 1740–1820* (Princeton: Princeton University Press, 2000).

11 Sydney Owenson (Lady Morgan), *The Wild Irish Girl*, ed. Kathryn Kirkpatrick (Oxford: Oxford University Press, 1999), p. 174.

12 On antiquarianism and Romantic fiction, see Katie Trumpener, *Bardic Nationalism: The Romantic Novel and the British Empire* (Princeton: Princeton University Press, 1997). On the footnotes in *Wild Irish Girl*, see Joep Leerssen, *Remembrance and Imagination: Patterns in the Historical and Literary Representation of Ireland in the Nineteenth Century* (Cork: Cork University Press, 1996), pp. 49–60.

13 Seamus Deane, *Strange Country: Modernity and Nationhood in Irish Writing Since 1790* (Oxford: Clarendon Press, 1997), pp. 30–2. For the novel's role in the formation of the gentry–professional classes, see Gary Kelly, *English Fiction in the Romantic Period 1789–1830* (London: Longman, 1989).

14 See Mary Jean Corbett, *Allegories of Union in Irish and English Writing, 1790–1870* (Cambridge: Cambridge University Press, 2000), ch. 2.

15 Robert Tracy, "Maria Edgeworth and Lady Morgan" (1985), rpt. in his *The Unappeasable Host: Studies in Irish Identities* (Dublin: University College Dublin Press, 1998), pp. 25–46.

16 Seamus Deane, *A Short History of Irish Literature* (Notre Dame: University of Notre Dame Press, 1986), pp. 97–8.

17 See Joep Leerseen, "The Cultivation of Culture: Towards a Definition of Romantic Nationalism in Europe," *Working Papers: European Studies, Amsterdam* (Amsterdam: University of Amsterdam, 2005).

18 Charles Robert Maturin, Preface to *The Milesian Chief: A Romance*, 4 vols., Vol. I (London: Colburn, 1812), p. v.

19 Seamus Deane, *A Short History of Irish Literature* (Notre Dame, Ind.: University of Notre Dame Press, 1986).

20 [John Banim], *The Anglo-Irish of the Nineteenth Century: A Novel*, 3 vols. (London, 1828), p. 121.
21 Michael Banim, *The Croppy: A Tale of the Irish Rebellion of 1798*, 3 vols., Vol. III (1828; rpt. New York: Garland, 1978), p. 316.
22 Martin Thom, *Republics, Nations and Tribes* (London: Verso, 1995).
23 [Ellen O'Connell Fitzsimon], "Irish Novels and Irish Novelists," *Dublin Review* 4 (1838), pp. 497, 503–4.

14

IAN DUNCAN

Scotland and the novel

Scottish fiction, meaning at once fiction produced in Scotland and fiction that made Scotland its topic, became one of the leading genres of European Romanticism in the decade after Waterloo. Its distinctive forms, the three-volume historical novel, magazine tale and fictitious regional memoir, were the product and fuel of a spectacular Edinburgh publishing boom in the first quarter of the nineteenth century, which was also characterized by innovations in the periodical genres of quarterly review and monthly magazine. The proportion of British fiction titles produced in Scotland rose steeply from a mere 0.5 percent in the first decade of the century to 4.4 percent in the 1810s and then to 12 percent in the 1820s, reaching 15 percent, or 54 out of 359 titles, in the peak years of 1822–5.[1] Following a nationwide financial crash in 1826, booksellers cut back the production of new novels, especially in Scotland, and invested instead in miscellanies, serials, reprints, and the genres of "useful knowledge." "Our publishers of the proud northern metropolis seem to have lost all pluck since the lamented death of their great father, Mr Constable," remarked *Fraser's Magazine* in 1830: "the vaunted Modern Athens is fast dwindling away into a mere spelling-book and primer manufactory."[2]

The meteoric career of Scottish fiction, as everyone at the time acknowledged, traced the career of an individual author, Walter Scott. The publication of *Waverley* in the summer of 1814 accelerated a modest rate of growth into a regional bonanza. The ruin of Scott and his principal publisher, Archibald Constable, in the 1826 crash precipitated a general decline of Scottish fiction, with little of note appearing after Scott's death in 1832. Meanwhile, the great series of Waverley Novels (as they came to be called) established the major trends in British Romantic fiction publishing: the displacement of poetry from the summit of the genre system by the novel, the heightened formal definition of the novel, the professionalization of production and marketing, the standardization of format for new works (three volumes, post-octavo, 31s./6d. the set), and even a masculine takeover of what had hitherto been characterized as a feminine kind of writing.[3] The formal predominance of Scott's novels, shaping as they were shaped by the infrastructures of Regency-era literary production and reception, accompanied the commercial predominance recently analysed by William St Clair. Scott sold more copies of his novels "than all the other novelists of the time put together."[4] The unprecedented print-runs of new titles such as *Rob Roy* (1818, 10,000 copies) were followed not just by reprints but by reissues in different formats, culminating in the publishing innovation of Scott's last years, the appearance of all his novels (followed, posthumously, by his other works) in a uniform edition corrected and with new introductions and notes by the author in a series of five-shilling monthly "small octavo" volumes, the so-called "Magnum Opus" edition (1829–33). "Scott and his partners achieved an ownership of the whole literary production and distribution process from author to reader, controlling or influencing the initial choice of subjects, the writing of the texts, the editing, the publishing, and the printing of the books, the reviewing in the local literary press, [and] the adaptations for the theatre," comments St Clair, with slight hyperbole.[5] "We have been now, for some years, inundated with showers of Scotch novels, thicker than the snow you see falling," complains the English narrator of Sarah Green's satire *Scotch Novel Reading* (1824). If the works of the "Great Unknown" seemed ubiquitous, their famous author's insistence on formal anonymity gave that ubiquity an uncanny cast, as though commercial mass-production were a kind of haunting. Scott's own preface to *The Fortunes of Nigel* (1821) stages an encounter with "the Eidolon, or Representation, of the Author of Waverley" in the inner labyrinth of Constable's shop: this phantasm, at once weird and humdrum, defends his right to be considered "a productive labourer" whose "bales of books" are as "profitable [a] part of the public stock" as "the goods of any other manufacture."

The characterization of a "close vertical and horizontal concentration of media ownership"[6] on the part of Scott and his associates suggests an aesthetic and ideological as well as commercial monopoly that could be expected to have stifled rival projects, and some commentators have cast Scott's impact on the Romantic novel in such terms. This essay considers the antithetical claim, that Scott's massive success encouraged rather than deterred the production of alternative forms of Scottish fiction. The experimental richness of Scott's novels – by no means confined to the first in the series – opened up the literary field, provoking further innovations, quite as much as their industrial predominance may have closed other possibilities down. The demand stimulated by the Waverley Novels made room for a proliferation of Scottish fiction by other hands, some of which consisted of more or less mechanical imitations (Sir Thomas Dick Lauder's

Lochandhu: A Tale of the Eighteenth Century, 1824, and *The Wolfe of Badenoch: A Historical Romance of the Fourteenth Century*, 1827), and some of which made claims to a rival originality. The most notable authors of "secondary Scottish novels" (in Francis Jeffrey's slighting phrase[7]) were James Hogg, John Galt, Susan Edmonstone Ferrier, John Gibson Lockhart, John Wilson, and Christian Isobel Johnstone: all of whom were associated, at one time or another, with the publisher who arose to challenge Constable's ascendancy in the postwar Edinburgh book trade, William Blackwood. (Two other novelists, Elizabeth Hamilton and Mary Brunton, produced Scottish variants of the Irish "national tale" before the appearance of *Waverley*.)

Following a temporary takeover of Scott from Constable (with the first series of *Tales of My Landlord*, 1816), Blackwood launched *Blackwood's Edinburgh Magazine* in 1817 as a rival to Constable's brace of Whig periodicals, and began publishing book-length works of fiction (Ferrier's *Marriage*, Hogg's *Brownie of Bodsbeck*) the following year. Blackwood went on to become the most prolific publisher of novels and tales – some of which first appeared in his magazine – in Scotland in the 1820s. Modern critics have described a Blackwoodian school of Scottish Romantic fiction in competition with Scott's, flourishing in the years when Scott himself forsook the making of modern Scotland for more exotic matter (after *Ivanhoe*, 1820). It typically consisted of comic and sentimental depictions of traditional, rural or small-town settings and manners, or of a materialist rather than supernatural mutation of Gothic exploring states of extreme sensation.[8] In the early 1820s Hogg and Galt emerged as the most original authors of Scottish prose fiction next to Scott, masters of the distinctive genres developed in the Blackwood orbit, regional tale and fictional autobiography. Blackwoodian regionalism and "tales of terror" would shape English-language fiction of the 1830s and 40s, from Dickens and the Brontës to Poe, while the historical novel remained the prestigious form of the novel as such in Britain in the decade or so following Scott's death.

Anglo-Irish writers had developed the national tale, a fiction addressing the internal formation of modern Britain upon the political and cultural absorption of its "Celtic fringe," in the decade or so before *Waverley*. Nevertheless it was Scott who established the "classical form of the historical novel" (as Georg Lukács defined it in *The Historical Novel*) as not just a national but a planetary genre. Across continental Europe (Alexander Pushkin to Alessandro Manzoni), from North America to the Indian subcontinent, distinctively colonial and anticolonial variants of Scott's national historical novel took root through the nineteenth century. Nor was Scott alone in reconstituting Scottish literature as a worldwide medium, coterminous with the commercial and administrative networks of empire. *Blackwood's* capitalized on its distribution throughout the settler colonies to address specifically colonial concerns and to redefine the miscellany as a quintessentially imperial genre.[9]

Contemporary reviewers noted this spectacular if belated rise of Scottish fiction. The novel, observed one, has assumed the role of classical epic to represent "the different modes of national existence . . . in modern times."[10] Another, writing the same year (1819), summed up what he understood to be the "important change" that had taken place "within these few years in the general taste and literature of Scotland": in a strange reversal of "the usual progress of the human mind," the "grave and metaphysical propensities of our countrymen" have succumbed to a "rage for works of fancy."[11] The reviewer characterizes a shift from the curriculum-based genres of the so-called Scottish Enlightenment – moral philosophy, the human and natural sciences – to the bookseller's genres of periodicals and fiction that flourished in Edinburgh after 1800. The shift tracks a general devolution of Scottish literary production from the academic infrastructure of the Enlightenment disciplines to the recognizably nineteenth-century conditions of an industrializing literary marketplace. Politics hastened if it did not by itself drive the change. The Anti-Jacobin reaction of the mid-1790s broke up the "Moderate" Whig consensus that had supplied the ideological medium of Enlightenment, as Pitt's Tory government tightened its regional monopoly over Scottish patronage and institutions. The founding of *The Edinburgh Review* in 1802, during the "thaw" of the Peace of Amiens, marks a watershed. Constable's pro-Reform quarterly renewed the liberal projects of Enlightenment – shut out from the universities – by relocating them in the marketplace. In turn, the *Edinburgh Review* dignified the commercial mode of periodical publication not only with the philosophical themes of Enlightenment (social history, political economy) but with its civic and professional ethos. Constable's high fees and formal anonymity guaranteed his authors' claim on professional status, underwriting the *Edinburgh Review's* rhetorical claim on a judicial authority over the modern commercial public sphere. Scott himself, trained in Enlightenment institutions and principles and (indeed) a schoolfellow of its editors, contributed to the early numbers of the *Edinburgh Review*. The transformation of the cultural status of British fiction effected by *Waverley* and its successors, as Ina Ferris has shown, followed Scott's dignifying investment of the novel, the commercial genre *par excellence*, with the tropes of "literary authority" established in the *Edinburgh Review* – the professionalized figure of an anonymous author as well as the Enlightenment discourse of philosophical history.[12]

Literary authority, as Ferris also argues, relied on a hierarchical association of genre and gender: history books and quarterly review essays were written and read by men, while fiction was produced and consumed by women. Scott's cultural elevation of the novel claimed what had hitherto been depreciated as a feminine commodity for a masculine domain of intellectual work. The strong traditions of British fiction in the first decade of the century had been shaped by women authors, including the dozen or so novels published in Scotland before *Waverley*, the most notable of which were Elizabeth Hamilton's *The Cottagers of Glenburnie* (1808) and Mary Brunton's *Self-Control* (1811). (Brunton's *Discipline* appeared five months after *Waverley*, at the end of 1814). Reviewers placed these works in a line of moral-reformist domestic fiction running from Frances Burney through Maria Edgeworth, who gave the form its "national" (Irish) development, and Hannah More, who infused it with an evangelical didacticism. Hamilton and Brunton draw on Edgeworth for their moralizing depictions of Scottish "national character," ranging from its metonymic characterization as a residual dirt that must be cleaned up in order for the regional society to prosper (*Cottagers of Glenburnie*), to a Romantic investment in the Celtic Highlands as source of a primitive virtue aloof from metropolitan depravity (*Discipline*).

Scott himself recognized a feminine tradition of domestic fiction that he distinguished from his own, and hailed Susan Ferrier as the Scots counterpart of Edgeworth in Ireland and Jane Austen in England. Ferrier admired Hamilton and Brunton (as well as More, Edgeworth, and Austen), and began writing *Marriage* under their influence in 1810. Her novels rehearse a fruitful (Edgeworthian) ambivalence, as they counterpoise Scotch squalor and metropolitan corruption (in *Marriage*) and yearn for a moral authenticity that may inhere in old-fashioned national character (such as Uncle Adam, in Ferrier's *The Inheritance*, 1824). Ferrier remained the only notable practitioner of domestic fiction in Scotland after 1814. (Brunton died in childbed in 1818, leaving the didactic fragment *Emmeline*.) The only other Scottish Romantic woman novelist to enjoy significant literary success, Christian Johnstone, kept her distance from the tradition: mocking it by literalizing it, in a quasi-fictional guide to domestic economy (*The Cook and Housewife's Manual*, 1826), or combining the depiction of Scottish manners with the more dissident Irish mutations of the national tale by Sydney Owenson and Charles Robert Maturin (in Johnstone's *Clan-Albin*, 1815, and *Elizabeth de Bruce*, 1827).

The 1820s *Blackwood's Magazine* series *Noctes Ambrosianae* (co-authored by Wilson, Lockhart, and others) exhibits the gendered cast of Edinburgh literary life in the guise of a private party at a tavern, a nostalgic apotheosis of the clubs and societies that incubated masculine literacy in Enlightenment Scotland. The *Noctes* offers the symposium of Tory good fellows as a fantastic masquerade of the commercial and patronage systems of the

Scottish culture industry. Conversation unfolds through a succession of whisky-fueled feats of boasting, brawling, singing, and tale-telling: a carnivalesque rebuke to the "Whig junta" of the *Edinburgh Review*. The rarity of female voices at the feast glosses the comparative tenuousness of the feminine tradition of domestic fiction in Scotland. Garside and Schöwerling show that the correlation between a net rise in novel production and a proportional decline in female authorship in the decade up to 1825 was even stronger in Scotland than in Great Britain at large. Their statistics confirm recent accounts of the rhetorical accession of masculine "history" over feminine "romance" in the critical reception of Scott's novels, and those novels' internal allegories of a male appropriation of archaic female powers.[13]

Not just Scott's example, then, but the patronizing and professionalizing ethos that framed it, the larger cultural legacy of the Scottish Enlightenment, contributed to a relative exclusion of women authors from the literary boom in postwar Edinburgh. Brunton and Ferrier, gifted as they were, followed the respectable path of female authorship mapped in the early career of Burney, eschewing public visibility and professional status. Johnstone, the most versatile of the women writers, presents the contrasting case of a successful professional career. Johnstone's forays into prose fiction were framed by her journalistic experience, first at the *Inverness Courier* (1812–26) and later (from 1832) at a succession of Edinburgh Radical magazines. Standing behind the name of her husband, master printer John Johnstone, she played an editorial role as well as that of main contributor. When *Elizabeth de Bruce* did not meet with the anticipated success, Johnstone turned from writing novels to the magazine genres of tale, essay, and review, and achieved her most influential literary work (after 1834) at *Tait's Edinburgh Magazine*. Nor, however, were male authors more successful when it came to sustaining a professional literary career: Scott's ruin, hastened by reckless expenditure on his country estate at Abbotsford, is shadowed by his protégé Hogg's perpetual struggle with insolvency, while Galt's adventures included colony-building in Upper Canada and a spell in debtors' prison. Wilson and Lockhart settled into literary careers as the editors of *Blackwood's* and the *Quarterly Review*, but both gave up writing fiction.

The "Moderate" consensus restored with the *Edinburgh Review* did not survive the resumption of war against France. The end of the war in 1815 unleashed a political and ideological polarization across the periodical press, hardened by economic recession, worsening social tensions, and the intensifying national debate over electoral reform. The epoch of the full-scale commercialization of Edinburgh literary culture, in short, was also that of its virulent politicization. Both tendencies find superlative expression in

Blackwood's Magazine, the most influential work of the postwar decade besides the Waverley novels, and the principal matrix for alternative forms of Scottish fiction. Founded as a Tory counter-blast to the pro-Reform press, *Blackwood's* momentous achievement was the construction of a "Romantic ideology" to oppose the Neo-Enlightenment liberalism (tied to the emergent science of political economy) of *The Edinburgh Review*. The magazine equipped Tory politics with an aesthetic ideology of cultural nationalism shaped by its avant-garde mixture of literary forms and discourses, key among which was fiction.

Although the quarterlies had condescended to notice novels, beginning with Edgeworth (who pioneered the novelization of Enlightenment philosophical history) and then Scott, they tended to cultivate a neoclassical suspicion of fiction as such. *Blackwood's*, in contrast, became the leading, experimental forum for publishing non-novelistic kinds of prose fiction in the early 1820s, establishing the modern short story as a genre and developing a variety of styles and formats, including serialization (Galt's *The Ayrshire Legatees* and *The Steam-Boat*, 1820–1; Hogg's *The Shepherd's Calendar*, 1823; David Macbeth Moir's *Mansie Wauch*, 1824). *Blackwood's* juxtaposed fictional with non-fictional articles (whereas earlier magazines had segregated them), and corrupted the latter with fictional devices such as disguised or fictitious contributors and narrative and dramatic frames. Ethnographic sketch and satirical mock-autobiography mutate into works of sheer invention, with historical and imaginary characters sharing the same page. The most elaborate of these satirical para- or pseudo-fictions included Lockhart's novelized anatomy of the Scottish cultural scene, *Peter's Letters to his Kinsfolk*, much of which appeared in *Blackwood's* before coming out in book form in 1819, and the serial symposium *Noctes Ambrosianae*, which took off (after several try-outs) in 1822.

Both these works promote the Blackwoodian cultural politics of an "organic" sentimental nationalism, by turns rowdy and nostalgic, through fictional techniques: in the *Noctes*, a series of festive dialogues among editorial personae ("Christopher North"), fictionalized versions of real people (Lord Byron, "the English Opium-Eater," "the Ettrick Shepherd," i.e. Hogg) and invented characters, some of whom have strayed from the pages of Scottish fiction. *Peter's Letters to his Kinsfolk* crowns Scott with the laurels of a Tory Romantic vision of national culture in the course of Lockhart's general critique of a cosmopolitan, proto-Jacobin Scottish Enlightenment and its present-day heirs, the Edinburgh reviewers. Lockhart attacks the liberal professionalism of the *Edinburgh Review*, arguing that its commercial base drives a fatal wedge between the reviewers' claims to judicial disinterest and their Whig *parti pris*. Scott's fiction, in contrast, occupies an aesthetic high ground of national representation, rising above mere politics. The symbolic appropriation of Scott stands on a larger platform than his role as literary viceroy of the "Dundas despotism" in Edinburgh, backer of Tory periodicals and patron of *Blackwood's* authors (including his future son-in-law). More plausibly than Sir Walter Scott, Laird of Abbotsford, the Author of *Waverley* could represent (although by no means uncontroversially) a Scottish culture in all its historical variety and complexity, thanks to the novel's newly won status as the literary form of national life. In the early nineteenth century the novel's rhetorical unification of a modern reading public, through the performative invocation of national life, made it the normative genre of an ascendant middle-class culture – in contrast to the reviews and magazines, the proliferation of which expressed the politicization of modern social divisions.[14] Edinburgh, arguably, was the decisive site for this development, and the Waverley novels its decisive agent. They themselves tell a version of this story: the history of a modernizing nation-formation out of the savage clash of factions, out of "politics" and "ideology" as such.

No less crucial than the topical assumption of Enlightenment historicism in Scott's novels, in this light, was their categorical reinvestment in a rhetoric of fiction, abstracted and historicized under the pre-modern title of "romance." David Hume's *History of England* provided the model of a Moderate historiography with its national narrative of Whig progress tempered by Tory sentiment and its apertures of sympathetic identification with "wavering heroes" such as Falkland and Clarendon. Hume also provided the philosophical justification for Scott's combination of history with romance. The intellectual plot of Enlightenment, in Hume's *Treatise of Human Nature*, dissolves the metaphysical foundations of reality and covers the resulting void with a sentimental commitment to "common life," everyday social intercourse, intermittently recognized as an imaginary construction of reality ratified by custom. Thus *Waverley* narrates not only the emergence of modern civil society through the final conquest of an ancient regime (Catholic, Jacobite, feudal, tribal), but a Humean dialectical progression from "metaphysical" illusion through melancholy disenchantment to a sentimental and ironic reattachment to common life. Scott works out this scheme in an internal allegory of the rise of the novel as modern national form, in which the movement from primitive imaginary modes of "romance" through an empirically exigent "history" yields a third, synthetic term, the combination of romance and history that is realized in *Waverley* itself. Scott's historical novel, the material medium of our work of reading, constitutes the vantage point of modernity as it produces the plot of its own production. Reflexively insistent on their fictional status, Scott's novels activate scepticism rather than belief as the subjective cast of their reader's (rather than their protagonist's) relation to history, which includes, in the logic of metafictional reflection, the reader's own historical situation.

Following Hume, then, Scott made fiction the performative technique of a liberal ideology, one that stakes its modernity upon the claim of having superseded primitive modes of belief or ideological identification – super- stition, fanaticism – through a capacity to stand apart from and reflect on the submerged life of history, the blind rage of politics. The Romantic Tory apotheosis of Scott would require (however) the excision of these roots in an Enlightenment culture compromised by Humean skepticism. Lockhart's account of Scott in *Peter's Letters to his Kinsfolk* accordingly shifts from a critical appreciation of the work of fiction to a cult of the author, around whom the category of "literary authority" can be more confidently reas- sembled. "Peter's" report of his pilgrimage to Abbotsford, to bask in its landlord's charisma, establishes the thoroughly counter-Enlightenment for- mation that Thomas Carlyle will later call "hero-worship." Scott's authority is of a kind that compels his readers' belief, according to Lockhart, just as his writing provides a necromantic medium for historical truth and national spirit. The identification of Scott's works with Tory Romanticism thus required a measure of symbolic violence, which did not go uncontested. William Hazlitt, a frequent target of *Blackwood's* contumely, proclaimed the universal merit of Scott's novels ("His works (taken together) are almost like a new edition of human nature") by cutting them off (in a reciprocal symbolic violence) from the deplorable political views of their author, exploiting the division of labor implicit in his anonymity. Scott's death in the year of the Reform Bill prompted Radical reviewers Christian Johnstone and Harriet Martineau to take up Hazlitt's reclamation of his achievement for a new, liberal and progressive "spirit of the age." The property not of a party interest but of all mankind, the Waverley novels belonged to the nation's future rather than its past.

The insistence on conventions of fictionality, framing a Humean closure on the theatre of common life, characterizes the aesthetic that Jerome McGann has called Scott's "Romantic postmodernity."[15] "Here ends the Astrologer": with these words Captain Mannering, renouncing an equivocal art, terminates the chain of romance devices that makes up Scott's second novel *Guy Mannering, or the Astrologer* (1815). The last chapter of *Old Mortality* (1816) zooms forward from the abyss of civil war to the ordinary present, where dressmaker Miss Martha Buskbody, connoisseur of "the whole stock of three circulating libraries in Gandercleuch and the next two market towns," bullies the work's putative editor into wrapping up his story according to the proper conventions. Conservative skepticism receives Scott's most exuberant treatment in *The Antiquary* (1816), a meta-Waverley Novel or Shandification of historical romance in which, despite the invocation of an unusually intricate plot, nothing happens: or rather, sensational events – manslaughter, infanticide, incest, a discovery of buried treasure, a French invasion, the repulse of a Roman invasion, the writing of an epic poem – turn out not to have happened, covering the one big event that must on no account be admitted to constitute the plot of the present: revolution.

It was with *Old Mortality*, the main work in the first set of *Tales of My Landlord*, that Scott's Humean rendition of national historical fiction became controversial. Scott applies the basic plot of *Waverley*, in which a "moderate" hero finds himself involved in a rebellion, to the religious civil wars of the late seventeenth century. His treatment of radical Presbyterianism, source of a Scottish tradition of popular democratic politics, proved far more divisive than his treatment of counter-revolutionary Jacobitism. Dissenting reviewers repudiated the novel's claim on a principled Whig Moderatism, struggling between revolutionary and absolutist extremes to be born as the dominant ideology of the modern age; they objected, in particular, to the depiction of the Covenanters, champions of Scotland's civil and religious liberties, as wild fanatics. Rival Covenanter historical fictions were published challenging Scott's: Hogg's *The Brownie of Bodsbeck* (1818), Galt's *Ringan Gilhaize* (1823). Both undo Scott's equation of the Covenanters with an archetypal revolutionary fanaticism, Hogg by stressing the natural piety of rural communities, Galt by distinguishing between the heroic epoch of the Scottish Reformation and its terrorist remnant, warped by government persecution. More striking is the articulation of their challenge in the deployment of literary form.[16] *The Brownie of Bodsbeck* defies the retrospective, rationalizing order of Enlightenment, realized in a unified complex plot and an abstract English narration, for an intermittent recital in which local actors tell their stories in what are represented to be their own voices. *Ringan Gilhaize* fuses memory and history into Ringan's single narration, transmitting the life-stories of his grandfather, father and himself, to curate the ideological legacy of the Reformation in early modern Scottish history. Ringan's narration renounces fictionality for a story that rests on the strong term of belief, faith: keystone of an agency that undergoes a tragic declension from revolutionary collectivism to solitary pathological obsession.

Hogg's and Galt's formal alternatives emerge through the opening made by Scott's fiction for the characteristically "Blackwoodian" fiction that followed. The *Tales of My Landlord* announce a distinctively regionalist representation of national life in the medium of a set of tales: "To his loving countrymen," goes the dedication, "whether they are denominated Men of the South, Gentlemen of the North, People of the West, or Folk of Fife, these Tales, illustrative of ancient Scottish manners, and of the Traditions of their Respective Districts, are respectfully inscribed." The most gifted of the Blackwood authors would develop this emphasis, making regional identity (the traditions of their respective districts) the foundation for their own claims on originality. Hogg's tales – *The Brownie of Bodsbeck* and its successors, *Winter Evening Tales* (1820) and *The Shepherd's Calendar* – ground their narrative matter and manner on the popular traditions of the Scottish Borders, centering on Ettrick, ranging to Liddesdale and Dumfries. Galt conceived of a series of "Tales of the West," emanating from and representing Glasgow and Ayrshire as a world socially and culturally distinct from polite Edinburgh. Hogg and Galt gave the tale its richest formal development, the first-person fictional memoir grounded in local patterns of experience and discourse. Their characteristic work – radically divergent in other respects – promoted vernacular Scots to the main narrative language, in contrast to Scott's framing of varieties of Scots speech within a general, obtrusively literary, imperial English. Galt had his own imitators, such as Moir (*Mansie Wauch*), Andrew Picken (*Tales and Sketches of the West of Scotland*, 1824) and Thomas Hamilton (*The Youth and Manhood of Cyril Thornton*, 1827). The novels and tales of Lockhart and Wilson – who also emerged, like Galt, from "the West" (but via Oxford) – forgo regional specificity for typical rather than particularized rural settings, drawing upon the moral–evangelical "feminine" tradition for a more sentimentally or sensationally intensive as well as didactic treatment (Lockhart's *Adam Blair*, 1822; Wilson's *Trials of Margaret Lyndsay*, 1823).

Galt distinguished his original achievement from Scott's: *Annals of the Parish* (1821) and *The Provost* (1822) are not "novels or romances" but "theoretical histories of society."[17] Drawing on the satirical form Edgeworth had pioneered in *Castle Rackrent*, Galt's imaginary autobiographies of a country minister and a small-town politician eschew the Scott model of plot-intensive romance for an alternative fictional development of conjectural history, a trompe-l'oeil representation of historical change in the micropolitics of provincial society. Galt clarifies the anecdotal, annalistic form of local memoir into a medium that registers the vibrations between local everyday life and an emergent global political economy, between objective processes of social change and the subjective horizons of experience, with unprecedented sensitivity.[18] Yet if these works exhibit the virtue Galt claimed as his "originality," his most ambitious works engage the commodified form of Scott's success, the three-volume national historical novel. Galt's finest novels, *The Entail* (1823) and *Ringan Gilhaize*, work out a strenuous and subtle debate with Scott's historical fiction in the early series of *Tales of My Landlord*. In *The Entail*, his masterpiece, Galt schematically recasts his rival's most formidable work, *The Heart of Mid-Lothian* (1818). Galt's novel, like Scott's, brings a family chronicle to bear on a legal crux that encodes a national-scale social and moral crisis, with Galt's indomitable anti-heroine, the Leddy Grippy, an exuberant parody of Scott's Jeanie Deans.

The comparison between Galt and Hogg charts a striking triangulation in the political economy of fiction in early 1820s Edinburgh. Galt challenges the Humean dialectic at work in the Waverley novels with a strong development of one of its terms, materialist social history, and a refusal of the other, antiquarian romance. Hogg, in contrast, asserts vernacular principles of storytelling in defiance of an Enlightenment cultural teleology. Hogg's tales, pioneered in his weekly miscellany *The Spy* in 1810–11 before their bravura development the following decade, experiment with a range of forms and styles (exemplified in *Winter Evening Tales*): novella-length satirical autobiography ("Renowned Adventures of Basil Lee," "Love Adventures of Mr George Cochrane"), autoethnographic sketch or anecdote ("The Shepherd's Calendar"), ghost story ("Country Dreams and Apparitions"). Hogg's more ambitious narratives offended polite taste by disrupting the conventions within which "folk" material was expected to be packaged, and by laying presumptuous claim to metropolitan styles and genres. In the 1820s Hogg too moved from the shorter forms of the tale to take on the prestigious, and profitable, form of multi-volume historical novel defined by Scott. *The Three Perils of Man: War, Women and Witchcraft* (1821), a medieval "Border Romance," rebuts Scott's brilliant antiquarian fictions (*Ivanhoe, The Monastery*) with a ferociously comic performance of what can only be called a proto-postmodern magic realism. Sorcerers and demons share narrative space with historical barons and peasants amid outbursts of slapstick cruelty. *The Three Perils of Woman: Love, Leasing and Jealousy* (1823) tracks the dissolution, rather than development, of the domestic national tale into historical romance *à la Waverley*. The final scenes of *The Three Perils of Woman*, set in the desolated Highlands after Culloden, enact a traumatic meltdown of cultural meaning, by turns farcical and harrowing.

Scott himself strove in the field of formal and political contestation that made up Scottish fiction in the 1820s. In 1823 the Author of *Waverley* returned to modern Scotland, after a series of romances with medieval and Renaissance settings, for an experiment in the self-avowedly alien genre of female-authored novel (according to Scott) of contemporary domestic manners: *Saint Ronan's Well* veers queasily between satire and melodrama.

Redgauntlet: A Tale of the Eighteenth Century (1824) undertakes a full-dress reclamation of Scott's signature form of Scottish historical romance. *Redgauntlet*'s historical retrospect includes an anthology of eighteenth-century genres – letters, journal, popular lyric, folk tale, Gothic novel, family history, law case, rogue's memoir, stage comedy – as well as of the Scottish Waverley novels themselves, as Scott rewrites the plot of Jacobite rebellion enmeshed with family romance related in *Waverley* and *Rob Roy*.[19] In the summer of 1765 a last attempt at Jacobite insurrection dissolves into anti-climax and non-event: a failure to reenter history confirmed in the historiographical status of the plot as Scott's own fictional invention. (No such return of Prince Charlie took place *vingt ans après*.) Scott's resort to comedy for the elegiac key of failure decisively empties history of its metaphysical charge. Perhaps his finest work, *Redgauntlet* reaffirms – with dazzling virtuosity – the aesthetic of Romantic skepticism inaugurated ten years earlier in *Waverley*.

This reaffirmation, mediated through the novel's insistence on formal miscellany, rebuts the aesthetic and ideological challenge posed by Galt in *Ringan Gilhaize*, which Scott burlesques in the inset story of the Redgauntlet family curse. (Galt returned the compliment by inserting a burlesque of this episode, in a chapter called "Redgauntlet," in his next novel *Rothelan*, 1824.) Hogg's masterpiece *The Private Memoirs and Confessions of a Justified Sinner*, published in the same month as *Redgauntlet* (June, 1824), has also been read as a reply to Galt's narrative of terrorist declension of the Covenant in *Ringan Gilhaize*, as well as a critical deconstruction of Scott's historical fiction.[20] Hogg splits his novel between the competing forms of imaginary memoir, its subjective horizon intensified into psychopathic delirium, and fictitious history, curated by an enlightened editor: far from resolving into a "moderate" synthesis, antinomies and antagonisms proliferate disastrously across the text. Both *Redgauntlet* and *Confessions of a Justified Sinner* share conspicuous formal and thematic features, including an elaborate self-reflexiveness about their material and cultural status as "tales of the eighteenth century," fictions of Scottish modernization, and as printed books, published at the end of the decade of national historical fiction inaugurated with *Waverley*. While *Redgauntlet* reaffirms the Humean paradigm of historical romance, *Confessions of a Justified Sinner* decomposes the ingredients of Scottish cultural modernity into a waste material residue, represented through the metonymic identification, in the final pages, of the sinner's unhallowed corpse with the text we are reading. A nauseating disintegration taints the author, his work, and the reader; and indeed, Hogg's masterpiece would remain all but unreadable until the twentieth century.

NOTES

1 Peter Garside and Rainer Schöwerling, *The English Novel 1770–1829: A Bibliographical Survey of Prose Fiction Published in the British Isles, Vol. II: 1800–1829* (Oxford: Oxford University Press, 2000), p. 76.
2 *Fraser's Magazine* 1: 2 (March, 1830), p. 236.
3 Garside and Schöwerling, *The English Novel 1770–1829*, p. 15.
4 William St Clair, *The Reading Nation in the Romantic Period* (Cambridge: Cambridge University Press, 2004), p. 221.
5 Ibid., p. 170.
6 Ibid.
7 "Secondary Scottish Novels," *Edinburgh Review* 39 (October 1823), pp. 158–79.
8 See F. R. Hart, *The Scottish Novel: From Smollett to Spark* (Cambridge, Mass.: Harvard University Press, 1978), pp. 31–84; Robert Morrison and Chris Baldick, eds., *Tales of Terror from Blackwood's Magazine* (Oxford: Oxford University Press, 1995); Peter Garside, "Hogg and the Blackwoodian Novel," *Studies in Hogg and his World* 15 (2004), pp. 5–20.
9 For both developments – the national tale before Scott, the imperial reach of Scott and *Blackwood's* – see Katie Trumpener, *Bardic Nationalism: The Romantic Novel and the British Empire* (Princeton: Princeton University Press, 1997), pp. 137–51, 243–91.
10 "Thoughts on Novel Writing," *Blackwood's Edinburgh Magazine* 4 (January 1819), pp. 394–6.
11 "Edinburgh Novels," *Edinburgh Magazine, or Literary Miscellany* 3 (June 1819), p. 60.
12 Ina Ferris, *The Achievement of Literary Authority: Gender, History, and the Waverley Novels* (Ithaca: Cornell University Press, 1991), pp. 19–59.
13 Garside and Schöwerling, *The English Novel 1770–1829*, pp. 72–5, 90; Ferris, *Achievement of Literary Authority*, pp. 79–104; Ian Duncan, *Modern Romance and Transformations of the Novel: The Gothic, Scott, Dickens* (Cambridge: Cambridge University Press, 1992), pp. 131–71.
14 Clifford Siskin, *The Work of Writing: Literature and Social Change in Britain, 1700–1830* (Baltimore: Johns Hopkins University Press, 1998), pp. 155–190; Jon Klancher, *The Making of English Reading Audiences, 1790–1832* (Madison, Wis.: University of Wisconsin Press, 1987), pp. 18–46.
15 Jerome McGann, "Walter Scott's Romantic Postmodernity," in Leith Davis, Ian Duncan, and Janet Sorensen, ed., *Scotland and the Borders of Romanticism* (Cambridge: Cambridge University Press, 2004), pp. 113–29.
16 For a discussion see Ferris, *Achievement of Literary Authority*, pp. 161–94.
17 John Galt, *Autobiography*, 2 vols., Vol. II (London, 1833), pp. 219–20.
18 See Trumpener, *Bardic Nationalism*, pp. 153–6.
19 See Leah Price, *The Anthology and the Rise of the Novel: From Richardson to George Eliot* (Cambridge: Cambridge University Press, 2000), pp. 54–65.
20 Douglas Mack, "'The Rage of Fanaticism in Former Days': James Hogg's *Confessions of a Justified Sinner* and the Controversy over *Old Mortality*," from Ian Campbell, ed., *Nineteenth-Century Scottish Fiction: Critical Essays* (Manchester: Carcanet, 1979), pp. 37–50; Gary Kelly, *English Fiction of the Romantic Period 1789–1830* (London and New York: Longman, 1989), pp. 260–73.

Historiography

Altick, Richard D., *The English Common Reader: A Social History of the Mass Reading Public 1800–1900*, Chicago, University of Chicago Press, 1957

Bibliothèque universelle des nouvelles, 224 volumes, 1775–89

Butler, Marilyn, *Romantics, Rebels, and Reactionaries: English Literature and its Background 1760–1830*, Oxford, Oxford University Press, 1982

The Corvey Project, www.shu.ac.uk/schools/cs/corvey/articles/

Dunlop, John, *The History of Fiction: Being a Critical Account of the Most Celebrated Prose Works of Fiction, from the Earliest Greek Romances to the Novels of the Present Age*, London, Longman, Hurst, Rees, Orme, and Brown, 1814

Garside, Peter, James Raven, and Rainer Schöwerling, eds., *The English Novel 1770–1829: A Bibliographical Survey of Prose Fiction Published in the British Isles*, 2 vols., Oxford, Oxford University Press, 2000

Kelly, Gary, *English Fiction of the Romantic Period*, London and New York, Longman, 1989

Klancher, Jon, *The Making of English Reading Audiences, 1790–1832*, Madison, Wisconsin, University of Wisconsin Press, 1987

McCalman, Iain, *Radical Underworld: Prophets, Revolutionaries and Pornographers in London 1795–1840*, Oxford, Oxford University Press, 1988

Martin, Angus, *La Bibliothèque universelle des romans 1775–1789: Présentation, table analytique, et index*, Oxford, The Voltaire Foundation at the Taylor Institution, 1985

Millgate, Jane, *Scott's Last Edition: A Study in Publishing History*, Edinburgh, Edinburgh University Press, 1987

Reeve, Clara, *The Progress of Romance and The History of Charoba, Queen of Aegypt* (reproduced from the Colchester edition of 1785), New York, The Facsimile Text Society, 1930

Tompkins, J. M. S., *The Popular Novel in England 1770–1800* (1932), Lincoln, Nebraska, University of Nebraska Press, 1961

Sadleir, Michael, *XIX Century Fiction*, 2 vols., London, Constable; Berkeley, University of California Press, 1951

St Clair, William, *The Reading Nation in the Romantic Period*, Cambridge, Cambridge University Press, 2004

Publishing history

Altick, Richard D., *The English Common Reader: A Social History of the Mass Reading Public 1800–1900*, Chicago, University of Chicago Press, 1957

Ashton, John, *Chap-books of the Eighteenth Century*, London, Chatto & Windus, 1882

Brack, O. M., Jr., ed., *Writers, Books and Trade: An Eighteenth Century Miscellany for William B. Todd*, New York, AMS Press, 1994

British Fiction, 1800–1829: A Database of Production, Circulation, and Reception, www.british-fiction.cf.ac.uk

Collins, A. S., *The Profession of Letters: A Study of the Relation of Author to Patron, Publisher and the Public, 1780–1832*, London, G. Routledge, 1928

Cruse, Amy, *The Englishman and His Books in the Early Nineteenth Century*, London, G. G. Harrap, 1930

Franklin, Caroline, E. J. Clery, and Peter Garside, eds., *Authorship, Commerce, and the Public: Scenes of Writing, 1750–1850*, New York, Palgrave, 2002

Garside, Peter, James Raven, and Rainer Schöwerling, *The English Novel, 1770–1829: A Bibliographical Survey of Prose Fiction Published in the British Isles*, 2 vols., Oxford, Oxford University Press, 2000

Howe, Ellic, *The London Compositor*, London, Bibliographical Society, 1947

Isaac, Peter, ed., *Six Centuries of the Provincial Book Trade in Britain*, Winchester, St Paul's Bibliographies, 1990

Johns, Adrian, *The Nature of the Book: Print and Knowledge in the Making*, Chicago, University of Chicago Press, 1998

Jordan, John O., and Robert L. Patten, eds., *Literature in the Marketplace*, Cambridge, Cambridge University Press, 1995

Myers, Robin and Michael Harris, eds., *Development of the English Book Trade, 1700–1899*, Oxford, Oxford Polytechnic Press, 1981

Spreading the Word: The Distribution Networks of Print, 1550–1850, Winchester, St. Paul's Bibliographies, 1990

Censorship and the Control of Print in England and France, 1600–1910, Winchester, St. Paul's Bibliographies, 1992

The Stationers' Company and the Book Trade, 1550–1990, Winchester, St. Paul's Bibliographies, 1997

Raven, James, *Judging New Wealth, Popular Publishing and Responses to Commerce in England, 1750–1800*, Oxford, Clarendon Press, 1992

The Business of Books: Booksellers and the English Book Trade, New Haven, Yale University Press, 2007

Raven, James, ed., *Free Print and Non-Commercial Publishing since 1700*, Aldershot, Ashgate, 2000

Raven, James, Helen Small, and Naomi Tadmor, eds., *The Practice and Representation of Reading in England*, Cambridge, Cambridge University Press, 1996

Sher, Richard, *The Enlightenment and the Book: Scottish Authors and their Publishers in Eighteenth-Century Britain, Ireland, and America*, Chicago, University of Chicago Press, 2006

Gothic fiction

Blackwell, Mark R., "The Gothic: Moving in the World of Novels," in *A Concise Companion to the Restoration and Eighteenth Century*, ed. Cynthia Wall, Oxford, Blackwell, 2005, pp. 144–61

Brown, Marshall, *The Gothic Text*, Stanford, Stanford University Press, 2005

Canuel, Mark, ' "Holy hypocrisy" and the Rule of Belief: Radcliffe's Gothics,' in Mark Canuel, *Religion, Toleration and British Writing, 1790–1830*, Cambridge Studies in Romanticism, Cambridge, Cambridge University Press, 2002, pp. 55–85

Castle, Terry, *The Female Thermometer: Eighteenth-Century Culture and the Invention of the Uncanny*, Oxford, Oxford University Press, 1995

Clery, E. J., *The Rise of Supernatural Fiction, 1762–1800*, Cambridge Studies in Romanticism, Cambridge, Cambridge University Press, 1995

Conger, Syndy M., "Sensibility Restored: Radcliffe's Answer to Lewis's *The Monk*," in *Gothic Fictions: Prohibition/Transgression*, ed. Kenneth W. Graham, New York, AMS Press, 1989, pp. 113–49

Duncan, Ian, *Modern Romance and Transformations of the Novel: The Gothic, Scott, Dickens*, Cambridge, Cambridge University Press, 1992

Ellis, Kate Ferguson, *The Contested Castle: Gothic Novels and the Subversion of Domestic Ideology*, Urbana, University of Illinois Press, 1989

Gamer, Michael, *Romanticism and the Gothic: Genre, Reception, and Canon Formation*, Cambridge Studies in Romanticism, Cambridge, Cambridge University Press, 2000

Hogle, Jerrold E., ed., *The Cambridge Companion to Gothic Fiction*, Cambridge, Cambridge University Press, 2002

Kilgour, Maggie, *The Rise of the Gothic Novel*, London, Routledge, 1995

Lynch, Deidre, "Gothic Libraries and National Subjects," *Studies in Romanticism* 40, 1 (Spring 2001), pp. 29–48

Miles, Robert, *Gothic Writing: A Genealogy, 1750–1820*, London, Routledge, 1993

Sedgwick, Eve Kosofsky, *The Coherence of Gothic Conventions* (1980), New York, Methuen, 1986

Summers, Montague, *The Gothic Quest: A History of the Gothic Novel*, London, Fortune Press, 1938

Watt, James, *Contesting the Gothic: Fiction, Genre and Cultural Conflict, 1764–1832*, Cambridge Studies in Romanticism, Cambridge, Cambridge University Press, 1999

Williams, Anne, *Art of Darkness: A Poetics of Gothic*, Chicago, University of Chicago Press, 1995

Historical fiction

Alliston, April, Introduction, Sophia Lee, *The Recess; or, A Tale of Other Times*, Lexington, Kentucky, University Press of Kentucky, 2000, pp. ix–xliv

Butler, Marilyn, *Peacock Displayed: A Satirist in His Context*, London, Routledge, 1979

Chandler, James, *England in 1819: The Politics of Literary Culture and the Case of Romantic Historicism*, Chicago, University of Chicago Press, 1998

Christensen, Allan Conrad, *The Subverting Vision of Bulwer Lytton: Bicentenary Reflections*, Newark, University of Delaware Press; Cranbury, New Jersey, Associated University Presses, 2004

Clemit, Pamela, *The Godwinian Novel: The Rational Fictions of Godwin, Brockden Brown, Mary Shelley*, Oxford, Oxford University Press, 1993

Duncan, Ian, *Scott's Shadow: The Novel in Romantic Edinburgh*, Princeton, Princeton University Press, 2007

Duncan, Ian, Ann Rowland, and Charles Snodgrass, eds., "Scott, Scotland and Romantic Nationalism," special issue of *Studies in Romanticism* 40, 1 (Spring 2001)

Ferris, Ina, *The Achievement of Literary Authority: Gender, History, and the Waverley Novels*, Ithaca, Cornell University Press, 1991

Fleishman, Avrom, *The English Historical Novel; Walter Scott to Virginia Woolf*, Baltimore, Johns Hopkins University Press, 1971

Hayden, John, *Scott: The Critical Heritage*, New York, Barnes & Noble, 1970 (especially comments and essays by Austen, Edgeworth, Jeffrey, Croker, Peacock, Sydney Smith, Coleridge, Hazlitt, Heine, Goethe, Stendhal, Bulwer-Lytton, Carlyle, Cardinal Newman, R. L. Stevenson, and John Ruskin)

Hogg, James, *Collected Works*, Stirling/South Carolina Research Edition, edited by Douglas Mack, Edinburgh, Edinburgh University Press, in progress

Lynch, Deidre Shauna, "Historical Novelist," [on Mary Shelley's historical fiction] in *The Cambridge Companion to Mary Shelley*, ed. Esther Schor, Cambridge, Cambridge University Press, 2003

Lukács, Georg, *The Historical Novel*, trans. Hannah and Stanley Mitchell, Lincoln, University of Nebraska Press, 1983

McGann, Jerome, "My Kinsman Walter Scott," in *The Scholar's Art: Literary Studies in a Managed World*, Chicago, University of Chicago Press, 2006, pp. 71–87

Maigron, Louis, *Roman historique à l'époque romantique: Essai sur l'influence de Walter Scott* (1898), Geneva, Slatkine Reprints, 1970

Maxwell, Richard, "Inundations of Time: A Definition of Scott's Originality," *ELH* 68, pp. 419–468

"Phantom States: *Cleveland*, *The Recess*, and the Origins of Historical Fiction," in Margaret Cohen and Carolinel Dever, eds., *The Literary Channel: The Inter-National Invention of the Novel*, Princeton, Princeton University Press, 2002, pp. 151–82

Pittock, Murray, *The Invention of Scotland: The Stuart Myth and the Scottish Identity, 1638 to the Present*, London, Routledge, 1991

Rigney, Ann, *Imperfect Histories: The Elusive Past and the Legacy of Romantic Historicism*, Ithaca, Cornell University Press, 2001

Scott, Walter, *The Waverley Novels*, Edinburgh Edition, ed. David Hewitt, Edinburgh: Edinburgh University Press, in progress

Trumpener, Katie, *Bardic Nationalism: The Romantic Novel and the British Empire*, Princeton, Princeton University Press, 1997

Wainwright, Clive, *The Romantic Interior: The British Collector at Home 1750–1850*, New Haven and London, Yale University Press, 1989

Welsh, Alexander, *The Hero of the Waverley Novels; With New Essays on Scott*, Princeton, New Jersey: Princeton University Press, 1992

Wilt, Judith, *Secret Leaves: The Novels of Walter Scott*, Chicago, University of Chicago Press, 1985

Locale, nature, and fiction

Barrell, John, *The Dark Side of the Landscape: The Rural Poor in English Painting 1730–1840*, Cambridge, Cambridge University Press, 1980
English Literature in History, 1730–80: An Equal, Wide Survey, New York, St. Martin's Press, 1983
Bewick, Thomas, *History of British Birds*, Vol. I, Newcastle, Beilby and Bewick, 1797
Bohrer, M. A., "Tales of Locale: The Natural History of *Selborne* and *Castle Rackrent*," *Modern Philology* 100 (2003), pp. 393–416
Costain, K. M., "The Community of Man: Galt and Eighteenth-Century Scottish Realism," *Scottish Literary Journal* 8 (1981), pp. 10–29
Crabbe, George, *The Complete Poetical Works*, eds. N. Dalrymple-Champneys and A. Pollard, 3 vols., Oxford, Clarendon Press, 1988
De Certeau, Michel, *The Practice of Everyday Life*, trans. S. Rendall, Berkeley, University of California Press, 1984
Edgeworth, Maria, *Novels and Selected Works*, 12 vols., London, Pickering & Chatto, 1999–2003, Vol. I, eds. J. Desmarais, T. McLoughlin, and M. Butler
Edgeworth, Maria, and R. L. Edgeworth, *Practical Education*, 2nd edn., London, J. Johnston, 1798
Galt, John, *Annals of the Parish and The Ayreshire Legatees*, 2 vols., Edinburgh and London, Blackwood, 1895
"Garden History Style Guide," www.gardenvisit.com/s/estyle2/estyle.htm
Goldsmith, O., and T. Parnel, *Poems by Goldsmith and Parnell*, London, Shakespeare Printing Office, 1795
Gray, Thomas, "Elegy Written in a Country Churchyard," *The Longman Anthology of British Literature: The Restoration and the Eighteenth Century*, 3rd edn., Vol. IC, New York, Pearson Longman, 2006, pp. 2854–7
Mitford, Mary Russell, "Our Village," *Works*, Philadelphia, Crissy and Markley, 1856
Nichols, J., *The History and Antiquities of the County of Leicestershire*, 4 vols., London, John Nichols, 1795–1815
White, Gilbert, *The Natural History of Selborne*, ed. R. Mabey, London, Everyman, 1993
Williams, Raymond, *The Country and the City*, New York, Oxford University Press, 1973
Withers, C. J., "Statistical Accounts of Scotland," in www.electricscotland.com/webclans/satistical_accounts.htm

Poetry and the novel

Adorno, Theodor, "Parataxis: On Hölderlin's Late Poetry," *Notes to Literature*, Vol. II, trans. Shierry Weber Nicholsen, New York, Columbia University Press, 1992, pp. 109–49
Austen, Jane, *Northanger Abbey, Lady Susan, The Watsons, and Sanditon*, ed. John Davie, Oxford, Oxford University Press, 1990
Brown, Marshall, *The Shape of German Romanticism*, Ithaca, Cornell University Press, 1979

"Theory of the Novel," in *The Cambridge History of Literary Criticism*, Vol. V: *Romanticism*, ed. Marshall Brown, Cambridge, Cambridge University Press, 2000, pp. 250–71

Clayton, Jay, *Romantic Vision and the Novel*, Cambridge, Cambridge University Press, 1987

Curran, Stuart, "General Introduction," in *The Works of Charlotte Smith*, Vol. I (containing *Manon L'Escaut* and *The Romance of Real Life*), ed. Michael Gamer, London, Pickering and Chatto, 2005, pp. vii–xxvii

Deresiewicz, William, *Jane Austen and the Romantic Poets*, New York, Columbia University Press, 2004

Dubrow, Heather, *The Challenges of Orpheus: Lyric Poetry and Early Modern England*, Baltimore, Johns Hopkins University Press, 2007

Eller, Ruth, "The Poetic Theme in Scott's Novels," in *Scott and His Influence: The Papers of the Aberdeen Scott Conference, 1982*, ed. J. H. Alexander and David Hewitt, Aberdeen: Association for Scottish Literary Studies, 1983, pp. 75–86

Favret, Mary, "Telling Tales about Genre: Poetry in the Romantic Novel," *Studies in the Novel* 26 (1994), pp. 281–300

Felluga, Dino, "Novel Poetry: Transgressing the Law of Genre," *Victorian Poetry* 41 (2003), pp. 90–9

Fess, Gilbert M., "Balzac and the Poets," *PMLA* 47 (1932), pp. 1158–66

Gamer, Michael, "Maria Edgeworth and the Romance of Real Life," *Novel: A Forum on Fiction* 34 (2001), pp. 232–66

Isaac, Bonnie J., "'Tous les refrains sont bons': Balzac and Poetry: *Lost Illusions*," *MLN* 98 (1983), pp. 728–44

Kelly, Gary, *English Fiction of the Romantic Period, 1789–1830*, London, Longman, 1989

Kroeber, Karl, *Romantic Narrative Art*, Madison, University of Wisconsin Press, 1960

Laughlin, Corinna, "The Ossianic Novel," unpublished dissertation, University of Washington, 1998

Lukács, Georg, *The Theory of the Novel*, trans. Anna Bostock, Cambridge, Massachusetts, The MIT Press, 1971

Neuburger, Paul, *Die Verseinlage in der Prosadichtung der Romantik*, Leipzig, Mayer und Müller, 1924

Posnock, Ross, *Henry James and the Problem of Robert Browning*, Athens, Georgia, University of Georgia Press, 1985

Pütz, Peter, "Wenn Effi läse, was Crampas empfiehlt...: Offene und verdeckte Zitaten im Roman," in *Theodor Fontane*, ed. Heinz Ludwig Arnold, Munich, Text & Kritik, 1989, pp. 174–84

Robson, Catherine, "Standing on the Burning Deck: Poetry, Performance, History," *PMLA* 120 (2005), pp. 148–62

Rothery, C. I., "Scott's Narrative Poetry and the Classical Form of the Historical Novel," in *Scott and His Influence: The Papers of the Aberdeen Scott Conference, 1982*, ed. J. H. Alexander and David Hewitt, Aberdeen, Association for Scottish Literary Studies, 1983, pp. 63–74

Schlegel, Friedrich, *Literary Notebooks*, ed. Hans Eichner, London, Athlone Press, 1957

Scott, Walter, *Sir Walter Scott on Novelists and Fiction*, ed. Ioan Williams, New York, Barnes and Noble, 1968

Siskin, Clifford, *The Work of Writing: Literature and Social Change in Britain, 1700–1830*, Baltimore, Johns Hopkins University Press, 1998

Smith, Charlotte, *The Old Manor House*, ed. Anne Henry Ehrenpreis, Oxford, Oxford University Press, 1989

Celestina, ed. Loraine Fletcher, Peterborough, Ontario, Broadview, 2004

Staiger, Emil, *Basic Concepts of Poetics*, trans. C. Hudson and Luanne T. Frank, University Park, Pennsylvania State University Press, 1991

Starr, G. Gabrielle, *Lyric Generations: Poetry and the Novel in the Long Eighteenth Century*, Baltimore, Johns Hopkins University Press, 2004

Striedter, Jurij, "Poetic Genre and the Sense of History in Pushkin," *New Literary History* 8 (1977), pp. 295–309

Orientalism and Empire

Aravamudan, Srinivas, *Tropicopolitans: Colonialism and Agency, 1688–1804*, Durham, Duke University Press, 1999

Ballaster, Ros, *Fabulous Orients: Fictions of the East in England 1662–1785*, Oxford, Oxford University Press, 2005

Bewell, Alan, *Romanticism and Colonial Disease*, Baltimore, Johns Hopkins University Press 1999

Brantlinger, Patrick, *Rule of Darkness: British Literature and Imperialism, 1830–1914*, Ithaca, Cornell University Press, 1988

Caracciolo, Peter L, ed., *The Arabian Nights in English Literature: Studies of the Reception of the Thousand and One Nights into British Culture*, Basingstoke, Macmillan, 1988

Chakravarty, Gautam, *The Indian Mutiny and the British Imagination*, Cambridge, Cambridge University Press, 2005

Fulford, Tim, and Peter Kitson, eds., *Romanticism and Colonialism: Writing and Empire, 1780–1830*, Cambridge, Cambridge University Press, 1998

Leask, Nigel, *British Romantic Writers and the East: Anxieties of Empire*, Cambridge, Cambridge University Press, 1992

Majeed, Javed, *Ungoverned Imaginings: James Mill's The History of British India and Orientalism*, Oxford, Oxford University Press, 1992

Makdisi, Saree, *Romantic Imperialism: Universal Empire and the Culture of Modernity*, Cambridge, Cambridge University Press, 1998

Moore-Gilbert, Bart, ed., *Writing India, 1757–1990: The Literature of British India*, Manchester, Manchester University Press, 1996

Nussbaum, Felicity, *Torrid Zones: Maternity, Sexuality, and Empire in Eighteenth-Century English Narratives*, Baltimore, Johns Hopkins University Press, 1995

Rajan, Balachandra, *Under Western Eyes: India from Milton to Macaulay*, Durham, Duke University Press, 1999

Richardson, Alan, and Sonia Hofkosh, *Romanticism, Race, and Imperial Culture, 1780–1834*, Bloomington, Indiana University Press, 1996

Rousseau, G. S., and Roy Porter, *Exoticism in the Enlightenment*, Manchester, Manchester University Press, 1990

Said, Edward, *Orientalism*, London, Routledge, 1978

Teltscher, Kate, *India Inscribed: European and British Writing on India, 1600–1800*, Oxford, Oxford University Press, 1995

Trumpener, Katie, *Bardic Nationalism: The Romantic Novel and the British Empire*, Princeton, Princeton University Press, 1997

Yeazell, Ruth Bernard, *Harems of the Mind: Passages of Western Art and Literature*, New Haven, Yale University Press, 2000

Intellectual history and political theory

Aspinall, Arthur, *Politics and the Press, 1780–1850 (1949)*, Brighton: Harvester, 1973

Barrell, John, *Imagining the King's Death: Figurative Treason, Fantasies of Regicide, 1793–96*, Oxford, Oxford University Press, 2000

    The Spirit of Despotism: Invasion of Privacy in the 1790s, Oxford, Oxford University Press, 2006

Craciun, Adriana, and Kari E. Lokke, ed., *Rebellious Hearts: British Women Writers and the French Revolution*, Albany, New York, State University of New York Press, 2001

Eisenstein, Elizabeth L., *Print Culture and Enlightenment Thought*, Chapel Hill, Hanes Foundation, 1986

Gregory, Allene, *The French Revolution and the English Novel*, New York, Haskell House, 1966

Grenby, M. O., *The Anti-Jacobin Novel: British Conservatism and the French Revolution*, Cambridge, Cambridge University Press, 2001

Keane, Angela, *Women Writers and the English Nation in the 1790s*, Cambridge, Cambridge University Press, 2000

Kelly, Gary, *The English Jacobin Novel, 1780–1805*, Oxford, Oxford University Press, 1976

    Women, Writing, and Revolution, 1790–1827, Oxford, Clarendon Press, 1993

Klancher, Jon, *The Making of English Reading Audiences, 1790–1832*, Madison, Wisconsin, University of Wisconsin Press, 1991

Kramnick, Isaac, *Republicanism and Bourgeois Radicalism: Political Ideology in Late Eighteenth-Century England and America*, Ithaca, Cornell University Press, 1990

McCalman, Iain, *Radical Underworld: Prophets, Revolutionaries and Pornographers in London, 1795–1840*, Cambridge: Cambridge University Press, 1988

Mee, Jon, *Dangerous Enthusiasm: William Blake and the Culture of Radicalism in the 1790s*, Oxford, Clarendon Press, 1992

Smith, Olivia, *The Politics of Language, 1791–1819*, Oxford, Clarendon Press, 1984

Tavor Bennett, Eve, *The Domestic Revolution: Enlightenment Feminisms and the Novel*, Baltimore and London, Johns Hopkins University Press, 2000

Watson, Nicola, J., *Revolution and the Form of the British Novel, 1790–1825*, Oxford, Clarendon Press, 1994

Wood, Marcus, *Radical Satire and Print Culture, 1790–1822*, Oxford, Clarendon Press, 1994

Women writers and the woman's novel

Alliston, April, *Virtue's Faults: Correspondences in Eighteenth-Century British and French Women's Fiction*, Stanford, Stanford University Press, 1996

Barker-Benfield, G. J., *The Culture of Sensibility: Sex and Society in Eighteenth-Century Britain*, Chicago, University of Chicago Press, 1992

Buss, Helen M., D. L. MacDonald, and Anne McWhir, eds., *Mary Shelley and Mary Wollstonecraft: Writing Lives*, Waterloo, Ontario, Wilfrid Laurier University Press, 2001

Butler, Marilyn, *Jane Austen and the War of Ideas*, New York, Oxford University Press, 1987

  Maria Edgeworth: A Literary Biography, New York, Oxford University Press, 1972

Doody, Margaret, *Frances Burney: The Life in the Works*, New Brunswick, Rutgers University Press, 1988

Epstein, Julia, *The Iron Pen: Frances Burney and the Politics of Women's Writing*, Madison, University of Wisconsin Press, 1989

Gallagher, Catherine, *Nobody's Story: The Vanishing Acts of Women Writers in the Marketplace, 1670–1820*, Berkeley, University of California Press, 1994

Gilbert, Sandra M., and Susan Gubar, *The Madwoman in the Attic: The Woman Writer and the Nineteenth-Century Literary Imagination*, New Haven, Yale University Press, 1979

Greenfield, Susan C., *Mothering Daughters: Novels and the Politics of Family Romance, Frances Burney to Jane Austen*, Detroit, Wayne State University Press, 2002

Homans, Margaret, *Bearing the Word: Language and Female Experience in Nineteenth-Century Women's Writing*, Chicago, University of Chicago Press, 1986

Johnson, Claudia L., *Equivocal Beings: Politics, Gender, and Sentimentality in the 1790s: Wollstonecraft, Radcliffe, Burney, Austen*, Chicago, University of Chicago Press, 1995

  Jane Austen: Women, Politics, and the Novel, Chicago, University of Chicago Press, 1988

Kelly, Gary, *Women, Writing, and Revolution 1790–1827*, New York, Oxford University Press, 1993

Kowaleski-Wallace, Elizabeth, *Their Fathers' Daughters: Hannah More, Maria Edgeworth, and Patriarchal Complicity*, New York, Oxford University Press, 1991

Lynch, Deidre Shauna, *The Economy of Character: Novels, Market Culture, and the Business of Inner Meaning*, Chicago, University of Chicago Press, 1998

Maurer, Shawn Lisa, "The Female (as) Reader: Sex, Sensibility, and the Maternal in Wollstonecraft's Fictions," *Essays in Literature* 19 (1992), pp. 35–54

Mellor, Anne K., *Mary Shelley: Her Life, her Fiction, her Monsters*, New York, Routledge, 1989

  Romanticism and Gender, New York, Routledge, 1993

Moers, Ellen, *Literary Women*, Garden City, Doubleday, 1976

Poovey, Mary, *The Proper Lady and the Woman Writer: Ideology as Style in the Works of Mary Wollstonecraft, Mary Shelley, and Jane Austen*, Chicago, University of Chicago Press, 1984

Richardson, Alan, *Literature, Education, and Romanticism: Reading as Social Practice, 1780–1832*, New York, Cambridge University Press, 1994

Spacks, Patricia Meyer, *Novel Beginnings: Experiments in Eighteenth-Century English Fiction*, New Haven, Yale University Press, 2006

Spencer, Jane, *The Rise of the Woman Novelist*, New York, Basil Blackwell, 1986

Spender, Dale, *Mothers of the Novel: 100 Good Women Writers Before Jane Austen*, New York, Pandora Press, 1986

Staves, Susan, *Married Women's Separate Property in England, 1660–1833*, Cambridge, Massachusetts, Harvard University Press, 1990

St Clair, William, *The Godwins and the Shelleys: A Biography of a Family*, New York, W. W. Norton, 1989

Sussman, Charlotte, "Daughter of the Revolution: Mary Shelley in Our Times," *JEMCS* 4 (2004), pp. 158–86

Todd, Janet, *The Sign of Angelica: Women, Writing, and Fiction, 1660–1800*, New York, Columbia University Press, 1989

  Mary Wollstonecraft: A Revolutionary Life, London, Weidenfeld and Nicolson, 2000

Turner, Cheryl, *Living by the Pen: Women Writers in the Eighteenth Century*, New York, Routledge, 1992

Van Sant, Ann Jessie, *Eighteenth-Century Sensibility and the Novel: The Senses in Social Context*, New York, Cambridge University Press, 1993

Zonana, Joyce, " 'They Will Prove the Truth of My Tale': Safie's Letters as the Feminist Core of Mary Shelley's *Frankenstein*," *Journal of Narrative Technique* 21 (1991), 170–84

Children's literature

Carpenter, Humphrey, and Mari Prichard, *The Oxford Companion to Children's Literature*, Oxford, Oxford University Press, 1984

Cutt, M. Nancy, *Mrs. Sherwood and her Books for Children*, London, Oxford University Press, 1974

David, Linda, *Children's Books Published by William Darton and his Sons*, Bloomington, Lilly Library, 1992

Demers, Patricia, *Heaven upon Earth: The Form of Moral and Religious Children's Literature, to 1850*, Knoxville, University of Tennessee Press, 1993

Goodenough, Elizabeth, Mark A. Heberle, and Naomi Sokoloff, eds., *Infant Tongues: The Voice of the Child in Literature*, Detroit, Wayne State University Press, 1994; Oxford, Oxford University Press, 1995

Hunt, Peter, ed., *Children's Literature: An Illustrated History*, Oxford, Oxford University Press, 1995

Jackson, Mary V., *Engines of Instruction, Mischief and Magic: Children's Literature in England from the Beginnings to 1839*, Lincoln, University of Nebraska Press, 1989

McGavran, James Holt, Jr., ed., *Romanticism and Children's Literature in Nineteenth-Century England*, Athens, University of Georgia Press, 1991

Moon, Marjorie, *Benjamin Tabart's Juvenile Library: A Bibliography of Books for Children Published, Written, Edited and Sold by Mr. Tabart, 1801–1820*, Winchester, Hampshire, St. Paul's Bibliographies; Detroit, Omnigraphics, 1990

Moon, Marjorie, ed., *John Harris's Books for Youth 1801–1843: A Check-List*, Cambridge, Marjorie Moon and A. J. B. Spilman, 1976

O'Malley, Andrew, *The Making of the Modern Child: Children's Literature and Childhood in the Late Eighteenth Century*, New York, Routledge, 2003

Pickering, Samuel, *John Locke and Children's Books in Eighteenth-Century England*, Knoxville, University of Tennessee, 1981

Richardson, Alan, *Literature, Education, and Romanticism: Reading as Social Practice, 1780–1832*, New York, Cambridge University Press, 1994

Thwaite, M. F., *From Primer to Pleasure: An Introduction to the History of Children's Books in England, from the Invention of Printing to 1900*, London, The Library Association, 1963

Whalley, Joyce Irene, *Cobswebs to Catch Flies. Illustrated Books for the Nursery and Schoolroom 1700–1900*, Berkeley: University of California Press, 1975

Sentimental fiction

Armstrong, Nancy, *Desire and Domestic Fiction: A Political History of the Novel*, Oxford, Oxford University Press, 1987

Brissenden, R. F., *Virtue in Distress: Studies in the Novel of Sentiment from Richardson to Sade*, New York, Harper & Row, 1974

Brown, Gillian, *Domestic Individualism: Imagining Self in Nineteenth-Century America*, Berkeley, University of California Press, 1990

Chandler, James, *England in 1819: The Politics of Literary Culture and the Case of Romantic Historicism*, Chicago, University of Chicago Press, 1998

Ellis, Markman, *The Politics of Sensibility: Race, Gender and Commerce in the Sentimental Novel*, Cambridge, Cambridge University Press, 1996

Ferris, Ina, *The Achievement of Literary Authority: Gender, History, and the Waverley Novels*, Ithaca, Cornell University Press, 1991

Festa, Lynn, *The Sentimental Figures of Empire*, Baltimore, Johns Hopkins Press, 2006

Johnson, Claudia L., *Equivocal Beings: Politics, Gender, and Sentimentality in the 1790s*, Chicago, University of Chicago Press, 1995

Jones, Chris, *Radical Sensibility: Literature and Ideas in the 1790s*, London, Routledge, 1993

Lynch, Deidre Shauna, *The Economy of Character: Novels, Market Culture, and the Business of Inner Meaning*, Chicago, University of Chicago Press, 1998

Mullan, John, *Sentiment and Sociability: The Language of Feeling in the Eighteenth Century*, Oxford, Clarendon Press, 1988

Pinch, Adela, *Strange Fits of Passion: Epistemologies of Emotion, Hume to Austen*, Stanford, Stanford University Press, 1996

Tave, Stuart, *The Amiable Humorist: A Study in the Comic Theory and Criticism of the 18th and 19th Centuries*, Chicago: University of Chicago Press, 1974

Tompkins, J. M. S., *The Popular Novel in England: 1770–1800*, Lincoln, University of Nebraska Press, 1961

Trumpener, Katie, *Bardic Nationalism: The Romantic Novel and the British Empire*, Princeton, Princeton University Press, 1997

Working-class fiction

Altick, Richard D., *The English Common Reader: A Social History of the Mass Reading Public, 1800–1900*, 1957; 2nd edn., Columbus, Ohio State University Press, 1998

Kelly, Gary, "Streetprint: Revolution and Romanticism," www.crcstudio.arts.ualber-ta.ca/streetprint/index.php?c=1

Neuburg, Victor E., *Popular Literature: A History and Guide*, London, Woburn Press, 1977

O'Malley, Andrew, *The Making of the Modern Child: Children's Literature and Childhood in the Late Eighteenth Century*, New York and London, Routledge, 2003

Rose, Jonathan, *The Intellectual Life of the British Working Classes*, New Haven and London, Yale University Press, 2001

Rule, John, *The Labouring Classes in Early Industrial England, 1750–1850*, London and New York, Longman, 1986

Shepard, Leslie, *The History of Street Literature*, Newton Abbot, David and Charles, 1973

Thompson, E. P., *The Making of the English Working Class*, 1963, Harmondsworth, Penguin Books, 1968

    Customs in Common, New York, The New Press, 1993

Vincent, David, *Bread, Knowledge and Freedom: A Study of Nineteenth-Century English Working Class Autobiography*, London, Europa Publications, 1981

The Irish novel

Backus, Margot Gayle, *The Gothic Family Romance: Heterosexuality, Child Sacrifice, and the Anglo-Irish Colonial Order*, Durham, North Carolina; London, Duke University Press, 1999

Burgess, Miranda J, "Violent Translations: Allegory, Gender, and Cultural Nationalism in Ireland, 1796–1806," *Modern Language Quarterly* 59 (1998), pp. 33–70

Butler, Marilyn, *Introduction to Castle Rackrent and Ennui*, London, Penguin, 1992, pp. 1–54

Corbett, Mary Jean, *Allegories of Union in Irish and English Writing, 1790–1870*, Cambridge, Cambridge University Press, 2000

Cronin, Michael, *Translating Ireland: Translation, Languages, Cultures*, Cork, Cork University Press, 1996

Deane, Seamus, *A Short History of Irish Literature*, Notre Dame, Indiana, University of Notre Dame Press, 1986

    Strange Country: Modernity and Nationhood in Irish Writing Since 1790, Oxford, Clarendon Press, 1997

Dennis, Ian, *Nationalism and Desire in Early Historical Fiction*, London, Macmillan, 1997

Dunne, Tom, "Haunted by History: Irish Romantic Writing 1800–50," in *Romanticism in National Context*, ed. Roy Porter and Mikulás Teich, Cambridge, Cambridge University Press, 1988, pp. 68–91

Eagleton, Terry, *Heathcliff and the Great Hunger: Studies in Irish Culture*, Notre Dame, Notre Dame Press, 1998

Ferris, Ina, *The Romantic National Tale and the Question of Ireland*, Cambridge, Cambridge University Press, 2002

Flanagan, Thomas, *The Irish Novelists 1800–1850*, New York, Columbia University Press, 1958

Foley, Tadhg, and Seán Ryder, eds., *Ideology and Ireland in the Nineteenth Century*, Dublin, Four Courts Press, 1998

Kelleher, Margaret, and James H. Murphy, eds., *Gender Perspectives in Nineteenth-Century Ireland: Public and Private Spheres*, Dublin, Irish Academic Press, 1997

Kelly, Gary, *English Fiction of the Romantic Period 1789–1830*, London, Longman, 1989

Kreilkamp, Vera, *The Anglo-Irish Novel and the Big House*, Syracuse, Syracuse University Press, 1998

Leerssen, Joep, *Remembrance and Imagination: Patterns in the Historical and Literary Representation of Ireland in the Nineteenth Century*, Notre Dame, University of Notre Dame Press, 1997

McCormack, W. J., *Ascendancy and Tradition in Anglo-Irish Literary History from 1789 to 1939*, Oxford, Clarendon Press, 1985

Moynahan, Julian, *Anglo-Irish: The Literary Imagination in a Hyphenated Culture*, Princeton, Princeton University Press, 1995

Sloan, Barry, *The Pioneers of Anglo-Irish Fiction 1800–1860*, Gerrards Cross, Colin Smythe, 1986

Tracy, Robert, *The Unappeasable Host: Studies in Irish Identities*, Dublin, University College Dublin Press, 1998

Trumpener, Katie, *Bardic Nationalism: The Romantic Novel and the British Empire*, Princeton, Princeton University Press, 1997

Scotland and the novel

Davis, Leith, Ian Duncan, and Janet Sorensen, eds., *Scotland and the Borders of Romanticism*, Cambridge, Cambridge University Press, 2004

Duncan, Ian, *Modern Romance and Transformations of the Novel: The Gothic, Scott, Dickens*, Cambridge, Cambridge University Press, 1992

Scott's Shadow: The Novel in Romantic Edinburgh, Princeton, Princeton University Press, 2007

Ina Ferris, *The Achievement of Literary Authority: Gender, History and the Waverley Novels*, Ithaca, New York, Cornell University Press, 1991

Fielding, Penny, *Writing and Orality: Nationality, Culture, and Nineteenth-Century Scottish Fiction*, Oxford, Clarendon Press, 1996

Garside, Peter, "Hogg and the Blackwoodian Novel," *Studies in Hogg and his World* 15 (2004), pp. 5–20

Garside, Peter, and Rainer Schowerling, *The English Novel 1770–1829: A Bibliographical Survey of Prose Fiction Published in the British Isles. Volume II: 1800–1829*, Oxford, Clarendon Press, 2000

Hart, F. R., *The Scottish Novel: From Smollett to Spark*, Cambridge, Massachusetts, Harvard University Press, 1978

Jones, Catherine, *Literary Memory: Scott's Waverley Novels and the Psychology of Narrative*, Lewisburg, Pennsylvania, Bucknell University Press, 2003

Kelly, Gary, *English Fiction of the Romantic Period 1789–1830*, London, Longman, 1989

Lee, Yoon Sun, *Nationalism and Irony: Burke, Scott, Carlyle*, New York, Oxford University Press, 2004

Mack, Douglas, "'The Rage of Fanaticism in Former Days': James Hogg's *Confessions of a Justified Sinner* and the Controversy over *Old Mortality*," in Ian Campbell, ed., *Nineteenth-Century Scottish Fiction: Critical Essays*, Manchester, Carcanet, 1979, pp. 37–50

Maxwell, Richard, "Inundations of Time: A Definition of Scott's Originality," *ELH* 68 (2001), pp. 419–68

St Clair, William, *The Reading Nation in the Romantic Period*, Cambridge, Cambridge University Press, 2004

Siskin, Clifford, *The Work of Writing: Literature and Social Change in Britain, 1700–1830*, Baltimore, Johns Hopkins University Press, 1998

Trumpener, Katie, *Bardic Nationalism: The Romantic Novel and the British Empire*, Princeton, Princeton University Press, 1997

"The Peripheral Rise of the Novel: Scotland, Ireland, and the Politics of Form," in Liam MacInvernay and Raymond Ryan, eds., *Ireland and Scotland: Culture and Society 1707–2000*, Dublin, Four Courts, 2004, pp. 164–82

Welsh, Alexander, *The Hero of the Waverley Novels; With New Essays on Scott*, Princeton, New Jersey, Princeton University Press, 1992

INDEX

Cambridge Companions to ...

AUTHORS

Edward Albee edited by Stephen J. Bottoms

Margaret Atwood edited by Coral Ann Howells

W. H. Auden edited by Stan Smith

Jane Austen edited by Edward Copeland and Juliet McMaster

Beckett edited by John Pilling

Aphra Behn edited by Derek Hughes and Janet Todd

Walter Benjamin edited by David S. Ferris

William Blake edited by Morris Eaves

Brecht edited by Peter Thomson and Glendyr Sacks (second edition)

The Brontës edited by Heather Glen

Frances Burney edited by Peter Sabor

Byron edited by Drummond Bone

Albert Camus edited by Edward J. Hughes

Willa Cather edited by Marilee Lindemann

Cervantes edited by Anthony J. Cascardi

Chaucer, second edition edited by Piero Boitani and Jill Mann

Chekhov edited by Vera Gottlieb and Paul Allain

Coleridge edited by Lucy Newlyn

Wilkie Collins edited by Jenny Bourne Taylor

Joseph Conrad edited by J. H. Stape

Dante edited by Rachel Jacoff (second edition)

Charles Dickens edited by John O. Jordan

Emily Dickinson edited by Wendy Martin

John Donne edited by Achsah Guibbory

Dostoevskii edited by W. J. Leatherbarrow

Theodore Dreiser edited by Leonard Cassuto and Claire Virginia Eby

John Dryden edited by Steven N. Zwicker

George Eliot edited by George Levine

T. S. Eliot edited by A. David Moody

Ralph Ellison edited by Ross Posnock

Ralph Waldo Emerson edited by Joel Porte and Saundra Morris

William Faulkner edited by Philip M. Weinstein

Henry Fielding edited by Claude Rawson

F. Scott Fitzgerald edited by Ruth Prigozy

Flaubert edited by Timothy Unwin

E. M. Forster edited by David Bradshaw

Brian Friel edited by Anthony Roche

Robert Frost edited by Robert Faggen

Elizabeth Gaskell edited by Jill L. Matus

Goethe edited by Lesley Sharpe

Thomas Hardy edited by Dale Kramer

Nathaniel Hawthorne edited by Richard Millington

Ernest Hemingway edited by Scott Donaldson

Homer edited by Robert Fowler

Ibsen edited by James McFarlane

Henry James edited by Jonathan Freedman

Samuel Johnson edited by Greg Clingham

Ben Jonson edited by Richard Harp and Stanley Stewart

James Joyce edited by Derek Attridge (second edition)

Kafka edited by Julian Preece

Keats edited by Susan J. Wolfson

Lacan edited by Jean-Michel Rabaté

D. H. Lawrence edited by Anne Fernihough

Primo Levi edited by Robert Gordon

David Mamet edited by Christopher Bigsby

Thomas Mann edited by Ritchie Robertson

Herman Melville edited by Robert S. Levine

Christopher Marlowe edited by Patrick Cheney

Arthur Miller edited by Christopher Bigsby

Milton edited by Dennis Danielson (second edition)

Molière edited by David Bradby and Andrew Calder

Toni Morrison edited by Justine Tally

Nabokov edited by Julian W. Connolly

Eugene O'Neill edited by Michael Manheim

George Orwell edited by John Rodden

Ovid edited by Philip Hardie

Harold Pinter edited by Peter Raby

Sylvia Plath edited by Jo Gill

Edgar Allan Poe edited by Kevin J. Hayes

Alexander Pope edited by Pat Rogers

Ezra Pound edited by Ira B. Nadel

Proust edited by Richard Bales

Pushkin edited by Andrew Kahn

Philip Roth edited by Timothy Parrish

Salman Rushdie edited by Abdulrazak Gurnah

Shakespeare edited by Margareta de Grazia and Stanley Wells

TOPICS